THE
PSYCHOLOGY
OF GREAT
TEACHING

THE PSYCHOLOGY OF GREAT TEACHING

(ALMOST) EVERYTHING TEACHERS OUGHT TO KNOW

PEDRO DE BRUYCKERE
CASPER HULSHOF
LIESE MISSINNE

SAGE Publications Ltd
1 Oliver's Yard
55 City Road
London EC1Y 1SP

CORWIN
A SAGE company
2455 Teller Road
Thousand Oaks, California 91320
(0800)233-9936
www.corwin.com

SAGE Publications India Pvt Ltd
B 1/I 1 Mohan Cooperative Industrial Area
Mathura Road
New Delhi 110 044

SAGE Publications Asia-Pacific Pte Ltd
3 Church Street
#10-04 Samsung Hub
Singapore 049483

Editor: James Clark
Senior assistant editor: Diana Alves
Production editor: Victoria Nicholas
Copyeditor: Jane Fricker
Proofreader: Thea Watson
Indexer: Martin Hargreaves
Marketing manager: Lorna Patkai
Cover design: Wendy Scott
Typeset by: C&M Digitals (P) Ltd, Chennai, India

© Pedro De Bruyckere, Casper Hulshof and Liese Missinne 2022

First published 2022

Apart from any fair dealing for the purposes of research, private study, or criticism or review, as permitted under the Copyright, Designs and Patents Act, 1988, this publication may not be reproduced, stored or transmitted in any form, or by any means, without the prior permission in writing of the publisher, or in the case of reprographic reproduction, in accordance with the terms of licences issued by the Copyright Licensing Agency. Enquiries concerning reproduction outside those terms should be sent to the publisher.

Library of Congress Control Number: 2021951974

British Library Cataloguing in Publication data

A catalogue record for this book is available from the British Library

ISBN 978-1-5297-6751-3
ISBN 978-1-5297-6750-6 (pbk)

CONTENTS

ABOUT THE AUTHORS

Pedro De Bruyckere is an educational scientist at the Artevelde University College of Applied Sciences in Ghent, Belgium and Utrecht University, the Netherlands. He wrote *The Ingredients for Great Teaching* and co-authored the two *Urban Myths about Learning and Education* books.

Casper Hulshof is a psychologist who teaches Educational Science at Utrecht University, the Netherlands and co-author of the *Urban Myths about Learning and Education* books.

Liese Missinne is an educational scientist and teacher trainer at the Artevelde University of Applied Sciences in Ghent, Belgium, training future teachers for secondary education.

ACKNOWLEDGEMENTS

You can see the names of the three of us on the cover of this book, but it would never have been possible without the support and help of many others. Thank you to our friends and family for their support. A special word of thanks to Eva-Ann De Smet for supporting us in the extensive literature study that forms the basis of this work. We would like to thank Professor Wim Van den Broeck for reading the chapter on nature/nurture. We thank the anonymous reviewers who went through the book for the many comments that made the book better. Thanks to Sage, the designers and editors, for the hard work and patience that was sometimes required. Also a special thank you for Ian Connerty who helped us with the translation!

HOW THIS BOOK IS STRUCTURED

Even though everything in psychology (up to a point) is connected to everything else, books on the subject tend to have the same structure. First come the biological and physiological processes, and the anatomy of the brain. This is followed by the development and working of the senses and the creation of the higher mental processes. Unfortunately, the subjects that are most relevant for teachers, caregivers and parents, such as personal and social development, learning and motivation, often fall between the cracks in this structure. For this reason, you will find them in a different place in each book on psychology. However, in our opinion it is precisely these themes that form the glue which binds the different standard elements of psychology together. Consequently, we regard these themes as the most appropriate way to subdivide the different sections of this book. In this way, we can discuss the matters that are of most interest to teachers, caregivers and parents, without feeling obliged to run through all the different 'standard' elements of the psychological discipline.

The book is therefore divided into four sections:

- Part 1: I

  In the first section, we look at the development of the individual. If you want to support children and young people in their development, it is useful to know how this development actually takes place. We will start with the various motors of development. Are we the product of our genes or of our environment? Next, we look at the development of personality, attachment, cognitive development, moral development and linguistic development. At the same time, it will become evident – for example, in the discussion of the crucial significance of play – that the role of others becomes increasingly important. This leads us on to Part 2.

- Part 2: Others

  We do not live and develop ourselves in isolation. We do this in interaction with our environment and the people who populate it: parents, family, friends, teachers, caregivers and so many others. How important is this environment and how can it best be organised for learning and living?

- Part 3: Learning

  In addition to providing the best possible support for the development of children and young people, as parents, caregivers or teachers we also want them to learn. This starts with perception, which makes the systematic build-up of expertise possible.

- Part 4: Behaviour

  The final section of the book deals with the behaviour that we display. We will look at the control room inside our head: our cognitive functions. We will examine how we can best motivate children and young people, before ending with a number of other ways in which we can give them a push in the right direction.

If, for example, you want to know how to prevent a child from being bullied, a number of the elements that are discussed separately at different places in the book come together. For this reason, throughout the book we have inserted a number of teacher takeaways with practical advice on specific subjects. They do not discuss different domains of psychology but combine models and insights from different branches of these domains and translate these into useful advice and tools to help your son or daughter, your pupils, or any other child or young person under your care.

INTRODUCTION: ALMOST EVERYTHING?

What is the aim of this book? Put simply, we want to discuss (almost) everything about psychology that you need to know as a teacher, caregiver or parent. In short, to create an all-embracing psychological handbook for anyone who works with and guides the development of children and young people. It is a bold claim, and one that might seem doomed to failure. Even so, that was our starting point. But if we wish to discuss almost everything, how come the result is just a single volume and not an encyclopaedia that would fill half a shelf in a library? This is only possible because the book deals with almost everything that you need to know about psychology *for use in everyday life and practice*.

Choices

This required us to make a number of very explicit choices, which we would like to explain before you start reading the core of the book.

Our first golden rule was to *'limit history to the minimum necessary to understand each subject'*. As a discipline, psychology has a relatively short but nonetheless fascinating history, in which the three authors love to delve. Many books about the various branches of the discipline quite rightly devote numerous pages to this history and if you are a student of psychology this history can be useful to understand how certain ideas emerged and developed, before... ultimately being disproved or superseded. We saw no point in writing 20 pages about Freud, only to conclude that the basis for his theories is weak and that nowadays his conclusions are hotly disputed.[1]

A second golden rule, linked to the first, was to make the information we provide *'as current as possible'*. In recent times, psychology has been through a number of difficult and stormy years, thanks to what is generally referred to as the replication crisis. In our second educational myths book *More Urban Myths about Learning and Education*, we investigated a number of classic psychological studies for which the results are not replicable today or for which, even worse, the results were faked at the time. 'Not replicable' means that the researchers of the original study repeated the same or similar experiments on a number of other occasions but were not able to obtain the same or similar results. Some well-known examples include:

- Zimbardo's Stanford prison research;[2]
- Milgram's electric shock experiments;[3]
- The bystander effect of Darley and Latané;[4]
- The pencil-in-the-mouth research of Strack, Martin and Stepper.[5]

Except for this introduction, we have tried to avoid mentioning this kind of questionable research, except where it is necessary to contradict and correct a number of widespread misconceptions. At the same time, during our examination of psychological textbooks we noted that many of the most recent studies – preferably with replications – were not included. With this present book we hope to make good for these omissions.

Our third golden rule was to always ask *'what do people who work with children and young people really need to know?'* We soon discovered that this meant that our book would not only need to discuss developmental psychology or to be a book about pure cognitive psychology. Psychology is a house with many different rooms, many of which can be relevant for parenting and education. For example, self-determination theory can shed light on the best way to motivate children and young people. Likewise, behavioural economics – one of the youngest branches of the psychological discipline and one that has resulted in the award of three Nobel Prizes in recent years – can help to explain how we make individual and collective errors of reasoning and how, using this knowledge, it is possible to change behaviour.

The fourth golden rule was *'practical thinking'*. This meant that in addition to explaining psychological theory, we also wished to focus on the practical consequences of these insights. For example, the bio-ecological system theory of Bronfenbrenner is interesting in its own right but from our perspective it is more useful as a way to better understand what is generally known in educational circles as community schools. Moreover, even relatively recent concepts like collective teacher efficacy can be linked to the work of Bronfenbrenner and his colleague Bandura. In the chapter in question, we also look at how you can use the implications of this knowledge in a practical school context. With a similar aim in mind, throughout the book we have inserted a series of subject-specific teacher takeaways that do not take a particular theory as their starting point but examine a range of relevant topics, such as divorce, bullying and motivation, from the perspective of various theories that are mentioned in different parts of the book.

The final golden rule is also the main reason why we deliberately added '(almost)' to the subtitle of this book. Leaving aside the fact that we are aware of our own fallibility and have therefore perhaps overlooked or forgotten some things, at the end of the day we had no alternative, albeit with pain in our heart but to *'make choices'*. This meant that we felt it was necessary to exclude any detailed reference to learning and developmental disorders. There were various reasons for this decision but the most important of them was our limited personal knowledge of this specialist field. Together, the three authors of this book have more than 40 years of experience in the teaching of developmental psychology, cognitive psychology and other related subjects but none of us is an expert in the field of learning disorders. Moreover, the domain of learning and developmental disorders and the best way to deal with them is so wide ranging that our book would need to have been twice as long to cover it adequately. We are convinced that a book with an approach like ours needs to be written on this important topic but we are not the best people to do it.

More

The choices that we made when writing the book are not 'innocent' or coincidental. First and foremost, they are an attempt to provide a conscious answer to the justified criticism that there is more to education than cognitive psychology and learning. At the same time, we also recognise that the raising of children can benefit from useful background information that goes beyond a few basic notions of developmental psychology.

With this in mind, in the following pages we have made a distinction between 'need to know' and 'nice to know'. 'Nice to know' is interesting (and sometimes amusing) background information that is not directly relevant to the essence of the theory under discussion but can nevertheless help us to understand that theory better. This information can be found in a series of separate boxes interspersed throughout the text. If you prefer, you can read the basic 'need to know' text without reading these separate 'nice to know' boxes.

HOW DO WE KNOW SOMETHING IN PSYCHOLOGY?

In this book we want to provide you with current and practical insights into elements of psychology that may be useful to parents, teachers and caregivers in their efforts to raise and educate young people. But how exactly does the science of psychology 'know' how children grow up, develop and deal with each other in a particular way? In other words, what is the basis for the conclusions that psychologists make?

Observation

People have been thinking about the nature of child development for centuries but one of the first scientists to approach the subject systematically was Charles Darwin,[6] who in 1877 published a short article about his son William (who he often referred to as Doddy), based on the diaries that he had kept 37 years earlier, following the child's birth. Darwin used one of the most important methods for learning about a child's development: observation. In a scientific sense, observation is not just a matter of watching but involves focused and systematic monitoring and detailed description of everything the child does. In the case of Doddy, Darwin was curious to find out more about the possible link between a child's play and the child's development, as well as to establish whether or not human communication is something innate.[7] Another giant in the history of developmental psychology, the Swiss scientist Jean Piaget, employed a similar technique. At first, he observed and analysed the behaviour of his own three children, which he later supplemented with the observation of other children.[8] However, Piaget also took the process a stage further. Whereas with 'ordinary' observation the observer attempts to influence the child under observation as little as possible, Piaget elaborated a 'clinical method' of observation, in which the observer not only observes but occasionally alters the nature of the observed child's environment in order to better understand the child's behaviour and to assess what it does or does not know. These were not yet experiments as such (more about that in a moment) but they did have a significant impact on the nascent discipline of developmental psychology.

This kind of observation and, particularly, the clinical method presents two major challenges:

- As an observer, you need to maintain the necessary degree of scientific detachment, which was not easy for Darwin and Piaget, since they were dealing with their own children.
- It is very difficult to know if it is possible to generalise what you have observed. People and children are so different that observing something in a limited sample of them does not mean that this will necessarily be the case with all of them.

Observations of this kind can be very useful for the formulation of hypotheses and theories; for example, about what a child can or cannot do at a particular age. However, other methods then need to be applied to check whether or not these hypotheses and theories are accurate. Today, the development of a scientific theory runs broadly as follows:

1. Researchers develop a hypothesis based on observation or by reflecting on existing theories.
2. An assessment is made of how and to what extent the hypothesis can best be investigated on the basis of data collection.
3. The results of the data collection are analysed.
4. The final results are published after independent and anonymous checking (peer review) by other scientists and possibly following repetition of the relevant research (replication).

The testing of hypotheses via research

Development and behaviour do not simply 'happen'. A child develops through a process of maturation, accumulated experiences, learning and/or independent decisions, which often influence each other in a cumulative manner. If, as a researcher, you want to find out how a certain evolution came about or why a child demonstrates a certain kind of behaviour, you need to make use of a series of investigative methods. The first challenge you face is to move beyond the straightforward identification of correlations.

From correlation to causal relationship

Imagine: Susan takes the bus to school at 8 o'clock each morning. For the past few days, she has noticed a handsome young man standing at the bus stop on the other side of the street. Today is Wednesday. He was already standing there all last week and he was standing there again on Monday and Tuesday of this week. And yes, today he is once more standing in the same spot! It therefore seems likely that he will be standing there again tomorrow... This scenario combines two elements that seem to coincide frequently: the first is the fact that Susan takes the bus to school at 8 o'clock each morning; the second is the fact that at the same time a boy is standing at the bus stop on the other side of the street. This is a correlation. But... Susan is not the reason why the young man is standing there. He is simply waiting for his own bus to take him to school, work or somewhere else. In other words, there is a correlation between Susan and the young man but not a causal relationship.

However, on Wednesday morning the young man crosses the road and asks Susan if she would like to go out for a drink with him on Friday night. It is now clear that Susan is the reason for the behaviour of the young man. Consequently, with this scenario it is possible to speak of a causal relationship between him and Susan.

It is often one of the greatest challenges in research to try and demonstrate a causal relationship. In comparison, it is usually much easier to identify a correlation.[9]

Sadly, these two phenomena are regularly confused in the media. You read, for example, that children who spend more time in front of a screen more frequently suffer from obesity. This is often portrayed as being a causal relationship but that is not necessarily the case. There are indeed many studies that demonstrate a correlation but there can be many different reasons for this. For example, it is possible that children from poorer families spend more time in front of screens because both their parents are out working all day to make ends meet, as a result of which the children are left alone without supervision and also have less access to sport (because sport also costs money). In this scenario, screen time is more an effect than a cause. It is certainly possible to use screen time as a predictor of possible obesity but reducing screen time will not necessarily reduce obesity: research studies that have tried to achieve this effect have so far concluded that the impact of reduced screen time on weight is minimal.[10]

What are the possible types of connection between screen time and obesity?

1. A correlation between screen time and obesity, where it is not clear which is cause and which is effect:

2. A clear causal relationship, in which more screen time leads to more obesity

3. A clear causal relationship in which obesity leads to more screen time:

4. A correlation between screen time and obesity caused by a distorting factor - namely, the socio-economic background of the child - which can have an impact on both screen time and obesity:

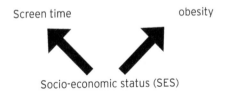

Screen time   obesity

Socio-economic status (SES)

In search of causal relationships via experiments and the use of reliable tools

One of the main aims of research is to eliminate the influence of possible distorting factors by isolating and controlling them. This means that in *experiments*, for example, the researchers attempt to gain as much control as they possibly can over any other influences that might have an effect on what they are trying to measure. However, if you fail to identify and neutralise a disruptive factor, it is likely that the conclusions you draw on the basis of the experiment will be flawed.

It is for this reason that many research studies work with different groups of test subjects, so that the experimental group – for example, the group that has to take a medicine that is being tested – can be compared with a control group – who are administered a placebo or some other harmless medicine. Even so, that is still not enough to be certain that other elements are not playing an influencing role. Other measures to counteract this possibility include the following:

• It is common practice to divide the test subjects between two or more groups on a random basis, since this makes it possible to check for all possible distorting variables, which you cannot do if you seek to keep the variables amongst the test subjects constant between the different groups. If, however, you distribute the test subjects between the groups randomly, this means that there can be no systematic differences between the groups, except for the manipulated variable: the thing you are testing and trying to measure. This means in turn that if there is a difference between the results of the groups, that difference must be attributable to the experimental (manipulated) variable. Because this method – known as randomised controlled trials or RCTs – also takes account of unknown distorting variables, it is generally regarded as the gold standard for good research. That being said, we shall see later that this approach is not always possible or desirable.

• It is also common practice not to tell the test subjects which group they belong to: the experimental group or the control group. This knowledge could become a distorting variable in its own right. If someone knows that they are receiving the trial medicine rather than the harmless placebo, this could have an effect on their behaviour.

- For much the same reason, it is also usual not even to inform the test leaders who belongs to which group, unless this is absolutely necessary for the effective implementation of the experiment.

In addition, researchers will always seek to make use of tools that are reliable and have been validated, so that they can establish whether or not there are genuine differences between the results of their test groups. In some cases, this is relatively easy. If you are testing a dieting pill, all you need is a decent set of weighing scales. You weigh your test subjects in both groups at the beginning and end of the experiment (known as the pre-test and the post-test), recording the results on an appropriate scale (presumably in kilograms and grams) and then comparing the differences. However, things are not always quite as simple for psychological experiments, so the necessary scales and tools to measure the effect of an approach often need to be developed specially. In this way, for instance, IQ tests are a good example of tools that make it possible to measure a person's intelligence as objectively as possible.

In recent decades, a large number of tools of this type for use in psychological research have been developed. Sometimes these tools are no more than question lists; sometimes they are observation lists, which allow researchers to carefully monitor different aspects of the behaviour of children or adults. One of the most well-known of these tests is designed to establish the extent to which a child is safely attached. It involves what is effectively a role-playing game in which the child has to progress through various steps, each of which is closely watched to observe his/her reaction in different situations. It is crucial for the quality and reliability of such tools that each step is carried out in exactly the same way.

Valid and reliable tools

It is often emphasised that tests and exams in schools need to be both valid and reliable. Some argue that there is a need for standardised tests. But what do these comments actually mean?

Validity: a test is valid if it measures what you want to measure.

Reliability: a test is reliable if it gives the same results when repeated.

Reliability is a necessary condition for validity but is not enough by itself.[11]

For instance, it is possible to use tests of this kind to establish whether or not the viewing of violent images can have an effect on the behaviour of children.

One such example is the famous Bobo doll experiment conducted by Bandura, in which children first watched on video various versions of how an adult attacked a life-sized doll (Bobo) and were then placed in a room with the same doll. Such experiments are often carried out in a laboratory setting, where it is easier to keep everything under tighter control but it is also possible for them to be conducted in the real world.

It is not possible to research everything via experiments

Imagine that you want to investigate whether smoking in the car is damaging for the health of children. It is difficult to justify in ethical terms the setting up of an experiment that deliberately exposes children to this danger. For this reason, there are certain hypotheses that cannot be tested by experiment and are therefore investigated by (amongst other things) a process of *naturalistic observation*, in which, for example, behaviour is observed in the real-life environments of our everyday world.

For both experiments and naturalistic observation, researchers can make use of observation schedules (with points to be monitored), existing data sources (such as official government data), recordings, interviews and *question lists* that can be used to conduct *survey research*. In our 'smoking in the car' example, this latter technique could be used to find out how many children sit in cars with smoking adults and what immediately noticeable effects, if any, it has on them. The sample population for the survey would need to be sufficiently large to ensure that it is representative of the total population and the question list would need to be both valid and reliable. With a survey of this kind, it will only be possible to assume (rather than prove) a causal relationship between smoking in the car and its effects on children but the data from the survey should at least be able to establish a correlation which shows that, for example, children who travel in smoke-filled cars are more frequently sick than others.[12]

A survey approach can be useful to support general conclusions like '15-year-old children living in cities feel happy less often than their age peers living outside of cities'. However, surveys cannot help you to discover in any depth what 15-year-olds are feeling or to establish which factors play a role in generating those feelings. This would require the use of alternative research methods, such as *case studies*, in which one or more test subject is followed and investigated in detail. The results of these studies are relevant and often do much more than scratch the surface but are less capable of generalisation than survey results.

In search of evolutions and developments via longitudinal and cross-sectional research

If you want to map evolutions and developments, one-off experiments, observations and surveys will not be appropriate. Evolutions and developments take place over time, and you will need to employ research methods that take account of this fact. In this context, it is customary to make a distinction between longitudinal research and transversal (or cohort or cross-sectional) research.

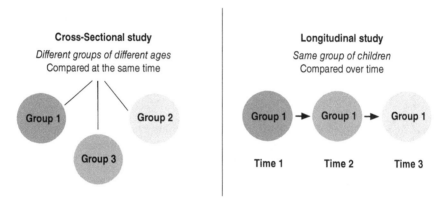

Figure 0.1   The difference between cross-sectional research and longitudinal research

With *longitudinal research*, the same children are monitored and questioned regularly over a longer period of time, so that evolutions in their condition can be recorded and analysed. The advantage of this kind of research is that such evolutions do indeed become visible but the disadvantage is the length of time it takes. However, this does not always need to be the case: taking measurements every minute over a period of one hour is also a longitudinal approach. That being said, this tends to be the exception rather than the rule. Most longitudinal studies last for years, in some cases even for decades. For example, researchers wanted to find out whether the use of social media was having a negative effect on the development of teenagers and their emotions. In 2021 the so-called Facebook Files showed that internal, non-peer reviewed research did show a possible negative effect and earlier research had also indicated that there was a possible correlation but the nature of the relationship was not clear. To investigate these matters further, earlier it had been decided to follow 500 adolescents over a period of eight years. This required the investment of significant time, effort and money, at the end of which it was finally possible to conclude that social media have little or no effect on teenage development and emotions.[13] Still, in comparison with some other studies, this timeframe was relatively short. One of the longest running longitudinal studies on record was begun in 1921 by Lewis Terman and involved the questioning every five years of 1,500 children with a high IQ. Although Terman himself died in 1956, the study continued long after his death with the remaining survivors of the test population and new research based on the study's findings is still being published today.[14]

If, as a researcher, you lack the necessary patience or financial resources to work in this manner, you might prefer to set up a *cross-sectional (or cohort or transverse)* study. This involves children and young people of different age groups being questioned at the same moment in time, following which the group results are compared. This kind of research is shorter and cheaper but potentially distorting factors can play a much greater role than in longitudinal research, because as people get older, they may be affected by experiences in their lives that the younger respondents have not yet undergone.

Confirmation and new insights based on brain research

In recent years, developments in neurological research have begun to play an increasingly important role in various psychological domains. For example, books about the adolescent brain have inspired both parents and teachers alike. However, this research is often no more than confirmation of what has already been established using other research methods. In this way, brain research has confirmed, for example, that teenagers are more occupied with themselves[15] and that prior knowledge is important for the learning of new material.[16] Sometimes the research does produce new insights, as we will describe later in the section on cognitive development, where research by Stanislas Dehaene has shown that infants can calculate basic maths at a much earlier age than was originally thought. Similarly, neurological studies have provided a possible (and partial) explanation for why some things happen, such as risk-taking behaviour in adolescence, which we will look at in the section on executive functions.[17] In this book we have used many sources from this highly specialised field of science. However, rather than explaining how the brain is constructed and functions, we have preferred to concentrate on what this all means for everyday practice in schools and the home.

Choices, choices, choices

This summary should have made clear that there is no single research method that offers the best solution in every situation. As a result, when researchers publish their findings, they always explain what methodological choices they have made and why. This is interesting in its own right but it is even more interesting when different researchers using different reasoning and different methods all investigate the same subject, particularly if their results all seem to be broadly comparable. This is known as *triangulation* and gives added weight to the relevant findings.

At the same time, it can also be useful to repeat some studies in exactly the same manner, to check whether or not the results of the first study were simply a matter of chance. This kind of 'double-check' research was not carried out quite as often before. When the practice became more frequent, it led to what is now known as the replication crisis.

The replication crisis

In 2011, Simmons, Nelson and Simonsohn demonstrated that it is possible using frequently employed scientific methods and statistical techniques to obtain results, either consciously or unconsciously, that seem to have been obtained in the correct manner but do not necessarily correspond with reality. In this way, for example, they were able to 'prove' that people get younger when they regularly listen to The Beatles' song *When I'm 64*.[18] Their work inspired a large-scale study that investigated 100 important psychological research projects of recent decades and came to the alarming conclusion that it was only possible to replicate the results successfully in just 36% of the cases. In other words, the results in the remaining 64% – almost two-thirds – were open to question.[19] There were quite large differences between the different domains of psychology. In cognitive psychology – the study of how we learn – almost half of the results were replicable. But in social psychology this figure plummeted to just a quarter. To make matters worse, this followed previous severe criticism of this branch of the psychological discipline in the media as a result of the large-scale fraud perpetrated by the Dutch researcher Diederik Stapel. In this context, it is important to underline that there is a huge difference between failed replications and fraud. The former can often be a case of bad luck and chance; the latter is always criminal (although, fortunately, it occurs much less frequently).

After 2015, a second major replication project was launched. Once again, it concluded that as many as half of the controlled studies, some of them classics in their field, were not replicable.[20] While 50% is better than 36%, it shows that the room for further improvement is still significant.

What do you do if you want to test if something is replicable? Just ask the people in the street!

In 2020, Suzanne Hoogeveen and colleagues published the results of an interesting study in which they asked non-scientists to estimate how great was the likelihood that the results of various psychological studies could be successfully replicated. What transpired? It turned out that the predictions of the 'amateurs' were remarkably accurate. But a degree of caution is needed - because, as far as we know, the results of this study have not yet been replicated...[21]

As these statistics show, the replication crisis is still a live issue, and one that has not made the writing of this book any easier. At the same time, it would be a mistake to think that psychology is 'unscientific'. If anything, the opposite is true. The fact that these problems have been discovered and are being corrected is evidence that the scientific methods we describe in this book, which require a constantly questioning mindset and proper replication, can and do work. Sadly, there are other domains in the world of science where replication is by no means so far advanced.

Moreover, it is often overlooked that many of psychology's most crucial insights, such as the Big Five theory and its derivatives in personality psychology, have been successfully replicated.[22] Similarly, the Many Labs research project, which conducts multiple replication studies of the same research in different countries, has demonstrated that successful replications are seemingly robust across different geographical locations. As a result, the insights in question are now more strongly supported after the replication crisis than they were before.[23]

Endnotes

1. Buekens, 2006.
2. Haney et al., 1972.
3. See: Milgram, 1963; Milgram, 1974.
4. Darley & Latané, 1968.
5. Strack et al., 1988.
6. Butterworth, 2014.
7. Darwin, 1877.
8. Beilin, 1992.
9. Pearl & Mackenzie, 2018.
10. Wahi et al., 2011.
11. De Bruyckere, 2018.
12. Pearl & Mackenzie, 2018.
13. Coyne et al., 2020.
14. See for example: Warne & Liu, 2017.
15. Van den Bos et al., 2011.
16. Van Kesteren et al., 2014.
17. Crone & Dahl, 2012.
18. Simmons et al., 2011.
19. Open Science Collaboration, 2015.
20. Klein et al., 2018.
21. Hoogeveen et al., 2020.
22. Soto, 2019.
23. Klein et al., 2018.

1

'I'

This first large section deals with different elements of developmental psychology that are necessary to understand the development of the individual child or young person and to guide him/her in the best possible way.

- We will start with the motors of development, nature and nurture and how they relate to each other, in part to make clear that although we are given many things by nature, education and upbringing can still play a significant role.
- Next, we will divide development into its different domains. This will make them easier to discuss, although it must be borne in mind that they all interact with each other. We will examine:
  - how personality and identity develop;
  - the role that attachment plays in the development of the individual;
  - how we learn the difference between good and bad, which we will discuss in chapter 1.4 on moral development; in particular, we will look at what we call the theory of mind;
  - the role of intelligence, with attention to both the positive and negative sides of IQ;
  - how, in terms of cognitive development, children can do much more at an early age than was once thought and how 'the other' comes into the picture via dynamic system theory;
  - the essential role that communication plays from an early age in our growth as a person; we will discuss this in the chapter on linguistic development;
  - how our body evolves a great deal and often very quickly throughout our life; this can have a major psychological impact, which we will discuss in the chapter on physical development;
  - how this body also makes sexuality possible, the evolution of which will be discussed in the chapter on sexual development;
  - the many forms of playing; in particular, we will look at how children and young people change in the way they play together with others; the discussion of this final development in the first large section of the book forms an ideal stepping stone to the second part, dealing with others.

1.1

WHAT DETERMINES WHO I AM? NATURE, NURTURE OR SOMETHING ELSE?

— What questions does this chapter answer? —

1. To what extent is something innate or learnt?
2. How do we know if something is innate or learnt?
3. How do nature and nurture influence each other throughout our lives?
4. What role can we play in upbringing and education?

Why are you as tall as you are? Why are you good at mathematics? Or at languages? Why are some people more quickly addicted than others? As you get older, you start to notice yourself adopting certain mannerisms, phrases and other small habits in which you can recognise your parents. How have they passed these things on to you?

A historical and current dichotomy

This series of questions has been occupying the scientific community for many years. It focuses on the contrasting roles of aptitude and environment, nature and nurture, and innate ability and learning. Throughout history, this has been a domain that has seen a variety of widely differing theories put forward. In the

18th century, the British Enlightenment philosopher John Locke – following the Greek philosopher Aristotle and the Italian theologian Thomas Aquinas – argued that a child was born as a blank sheet of paper. His forerunners referred to this as a 'tabula rasa'.[1] According to this vision, almost everything is learnt. You could describe it as a kind of pedagogical optimism. As a result, everyone has it in them to run a marathon, play the piano and much, much more.

In contrast, Locke's Romantic counterpart, Jean-Jacques Rousseau, thought that the child was by no means a blank page but was by nature good. In his classic book *Emile*, he described how it was the child's environment that ruined or 'corrupted' him/her, rather than making the child a better person.[2] In other words (and ironically enough), Rousseau still sees an influential role for the child's environment but it is essentially a negative one. Even so, Rousseau's ideas continue to be seen as an example of the 'nature' point of view, in contrast to Locke's 'nurture' perspective. However, in both cases the child occupied a fairly central position, which represented a break with previous thinking on such matters.

Traces of the nature–nurture dichotomy today

The influence of Rousseau in today's education is still significant and is seen in, amongst other things, various educational innovations and pedagogies,[3] but above all in the image of the child as an active discoverer. This latter concept translates, for example, into the idea that children should find out everything for themselves or that you should only introduce them to new things when they are ready for them.

However, at the start of the present century there was also a renewed focus on the importance of innate ability, thanks in part to the book *The Blank Slate* by Steven Pinker.[4] Pinker wrote this book as a reaction to his experience that the 'tabula rasa' theory was still a subject of contention in contemporary society. In particular, the educational world seems to have difficulty in coming to terms with the concept of inborn differences between children,[5] possibly because this can all too easily be associated with determinism: the idea that if something is determined genetically, it is immutable and that consequently your future is already fixed at birth.

We shall see that the truth is actually more complex and more nuanced. In psychology, the discussion now seems primarily to be about the size of the respective contributions of nurture and nature in shaping the characteristics and attributes of people.

How can this be researched?

Much of the research into the relative influence of innate ability and environmental factors makes use of twins. This kind of research looks at the impact of heredity and is therefore often confused with molecular genetic research that examines DNA. However, these two things are not the same.

Let's start with hereditary research involving twins. To investigate whether something in a person's make-up is the result of innate ability or their environment, it is necessary to ensure that one of those two factors is constant. In reality, of course, it is impossible to keep the child's environment 100% consistent. Parents do not deal with each of their children equally and there are hundreds of other people with whom the children will eventually come into contact. In other words, we need to concentrate on the 'innate ability' factor. Two children from the same parents have a degree of overlap in their genetic material, which they have inherited from their mother and father. Except, that is, if the two children are identical twins. In that case, the overlap is complete. This explains why hereditary research often focuses on twin research involving the participation of monozygotic (single egg and single sperm) twins, because they share the same genetic material. It is then reasoned that if differences are later discovered between the two twins, this must be the result of the influence of their environment. A further distinction can also be made between identical twins who grow up together and identical twins who grow up apart, perhaps as a result of divorce or adoption. In this latter case, their environment can be really different.

As a consequence of such research, we are now in a position to make fairly definite conclusions about the innate aptitudes and abilities we inherit, although by using this kind of research design, we do not know which genes are responsible for this process.

In contrast, molecular genetic research does examine which parts of our DNA, or rather which combinations of genes, are responsible for particular characteristics. In this way, for example, it was possible for researchers to establish that if one of two children in the same family possesses a certain gene combination, this child is more likely to go to university than its sibling who does not have this same combination.[6]

Watching TV is (partially) hereditary

Studies of this kind allow us to identify with certainty a variety of characteristics that are determined, at least in part, by heredity. For example, it has been established that the number of hours of television you watch each day is partially determined by hereditary factors.[7] This is equally true for your political convictions,[8] whether or not you will seek creative work,[9] or whether or not you are likely to have a divorce in later life.[10] But be careful: this information needs to be interpreted correctly. As we shall see shortly, this does not mean that if your parents or your (twin) brother or sister experience divorce that you will also per se experience it. It simply means that the likelihood that you will experience it is greater.

What do we know for certain?

It is not really possible to make 100% definitive pronouncements but in the year 2000 Eric Turkheimer nevertheless formulated three 'laws' applicable to the 'nature–nurture' debate,[11] which were supplemented in 2015 by the addition of a fourth law proposed by Chabris and colleagues.[12] These laws indicate what we know with a reasonable degree of certainty, because the different elements appear consistently in research findings:

1. **All human characteristics are partially hereditary.**

    Identical twins who grow up apart more closely resemble each other than non-identical twins who grow up apart, who in turn are more similar to each other than two people who are not related and grow up apart.

2. **The effect of genes is greater than the effect of a shared environment.**

    Once they become adults, the differences between identical twins who grew up together are not much greater than the differences between identical twins who did not grow up together.

3. **A great deal of our behaviour cannot be explained exclusively by either heredity or a shared environment.**

    Even identical twins who grow up together are not 100% similar and do not behave in precisely the same way. In addition to a shared environment, they also have their own unique environment populated by different people and different experiences, which they encounter separately.

4. **Most of the characteristics we acquire through heredity are shaped by many different genes with small effects.**

    For example, there is no single gene that is responsible for boosting a person's IQ by five points. On the contrary, there are thousands of different genes that each contribute in their own small way to our IQ.

Does natural aptitude increase or decline as you get older?

If we accept that nature and nurture are together responsible for close to 100% of the way in which our characteristics differ from those of others, it is not unreasonable to ask how much of that percentage is the result of innate factors and how much is the result of our environment. And do those proportions remain consistent over time? It seems plausible to assume that the role played by the environment will increase as we get older, since this environment provides us with an increasing number of new experiences but research suggests that this is not the case. The role played by genes and heredity in determining your levels of cognition and intelligence actually becomes more significant as you get older, because you increasingly distance yourself from the parental environment in which you grew up and start to live a more independent life, in which the impact of your own unique environment

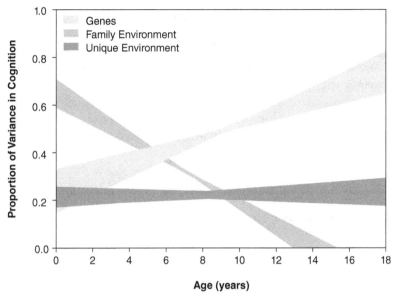

Figure 1.1 How genes and the environment influence the variance in cognition

remains fairly constant.[13] Or to put it more simply: the older you get, the greater the influence of your genes.

This insight is reasonably stable and has been replicated on multiple occasions with success. In other words, the research has been carried out a number of times with different sample populations but with consistently comparable results.[14]

Are some characteristics pure nature or pure nurture?

Imagine that you are born with Huntington's disease, which you can only acquire as the result of a genetic defect and which will confront you with increasingly serious motor complaints as you get older, ultimately leading to the deterioration of your mental faculties and to associated psychiatric problems. On average, people suffering from this condition live less long than people who do not have it.[15] This is an example of the powerful impact of 'nature' but it does not mean that the environment – 'nurture' – does not play a role. Medicines are being developed that can slow down the development of some of the disease's symptoms.[16] And perhaps it might sound slightly macabre but you can never be 100% certain that the disease will actually kill you. You might, for example, die in a car crash at an early age. A different example? Consider the language you speak. This, you might think, is pure nurture, since it is determined by your environment. Self-evidently, a child born in China to Chinese parents will be more likely to speak Chinese than a child born to French parents living in France. But what if you are unable to speak as a result of a genetic abnormality? In that case, it is nature that plays the defining role.

What is there in addition to nature and nurture?

Turkheimer's third law makes clear that factors other than innate aptitude and environment are also at play. If this were not the case, identical twins growing up in the same environment would develop in a highly similar way, but that is not what happens. In part, this can be explained by the fact that the environment of two people, even twins, cannot be 100% identical but in part it is also the result of the influence of other elements, such as interaction, transaction and a person's own free choices.

The gene-environment correlation

Nowadays, considerable scientific attention is being devoted to the so-called gene-environment correlation. The starting point is the assumption that genes and environment influence each other through various processes. On the one hand, you might have an innate disposition for addiction but you will only become addicted if the conditions of your environment make this possible. Similarly, you could reasonably contend that environmental factors will only lead to psychological disorders if the person in question is innately susceptible to such disorders. But the reverse can also be true: for example, a genetic predisposition to seek out excitement might persuade you to search for more potentially dangerous environments.[17]

Interaction

Most twin research makes it possible to identify the scale of the role played by heredity and the scale of the role played by environment. Around nine years of age, the influence of heredity accounts for 41% of the differences in intelligence. By the age of 17 years, the impact of hereditary material on differences in intelligence has risen to 66%.[18] This does not mean that the intelligence of every nine-year-old child is determined for 41% by hereditary factors – both heredity and environment continue to play a full and constant role – but it does mean that 41% of the differences in intelligence with other children can be attributed to heredity. For some children the influence of environment will be greater than for others, whereas in some cases the opposite will be true: the influence of heredity will be greater. A possible vision of this interaction process can be represented as shown in Figure 1.2.

The better or more ideal the environment in which a child grows up, the more closely that child will develop in accordance with its genetic potential. The worse or more damaging the environment, the closer the child will develop to the bottom level of its potential learning capabilities. It is inborn ability that sets the maximum and minimum limits but it is environment that determines the level to which a child will develop between those limits.

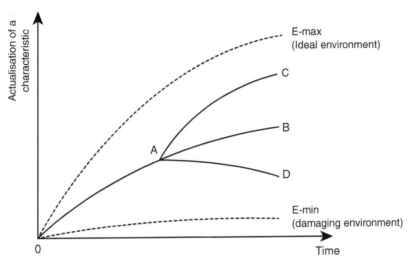

Figure 1.2 Interaction between environment and nature

This leads on to an interesting question. Imagine that every child were able to grow up in the best possible circumstances: healthy parents, adequate financial resources, sufficient stimulation and challenges, the best school with the best teachers, etc. What then would be the percentage impact of heredity on intelligence differences? The answer is clear: close to 100%.

This provides us with the following important insights:

- The better and more stimulating the environment in which a child grows up, the greater the influence of the hereditary material that the child has received through its genes.
- The worse the environment in which a child grows up, the greater the influence of that environment becomes.

Dutch reading education is so consistent that reading ability is almost exclusively determined by genetic factors

In 2018, Elsje van Bergen and her colleagues investigated reading ability and the prevalence of dyslexia in 6,000 pairs of Dutch twins. The researchers concluded that heredity and environment both play a role but also provided a good illustration of the insight we have just described above. Van Bergen argues that 'In the Netherlands education is so good and so egalitarian that the difference in reading ability between children can be attributed primarily to genetic differences. This is a compliment for the Dutch educational system. It does not matter how rich or poor your parents are: the real difference is in your genes. As a result, one child will pick up reading quite quickly and naturally, while another will be at a greater genetic risk of contracting dyslexia.'[19]

Maturation and learning influence each other

A distinction is often made between maturation and learning. Maturation can be described as something that is naturally present in a child and is gradually brought to the surface for further evolution and enhancement. Learning is something that is offered to a child by their environment. It is clear, however, that maturation and environment inevitably have an impact on each other. For example, a child might not yet be able to walk because their muscles are not strong enough, even though every baby is born with an innate walk and dance reflex. How do we know? If you pick up the baby and hold them just above the ground, they will automatically make walking-dancing motions with their legs. This reflex disappears after a few months and the child will only really learn to walk once their muscles have developed sufficiently to bear their weight.

Transaction

Criticism has been raised about the possibility of a too simple interpretation of interaction. If you look at nature and nature too simplistically, the process of interaction is effectively reduced to the equivalent of two separate buckets from which different things can be extracted. But that cannot be correct, because we know that these two aspects do indeed interact on each other. Nobody would ever attempt to assess the impact of, say, the brass section on the total experience of listening to an orchestra as a whole. And it is the same with development: it is much more than the sum of the different parts of nature and nurture.

This ability of nature and nurture to affect and enhance each other is central to a transactional vision of the kind found in the model elaborated by Sameroff,[20] in which the influence of both elements is felt throughout a child's development.

We can make this model concrete on the basis of the following two examples:

- A child is born with a reduced natural aptitude for the learning of language. As a result, the environment is less inclined to engage the child in conversation, so that the child's linguistic development is further hampered by that environment through a lack of adequate stimulation. In turn, the child will feel less inclined to seek interaction with their teachers, so that the child will be asked fewer questions at school, again resulting in reduced stimulation to develop their own powers of thought.
- A child is born with an extremely difficult character. In this very specific situation, it is not easy for the parents to like their child. Tired and driven to distraction by the child's behaviour, this can sometimes lead the parents to mistreat their offspring. As a result, the child's behaviour becomes even more negative, which can have an effect on the child's interaction not only with the parents but also with teachers, others in the neighbourhood, etc.[21]

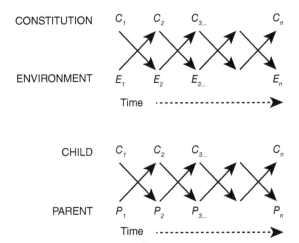

Figure 1.3 Transaction between nature and nurture

In both these examples, we can see how various (in this case negative) interactions have an impact on shaping the evolution of the child's development. The underlying premise is that the influence of both innate disposition and the environment changes over time and that, consequently, the nature of their mutual interaction also changes and has a corresponding impact on how further interactions will take place in the future.

Do we have a role to play: self-determination?

This is the most difficult factor of all to assess: the role of free will. Imagine that you are born with a natural talent for tennis. Your environment encourages you to play but... you don't want to. This is where a third factor comes into play in addition to nature and nurture: self-determination, or your ability to decide for yourself. However, this is a factor that is very difficult to investigate scientifically; it is more a matter for the philosophers. To complicate matters still further, it is also possible to ask to what extent free will is actually free. After all, your personal concept of free will is formed by your character (which, to a large extent, is a question of nature) and by your interactions or transactions with your environment (which is a question of nurture).[22] At the present time, there is even a serious debate taking place in scientific circles with regard to the very existence (or non-existence) of any such a thing as 'the self', a subject to which we will return later in the book when we discuss personality.

Does our environment also influence our genes? Epigenetics

A less well-known but steadily growing branch of research is the study of epigenetics. Is it possible that certain experiences of your grandparents and great-grandparents –

for example, suffering hunger and deprivation during the Second World War – can still have an influence on you today? These were experiences that were not originally part of their DNA, and the structure of that DNA was not changed as a result of what happened to them. Even so... it is claimed that information of this kind can still be passed on genetically from generation to generation. At first hearing, this might sound a bit too much like science fiction but there are serious indications that life experiences can indeed be transmitted via hereditary material. Not in the form of genetic abnormalities but more as a kind of 'marker' in the shape of additional molecules superimposed on our genetic material, which a gene can activate or deactivate in response to what a person does (or fails to do).

The 'science fiction' aspect of this research was very evident in a study carried out in 2003 amongst more than 1,000 children.[23] The results showed that the stress sensitivity of children whose mothers were also exposed to powerful stress sensations during their pregnancy – in other words, after the child's DNA had already been determined – was much higher than the sensitivity levels of children whose mothers had not been exposed to stress.

Translated into concrete, everyday terms, this means that it is important, for example, in cases of teenage pregnancy to ensure that the young mother-to-be is not subjected to unnecessary additional stress, since this could have a direct impact on the mental health of her child.

Sensitive periods

There are periods when we are more receptive for certain stimulations emanating from our environment. This may, for example, allow us to pick up a language more quickly. We refer to these periods as sensitive periods,[24] although in the past they were also referred to as critical periods. This latter description was based on the idea that if you did not learn a particular skill at a particular stage in your life, you would no longer be able to learn it subsequently. We now know that in many cases this is still possible; hence the adoption of the more appropriate 'sensitive' as opposed to 'critical'. These sensitive periods are the periods during which learning to talk, acquiring a musical ear and many other such skills is easier than at other times in our life.[25] However, it is not certain that you will be able to attain the same level with the same ease later on.[26]

What does all this mean in practice?

If we seek to quantify the influence of genetics and heredity on education, the answer is simple and straightforward: very little. This was the conclusion of a summary of frequently asked questions that was published in the report of a research study into the extent that heredity has an impact on school performance and even the prevalence of truancy.[27]

Even if research can show that between 57 and 58% of the differences between children in school performance can be attributed to hereditary factors,[28] there are still many other percentages that can have a significant cumulative effect. Moreover, this figure of 58% is an average and also varies depending on the subject in question: being good or poor at mathematics is most susceptible to genetic influences, while performance in artistic subjects is less susceptible. Additionally, the environment in which the child grows up is also relevant.

This insight – that heredity and environment both play an important role, especially if the environment is sub-optimal – is a challenge that must inspire everyone around the child or young person to do their utmost to improve that environment – that nurture – to the greatest possible extent.

This desire to make the environment as optimal as possible is also the starting point for various transactional models that are current in both developmental psychology and pedagogics, as a result of which we will also be looking at them again later in the book.

Endnotes

1. See amongst others: Duschinsky, 2012; Hicks, 2015; Locke & Nidditch, 1979.
2. See amongst others: Doorman, 2015; Rousseau, 2010.
3. De Bruyckere et al., 2015b.
4. Pinker, 2003.
5. See amongst others: Haworth & Plomin, 2012; Hayden, 2013.
6. Domingue et al., 2015.
7. Plomin et al., 1990.
8. See amongst others: Settle et al., 2009; Klemmensen et al., 2012.
9. Roeling et al., 2017.
10. McGue & Lykken, 1992.
11. Turkheimer, 2000.
12. Chabris et al., 2015.
13. Tucker-Drob et al., 2013.
14. Plomin et al., 2016.
15. Solberg et al., 2018.
16. Moreno-Delgado et al., 2020.
17. Van Reekum & Schmeets, 2008.
18. Haworth et al., 2010.
19. See amongst others: Van Bergen et al., 2018. See also: Nederlandse Organisatie voor Wetenschappelijk Onderzoek, 2018.
20. See amongst others: Sameroff, 2009; Sameroff, 1975.
21. The second example is a free interpretation of Van der Horst et al., 2016.

22. Turkheimer, 2018.
23. Caspi, 2003.
24. Uylings, 2006.
25. Michel & Tyler, 2005.
26. Dehaene, 2020.
27. See: Rietveld et al., 2013; but also: Okbay et al., 2016.
28. See amongst others: Shakeshaft et al., 2013.

1.2

HOW DOES PERSONALITY DEVELOP? WHO AM I?

┤ What questions does this chapter answer? ├

1. What is the difference between temperament, character, personality and identity?
2. What are the different dimensions of personality?
3. How does our personality develop and are we able to have an impact on this process?
4. What does personality theory teach us in terms of practice?

Can you change your partner? Can you change the character of your children? These seem simple enough questions but the answers can have far-reaching consequences. Is someone's personality stable or does it evolve over time? Are the personality characteristics of young children the same as when they later become teenagers and are these characteristics predictive of their personality as adults?

Over the years, many different theories have been advanced to explain how personality develops during childhood and adolescence, with the ideas of Freud as a classic example. Today, many of these theories are the subject of contention and even controversy.[1] This is even more the case with typologies of the Myers–Briggs Type Indicator (MBTI) variety, a corruption of the original theories of Jung that is pure pseudo-science at its worst.[2] In this chapter we will look at the nature of temperament, character, personality and identity, based on the most important contemporary theories and insights, before discussing what this can mean for a child's upbringing and education.

Dimensions versus typologies

You will notice that in this chapter we will continually talk about dimensions. These differ fundamentally from typologies. According to typologies like MBTI, everyone belongs to a particular type. For example, you are either introvert and inward-looking or you are extrovert and focused on others, with whom you are open. With this method of classification, you cannot be a bit of both. But with dimensions, you can. Dimensions view you as a scale, in which everyone finds a position somewhere between extremely introvert and extremely extrovert. This means that dimensions have room for nuance. MBTI only allows for 16 different kinds of people. With dimensions, countless different combinations are possible.

Ordering from nature to nurture

We often use different words to describe the way someone is but in psychology words like temperament, character, personality and identity do not mean the same. We will discuss them here in an order that reflects the extent to which they are either innate or learnt – yes, nature and nurture again – as a result of interaction with the environment.

Temperament

A child, even if only a few months old, can already be excitable or calm, react positively or negatively to their environment, or can be compliant or disruptive. These are all characteristics that are fixed in the child's brain at birth. This 'nature' aspect of our behaviour is quasi-immutable.[3] Temperament can therefore be defined as the consistent or unchangeable differences in your behaviour based on your biological origins, which are relatively independent of learning, values and attitudes.[4] This does not mean that there are no changes in how you can see the temperament of a child develop, particularly during the first year of life.[5] This helps to explain why the classic assessment of temperament is usually divided into three dimensions, namely: surgency/extraversion, negative affectivity and effortful control. During the child's first year, this final factor is referred to as orientation/regulation.[6]

What do these different dimensions actually mean? Van Cauwenberge and colleagues summarise them as follows:

- Surgency/extraversion indicates the extent to which children react with positive emotions.
- Negative affectivity indicates the extent to which children respond with negative emotions.
- Effortful control indicates the self-regulation of behaviour, attention and emotional reactions.[7]

On the basis of the professional literature, we would like to add a fourth dimension to this list:

• Activity, indicating the extent to which the child's behaviour is active or passive.[8]

The first two dimensions relate to the automatic responses of children to stimulation, while the third relates to the level of control the child has over their emotions. Because newborn babies are not yet capable of regulating their reactions voluntarily, they are offered external help, which is reflected in the alternative orientation/regulation dimension. This examines the extent to which the child shows the first signs of control and is able to direct their attention. It therefore includes aspects such as the ability to persist, to be attentive, to plan and to adjust emotions according to the situation. Consequently, it is possible to see a link with the 'nature' contribution to the executive functions that we describe later in this book. The fourth dimension that we have added relates to a highly visible element that most parents will be all too familiar with: how calm or animated their child is by nature.

Can you change someone's temperament? Probably not, or only marginally at best.

Character

If temperament is determined almost exclusively by heredity, various definitions of character focus on the qualities in people that are developed primarily through interaction with the environment, a process in which nature and nurture impact on each other. As a result, character traits are less hereditary and for this reason also develop later than the temperament dimensions. They are also influenced by maturation and therefore have a biological origin.[9] Character is also more concerned with matters like willpower and morality. This latter aspect is influenced exclusively by the environment, because it relates to the entirety of actions and behaviours that are seen in a society as being correct and desirable.[10]

Can you change someone's character? Probably, up to a certain point.

Personality

There is no generally accepted definition about the nature of personality. According to the biosocial model of Cloninger, the simplest definition is that personality is the combination of all a person's character traits and temperament dimensions.[11] This same line of reasoning can be recognised in another useful working definition: personality is a person's defining set of behaviours, knowledge, opinions and emotional patterns that develop under the influence of biological factors and environmental factors.[12]

Whereas a baby or young child reacts exclusively on the basis of their innate temperament, soon thereafter a variety of different character traits start to develop as a result of interaction with the environment. Taken together, these form the maturing child's personality. This personality can later be seen in how you react, how you work together with others, in your personal convictions and beliefs, and in the extent to which you can be moved or affected in certain situations.

One of the most important personality classifications makes use of five different factors or dimensions, which are generally known as the Big Five.[13] [14] These five factors or dimensions are:

- Extraversion (outgoing/energetic vs. solitary/reserved)
- Agreeableness (friendly/helpful vs. challenging/self-centred)
- Conscientiousness (efficient/organised vs. easy-going/careless)
- Neuroticism (sensitive/nervous vs. secure/confident)
- Openness to experience (inventive/curious vs. consistent/cautious)

The Big Five as dictionary wisdom

Some of the ways in which the concept of the Big Five was developed in the years between its introduction in 1936 and the 1980s are somewhat curious. One method made use of two standard dictionaries, with researchers collecting together all the words that we use to describe a person. These words were then clustered together in non-overlapping groups.[15]

This basic classification is still often used in research but in recent times has undergone an evolution, since it is now widely accepted that not all aspects of personality can be covered within the five dimensions of the Big Five model. This has resulted in the emergence of the HEXACO model, which consists of the following elements:

H. Honesty-Humility

E. Emotionality

X. eXtraversion

A. Agreeableness

C. Conscientiousness

O. Openness to experience[16]

Can these dimensions also be applied to children and adolescents? Since this is open to question, an alternative scale of six dimensions – the Little Six – has been developed that is more specifically applicable for mapping the personality of children and teenagers. The six dimensions are:

- Extraversion
- Agreeableness
- Conscientiousness
- Neuroticism
- Openness to experience
- Activity

It is interesting to note that these six dimensions of personality evolve in different ways throughout a child or teenager's development. According to Soto, agreeableness, conscientiousness and openness to experience at first decline in importance, before improving again later on, whereas extraversion and activity decline progressively throughout the development. Research further suggests that girls display on average more agreeableness than boys and also more conscientiousness. However, during adolescence girls are less emotionally stable and therefore more prone to neuroticism, again on average.[17]

It is equally noteworthy that the differences between children and young people tend to grow throughout their youth and until the end of early adolescence, at which point the differences become more or less stable. This has been observed in research carried out in both the United States and Russia, so that the phenomenon does not appear to be culture dependent.[18]

Among the many other classification systems, there is one that focuses on the darker aspects of personality. This is the so-called Dark Triad,[19] which consists of:

- *Machiavellianism,* named after the famous medieval author who first coined the phrase 'the end justifies the means'. This relates to a person's willingness to make use of manipulation or deception to achieve his or her own goals.
- *Narcissism,* named after Narcissus, a character in Greek mythology who was obsessed by his own looks and personality. This finds expression in personality traits such as egotism, dominance, ambition and lack of empathy.
- *Psychopathy* is the darkest aspect of the Dark Triad, in which a lack of empathy is coupled with impulsiveness and a desire to seek satisfaction through excitement.

Can you change someone's personality? If we accept that personality is the sum of temperament and character, then the answer is again: yes, up to a certain point.

Growth mindset?

Carol Dweck regards personal opinions as an important motor for changing someone's personality.[20] If you can change someone's opinion about how stable their personality is (or is not), then it becomes much easier to change that personality. This corresponds perfectly with the theory of Growth Mindset, for which Dweck is most famous.

(Continued)

According to Dweck, there are two ways of looking at success and failure: you are either convinced that you possess a set of skills that are more or less unchangeable, in which case you have a fixed mindset; or else you believe that your set of skills can always be improved through further effort, in which case you have a growth mindset.[21] Mindset is a concept that has firmly established itself in the educational repertoire in a relatively short period of time. However, the most important conclusion that needs to be borne in mind is that knowledge about your own mindset seems to have only a limited effect on your behaviour, so that a mindset approach is not a miracle remedy for turning low-performing pupils into model pupils.[22]

Nevertheless, the fact remains that as a teacher it is better not to give person-oriented feedback (for example, 'you are a clever girl'), preferring instead to offer feedback that is focused on the task or process (for example, 'no "I before E" mistakes this time' or 'well done, you are making good progress'). The reason why this latter approach works is that it provides pupils with something they can use to move forward. In other words, it allows them to learn from their mistakes. Just being told 'you are clever' does not really help you very much. You can find more on this in the book *The Ingredients for Great Teaching*[23].

How does your personality respond to others? The interpersonal circumplex or interpersonal circle

Perhaps you have already heard of Leary's Rose (although Leary himself never referred to it as such)? This circle, which includes key dimensions like dominance and affection, is often simplified for use in the educational world and describes how someone reacts to others, with 'above' being highly dominant and 'together' being highly affectionate (Figure 1.4).

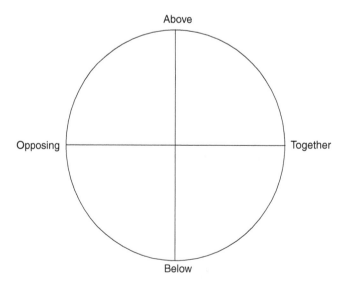

Figure 1.4   The simplified version of the interpersonal circumplex

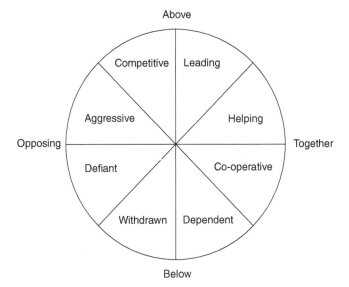

Figure 1.5 The eight segment version of the interpersonal circumplex

The resulting four quadrants are often further subdivided into two, producing a total of eight segments (Figure 1.5).

To make things even more complex, it is possible to add further gradations of behaviour within the circle, such as you can see in the original circle developed by Leary and published in 1957 (Figure 1.6).[24] The different letters describe one of the 16 interpersonal themes Leary described, with A standing for dominant behaviour. In his work Leary was influenced by Erikson amongst others, but he wanted his work to be a functional tool to describe and evaluate how people interact with each other. You can see in this model how the behaviour that is being described in the different gradations always is linked to somebody else. A person provokes obedience, a person submits to somebody else, etc. Also note, however, that Leary's classification groups are not strictly in line with the simplified model depicted above but are more concerned with describing aspects of personality, which was in keeping with Leary's original intention for his model.

Leary's Rose is just one of the many versions of what is referred to as the interpersonal circumplex or interpersonal circle, which was initially developed for research into personality and psychotherapy.[25]

Throughout the years, this link with personality has emerged on numerous occasions. For example, various versions of the circle can be linked to the Big Five.[26] Other versions of the model have also been used to map psychological disorders.

One important idea that is frequently used in education and leadership training goes beyond the straightforward description of personality. This idea is based on the assumption that certain types of behaviour exhibited by one person can have an impact on determining the behaviour of another person. According to Carson, dominant behaviour in one person can trigger submissive behaviour in someone

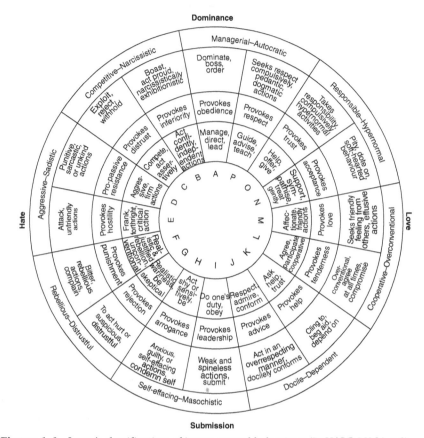

Figure 1.6 Leary's classification of interpersonal behaviour (BoH/CC-BY-SA-4.0)

else and vice versa, these being the two opposing types of behaviour on the vertical 'dominance' axis. However, he also concluded that togetherness behaviour could trigger similar behaviour in someone else and that opposing behaviour could have this same copy-cat effect, these being the corresponding forms of behaviour on the horizontal axis.[27]

We now know that reality can actually be much more complex but the model can still be superimposed onto that complex reality to describe in simple terms how one person reacts to another.

Identity

In addition to concepts like temperament, character and personality, concepts like identity and the self are also important aspects of a person's psychological make-up. If we wish to talk about identity, reference will inevitably need to be made to the work of Erik Erikson, who built on the foundations laid by Freud but took a completely different starting point for his theories. While Freud viewed personality from a psychosexual perspective, Erikson focused on the psychosocial development of children and young people and the evolution of their identity. It is self-evident that in matters relating to identity the environment inevitably plays an important role.

According to Erikson, identity is a subjective sense of self that allows you to feel that you are consistently the same person at different times and in different circumstances. Perhaps your behaviour at home is different from your behaviour at work. Perhaps you move to another country, or get married, or have children. But in all these changing circumstances you continue to recognise yourself as who you are. Erikson refers to this as a feeling of continuity.[28]

Identity of a person or a group?

The question of identity is currently attracting renewed attention in the scientific community. This relates not so much to individual identity as described in psychology but more to questions relating to a social or collective identity. Even so, all these phenomena are essentially linked, because the way others see us has a powerful influence on the way we see ourselves. Imagine that you are a member of the supporters' club of your favourite football team. In that case, part of your personal identity will be determined by your club membership. In response to the questions 'who are you?' or 'what are you?', you will answer that (among other things) 'I am a supporter of...'. At the same time, the opinions and convictions of the supporters' club are determined by its members. If the majority of the supporters are not in favour of the new trainer, this will quickly become the opinion of the group as a whole.

This example corresponds with the manner in which Polletta and Jasper describe how personal and collective identities interact on each other. As an individual person, you can identify with the convictions, values and ideas that form the identity of the group to which you belong. At the same time, the collective identity of that group is formed by the identities of its various group members, including yourself.[29]

Erik Erikson makes a distinction in his model between eight different phases of identity development, in each of which a crisis needs to be resolved between two extremes. As a baby, do you develop a basic form of trust or mistrust? If the latter, will you eventually experience problems in all the subsequent phases? For example, in the second phase, where the crisis needs to be resolved between autonomy and shame, your mistrust will probably make you less inclined to quickly stand on your own two feet. Erikson's eight phases are as follows:

1. Babyhood (0–1 year): development of (basic) trust or mistrust
2. Infancy (2–3 years): development of autonomy or shame

3. Early childhood (4–6 years): development of initiative or blame
4. Late childhood (7–13 years): development of industry or inferiority
5. Adolescence (14–25 years): development of identity or role confusion
6. Early adulthood (25–40 years): development of intimacy or isolation
7. Mid-adulthood (40–65 years): development of generativity or stagnation
8. Late adulthood (plus 65 years): development of integrity or despair

The most important phase in Erikson's theory is phase 5, in which the crisis is between the development of an identity or role confusion.

The Erikson model is given plenty of attention in textbooks but is significantly less used in research. Having said that, much of this research has nevertheless confirmed many of Erikson's hypotheses, especially with regard to adolescence but with the possible exception of the timing. Nowadays, it is more generally accepted that the developmental 'identity crisis' takes place towards the end of the adolescent period and even during the early adult period, although it is not yet clear whether this has always been the case or is a result of a more recent societal evolution.[30]

Building on Erikson's work, James Marcia has elaborated a more concrete structure to describe precisely what happens during the process of identity development. He distinguishes between four different categories:

- **Identity achievement**: As an adolescent, you have sufficiently investigated who you are and have experimented sufficiently to have acquired a clear and secure identity of your own.
- **Foreclosure**: You have chosen an identity for yourself but have not sufficiently experimented, so that you have never had a crisis that caused you to doubt who you really are. Alternatively, perhaps someone made a choice of identity for you, which you felt obliged to accept; for example, continuing the family business.
- **Moratorium**: This is a 'step-by-step' or 'wait-and-see' approach. You experiment with different kinds of identity before moving on to the next step, which, ultimately, may lead to achievement.
- **Identity diffusion**: This is different from the moratorium, in the sense that you have experimented with your identity but have never made a definitive choice. This can be interesting but it may mean, for example, that you have difficulty in forming close attachments.[31]

Not every adolescent will find himself or herself permanently fixed in one of these categories and all four can appear at some stage in a teenager's life.[32] Moreover, differences can also occur in the way that teenagers explore the different identity options available to them. According to Berzonsky[33], there are three broad methods of exploration:

- Informational
- Normative
- Diffuse-avoidant

The informational method involves actively going in search of the various possibilities, while a normative approach usually sees adolescents complying with the expectations of others. Exponents of the diffuse-avoidant method generally tend to postpone making any firm identity choice.

Smits and colleagues argue that these three different methods can be linked to other characteristics. An informational approach is the healthiest, whereas adolescents who adopt the normative approach tend to end up with more prejudices and have more difficulty relating to others. Worst of all is the diffuse-avoidant approach, which can leave young people feeling less than comfortable with who they are.[34] In terms of additional support for these processes, the theory of self-determination (which is discussed elsewhere in the book) can be a useful tool.[35]

How typical is the 'difficult teenager'?

It is almost a cliché: during their adolescent years teenagers are constantly wrestling with themselves and their identity, creating problems for their surrounding environment. This image dates back to 1904, when Granville Stanley Hall described how massive hormonal changes during puberty can result in rebellion and conflicts with parents.[36] The picture painted by Erikson and Marcia in their theories seemed to confirm this. Even so, this is a subject that needs to be approached with a good deal of nuance. Although the 'difficult teenager' stereotype has inspired many TV series and books, research conducted during the 1960s concluded that most adolescents do not go through a 'Sturm und Drang' period, with as few as between one and two out of every ten teenagers experiencing more difficulty during this stage of their life.[37] Most of the research conducted in more recent years has reached the same conclusion.[38] This applies equally to the newer variants of the idea that adolescence is a period of uncertainty and anxiety. Even the more logical of these new theories, such as the quarter-life crisis, which shifts the identity crisis into the phase of early adulthood,[39] seem not to apply to the large majority of young people.[40] If young people do experience their adolescence as being more difficult, this is more often caused by factors in their immediate environment[41] or by wider societal factors such as economic crisis,[42] which increase the likelihood of aggression or feelings of identity discomfort. However, nature and natural disposition can also play a role, which can often be linked to later problems during adulthood.[43]

What does all this mean in terms of educational practice?

Personality theory offers a number of takeaway lessons that can be of use during a young person's upbringing and education:

1. **Be wary of using types and typologies.**

We need to be careful about the use of typologies when dealing with personality and, by extension, should avoid, where possible, the use of broader types like 'pupils' or 'children'. Subdividing young people into categories like 'you are a thinker, trier, doer, decider, dreamer, etc.' is likewise not a good idea.[44]

2. **Be aware that you cannot change everything about a young person.**

You can, however, change some things, if you go about it the right way. For example, personality can be influenced up to a certain point. You will never succeed in converting an introvert child that draws little energy from social activities in large groups into a full-blown extrovert but you can help that child to deal with those situations and to find a place for himself/herself within them. As a result, the child's interaction with the environment and their reaction to that environment can change.

3. **Get to know the children and pupils under your care.**

The dimensions of the Big Five (introvert/extravert, helpful/self-centred, conscientious/careless, nervous/confident, curious/cautious), if used with care, can be a valuable aid for getting to know and understand the pupils you teach. Who are those pupils? Why is this one such a perfectionist? Why is that one so sloppy? Why does one child blossom during social activities, whereas others retreat into their shell? Why is this girl quicker on the uptake than that boy? But be careful: remember that personality can only explain part of a young person's behaviour. Even so, insight into the Big Five dimensions will assist you to think about the specific (educational) needs of individual pupils and will make it possible for you – as a teacher, educator or parent – to better respond to those needs.

4. **Be aware that the growth mindset theory cannot work miracles.**

Focusing exclusively on the development of a growth mindset will not improve a pupil's performance. This performance is affected by a number of different factors. Attributing everything to hard work will result in a negative narrowing of perspective. Of course, it is important to continue to believe in every pupil and to strive to extract the maximum from their potential. But it is even better if you believe in your pupils as a team (collective teacher or student efficacy).

Endnotes

1. See amongst others: Buekens, 2006; Crews, 1996.
2. For a summary of the literature, see De Bruyckere et al., 2019.

3. Cloninger, 2004.

4. Rothbart et al., 2000.

5. Rothbart, 1989.

6. Van Cauwenberge et al., 2012.

7. Note that different classifications are possible, including Cloninger's.

8. For a list of articles arguing this point, see: Soto, 2016.

9. Saucier & Srivastava, 2015.

10. Zohar et al., 2019.

11. Cloninger et al., 1993.

12. Corr & Matthews, 2009.

13. Bell, 2007.

14. Digman, 1990.

15. Allport & Odbert, 1936.

16. Lee & Ashton, 2014.

17. Soto, 2016.

18. Mõttus et al., 2017.

19. Lee & Ashton, 2014.

20. Dweck, 2008.

21. Dweck, 2006.

22. For a discussion of growth mindset, see: De Bruyckere et al., 2019.

23. De Bruyckere, 2018

24. Leary, 1957.

25. Freedman et al., 1951.

26. Hofstee et al., 1992.

27. Carson, 1969; the work cited is from a 2019 republication.

28. Erikson, 1968.

29. Polletta & Jasper, 2001.

30. Steinberg & Morris, 2001.

31. Marcia, 1966.

32. Feldman, 2012.

33. Berzonsky, 2008

34. It does not seem illogical to also make the link here with attachment.

35. Smits et al., 2010.

36. Hall, 1916.

37. Offer, 1969.

38. Larson, 2000.

39. Arnett, 2004.

40. Arnett, 2007.

41. See amongst others: Conger et al., 1994; Ronen et al., 2016.

42. See amongst others: Lazaratou et al., 2017; Parker et al., 2016.

43. Gowers, 2005.

44. In our first edumyths book, *Urban Myths about Learning and Education* we look more closely at the non-existence of learning/teaching styles.

1.3

ATTACHMENT AS AN IMPORTANT STARTING POINT

What questions does this chapter answer?

1. What are the different kinds of attachment?
2. What is a safe or secure attachment and why is it important?
3. What does attachment theory teach us in terms of practice for the upbringing of children and education?

What is the importance of a close relationship between a mother and a child? Or rather: between the child and the people raising the child, including teachers? What influence does attachment have on our development and what does it say about our behaviour? These are just a few of the many questions that we can ask about attachment theory, a theory that has now been around for a number of decades and has given us a number of interesting insights into the development of children and young people.

For many years attachment theory was one of the most important theories in psychology, based on the work of the British psychologist John Bowlby. During the 1930s, Bowlby became fascinated by the way in which children grew up in motherless or deprived families. This eventually led in the 1950s to the formulation of his theory of attachment, which was further elaborated by Mary Ainsworth.[1] Both researchers concluded early on that the extent to which a child is securely attached to the mother or caregiver has an important influence on that child's later development.[2] Even more importantly, it was clear that the adult plays a crucial role in the creation of that secure attachment.[3] But what exactly is secure attachment and how can it be formed? And what is the current thinking about the theory today?

What is secure attachment?

Let us imagine that a one-year-old child is sitting with one of their parents (let's say the mother) in a room where the child has never been before. There are toys on the floor and the mother plays for a few minutes with the child but then lets the child explore the room and the toys further for themselves. Suddenly, a stranger enters the room, talks briefly to the mother and then seeks to engage with the child. Moments later, the mother goes outside, leaving her child in a strange room with a strange person. After some minutes, the mother returns, and the stranger goes outside. A short time later, the mother also leaves again, so that the child is now alone in the room. The stranger comes back and tries to comfort the child. Then the mother also comes back and tries to comfort the child.

How do you think the child will react in these circumstances? By crying? Will the mother be able to comfort the child? Will the stranger be able to comfort the child? The child's reaction and, above all, the extent to which the mother is able to comfort them will reveal much about the nature of the attachment that the child has developed. These various steps are part of a test (known as the Strange Situation test) that Mary Ainsworth devised to see if a child is securely or insecurely attached.[4] Attachment can be seen as a stable and lasting connection between two individuals, often (but not always) in the first instance between a mother and her child.

During the test, the researchers (either via cameras or concealed behind a two-way mirror) look in particular to see how the child reacts to the parent or caregiver. To what extent does the child seek, maintain or even avoid contact with the parent? And to what extent is the child comforted and consoled?

Mary Ainsworth distinguished three kinds of attachment: one secure and two insecure:[5]

- A **securely attached child** will become moderately or even seriously upset if the parent or caregiver leaves the room. Each time the parent or caregiver returns to the strange room, the child will attempt to communicate or seek physical contact with him/her, and he/she will be able to comfort the child quite quickly, so that the child is soon once again playing with the toys. This is the secure form of attachment.
- An **avoidant-insecurely attached child** is less upset than a securely attached child when the parent or caregiver leaves the room. When the parent or caregiver returns, the child will seek to avoid him/her, either by turning its back or deliberately looking away. Instead, the child focuses their attention primarily on the toys. This is the first form of insecure attachment.
- An **ambivalent-insecurely attached child** becomes very upset and even afraid when the parent or caregiver leaves the room but will often react ambivalently when the parent or caregiver returns. For example, the child wants physical contact and will seek to be picked up but once this has happened will also seek to pull away. The child will also be harder to comfort

and will take longer before returning to play with the toys. This is the second form of insecure attachment.

Later research, primarily by Main and Solomon, identified a fourth type of attachment:[6] **disorganised or disoriented attachment**, which is the most extreme form of insecure attachment. The child will display clear signs of being frightened and will react in a confused manner, seeking alternately to cling on to and pull away from the parent or caregiver, or by alternating periods of almost complete immobility with periods of frenzied movement. It is suspected that this fourth type of attachment is caused by abuse or trauma at a very early age, so that the child quickly realises that the 'safe haven' that the parent or caregiver should represent can also be a source of danger.[7]

Over the years, much further research has been done to establish to what extent children and adults are securely and insecurely attached. The majority of the research consistently suggests that in the majority of cases the attachment is secure. On average, this is what happens in 58% of cases but this figure can vary, depending on the region, target group, etc. Avoidant-insecure attachment occurs in 23% of cases, with ambivalent-insecure attachment accounting for the remaining 19%.[8] However, these averages can conceal significant variations. In groups with a low socio-economic status, the distribution is 50% for secure, 33% for avoidant-insecure and 18% for ambivalent-insecure.[9] The more extreme form of disorganised or disoriented attachment occurs relatively infrequently, although it is again more common in certain levels of society.[10] A number of the published articles relating to attachment suggest that insecure attachment can be passed on from generation to generation. One research study conducted in the late 20th century concluded that only 14% of the parents of children with behavioural problems had experienced secure attachment during their own childhood.[11] Certain conditions in the domestic environment – for example, the stress caused by relational problems in the family – can also increase the likelihood of insecure attachment.[12]

What determines the secureness or otherwise of attachment?

Like almost every other subject discussed in this book, the level of secure attachment that a child feels is determined by a variety of different factors, although in this instance nurture seems more important than nature.[13] At the very earliest age, the mother plays a modest but clear role in the child's environment, which has more impact than the joint influence of the parents combined.[14] In particular, it is the sensitive responsiveness and mind-mindedness of these first primary caregivers that is crucial for the development of secure attachment in a safe climate.

What is *sensitive responsiveness*? You can describe it as the extent to which a mother or other primary caregiver can identify the needs of the child and respond to them. Ainsworth described a number of instances of insensitive responsiveness in mothers, which included feeding the child at moments when the child clearly wanted social interaction or playing with the child when the child was obviously hungry.[15] For Ainsworth, a mother's level of sensitive responsiveness was a good predictor for the subsequent level of secure attachment, although later research has partially modified this opinion.[16] It now seems that the more recent concept of *mind-mindedness* is a more reliable predictor.[17] This is 'the capacity as primary caregiver to be mentally attuned to the thoughts and feelings of the young child'. This is similar to sensitive responsiveness but goes a stage further in the sense that the parent or caregiver recognises that the child is an autonomous being with a mind of their own, rather than an entity with needs that must be satisfied. Mind-mindedness therefore implies that the parent or caregiver needs to ask himself/herself why a child does something. In this way, a mind-minded adult will understand, for example, that the child can be overstimulated by the game they are playing and should therefore stop. In other words, it is not simply a question of responding to what the child needs but also requires genuine interaction with the child, so that the child can gradually learn how to express what they feel and/or want. As a result, the parent or caregiver slowly but surely teaches the child how to master their emotions, by first doing it for the child, who eventually evolves through example towards greater self-control.[18] We will return to mind-mindfulness in the chapter on the development of moral thinking and the theory of mind.

The evolution of attachment

Attachment seems to have a biological basis. Although the behaviour only becomes apparent around the eighth month of life, it has its origins much earlier.[19] Perhaps understandably, researchers originally focused on these early months and years. However, we know now that attachment plays a role throughout a person's life, although the nature of this attachment and the people with whom we form attachment evolves with time.

As a young baby, you will become attached initially to your mother or your first primary caregiver, gradually extending this to the rest of your family. However, as you get older you will increasingly form attachments with a growing number of other people in your environment, although these new attachments will continue to be coloured by that first initial attachment. After your parents and family, you will form relationships with teachers, coaches, friends and peers. The quality of these relationships and friendships can have an influence on how you later develop as an adolescent and adult.[20] The nature of these contacts also changes over time. Whereas the attachment of young children is nurtured in a very physical and intimate way, these aspects become less important as children get older, so that today we can now see, for example, that attachment between adolescents can be stimulated through contact via messages on a mobile phone.[21]

A research study from 2019 suggests that the depth of attachment remains fairly stable throughout life,[22] although limited evolutions can take place as a result of the things that happen to you. Avoidant-insecure and ambivalent-insecure attachment both seem to decline with the passage of time. In particular, a good and healthy relationship can help to reduce the avoidant-insecure variant.

A love relationship is also a form of attachment

In the 1980s, a number of researchers described how the same mechanisms that play a role in the attachment of newborn infants can also be seen in healthy romantic relationships between adults. Here are some examples of the similarities:[23]

- Both partners feel safe if the other is near at hand and reacts responsively.
- Both partners have close, intimate and physical contact.
- Both partners show a mutual fascination for each other.
- Both partners can feel insecure if the other is not around.
- Both partners share discoveries with each other.
- Both partners play with the facial expressions of the other and try to influence them.

And yes, sometimes the chatter between love birds can sound just like baby talk!

Why is secure attachment so important?

The level of secure attachment in a child can be linked to various other elements in the later life and adulthood of that child:[24]

- A securely attached child will find it easier at a younger age to assess what others are feeling. Research shows that the children of parents who deal with their offspring in a good mind-minded manner can achieve this by the time they are five years old.[25]
- A securely attached child will make relationships more easily in later life, because attachment has an impact on the way we look at others and how far we are prepared to trust them. The social competencies of securely attached children are often better than those of insecurely attached children.[26]
- Attachment not only determines the way we look at others but also how we look at ourselves. In other words, it has an influence on your self-image and the development of your personality and identity.
- Insecure attachment during the years of childhood increases the risk of developing psychopathologies in later life[27] and the likelihood of suicide.[28]
- Secure attachment makes it easier for the child to adjust at school.[29]

Attachment and mind-mindedness in child day care

If we now know that attachment is not only important during the very first months and years of life, it is logical that growing attention is also being paid to matters like mind-mindedness in professional environments, such as child day care centres and pre-school nurseries,[30] where it has become evident that dealing with young children in a mind-minded way can have an important beneficial impact on their development.[31]

Ruben Fukkink[32] has summarised the most important pedagogic consequences as follows:

- Creating a safe climate means having a fixed group of adults, so that the child repeatedly sees the same faces. Fixed routines also contribute to a feeling of safety, not only between the staff and the children but also between the children themselves.
- Pedagogic staff must not treat children as though they are highly dependent and must avoid too many conflictual interactions with them.
- Pedagogic staff must adopt a sensitive attitude to children of all ages and must be able to pick up the signals given by children, interpret these correctly and respond accordingly.
- Interactions with the children must not be purely routine. In addition, pedagogic staff must also show a sensitive and responsive attitude in the group context of childcare and in their dealings with several children at the same time, not just in one-to-one situations. This feeling of sensitivity at group level is thought to be an important predictor for the secure attachment of young children.

Attachment: yes, but...

Like many other psychological theories, in recent years some of the work relating to attachment has also come in for criticism. This has resulted in two important nuances:

- Viewed in historical terms, a great deal of attachment research focused primarily on mothers, whereas a child can also become attached to others in their environment. It is now clear that children can become attached to different people in different ways. A child can be securely attached to their mother, insecurely attached to their father and attached in yet another different way to, say, their grandparents. Although a good relationship between the father and child has little impact on the child's initial attachment, a bad relationship between father and child can negatively affect the child's bond with the mother.[33]

- In addition to the wider influence of the environment, we now know that there is also a connection between attachment and natural disposition, in other words, nature. Some children seem to have a greater natural propensity for certain kinds of attachment.[34] Other pre-birth factors – such as the use of drugs or alcohol by the mother during the pregnancy – can also have an effect.[35]

What does all this mean in terms of raising children and educational practice?

1. **Secure attachment is the basis for a good relationship.**

   Both in education and in child raising, having a good relationship with the child is important. This is something that you can fall back on at moments when, as a teacher or a caregiver, you make a 'mistake'; for example, if you unexpectedly get angry or overreact. There is nothing wrong with this; it will inevitably happen, because you are only human! If you have a good attachment, bond or relationship with the child, this kind of short 'breakdown' is quickly repaired and forgotten. You apologise and say what you did wrong and why you did it. In this way, you not only teach the children that making mistakes is a natural part of life but also how you can correct the situation.

2. **Invest in good attachment with the child.**

   You can do this by creating an environment in which the child feels safe and at ease. This means somewhere where the child can be themselves and where the child's emotions can be recognised, named and given a place. In other words, a clear and well-defined safe space in which to play. Within this space, it is the task of the teacher or caregiver to learn how to assess the (educational) needs and requirements of the child and to respond to them appropriately. What does the child need in this situation? A friendly chat or greater focus on the study material, which will allow the child to forget the bad situation at home?

3. **Be aware that insecurely attached children can often deal less well with their emotions (which can sometimes find expression in behavioural problems).**

   First and foremost, you need to be kind and understanding. Help the child or pupil to deal better with their emotions by practical examples, modelling, naming and recognition, until the child gradually gets greater self-control over their own emotional reactions. We will look at this more closely in the chapter on executive function.

── Teacher takeaways ──────────────────────────

How do you support children in cases of death and grieving?

Obviously, this is something you want to spare every child and young person but it is, unfortunately, an inevitable fact of life that people and animals can die. How can you best guide children through the grieving process when this happens?

How do children react at different ages and how do you deal with this?

Children and young people react differently to loss than adults. There are also major differences between themselves, depending on their age. Himebauch and colleagues summarise these differences as follows:[36]

- 0 to 2 years: These children still have no conception of death but can still feel sorrow and can grieve, in part by absorbing the emotions and sadness that is evident in others in their environment.

  How do you deal with this? As far as possible, by maintaining your usual fixed routines and by keeping them in close contact with the important people in their immediate surroundings.

- 2 to 6 years: At this age, children often see death as something temporary and therefore reversible. They can devise the most fantastic explanations to account for what has happened, in some of which they place the blame on themselves.

  How do you deal with this? Offer them simple and clear explanations, avoid euphemisms and well-meaning falsehoods, correct wrong ideas and make clear that the deceased person will not be coming back.

- 6 to 8 years: At this age, most children understand that death is something permanent but do not think that it will happen to everyone, themselves included. They can experience anger, both towards the deceased and towards the environment that could not prevent the death. In some cases, they also experience fear, feelings of depression and physical complaints.

  How do you deal with this? In addition to providing clear and realistic information, it is important to involve the child in the various rituals surrounding death, such as the funeral. Schools can also play a role in this and, like the rest of the child's environment, must show understanding for the child's behaviour and offer support, where needed.

(Continued)

- 8 to 12 years: At this age, children already have an adult conception of death: it is permanent, irreversible and universal. They understand what is happening and what has caused it to happen. It is possible that the children will try to rationalise everything, because they cannot give their feelings a proper place, which may result in them seeming morbid and asking questions that some in their environment may find shocking because they seem to be so insensitive, even though it is never the child's intention to shock. Children in this age category also start to show an interest in religious and cultural customs, and the rituals surrounding death. Some may be troubled by feelings of guilt.

  How do you deal with this? Any feelings of guilt must certainly be discussed and clarified. Talk about your own feelings as an adult and also give the child plenty of opportunities to talk in response. Involve the child as much as they want to be involved in the final parting from those who are dying and in the funeral rites of those who have died.

- 12 to 18 years: At this age, teenagers have an adult understanding of death, which may result in them asking existential questions about life and its termination. In exceptional cases, this may be linked to risk behaviour that sees them flirt with their own mortality. Sometimes they are less interested in the adult rituals of death and, in consequence, can feel misunderstood. Powerful emotional reactions are possible, in which they are not always able to recognise their feelings or express them in words.

  How do you deal with this? Ensure that they have enough contact with peers and friends and provide plenty of opportunities to give them support, whilst at the same time respecting their independence.

You will note that the above descriptions make frequent use of words like 'often' and 'sometimes'. Like so many aspects of human development, there are no uniform reactions: children can react to death in a manner that is older or younger than their actual years.

It is also important to realise that illness or a death, particularly within the close family, can mean added responsibilities for the child, which is something that schools need to take into account.[37] Death of a loved one can affect the development of any child and feelings of loss and grief may emerge in the later phases of that development,[38] which underlines the importance of good guidance and support.[39]

Endnotes

1. Bretherton, 1992.
2. Bowlby, 1982.

3. Sroufe, 1996.
4. Ainsworth et al., 2015.
5. The descriptions are based on: Ainsworth & Bell, 1970; Van IJzendoorn et al., 1991.
6. Main & Solomon, 1990.
7. Beeney et al., 2017.
8. See amongst others: Bakermans-Kranenburg & Van IJzendoorn, 2009.
9. Van IJzendoorn & Bakermans-Kranenburg, 1996.
10. Granqvist et al., 2017.
11. Van Ijzendoorn & Bakermans-Kranenburg, 1996.
12. See amongst others: Cummings & Davies, 1994; Davies & Cummings, 1994.
13. Brussoni et al., 2000.
14. See amongst others: Belsky & Fearon, 2008; De Wolff & Van Ijzendoorn, 1997.
15. Ainsworth et al., 1974.
16. De Wolff & Van IJzendoorn, 1997.
17. See amongst others: Meins et al., 2011; Meins et al., 2003.
18. Zeegers et al., 2018.
19. Thompson, 2013.
20. Fraley et al., 2013.
21. Lepp et al., 2016.
22. Chopik et al., 2019.
23. Shaver & Hazan, 1987.
24. This summary is based on Thompson, 2013, supplemented with the further research mentioned.
25. Kirk et al., 2015.
26. Kenny & Gallagher, 2002.
27. Nicolai, 2001.
28. Zortea et al., 2021.
29. Rice et al., 1995.
30. Degotardi & Sweller, 2012.
31. Colonnesi et al., 2017.
32. Fukkink, 2017.
33. See amongst others: Brown et al., 2007; Benware, 2013.
34. Barbaro et al., 2017.
35. O'Connor et al., 2002.
36. Himebauch et al., 2008.
37. Wood, 2008.
38. Keirse, 2002.
39. Baum et al., 2014.

1.4

MORAL DEVELOPMENT: THE DIFFERENCE BETWEEN RIGHT AND WRONG, AND HOW WE LEARN IT

What questions does this chapter answer?

1. How do children develop a moral sense that allows them to distinguish between right and wrong?
2. What role does empathy play in our moral development and can this be trained?
3. How can we support our moral development?

Imagine that someone you love is suffering from a deadly disease. Fortunately, there is good news: a doctor has a medicine that will cure the sufferer.[1] However, the doctor is asking a high price for the medicine, so high that you will never be able to afford it. You plead with him to lower his price but without success. 'It is my discovery,' he says, 'and I want to make some money from it.' So, what do you do next? Given the circumstances, would you be justified in breaking into the doctor's office to steal the medicine? The answer to this question is not simply a straightforward matter of right and wrong. It is more a matter of arguments for and against. Is it permissible to steal in a good cause? Or should you follow the law at all times? And, more generally, do children think differently on these matters than adults? That is the subject of Lawrence Kohlberg's theory of moral development.

From what age does a child know that there are some things it is not allowed to do? And from what age does a child become helpful to others? When does a child know that something is morally right or wrong? These are questions that have occupied scientists for many years and the final answers have still not been given. At the present time, there are a number of different theories in circulation, each of which is subject to a degree of criticism. These theories, of which Kohlberg's is the most important, often see a link between cognitive development and moral development. At the same time, in recent decades new approaches have emerged that take as their starting point the concept of empathy: the extent to which one person can understand and share the feelings of another. In this chapter, we will look at both schools of thought and, in particular, see how we can help children and young people to deal with these complex matters.

Kohlberg's stages of moral development

Kohlberg sees the development of a moral sense as part of the development of a person's personality. This is not illogical, and the idea had already been incorporated into many previous approaches to personality development, such as Freud's, which foresaw the development of something like a conscience, an *uber-ich* or superego. Kohlberg based his theory of moral development on the processes associated with the development of thought in a child, building further on the work of Piaget, who had also elaborated his own theory to explain moral development in children. Like Piaget, Kohlberg identified different stages in a child's cognitive-moral growth. He argued that there are six such stages, grouped in pairs at three different levels.[2]

These three development levels are pre-conventional, conventional and post-conventional. The names of all three levels are based on the word 'convention', which can be defined as 'a treaty' or 'an agreement' but can also be seen as 'a rule'. According to Kohlberg, there are two stages before a child can understand rules, two stages when rules are very important for the child, and two stages when (older) children understand the relativity of rules.

This results in the following programme of development:

- First level: pre-conventional level

    o   Stage 1: Acting to avoid punishment[3]

    You do something or do not do something to avoid punishment. As a young child, you do not yet know why it is wrong to 'steal' a sweet but you refrain from doing it, because last time your mother was very angry and made you stand in the corner.

    o   Stage 2: Acting to further your own best interests

    You now realise that other people also have their own needs and desires, and you begin a process of exchange that allows you to satisfy your own needs and desires: 'If I help with the washing up, do I get a sweet?' This is the period when a child starts negotiating to achieve their own objectives, although Kohlberg contends that there is still no moral awareness involved.

- Second level: conventional level
  - o Stage 3: Doing good and the golden rule

    The child now understands that there are such things as rules or conventions and that 'doing good' or 'being good' are important. In concrete terms, this means that the child's motives for doing something must be good, which involves taking account of others rather than simply doing something for yourself. In other words, you do it because it is the right thing to do. The link with key social aspects of life is clear: mutual friendships and values like loyalty, trust, respect and gratitude become important. With his 'golden rule', Kohlberg describes a form of behaviour in which rules are absolute and cannot be infringed: 'No mummy, I can't do that, because my teacher said so.'

  - o Stage 4: Living together and acting according to your conscience

    The child now understands that rules are necessary to allow people to live together in harmony. 'If everyone behaves however they like, the result would be chaos!' You realise that personal values and the rules laid down by society can sometimes clash but you place compliance with the rules ahead of your own individual interests. 'I would like to help you but I can't, because it is not allowed.'

- Third level: post-conventional level
  - o Stage 5: Values and rules are relative

    Whereas in stage 4 'the letter of the law' was central, in stage 5 the older child now starts to realise that there is also such a thing as 'the spirit of the law' and that values, agreements and rules can vary from person to person and from society to society. You learn to make a distinction between moral rules and legal rules. Theft might be legally wrong but stealing a medicine to save the life of a loved one may be justified. Rules are now interpreted in light of the context and the circumstances of the situation.

  - o Stage 6: Universal ethical principles and values

    The young person now has their own set of rational values and also acts in accordance with universal principles, such as the equality of human rights and respect for the dignity of both people and animals.

According to Kohlberg, not everyone reaches this final stage of moral development. Nor does he set theoretical age categories by which each of the six stages should be completed. For example, in his work he described how one 13-year-old was still in stage 2, although in other cases it is possible to see a link between Kohlberg's stages and the age categories that Piaget proposed in his theory.

How do children view lying?

To some extent, the way in which children deal with the truth and lying is in keeping with Kohlberg's theory. Whereas younger children see the truth and lies in clear black-and-white terms, as they get older, they adopt a more nuanced approach that takes account of the reasons why someone has lied.[4] In this way, for example, a white lie might be excused or be regarded as a less serious 'fault'.

The limitations of the Kohlberg model

The literature contains a number of criticisms of Kohlberg's theories. The most frequently cited shortcomings and limitations are as follows:

1. **Does reaching stage 6 mean that you are a good person?**

    It is perfectly possible for someone in stage 6 to be a rational thinking, detached and cold person. Or as Straughan puts it: 'How to reach stage 6 and remain a bastard'.[5]

2. **What about girls and women?**

    Much of Kohlberg's research focused on boys and men from white middle-class backgrounds. Some critics argue that girls and women may develop in a different way.[6]

3. **Thinking is not the same as behaviour.**

    Kohlberg concentrates primarily on cognitive processes and the reasoning that decides whether or not something is right or wrong. But thinking something is not the same as doing something. We do not always do what we think, although older research suggests that there is probably a link.[7] It is also possible to ask whether the reactions we show in certain situations are always so carefully considered as Kohlberg implies. Think, for example, of the role of fallacies described in behavioural economics. Moreover, there are many other instances where people act on the basis of their 'gut-feeling' rather than on rational thought.[8]

Moral credit: 'I have already been good...'

In the news, you can sometimes read or hear stories about 'benefactors' who have given huge amounts of money to good causes, only to be later exposed as something less than honest and/or decent in their other activities. There are strong scientific indications

(Continued)

that a phenomenon exists that might best be described as moral licence or moral credit. What does this mean, exactly? People who have done something good sometimes think that this means they have 'earned' the compensatory right to do something bad. In other words, it is a way to buy off your conscience. 'I am a vegetarian [good for the climate], so I can take a plane for my holidays [bad for the climate].' Or: ' I do voluntary work, so cheating on my partner is not a problem.'[9] But be careful: the researchers into this phenomenon do not claim (and nor do we) that all people who do good also have a darker side!

Is moral behaviour innate or learnt? Theory of mind or the importance of empathy

This seems more like a philosophical or theological question: are people by nature good or bad? It is indeed a question that has been debated for many years, starting in the modern scientific community with the research carried out by Piaget in the 1930s.[10] In the first instance, his work was a reaction to a point of view that still sometimes emerges today; namely, that morality is imposed on a person by their environment, although he was equally sceptical about an overly individual approach which suggests that children develop a kind of personal intuition for what is right and wrong.[11] This latter argument is still current and plays an important role in what is known as theory of mind (ToM), where one of the central questions relates to the age at which a child can empathise with others. According to Hoffman, the extent to which a person can empathise with others is an important precondition for moral behaviour, in addition to the necessary cognitive processes described by Kohlberg.[12]

Theory of mind?

Theory of mind can be described as the ability to read the minds of others.[13] Of course, we cannot really do this but you get the general idea. You must have a good sense of what others are thinking. To do this naturally implies that these others are intelligent and independently thinking beings, just as you are also someone who is completely different from the rest of the world. It is as if you need to have a theory about how and why different minds to yours can exist: hence the name.

Theory of mind is often associated with research into autism and one of the prevailing hypotheses contends that children with autism have difficulty in assessing what others are thinking. At the same time, theory of mind also forms an important basis for current thinking about empathy, which means that it also has relevant implications for moral development. This reasoning argues that if you cannot empathise with what the other person is feeling, you will be less inclined to take account of those feelings. Simon Baron-Cohen even suspects that a poorly functioning empathic centre in the brain can help to explain in part the behaviour of psycho-paths and some criminals. But the emphasis here is on 'in part': it is not the case that everyone with a defective empathic centre will automatically become a criminal.[14]

How do you measure theory of mind? On the basis of 'false beliefs'

In order to determine the development of theory of mind in children, use is made of tasks that involve a specific form of reasoning, known as false beliefs. With false beliefs, stories are told, or scenes are acted in which someone is tricked. Consider, for example, the following story that is played out for the children using two puppets, Sally and Anne. Sally puts a bar of chocolate into a basket, watched by Anne. Sally then goes off for a short walk. While she is away, Anne takes the bar of chocolate and puts it in a box. The children are then asked to predict where Sally will look for the bar when she comes back from her walk. Children who already have theory of mind will know that Sally cannot know that Anne has moved the chocolate, and so they will answer 'in the basket'. Children who do not yet have theory of mind will answer 'in the box'. This test is known as the 'unexpected transfer test'. Another example of such a test is the 'deceptive box' task, which involves giving the children a box of a popular brand of sweets, only to find that the box contains pencils when they open it. When asked what they had expected to see, children without theory of mind will answer 'pencils', while those with theory of mind will say 'sweets'.

When do children develop theory of mind?

On average, most children are able to correctly solve the above mentioned 'false belief' exercises by the time they are four years old. However, this does not mean that children do not have theory of mind at an earlier age. Peter Mitchell sus-pects that the development process is a gradual one, so that children systematically acquire more and more theory of mind, so that their number of false ideas gradu-ally declines.[15]

Bearing in mind the caution and caveats that always need to be adopted when attempting to classify such matters, this development might progress as follows:

- 1 year
  - o Babies learn to understand that people do things for a reason and that you can communicate about how you feel, which may allow you to influence other people's actions. For example, they realise that people can laugh or cry because they feel happy or sad, and know that this can prompt reactions in, say, mummy and daddy. This relates back to aspects of what we discussed in the chapter on attachment and mind-mindedness.

- o   This opens the door for new forms of communication; for example, looking at a book together.
- 2 years
  - o   Children start to realise that what they see, think or feel is not necessarily the same as what others see, think or feel.
- 3 years
  - o   Children realise that what someone thinks takes place inside that person's head and that you do not necessarily need to see something in order to be able to think or talk about it.
  - o   They still make mistakes in 'false belief' exercises.
- 4 years
  - o   Children realise that a person's convictions and desires can play a role in how someone reacts.
  - o   They now give an increasing number of correct answers in 'false belief' exercises.
- 4–6 years
  - o   Children continue to systematically improve in 'false belief' exercises.

Bye-bye Piaget?

Theory of mind runs contrary to the arguments of one of the founding fathers of developmental psychology: Jean Piaget. Piaget gave a central place in his thinking to egocentrism and contended that it took children quite some time before they were able to empathise with others. According to his vision, children continue until the end of their early childhood to focus exclusively on their own perspective of the world and ignore others, which hinders communication and cooperation with these others. However, it was already becoming clear during the 1970s and 1980s that in specific circumstances children as young as two years old are capable of assessing the perspective of someone else.[16]

Does empathy make you a better person? Not necessarily. It has been suggested that people usually empathise better with the people who are most like them or who belong to their group, so that they have less empathy with 'the others' who are different.

How can moral development be supported?

It seems probable that moral development is in part innate and in part influenced by the child's environment.[17] So how can we help children to develop their sense of morality?

In young children, theory of mind can be stimulated in different ways:[18]

- Presenting children with situations that involve false beliefs.
- Imitation games and role play, in which the child has to imagine he/she is someone else.
- Reading stories that contain different perspectives.
- As parents, caregivers or teachers, talking about and explaining your own thoughts and feelings.
- Interaction with other children of different ages.

There is a considerable overlap between working to develop theory of mind and working to develop social skills (an overlap that is not illogical).

Books with people seem to be more effective than books with animals

Canadian researchers conducted a study to investigate the effect of reading books on moral development, in which one test group of young children was read stories involving people in the leading role, while a second group was read comparable stories in which animals featured most prominently. The social interactions of the two groups were then monitored and measured; for example, to what extent were the children inclined to share things with others. What happened? Children who had been read the more realistic stories with people were (slightly) more willing to share than the children who had listened to stories with animals. According to the researchers, these findings are in line with those of earlier research, which also concluded that realistic stories are more effective in shaping the development of children.[19]

As children get older, other forms of interaction and stimulation can be used, such as discussions, moral dilemmas, etc. However, the influence of friends and the role played by what young people do in their free time also becomes significantly greater. In particular, it seems that friends have an important impact on how socially or negatively young people behave.[20]

Teacher takeaways

How do you deal with bad news in the media?

Perhaps you would prefer your children, pupils or students to be kept away from worrying news about natural disasters and terrorist attacks but this is almost impossible in an increasingly mediatised world. For that reason, it is better to know

(Continued)

how you can best deal with your children and their concerns when they are confronted with bad news.

Peter Nikken has summarised how children of different ages react on average to bad news in the media:[21]

- **4-6 years:** These children relate everything to themselves and are unable to separate fact from fiction. It is therefore advisable to shield children of this age from bad news and to reassure them that nothing is going to happen to them.
- **From 7 years:** By this age, children are able to make the distinction between fiction and reality. This means that you can discuss bad news with them. However, it is important to put the news in its proper context and to again provide reassurance, where necessary.
- **9-12 years:** With children of this age, you can talk openly about the news. They have a need for the nuancing, clarification and explanation of bad news.

If we look at the process of moral development, particularly as expounded by Kohlberg, it needs to be borne in mind that some of the opinions expressed by children and teenagers may seem outspoken. Sometimes, these opinions will be outspokenly positive; sometimes, they will be outspokenly negative. In this latter instance, the opinions can sometimes be shocking for adults but they are not necessarily an indication of, for example, radicalisation.

How can you best deal with this?

Some concrete tips:

- Above all, listen to what the children and young people have to say. Answer their questions honestly and tell them what worries you about the situation.
- Even if the children do not take the initiative to discuss bad news, it is a good idea to ask them if they would like to talk about it but without forcing them.
- Give them the chance to express their emotions. This does not necessarily have to be in words; drawing what is on their mind is also possible. Do not hide your own emotions but attempt to explain them instead. Children and young people often want to do something positive in response to bad news; allow room for this.
- Point out the exceptional nature of natural disasters, terrorist attacks, wars, etc.
- Stick to the facts and do not make the situation more dramatic than it is. It is also important to mention the possibility of hoaxes - false stories and manipulated images - that often spread quickly via social media. Websites like snopes.com can help in this respect.
- Avoid complex and unclear explanations that children cannot understand and that will only make them even more confused and anxious.

- Make sure that certain children in the group or class are not targeted by others because of their convictions, opinions or beliefs. Make clear to these children that they can always come to you in the event of problems. Also intervene to nuance the outspoken comments of some children that might be hurtful for other children. Emphasise that everyone is shocked, moved or affected by what has happened.[22]

How can you discuss controversial matters in the classroom?

Natural disasters and terrorist attacks can certainly lead to discussions in the class-room, especially among teenagers. Such discussions are generally a good thing but they can be a challenge for teachers if feelings are running high. You do not want to put a brake on your pupils' development of their own opinions and thoughts but nor do you want some of them to be inadvertently hurt by the outspoken comments of their classmates, so that a degree of nuance is always necessary.

The following guidance can help:[23]

- Create a safe and respectful climate in the class.
- Prepare yourself properly for the discussion.
- Explore what your pupils already know or have experienced.
- Provide relevant information and check if there are still any unanswered questions.
- Help the pupils to make the connection between the events and their own lives.
- Give the pupils an opportunity to further explore the situation.
- Allow the pupils to formulate their own opinions.
- Continually monitor the tone and atmosphere of the discussion, so that things do not get out of hand.
- Search for possible links with the pupils' home situation.
- Allow the pupils to 'do something'.
- Good discussions in class are something you need to encourage and practise constantly.

Endnotes

1. This example is a variation of the so-called 'Heinz problem'. See Kohlberg, 1981.
2. Kohlberg, 1976.
3. Kolhberg described the different stages as follows:
   - Heteronomous morality
   - Individualism, instrumental purpose and exchange

- o   Mutual interpersonal expectations, relationships, and interpersonal conformity
- o   Social system and conscience
- o   Social contract or utility and individual rights
- o   Universal ethical principles

We prefer to use our own descriptions for these stages.

4. Talwar et al., 2016.
5. Straughan, 1986.
6. Gilligan, 1977.
7. Turiel & Rothman, 1972.
8. Arnold, 2000.
9. Merritt et al., 2010.
10. Piaget, 2013.
11. Carpendale, 2009.
12. Hoffman, 2001.
13. Long et al., 2010.
14. Baron-Cohen, 2012.
15. Mitchell, 2017.
16. See amongst others: Borke, 1975; Light, 1983.
17. Dahl, 2019.
18. Hofmann et al., 2016.
19. Larsen et al., 2018.
20. Hart et al., 2017.
21. Kennisnet, 2016.
22. These tips are based on: National Center for School Crisis and Bereavement, 2018; National Society for the Prevention of Cruelty to Children, 2017; Kennisnet, 2016.
23. Klasse, 2015.

1.5

INTELLIGENCE: MORE THAN JUST A FIGURE AFTER TAKING A TEST[1]

What questions does this chapter answer?

1. What is intelligence and how do you measure it?
2. To what extent is intelligence innate?
3. Why are intelligence tests useful (and why not)?
4. What does all this mean in terms of educational practice?

When is someone clever or intelligent? We have regularly posed this question to our students in recent years and have received many different answers. Someone who knows a lot? Someone who can easily solve problems? Perhaps someone with plenty of life experience? These are just a few of the answers we have had. It is probably no coincidence that the scientific community seems to find it equally hard to provide a single and generally accepted definition of intelligence. In fact, it has been said (not without a degree of truth) that there are almost as many definitions of intelligence as there are intelligence researchers![2] Based on a survey of widely used possible definitions, Legg and Hutter identified the following three elements as those that most frequently occur:

Intelligence...

- ...is a property that an individual agent has as it interacts with its environment or environments;
- ...is related to the agent's ability to succeed or profit with respect to some goal or objective; and
- ...depends on how able the agent is to adapt to different objectives and environments.[3]

Extrapolating on these three elements, they arrived at the following definition:[4]

> Intelligence measures an agent's ability to achieve goals in a wide range of environments.[5]

Perhaps the most surprising word in this definition is 'measures'. Although intelligence is much older than IQ tests and has been discussed by philosophers for centuries, in our modern age the subject has been taken over by psychologists, who often focus on the need for its measurement. This evolution has much to do with education.

IQ tests: their creation and development

The first useable IQ test was developed in 1904 by Alfred Binet and Theodore Simon, in response to a request by the French government. The introduction of compulsory education meant there was a need for a test to identify which pupils scored poorly, so that they could be helped to improve.[6] The test consisted of a series of questions and tasks that a wide range of pupils and (later) others were asked to complete. In the first instance, Binet used words like 'imbecile' and 'idiot' to describe those who performed particularly badly, as a means to determine what level of handicap could be attributed to them on the basis of their measured IQ.[7] As a result, these initially neutral terms became heavily charged with negative implications, so that over time their use became less acceptable. Later, Binet linked the test to an age-based result, so that the number of correct solutions would give an indication of the tested person's mental age. If you answered as many questions correctly as an average 15-year-old, you would have a mental age of 15 years. The original aim of both Binet and Simon and the French government was humane: they wanted to provide each child with education suited to the child's ability.[8]

A few years afterwards, in 1912, William Stern devised a way to convert this result into a number, by comparing the tested person's mental age with their actual or chronological age. The result was the person's intelligence quotient or IQ, this being the mental age divided by the chronological age. Some time later, it was suggested to multiply this answer by 100, in order to produce a figure that was easier to use.[9]

So how exactly did this work? Here is a concrete example:

- Imagine that a 10-year-old child answers as many questions as a 12-year-old.
  - Mental age: 12
  - Chronological age: 10
  - IQ: 12/10 x 100 = 120
- Imagine that a 10-year-old child answers as many questions as an 8-year-old.
  - Mental age: 8
  - Chronological age: 10
  - IQ: 8/10 x 100 = 80

Based on this system, it is clear that the average level of intelligence should, by definition, be 100. The majority of people (roughly 68%) have an IQ between 85 and 115 (a deviation by one standard deviation from the average of 100). If you have an IQ score of above 130 you belong to the 2.2% of the population that is highly intelligent. A further 2.2% of the population has an IQ lower than 75, which classifies them as being intellectually disabled.

In order to be able to make valid comparisons, it is important that everyone does the same test in the same way, so that no other factors can have an influence. For this reason, the entire procedure for taking an intelligence test is described in detail and must be followed to the letter. The test must also be calibrated regularly to take account of the rapidly changing nature of society. If, for example, you asked the participants as part of an intelligence test in the 1980s to describe a typewriter, that would have been a meaningful question at that time. If you were to ask that same question today, it would be more properly at home in a history test!

An intelligence test is therefore a standardised test or measuring instrument that can be used to compare the performance of one person against the performance of another person. Nowadays, there are several such tests, like the Stanford–Binet test, the Wechsler scales, including the Wechsler Intelligence Scale or WISC, now into its fourth version (IV) and the Wechsler Adult Intelligence Scale or WAIS, now into its third version (III), the Kaufman Assessment Battery for Children (KABC-II), etc.

The majority of these tests measure two different types of ability; namely, verbal ability and performance ability, which are combined to give a single end score.

The verbal questions set tasks like the following:

- Comparisons, such as the question: 'What is the correspondence between blue, green and yellow?'
- Concepts, such as the question: 'Why must people vote during elections?'
- Memorising series of numbers like 3-5-2, which can be made longer as the test candidates get older.

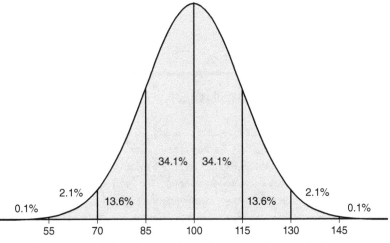

Figure 1.7 The typical distribution of intelligence in the population

Using a series of numbers to test verbal ability might seem strange but it has been shown that such questions are nonetheless a good predictor of verbal skills.[10]

Performance tests set tasks like replicating a design with building blocks or in drawings. The completion of lists, figures and other logical puzzles is also used.

There is usually a degree of agreement between a person's verbal and performance intelligence but not always. For example, it is perfectly possible for a child to have a higher score for the former and a lower score for the latter.

Fluid and crystallised

When dealing with intelligence, another distinction that needs to be made is the difference between fluid intelligence and crystallised intelligence, which together form general intelligence (often represented as the letter 'g'). This distinction dates back to the work of Hebb and Cattell[11] during the mid-20th century. Fluid intelligence is the ability to solve new problems, which requires skills such as understanding, problem-solving ability and learning ability. When faced with new challenges, you know how to deal with them because you possess the necessary mental capabilities, which are often to a large extent innate. Crystallised intelligence involves the use of acquired knowledge, skills and experience. You find yourself in situations that you recognise as problems that you have already encountered in the past, so that you first try to apply the same solution that worked on previous occasions. In theory, this kind of intelligence increases as a person gets older (providing the person receives schooling and can benefit from a stimulating environment) and finds expression in (amongst other things) general knowledge and vocabulary.[12]

It would be logical to assume that fluid intelligence is inborn and that crystallised intelligence is shaped by the environment but things are not that simple. It is certainly true that the basis of fluid intelligence is now widely regarded as being hereditary but the research results are not uniformly clear on this point.[13] Moreover, since you unquestionably need fluid intelligence in order to build up and better use (through practice) your store of crystallised intelligence, this too is also genetically determined to a certain extent.[14]

Are there other forms of intelligence?

A popular criticism of 'classic' intelligence is that it is too limited and fails to take account of other forms of wisdom and talent. Perhaps the most well-known alternative theory in this respect is the 'multiple intelligence' concept of Howard Gardner, which we discussed in our first educational myths book, where we concluded (with a certain degree of nuance) that people do indeed differ in matters of intelligence but that Gardner's theory has no predictive value - specific to intelligence, as has been the case with the overall approach ever since Binet and Simon - and that his classification was open to contestation.[15] In 2016,

Gardner wrote a short essay looking back at his career, in which his theory of multiple intelligences was covered at some length. He mentioned three elements which, in their way, were far more damning than the criticism we had given in our book.

Gardner stated that:

- he had never properly researched his theory;
- in his opinion, his theories are now out of date; and
- he used intelligence as a concept to get his work published.[16]

Is intelligence innate or learnt?

Initially, a significant number of researchers argued that intelligence was innate. And there is indeed a strong basis for claiming that intelligence is genetic... in part.[17] Because at the same time, this does not mean (like so many other aspects in this domain) that everything is predetermined at birth, so that the environment does not have an influence. Over time, the influence of heredity on intelligence increases from roughly 20% at birth to roughly 80% in later life.[18] The bad news is that this means that you will get progressively more like your parents as you age; the good news is that you will never be completely like them, not least because you have two different parents.

Moreover, there are enough other indications to suggest that the environment can also play an important role in intelligence. The most famous of these is probably the Flynn effect. Flynn described how the average score of a population in intelligence tests can increase over the years (although more recent evidence suggests that it can also decrease: the so-called Reversed Flynn effect). As mentioned earlier, the questions in IQ tests are regularly updated and recalibrated. Given this fact, Flynn asked himself whether the average IQ would remain consistent over time. It became apparent that from the 1930s onwards, a massive increase in average IQ level was recorded in the western world.[19] But the reasons for this growth in intelligence remain a mystery. Suggestions include more intellectually challenging television,[20] less lead in the atmosphere,[21] better guessing,[22] improved and wider access to education,[23] etc. However, it seems that the Flynn effect has now come to a halt in many European countries,[24] while recent research also suggests that a noticeable increase is still taking place in other parts of the world, such as China.[25] All these examples seem to confirm the influence that environmental factors can have on intelligence.

The influence of the environment becomes even clearer if we look at the effect that adoption can have on intelligence.[26] If you are fortunate enough to be a child that is adopted by a richer and better educated family, you can expect your IQ to increase by between 12 and 18 points in comparison with children who are not able to change their social class. Last but not least, one of the very best ways to improve someone's intelligence is... proper schooling! Every extra year that a child attends school increases their IQ by between 1 and 5 points.[27]

Scarcity

Mullainathan, Shafir and colleagues demonstrated in a series of experiments that stress and worry – for example, about your financial situation – can lead to a reduction in your intelligence of 12 to 13 points.[28] This is comparable to completing an IQ test after a drunken night out, as described by Mullainathan and Shafir in their book *Scarcity*.[29] They explain how this can result in a kind of tunnel vision. You can liken it to having a very full diary of appointments, so that you find yourself with a shortage – or scarcity – of time. It is this scarcity that has a negative effect on your level of intelligence. You tackle the most urgent matters first but all other matters are left unattended and allowed to run their course, until they too eventually become urgent problems. Pausing to consider what you should actually do first is simply not possible, because you do not have the necessary time for a pause! You are caught in the scarcity trap, so that your tunnel vision leads you inexorably in a single (and often wrong) direction.

The dark side of intelligence tests

Throughout history, intelligence and intelligence tests often have been associated with highly questionable ethical theories and have been the subject of heated debate. In particular, the concept of intelligence and, by extension, intelligence tests were exploited by the supporters of eugenics.[30] This is the idea that racial improvement is possible. The idea was first suggested by someone who is also important for the history of intelligence research: Francis Galton, a distant descendant of Charles Darwin. This familial link perhaps helps to explain why Galton devoted much of his thought to how the human race could be improved via natural selection.[31] The distinction between nature (innate) and nurture (learnt) also has its origins with Galton. Eugenics had a huge impact on the thinking of the Nazis and is closely linked to the Holocaust, as a result of which it is still a taboo subject today.[32] This is a link that has cast a shadow over the concept of intelligence and its investigation ever since.

While eugenics was no longer acceptable as a subject in scientific circles after the Second World War, IQ and IQ tests continued to exist but new works were soon published that again led to associations with racism. One of the most frequently cited and most controversial articles was written in 1969 by Arthur Jensen and was entitled 'How much can we boost IQ and scholastic achievement?'[33] In this long piece, Jensen described how various programmes to improve the school performance of children from socially deprived backgrounds in the United States had failed, because, in his opinion, 80% of intelligence was innate. Given the social structure in the US, this was interpreted as 'the black population is more stupid than the white one'. Similar public and scientific indignation[34] greeted the 1994 publication of *The Bell Curve* by Charles Murray and Richard Herrnstein.[35] Stuart Ritchie has commented that it is still very difficult to conduct research in the field of intelligence, which is something that we also discovered when trying in the past to describe and comment on the two above mentioned works. It is still a subject that makes people angry when you write about it.

So, what is the truth of the matter? As we have already mentioned, it is indeed true that intelligence has a genetic basis. But the effects of heredity at the individual level say nothing about the effects of heredity at the group level. Likewise, there is no evidence to show that heredity plays a role in the differences in intelligence between countries, as mentioned by Ritchie.

This brings us to a matter that is often associated with racism: cultural phenomena. Anastasi and Urbina argue that IQ tests favour white middle-class males.[36] Since their inception, IQ tests have traditionally been written and calibrated for the requirements of a particular culture, which is usually white and prosperous. This means that certain IQ questions will not be understood by and are therefore not appropriate for other cultures, as a result of which people from these cultures generally score lower. It was to try and counteract this disparity that the so-called Culture Fair Intelligence Test (CFIT) was designed by Raymond Cattell in 1949. His aim was to create a way of measuring and quantifying cognitive ability that was not influenced by socio-cultural and environmental factors.[37] Because language is possibly the main carrier of culture, culture fair tests consist mainly of performance-oriented visual puzzles such as mazes, the copying of symbols, the identification of similar figures, and other non-verbal tasks.

How 'biased' are intelligence tests?

Towards the end of the 20th century, two multidisciplinary teams of researchers were set up (the first in 1978, the second in 1994) to investigate possible biases in IQ tests that worked to the disadvantage of specific population groups and women. Both teams concluded that IQ tests 'as a whole' are not biased against either females or minority groups.[38] However, this requires a degree of nuance. The fact that there is no bias 'as a whole' does not mean that bias cannot exist at the level of individual questions. It is still possible that certain questions or tasks in IQ tests are easier or more difficult for certain target groups. The research teams concluded that this was indeed the case for a limited number of questions,[39] but argued that this did not mean that the tests, considered in their entirety, were biased. These 'biased' questions favoured different groups, so that they effectively cancelled each other out in the end score.[40] This myth was discussed in a book analysing 50 popular psychological myths, written by Scott Lilienfeld and his colleagues. Their conclusion is worth repeating: the fact that today's IQ tests no longer contain bias does not mean that there will be no differences in the performance of different groups. As a result, criticising the IQ test is a bit like 'shooting the messenger'. By placing the 'blame' on the test, it obviates the need to look for the real causes of the problem, which for Lilienfeld and his team were to be found in environmental factors.[41]

Why we continue to use intelligence tests: good but not absolute predictors

A higher IQ is associated with:

- better health and a longer life;[42]
- the extent of religious inspiration;[43]
- the extent of political commitment;[44]
- higher incomes;[45]
- better school results;[46]
- ...

We could add a number of other things to this list but the essence can be made clear by looking more closely at perhaps the most obvious of these associations: better school results. The correlation between IQ test results and school results is .50. This means that 25% of the difference between children's school results can be explained by IQ. This is certainly a high figure but it does not tell us everything.[47] Once again, a degree of nuance is necessary. Because schools are culturally defined, including the definition of what constitutes 'success', it would indeed be strange if a culture-specific test did not correlate with success in a culture-specific institution with culture-specific goals!

It also needs to be borne in mind that the correlation of .50 is an average. Different research studies have yielded different overall results and also differences for different subjects. For example, mathematics is significantly more influenced by intelligence and languages significantly less.[48] Nor should it be forgotten that schooling itself has an impact on IQ.

So, what are we saying? At the end of the day, IQ is a good predictor but not an absolute one. An absolute predictor would mean that a single test would allow us to predict perfectly what someone's life – school results, job prospects, income, etc. – should look like. This is clearly not the case, because so many other factors also play a role, such as personality characteristics and socio-economic status, to name but two. Even so, this does not alter the fact that the IQ test is a good predictor, is easy to implement and provides valuable input for the assistance and improvement of those taking it. In short, the original intention of Binet and Simon's IQ test is still as valid today as it was in 1904: to give extra support to those who need it, so that they can move forward in their life.

What does all this mean in terms of educational practice?

1. **Going to school improves your IQ.**

   It has been clearly demonstrated that schooling can increase your IQ. Even though intelligence is determined to a large extent by genetic factors, this does not mean that it cannot be influenced. Of course, you will not be able to realise your maximum potential without making the necessary degree of effort.

2. **Worries can have a negative effect on your IQ.**

Children are sometimes more intelligent than we think or can observe in the classroom. There are many children who are capable of more but who are held back by unfavourable conditions or the lack of the right learning opportunities.

3. **IQ is a good predictor for later school performance.**

It would be most unwise to 'throw the child away with the bathwater' by failing to take any account of IQ. It gives a first important insight into possible future performance at school and opens the door for possible remedial action, where needed. At the same time, it is equally important to continue to look further than IQ alone. You can compare it with a score in an average classroom test. A 3/10 or an 8/10 gives you a first useful indication of a child's performance but it is also necessary to find out why the child has performed either well or poorly. Does that 3/10 mean that the child's home situation is hampering their performance or is it simply that the child did not study hard enough?

Endnotes

1. This chapter is a reworking and expansion of our lemma relating to intelligence in *More Urban Myths about Learning and Education* (De Bruyckere et al., 2019). Reused with permission from Taylor & Francis © 2019. Originally published in Dutch as *Juffen zijn toffer dan meesters* by Lannoo Publishers © 2018.
2. Resing & Drenth, 2007.
3. Legg & Hutter, 2007.
4. Legg & Hutter, 2007.
5. Legg & Hutter, 2007.
6. Gregory & Zangwill, 1987.
7. Nicolas et al., 2013.
8. Ritchie, 2015.
9. Lamiell, 2003.
10. Slater & Bremner, 2017.
11. Brown, 2016.
12. Unsworth et al., 2014.
13. Kan et al., 2013.
14. Sternberg, 2008.

15. De Bruyckere et al., 2015a.
16. Gardner, 2016.
17. See amongst others: Benyamin et al., 2014; Burt, 1966; Davies et al., 2011; Posthuma et al., 2002.
18. Plomin & Deary, 2015.
19. See amongst others: Pietschnig & Voracek, 2015; Trahan et al., 2014.
20. Johnson, 2005.
21. Kaufman et al., 2014.
22. Woodley et al., 2014.
23. Flynn & Flynn, 2012.
24. See amongst others: Germany: Pietschnig & Gittler, 2015; France: Dutton & Lynn, 2015; Denmark and Norway: Teasdale & Owen, 2005; Finland: Dutton & Lynn, 2013.
25. Wang & Lynn, 2018.
26. Nisbett et al., 2012.
27. Ritchie & Tucker-Drob, 2018.
28. Mani et al., 2013.
29. Mullainathan & Shafir, 2013.
30. Chitty, 2007.
31. Galton, 1883.
32. Bashford & Levine, 2010.
33. Jensen, 1969.
34. Herrnstein, 1995.
35. Herrnstein & Murray, 1994.
36. Anastasi & Urbina, 1997.
37. Cattell, 1949.
38. See amongst others: Hartigan & Wigdor, 1989; Neisser et al., 1996; Wigdor, 1982.
39. Freedle & Kostin, 1997.
40. Freedle & Kostin, 1997 and Sackett et al., 2001.
41. Lilienfeld et al., 2011.
42. See amongst others: Gottfredson & Deary, 2004; Wrulich et al., 2014.
43. Lynn et al., 2009.
44. Deary et al., 2008.
45. Robertson et al., 2010.
46. Colom & Flores-Mendoza, 2007.
47. Neisser et al., 1996.
48. Deary et al., 2007.

1.6

COGNITIVE DEVELOPMENT: WHEN DO WE UNDERSTAND WHAT WE UNDERSTAND?

What questions does this chapter answer?

1. How do children develop their cognitive capabilities?
2. What factors influence our cognitive development?
3. What does all this mean in terms of educational practice?

Before you are born, development is already underway in many different areas. Your physical development is the most visible of these areas but your cognitive development is perhaps the most dramatic. Cognitive development is the way in which your cognitive functions are initiated, expanded and refined through your life. In other words, it is the development of the ways in which we store, process, retrieve and apply information, which are all aspects that we will discuss in more detail when we deal with learning in the third part of the book. Theories about cognitive development focus primarily on the development of thought and therefore stand in sharp contrast to the behaviourist perspective,[1] which – as the name implies – focuses on behaviour.

In the previous chapters we have already looked at a number of matters that are closely related to cognitive development. The 'nature–nurture' debate is one such matter: to what extent is cognitive development fixed and to what extent is it 'malleable'? In this respect, the rare cases of the so-called 'wolf children' or 'feral children' are both remarkable and instructive. One such child was Victor of Aveyron (France), who was found in woods in 1800, having spent the first years of his life in complete isolation. The doctor to whom he was entrusted, Jean Itard, closely monitored and recorded Victor's subsequent development.[2] He noted, for example, that it proved impossible to teach Victor language. The same applies to modern-day feral children, who are still occasionally discovered from time to time. One well-known case is that of Genie, a victim of neglect and abuse, who was found in Los Angeles in 1970, by which time she was 13 years old. Genie later developed well in many different areas but it again proved impossible for her to acquire normal language skills.[3] These cases, separated by almost 200 years, both suggest that in terms of linguistic development something fundamentally important is damaged or lost if that development is interrupted or neglected during the early years of life. This seemed to lend weight to the idea of critical periods, as mentioned in an earlier chapter. The problem is, however, that we often have no idea about how these children behaved before they were abandoned and/or neglected, making it impossible to have a clear causal explanation. As explained before, we now tend to think in terms of sensitive periods.

Another fundamental question about development is whether or not it is a continuous or a discrete process. This is essentially the difference between 'non-stop' development and a development that takes place in keeping with certain benchmarks or milestones: by this age you can do this, by that age you can no longer do that, etc.

Even if the underlying process of growth in general is continuous, cognitive development can be perceived to take place, at least to some extent, in leaps and bounds: a child can suddenly do something that it was incapable of doing just weeks or months before. This is the reason why most development theories now assume that cognitive development takes place in different stages. As a result, research into cognitive development often focuses on trying to identify and observe these different stages, although this is far from easy, because the mechanisms that initiate the transition from one stage to the next are far from clear.

Why this chapter makes no mention of stages

The development psychologist Robert Siegler has referred to this almost 'magical' process as 'the process of immaculate transition'.[4] Siegler is a so-called neo-Piagetian, which means that he builds on the work of Jean Piaget. It was Piaget who developed perhaps the best-known theory of cognitive development. Like many other development theories, such as the theory of psychosexual development elaborated by Sigmund Freud, Piaget's theory focused on the first years of life. Based on research that he largely conducted on his own children, the Swiss scientist put forward a number of key ideas relating to cognitive acquisition and function that have found their way into the world of education. These ideas have two fundamental starting points. First, that children are active and motivated pupils, for whom interaction with the physical environment is of crucial importance for their cognitive development. Second, that children think in a qualitatively different way from adults and that this way of thinking is related to the cognitive stage in which they find themselves at a particular moment in time. If you show a four-year-old child a diamond (◊) and ask them to draw it, you can expect to see many different variants in response, for example, a square with a tail! Young children do not draw what they see but what they think they see. It is sometimes claimed that this 'naivety' of thought leads to more creative expression than simply copying what you see. This was the theme of the well-known TED talk by Sir Ken Robinson entitled *Do schools kill creativity?*[5] At the opposite end of the spectrum, the American psychologist Keith Sawyer argues that schools are an essential breeding ground for the development of creative thinking: without knowledge, he says, there can be no creativity.[6]

Piaget's stages: popular but superseded

The 'stages' idea and the specific classifications it involves are probably the most well-known aspect of Piaget's theory of cognitive development. According to Piaget, each child's cognitive development goes through four separate stages: the sensorimotor stage (from 0 to 2 years); the pre-operational stage (from 2 to 7 years); the concrete operational stage (from 7 to 11 years); and finally the formal operational stage (from 11 years onwards). After this point has been reached, Piaget regarded a child's cognitive development as having been more or less completed. He accepted that the ages for the transitions between the various stages would vary from child to child but asserted that the sequential order of those stages would be the same for everyone. Each stage is characterised by a series of cognitive activities of which the child is (or is not) capable. In the sensorimotor stage, those activities relate primarily to object permanence, so that the child learns to understand that objects continue to exist, even when the child is not looking at them. The pre-operational stage deals with a wider range of matters, such as egocentrism (the child's initial inability to see things from another person's point of view) and conservation (the realisation that changing the characteristics of an object does not change the essential nature of that object: cutting a pizza into six slices - regrettably - produces no more pizza than if you cut it into four slices). These characteristics reflect the fact that children in this stage are not good at dealing with more than one aspect of a situation at the same time.[7] The concrete operational stage is the stage in which the child no longer experiences these challenges and gradually becomes more able to apply formal logical reasoning, although the ability to think abstractly is still lacking (hence the use of the term 'concrete' for this particular stage). This means that they fail to understand the logic of a connection like 'if A=B and B=C, then A=C must also be true'. These shortcomings are overcome in the formal operational stage, the final stage, in which reflection on abstract hypotheses becomes possible ('What would happen if the supply of electricity failed all around the world?').

We felt that it was necessary to outline the Piaget stages in a separate box, because no book about psychology can fail to include them. That being said, we took the deliberate decision not to describe them in detail, because many of Piaget's conclusions are now open to question or have been superseded. Research conducted in later years has established that Piaget's own research methods and observations resulted in an underestimation of the cognitive skills of young children. More modern and refined research methods have reached significantly different outcomes. Here are some examples.

If we look at newborn babies, it is clear that they are already capable of observing the world around them in a meaningful way, even though their eyesight is limited and blurred.[8] A common method used to measure the preferences of babies is the so-called 'fixation time' method. This essentially means measuring how long a child looks at something they are shown (the stimulus) before they turn their gaze away. Just a few days after birth, the baby is capable of making a distinction between a circle in which the nose, mouth and ears are not in the right positions and a circle in which they are arranged like a normal face. When both stimuli are offered, the fixation time for the real face is longer than for the fake face.

Some Piagetian critics have argued that this kind of facial recognition does not require very much in the way of cognitive development, which may be a valid comment. However, a second test is more convincing, since it demonstrates that even very young children seem to be capable of cognitive operations that are normally associated with higher mental skills, such as the recognition of purposive behaviour.[9] The American psychologist Amanda Woodward placed children aged between five and nine months in a chair, from where they could see two plinths. On top of the left-hand plinth there was a ball. On top of the right-hand plinth there was a teddy bear. The experiment consisted of two phases. During the first phase – the habituation phase – the researcher reaches out an arm towards the ball, touches it, and then withdraws the arm. This is repeated a number of times, until the child no longer devotes specific attention to the action. During the second phase, the positions of the ball and the bear are switched. The researcher then performs one of two action options: they can either repeat exactly the same movement as before and touch the bear, or else make a completely different kind of movement and now touch the ball that had been repositioned on the other plinth. In the first option, the movement is the same but the object is different. In the second option, the movement is different but the object is the same. Which action would be more likely to surprise the child? The results showed that even children as young as five months reacted with surprise when the researcher reached for the bear. The movement is the same as during the habituation phase but the purpose of that movement is now different. The children were less surprised if the movement was different but the purpose (touching the ball) remained the same. Conclusion: even very young children have a rudimentary understanding of intention, a skill that is only developed at a much later stage according to the theories of Piaget.

Another example of weakness in Piagetian thinking is the so-called 'three mountain task', devised by Piaget and Inhelder to show that children in the pre-operational stage can only think from their own perspective.[10] A child is sat in front of a table, on which three mountains of different sizes have been made from piles of earth/sand. In front of the mountains stands a house, which is not visible from the other side of the table, because the mountains are in the way. A doll is then set down on this far side of the table. The child is then asked what the doll can see. In addition to the mountains, the most common answer was that the doll can see the house. According to Piaget, this demonstrated that children at the age of four years still find it difficult to distinguish between their own perspective and the doll's perspective, which he interpreted as a clear sign of continuing egocentrism during this pre-operational phase. However, more specific later studies have shown that the reason why children react in this way during this kind of experiment is more closely related to the situation than to their own lack of perspective. The situation they are faced with is completely new and previously unknown to them, so that they easily become confused. If the 'three mountains' test is presented to them in a different way as a game of 'hide and seek' with a doll ('if you want to hide from the doll, where would you sit?'), the children understand the situation much better and respond differently: the majority know how to keep out of the doll's line of vision.[11] In other words, an ability to solve Piaget's test is to a significant extent dependent on the child's prior knowledge. To paraphrase Stanislas Dehaene:[12] If the child can make use of its prior knowledge, it better knows on which aspects of the task attention needs to be focused and which (automatic) reactions need to be suppressed.

A final example illustrates that some cognitive activities that Piaget associated with the formal operational stage can actually be performed by very young children. The activities in question are causal thinking or 'scientific' reasoning.[13] In an experiment conducted by Xu and Garcia a group of young children (some as young as eight months old) watched as a researcher pulled balls one after the other out of a closed box, the contents of which they had been shown in advance for familiarisation purposes.[14] Half of the balls in the box were red, the other half were white. If the large majority of the balls pulled out of the box were red, so that the majority of the balls remaining in the box when it was opened and shown to the children were white, this prompted a reaction of strong interest and surprise (measured by fixation time). The children's level of interest was much less when the number of red balls pulled from the box was roughly the same as the number left inside. This clearly suggests that even very young children have an understanding of probabilities: they can evaluate the probability of a sample in relation to a total population, which is also known as Bayesian reasoning.[15]

Seymour Papert, who for many years was a close colleague of Piaget, has emphasised that the essence of Piaget's thinking was the idea that much of the learning acquired by children takes place in a disorganised manner, without the input of teachers and schools. Giving a child the opportunity to be randomly active in its environment is therefore (in his opinion) more important than explicit instruction.[16] The examples cited above seem to confirm this in part but also show how a teacher can create situations in which learning and development can take place optimally.

The importance of others in cognitive development

It is this important role played by the environment and others in the development of thinking that is central to the work of Lev Vygotsky. This Russian educational psychologist is best known for his concept of the zone of proximal development. Note, in particular, the use of the word 'development'. Vygotsky does not talk about a zone of proximal learning. Instead, he defined his zone as:

> the distance between the actual developmental level as determined by independent problem-solving and the level of potential development as determined through problem-solving under adult guidance or in collaboration with more capable peers.[17]

Chaiklin[18] later clarified Vygotsky's reasoning: when he described the zone of proximal development, he was not thinking about the development of specific skills or knowledge. He viewed everything in relation to the development of the child as a whole. As a result, Chaiklin argued that the zone of proximal development can best be used to describe how a child or young person develops in interaction with the external world.

If we are dealing with education, the use of the term 'zone of proximal learning' or, better still, the concept of 'scaffolding' is more appropriate. The latter has been used by Ausubel (among others) to describe how a child learns new things on the basis of their prior knowledge.[19] With effective forms of scaffolding the teacher assesses a pupil's existing level of knowledge and sets new challenges reflecting that knowledge, which the pupil should be able to solve with a little additional help.

Some starting points for dynamic systems theory

A worthy replacement for Piaget's development theory is still in the process of construction. One of the promising potential alternatives is dynamic systems theory, although this goes much further than cognitive development alone. Dynamic systems theory originated in the realm of physics but Thelen and Smith converted its main concepts for application in the field of (developmental) psychology.[20] The theory focuses on the complex interactions between different systems (physical, cognitive, social) over different periods of time.[21]

It is worth repeating that although this DST (as it is known) is 'promising', it is still very much a work in progress. There are still many things about the theory on which scientists do not agree or have not been finalised but there is a general acceptance (as was the case with Vygotsky) that 'the other' plays a defining role.[22]

To better understand what the theory involves, particularly in terms of cognitive development, it may be useful to look at a number of DST's fundamental starting points, even if there is still some scientific disagreement about how they should be further developed.

One of the key concepts is the concept of *multicausality*, which is the idea that there are many different reasons for the way your behaviour develops, in which no one factor is more important than any other. Consider, for example, learning to talk. A baby will start by making babbling noises, to which the mother responds, to which the baby in turn responds by further refining their babbling. So which factor is most important for this development: the initial babbling of the baby or the reaction of the mother? Both are important to bring about the desired development.[23]

In the examples mentioned above to cast doubt on the transitional timings proposed by Piaget, several references were made to interaction. In the various experiments, it was (admittedly) an adult who tested the child and gave the child instructions. However, in the 'three mountains' test, for example, the performance of the child was dependent on two key success factors: the child's own ability (estimating what another person can see) and the way the task was conceived and described by the supervising adult (as a game of hide-and-seek). As a result, the outcome was determined by both the child and the adult.

A second starting point for DST is self-organisation. To keep the above example relating to multicausality as simple as possible, we only made mention of two contributory factors to the child's development of speech: the child's own babbling and the reaction of the mother. In reality, many more factors are involved in any given developmental situation and these various components all have an influence on each other. When the proponents of dynamic systems theory talk about self-organisation, they mean that the interaction between all these different mutually influencing factors takes place in accordance with a small number of simple rules. Yet even though they are simple, these rules are sufficient to make possible highly complex forms of behaviour.

Play the Game of Life

This may all sound fairly complicated but there is a simple way that you can test it for yourself. How? By playing the Game of Life (sometimes known as just Life), which was created by John Conway. If you are interested in experimenting with this game, just surf to https://playgameoflife.com/

The Game of Life is played on a grid like the one reproduced below.

What is the idea? You fill in a number of random cells on the grid and then press 'start'. Like DST interaction, the game has a number of simple rules:

- Each cell with just one or no neighbour dies from underpopulation.
- Each cell with four or more neighbours dies from overpopulation.

(Continued)

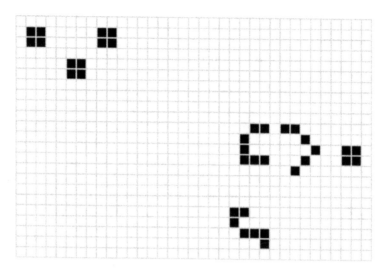

Figure 1.8   An example grid of the Game of Life

- Every cell with two or three neighbours survives to the next generation.
- An empty cell with three neighbours becomes a live cell.

Once you have filled in several cells on the grid and pressed the start button, you will see how complex patterns of cells can be created by using just these four simple rules.

Like in the Game of Life, self-organisation is not a one-off event but a process that is repeated continually. As a result, new forms of balance can be created, even though nothing else appears to change. This explains how dynamic systems theory is able to explain why we can simultaneously see both continuous behavioural change and observe what seem to be larger leaps forward in development. More important-ly still, DST can also explain why the same set of basic building blocks result in the creation of so many different types of people and why, for example, monozygotic twins can never be truly identical.

A third DST starting point relates to the interaction between differing time scales, known in the jargon as *the nesting of scales*.[24] When our behaviour changes – if, for example, a toddler starts to walk – different time scales are brought together. A person's reaction time can be measured in milliseconds, whereas the learning of a skill can take hours, days, months or even years. All those different time scales are combined in the single moment when the toddler takes that very first step (which is, in fact, a leap, as mentioned in the previous paragraph).

In summary, change in dynamic systems theory arises as a result of the complex interaction of a number of influential factors (often many), which frequently have very different timings but all adhere to the same simple set of rules.

The systems approach makes it possible to combine stable and dynamic aspects of development with each other, which in turn makes it possible to make more specific pronouncements about the transition from one developmental stage to another.[25] All in all, DST seems to take far greater and far better account of the complexity and dynamism of cognitive development than other theories dealing with the same subject. At the same time, many people claim that the theory is much harder to understand, making it difficult to take into account in daily educational practice. But is that really so? After all, parents, brothers and sisters but also teachers, the school and fellow pupils are all factors or components that can obviously have an influence on the (cognitive) development of a child or young person. And there is nothing overly complex about that.

In other words, dynamic systems theory as an explanatory model for the development of the individual child or young person makes clear why in the second part of this book we will concentrate at length on the impact of 'others'.

What does all this mean in terms of educational practice?

1. **Every child and pupil has its own unique cognitive development.**

    The cognitive development of every child is a gradual and continuous process but one that also experiences periodic leaps forward. This helps to explain the large differences that can sometimes occur between children and pupils.

2. **Teachers and caregivers must not only create the right conditions for development but also stimulate that development by engaging in interaction with the children and pupils concerned**.

    As a teacher, simply creating a dynamic learning environment is not enough. You also need to interact with your pupils: talk to them, discuss with them, give them guidance, etc. This significantly strengthens cognitive development through a process of mutual influencing. It is equally important for caregivers to be aware of the need to engage in various enabling interactions that can stimulate the child to grow.

— Teacher takeaways —

The importance of sleep

Children need a lot of sleep. Young people need a lot of sleep. In fact, we all need a lot of sleep. It may sound like stating the obvious but research has shown that the average number of hours of sleep per night for children and teenagers has declined in recent years, although it is an evolution that has been taking place for much longer.[26]

Why is sleep so important?

(Continued)

- Most scientists investigating the workings of the brain now suspect that during sleep the brain 'relives' a number of the previous day's waking moments as a way to reinforce the knowledge it has acquired and to integrate that knowledge into the existing memories of the sleeper. Researchers have demonstrated that even with children as young as nine months old sleep helps to fix knowledge in their brain.[27]
- Sufficient sleep assists powers of attention/concentration and helps you to learn.
- Children and young people who sleep sufficiently are better behaved and better able to control their emotions.
- Quality of life and mental and physical health are all improved by sufficient sleep.[28]

It is true that the differing amounts of sleep that people need are determined by genetic factors.[29] For this reason, the American Academy of Sleep Medicine[30] has developed a schedule to indicate how many hours of sleep children ideally need at different ages in their development:

- Less than 4 months: the variations between children are too great to be able to give any clear recommendation.
- 4 to 12 months: 12 to 16 hours of sleep per day, including naps.
- 1 to 2 years: 11 to 14 hours of sleep per day, including naps.
- 3 to 5 years: 10 to 13 hours of sleep per day.
- 6 to 12 years: 9 to 12 hours of sleep per day.
- 13 to 18 years: 8 to 10 hours of sleep per day.

What happens if children and young people do not get enough sleep?

- Sleep deficiency affects how the brain develops, so that a lack of sleep is much more serious for children and teenagers than it is for adults.[31]
- It increases the likelihood of being overweight, obesity and diabetes.[32]
- It increases the likelihood of feelings of anxiety[33] and depression.
- It increases the likelihood of attention, behaviour and learning problems,[34] and therefore the likelihood of poorer school results.[35]
- It increases the likelihood of accidents and injury.
- In teenagers, lack of sleep has been linked to a greater incidence of self-harm, suicidal thoughts and attempts at suicide.[36]

What happens if a child sleeps too much?

- It increases the likelihood of obesity and mental problems.[37]

What are the best things you can do as a parent or caregiver?

- Establish a sleep routine as early as possible in a child's development.[38]

- Make sure that your children get enough sleep. Avoid mistakes like keeping them up later in the evening in the hope that this will allow them (and you) to sleep in later in the morning.
- Setting a regular hour for a child to go to sleep is very important. You must persist with this, even with older teenagers and even if it leads to protests and arguments. Children and young people who go to bed at a fixed time, willingly or not, sleep more, with all the positive effects this entails.[39]
- Sleeping enough and keeping to regular sleeping hours as an adult will also help to improve the sleep behaviour of your children.[40]

Endnotes

1. Ormrod, 2020.
2. Itard's report on the development of Victor can be found in *Rapport sur Victor de l'Aveyron,* 1806.
3. The study of Genie's language acquisition skills is described in Susan Curtiss, *Genie: A Psycholinguistic Study of a Modern-day Wild Child* (1977).
4. Siegler, 1996.
5. Robinson, 2006. www.ted.com/talks/sir_ken_robinson_do_schools_kill_creativity
6. Sawyer, 2011. We devoted a chapter to the 'schools kill creativity' myth in our book *Urban Myths about Learning and Education* (De Bruyckere et al., 2015a).
7. One of the authors once tried to conduct a conservation experiment with his five-year-old daughter. The results can be viewed on YouTube: www.youtube.com/watch?v=rKnXeGWb1wo
8. Slater & Kirby, 1998.
9. Woodward, 1999.
10. The 'mountains' problem was originally described in Piaget & Inhelder (1967), *The Child's Conception of Space.*
11. Borke, 1975.
12. pp. 162–163 in Dehaene, 2020.
13. A summary of the developments in this field can be found in Gopnik, 2012.
14. Xu & Garcia, 2008.
15. See also: Zhu & Gigerenzer, 2006.
16. Wright, 2002.
17. Vygotsky, 1978, p. 86.
18. Chaiklin, 2003.
19. Ausubel et al., 1968.

20. Thelen & Smith, 1996.
21. Newman & Newman, 2020.
22. Perone & Simmering, 2017.
23. Thelen & Smith, 2007.
24. Smith & Thelen, 2003.
25. Sosnowska et al., 2020.
26. Matricciani et al., 2012.
27. Friedrich et al., 2015.
28. Paruthi et al., 2016.
29. Shi et al., 2019.
30. Paruthi et al., 2016.
31. Kurth et al., 2016.
32. Paul et al., 2016.
33. Simon et al., 2019.
34. Paruthi et al., 2016.
35. Titova et al., 2015.
36. Paruthi et al., 2016.
37. Paruthi et al., 2016.
38. Wolfson, 1998.
39. Peltz et al., 2019.
40. Komada et al., 2009.

1.7

LANGUAGE DEVELOPMENT: FROM BABBLING TO ...

What questions does this chapter answer?

1. What do we understand by language?
2. How do children develop language?
3. To what extent is language innate?
4. How can we stimulate the linguistic development of children?

You are currently reading this book. There is nothing special about that, is there? Well, yes there is. As human beings, we have developed an instrument that allows us to communicate with each other: language. We use words, make sentences, learn to talk and listen at an early age, and later we learn how to read and write.

But what exactly is language? There are many possible definitions. In linguistics, a historical distinction is made between language as an abstract concept (known as langue), specific language systems (such as French, Dutch and English), and the way these language systems are used (known as parole).[1]

Animals also communicate but there are fundamental differences between forms of animal communication and human language. It may be possible to speak of a langue in animal communication but human language has additionally developed agreed symbols and rules that we generally refer to as grammar.[2] As a result, we can describe human language as the systematic and meaningful organisation of symbols that form the basis for two-way communication between different people.

Is language innate or learnt?

This might seem like a silly question. If you are born into an English-speaking environment, you are hardly likely to spontaneously start speaking French, are you? Even so, Noam Chomsky has argued that certain elements of language may be innate. He claims that we are born with a kind of *language acquisition device*. This natural aptitude – a totality of various internal mental mechanisms – ensures that children can learn the language of their immediate environment quickly and efficiently.[3] Neurological research has shown that young children use the same brain structures to process language that adults use to process speech, which may indicate that there is a common evolutionary basis.[4] However, this idea is not without its critics. There may well be a number of mechanisms in each of us that allow us to pick up a language quickly but this is only possible as a result of social interaction, which also plays an essential role in linguistic development.[5]

A more nurture-based approach argues that language acquisition occurs in accordance with the laws of confirmation and conditioning, principles that we will discuss in the chapter on learning. This means, for example, that children learn how to better pronounce words through step-by-step shaping and positive confirmation. At first, you are happy if you think you can vaguely recognise the word 'water' in what your baby is babbling but through repetition and confirmation you systematically attempt to set the linguistic bar higher.[6] That being said, this explanation also has its limitations: in daily practice parents are not always consistently positive in their confirmation but in most cases this does not prevent the child from learning how to speak quickly and well.

As you have probably already suspected, there is a strong likelihood that language is acquired and developed through a process of interaction or transaction, in which natural aptitude and the environment mutually influence each other. Language recognition mechanisms are certainly present and confirmation definitely plays a role, as do other forms of interaction.[7] It is also possible that language has a function in terms of processing a child's own thoughts, in which the child employs egocentric use of language to order and adjust their thinking and behaviour via a kind of internal monologue.[8] This is something that you can see, for example, if the child performs the marshmallow test, when the child seeks inwardly to resist the temptation of eating the sweet on the table in front of them, so that they can gain the reward of a second sweet if they do the right thing.[9]

The building blocks of language

Human language consists of a number of different elements that have been researched by different branches of science:

- **Phonology**: The basic sounds that we use and combine to make words and sentences are known as phonemes. Phonemes should not be confused with letters, because the same letter can be pronounced in different ways. Think, for example, of the 'c' in 'circus' or the 'e' in 'leather'. English has 42 different phonemes. In Dutch – the native language of the authors of this book – there are 40 different phonemes,[10] of which at least 16 are vowels.[11] Given this explanation, you might be forgiven for thinking that phonemes are the same as sounds. However, things are not quite that simple, because some phonemes, like letters, can also be pronounced in different ways by people speaking in different regional accents. In Belgium, for example, there is a difference between the rolled French 'r' and the uvular 'r', both being pronounced in different parts of the mouth.

- **Morphology**: Phonemes are joined together to form *morphemes*. A morpheme is the smallest unit of meaning in language. Once again, you might think that this refers to words like 'book' but, again, the situation is more complex than it seems. 'Book' is indeed an example of a single morpheme but 'booklet', although still a single word, is actually two morphemes. The addition of the suffix '-let' results in a different meaning and indicates that the word to which it is added is small rather than large. As well as suffixes, it is also possible to add prefixes to words. For example, 'dis' is a prefix in the word 'disagree'.[12] Free morphemes are morphemes that can stand alone, such as the previously mentioned 'book'. Bound morphemes can only be used in combination with other morphemes, such as '-er' in the word 'farmer'.

- **Morphosyntax** is the term we use to describe the way in which people make use of the morphology of words to construct syntactically correct sentences. We know, for example, that a verb needs to be conjugated to reflect its subject (first person, second person, etc.). In this way, children gradually learn – without the need for formal lessons – that 'he walk' sounds wrong, whereas 'he walks' sounds right.

- **Semantics**: We have already mentioned that morphemes are the smallest unit of meaning in language. However, the words that we use to communicate need to be set in a particular order, so that they can acquire even more meaning. The totality of the rules that we use in a language to determine the meaning of words and sentences is known as semantics.

- **Pragmatics**: This is the domain within linguistics that looks at how people use language in particular contexts. We can say 'hello' as a greeting when we meet people but the same word can also be used as an expression of surprise in a phrase like 'hello, what's this?' Children who have difficulty coming to terms with these different interpretations will tend to understand language literally, which means that in turn they will also find it harder to understand humorous and figurative use of language. Pragmatics also deals with mechanisms such as taking turns to speak during a conversation, so that you alternate what you want to say with listening to what someone else wants to say.

These subdivisions of linguistics are relevant and useful for better understanding the development of language in children. In particular, it needs to be remembered that children are capable of comprehending language before they are capable of producing it themselves. We are all over the moon as soon as our baby speaks their first word but they actually start to make use of language to better understand the world around them long before that.

What's more, this understanding develops much more quickly than speech. Babies can learn to understand around 22 new words each month, whereas the comparable figure for learning to speak new words is just 9 per month, at least in the beginning.[13]

It is also worth pointing out that most of this development happens unconsciously. When we go to school at the age of four or five, we are asked to formally learn the rules of grammar that most of us have already picked up in our early years of infancy. The conscious description of such rules is far from easy. In fact, most adults (unless specialists in the field) would have difficulty in describing them. If asked, the four- and five-year-olds would also find it difficult to explain them but this does nothing to alter the fact that their command of language at this age is already fairly complete.[14]

The babbling of babies: the pre-linguistic phase

Language development starts at a very early age. During the first month of life, babies will already respond to a voice that is addressing them and give their attention to the person speaking. Babies can also recognise subtle differences in the use of language that they hear in their environment, differences that they will need to be aware of later on to understand their mother tongue.[15] At the age of four to five months, they will gradually be able to distinguish their own name from other similar sounding words; for example, Paul from ball or Pat from cat. At the age of five to six months, they will be able to notice the difference between two languages in the sense of language systems (like English and French), although there are indications that they may already have developed a preference for the dominant language in their environment.[16] At the same time, during this phase they will also find it increasingly difficult to distinguish phonemes regarded as single in their own language.[17]

As far as producing language is concerned, babies make efforts to communicate from a very early age in a manner that is not necessarily linguistic. This communication initially takes the form of sounds, facial expressions, gestures (learnt) imitation, etc.[18] Gradually, this develops into babbling or gibberish, which are meaningless noises that resemble speech but are not the same.

At the age of two to three months, the child will start to repeat variations of the same phoneme, usually one with a vowel sound. At the age of five months, this repetition will be made more complex through the addition of consonant sounds.[19]

A month later, this babbling will evolve yet further in the direction of language dependency, so that the sounds start to seem more and more like words. By the seventh month of life, the child starts to break up this stream of babbling sounds, in much the same way that sentences are broken up into individual words.[20] At eight months, the rhythm and tonality of the mother tongue will be injected by imitation into these separate sounds.[21] As already mentioned, a certain understanding and perception of some words will already have taken place spontaneously by this stage. By the time the child finally speaks their first word at the age of 10 to 12 months, they will know a number of meanings of the different words they hear.[22]

Mummy, daddy and the rest of the dictionary

The first words are spoken first and foremost for the pleasure they give (both to the speaker and the listeners). It is only later that they are used as a tool; for example, to ask for things.[23] Often, these first words relate to something or someone that frequently comes and goes in the young child's life, such as a parent or the household pet.

Between the age of 15 and 20 months, the child experiences a 'word spurt', which allows the child to accelerate the rate at which they are able to learn new words.[24] Between their second and seventeenth birthdays, the child will learn on average a further 60,000 words, at an average of 11 words per day.[25]

The influence of the environment on vocabulary

The earliest words a child speaks relate to objects from their environment, objects that their parents help to name and identify as part of a process known as *joint attention*. Because the environment can play an important role in the development of vocabulary, it is possible to see significant differences in the range of vocabulary in young children of the same age. The children of parents who read to them regularly from a very early age will have a huge advantage over their peers in terms of vocabulary by the time they reach nursery school.[26] Reading just one book[27] per day to a child will result in that child hearing 1.4 million words more than a child who is not read to. This corresponds with the results of a separate and more well-known research study, which concluded that by the age of four years children from families with a low socio-economic status have heard 30 million fewer words than children from families with a higher SES. Just as importantly, this huge difference is the result of specific linguistic interaction, which can have a further enhanced positive effect on vocabulary development. The '30 million word gap' article published by Hart and Risley in the 1990s has recently come in for criticism as a result of a new study that did not reach the same findings.[28] However, this new study has, in turn, also been heavily criticised.[29]

Why is all this so important? The reason is simple. A child's situation at the start of their school career is a good predictor for their school performance in later years.[30] In other words, if there is such a thing as a massive word gap, it is unlikely to be made good as the child gets older.

Quiet please! I'm learning words!

Research from 2016 suggests that background noise can have a negative effect on a young child's ability to pick up new words, if the noise level of the words is less than 10 dB louder than the ambient noise of the surroundings.[31]

Learning to communicate: pragmatic development

If you are talking with others, you need to learn various 'rules': how to wait your turn to say something, how to listen to what someone else is saying, how to keep to the subject of the conversation, etc. This pragmatic development also begins at an early age with what we call proto-conversations. This involves, for example, interaction between one of the parents and the child, in which the adult fills up the pauses in the child's babbling with proper words and sentences. At some time between the ages of eight and twelve months, the child will start to participate in these proto-conversations more consciously.[32] By the time of the child's first birthday, they will even be able to recognise some instances of miscommunication and may attempt to correct the misunderstanding by repeating themselves.[33]

From the age of two years onwards, the child can engage 'two-turn' conversations, which can be gradually expanded to increase the number of turns.[34] From the age of three years onwards, the child is capable of asking for clarification of things they do not understand.[35]

By five or six years old, the child starts to think consciously about their use of language. This is known as *metalinguistic awareness*. At this age, children are aware that language needs to conform to rules; rules which, up to this point, they have learnt implicitly.[36] This pragmatic realisation helps them in their communication with the outside world, if the information they hear is confusing or does not seem to be complete. From a child's seventh birthday onwards, this pragmatic insight continues to develop further and most children realise that their conversation partner can also make mistakes, so that there is a possibility of miscommunication on the other side of the dialogue. This prompts the child to ask for explanations more quickly.[37]

What about bilingualism?

More and more children are being raised bilingually, which means that they need to learn two languages.[38] This is easier if the two languages resemble each other.[39] For a long time, bilingualism was regarded as being beneficial for the child in terms of its possible positive effects on intelligence[40] or the working memory.[41] At the same time, it was also understood that there was a downside: the development of morphosyntax takes place more slowly[42] and the child will generally have a smaller vocabulary per language, although in total the child will know as many words as a child brought up in a single language.[43]

However, the insights relating to the positive effects of bilingualism on, for example, the executive functions of children have recently become a victim of the replication crisis in psychology.[44] Even the linguistic benefits of bilingualism no longer seem certain, at least not in every case.[45] It has also been suggested that bilingually raised children are not necessarily more kind towards other children, as had previously been assumed.[46] This is a research domain in which there are currently many contradictory findings, so that it seems unwise for us to make any conclusive pronouncements.

What does all this mean for daily practice?

1. **Children learn their mother tongue spontaneously and unconsciously**.

   Of course, this is on condition that they are surrounded by a healthy environment and can benefit from sufficient linguistic interactions of the right kind.

2. **Learning how to read and write or learning a second language are not spontaneous processes and therefore need to be explicitly learnt.**

   This means that children will not automatically learn how to read, not even in a stimulating and encouraging environment. Children can certainly show a spontaneous interest in books but they will not be able to 'teach themselves' to read. This requires specific attention to the technique of reading, which is something that needs to be imparted by adults.

3. **Read sufficiently to children (out loud).**

   A book before bedtime or at the start or end of the school day can make a huge difference to the vocabulary of young children.

4. **Ensure a sufficient number of qualitative linguistic interactions.**

   In addition to reading aloud to children, it is also important to talk with them sufficiently, so that they can improve their verbal linguistic skills.

─Teacher takeaways ─

Helping children to learn how to read

While most children learn how to speak and understand the dominant language of their environment relatively easily at a very early age, it is a different matter with learning how to read and write.

Learning technical reading

In this section we will be dealing with expertise relating to the distinction made by Geary between primary knowledge and secondary knowledge or, to put it in slightly different terms, the difference between what you learn naturally and easily and matters that are to a large extent culturally determined, so that you need much more support to learn them. Reading and writing belong to this second, culturally determined category, although this is not always what many people thought in the past.

Those who are convinced that learning to read is a natural process advocate the use of a *whole language method*. The reasoning behind such methods is that children are able to teach themselves to read, if only they are provided with a rich linguistic environment, in which they can discover their own meaning in the texts they are given.[47]

Nowadays, however, after many years of bitter 'reading wars', we now know that reading is more a form of secondary knowledge and is therefore better explicitly learnt via a structure or phonetics-based method.[48] In this latter approach children learn to read by acquiring insights into the ways that letters and sounds are related to each other.[49] The use of these insights needs to become second nature and this is only possible with repeated practice. For some parents, this might sound both strange and unnatural but it needs to be emphasised that reading is not a natural aptitude that we are automatically given at birth.

Learning reading comprehension

In recent years, reading comprehension has been the subject of heated discussion in our linguistic region. In many countries, the level of reading comprehension is in decline, which in the long term can have dramatic consequences for every other kind of learning. Have you ever stopped to think just how much children at school - but also elsewhere - need to make use of their reading comprehension? If you want to learn something, you have to be able to read and understand the text that contains the necessary information. And it is not just children at school: if you are given a set of safety instructions at work, it is vital that you are able to read and understand them correctly. Even as a parent, you need to be able to understand the letter from school about next month's school fete. So how can you best make sure that your own and your children's reading comprehension is up to scratch?

An important insight that can help you in this respect is the fact that reading comprehension is not an addition but a multiplication, as expounded in the simple vision on reading put forward by Hoover and Gough in 1990.[50] Their formula is:

Reading = decoding × (listening) comprehension.

Why do Hoover and Gough use a multiplication in the formula, rather than an addition? With an addition, the total sum continues to improve, even if one of the elements in the equation is less good. 20 + 1 still makes 21, and is therefore an improvement. This is not the case with multiplication. 20 × 1 is still only 20. 20 × 0 is 0!

Reading comprehension works like a multiplication. All the elements need to be positive if improvement is to be achieved. This means, for example, that a high motivation to read (20) will not compensate for a lack of technical reading ability (1 or 0) and vice versa, although they can both help each other up to a point. Likewise, a good vocabulary or good background information is scarcely able to compensate for other matters, although once again they can help to mutually strengthen each other to a limited degree.

Imagine that your technical reading skills are poor. Do you think that you will be motivated to read? Imagine that your technical reading skills are adequate but that you have very little background knowledge or a limited vocabulary. Will your technical skills help you to understand the content of more difficult texts? Research results suggest not.[51] In short: everything has an effect on everything else.[52]

How can you work to improve reading?

In recent years various reports have been published about how you can stimulate reading and reading comprehension in children. A first and crucial tip that appears in many of these reports is 'read aloud'. It is even better if you can make this reading interactive, by asking the children questions about the illustrations, characters and events in the story. This improves both their understanding and their vocabulary.[53]

The advantages of reading aloud to children from an early age go much further than simply being able to read better. Research shows that it can also help them with their cognitive, social-emotional, physical and creative development.[54] At the same time, we know that by itself reading aloud or reading together is not enough.[55] Houtveen has offered us the following further tips for the stimulation of reading in children, most of which appear in one form or another in almost all the published reports:[56]

- Read with a purpose: use texts that tell children what they want to know about a subject.
- Work at building up knowledge: prior knowledge leads to understanding of the text, understanding of the text leads to new knowledge, which can then be used to understand the following text.

(Continued)

- Work at building up vocabulary: the more words and concepts the children know, the quicker they will understand a text.
- Use different kinds of texts, both fiction and non-fiction.
- Involve the children in discussion. Discussions in which adults and children are cognitively, socially and affectively engaged together in the construction of meaning can help to contribute towards conceptualisation and comprehension.
- Help the children to become strategic readers. When comprehension does not come automatically, good readers make use of targeted and conscious reading strategies to solve comprehension problems and/or make decisions about how to approach a reading task.
- Explain textual structures: paragraphs, headings, anaphora, etc.
- Integrate reading and writing.
- Provide a stimulating and motivating reading environment. The intrinsic motivation of children increases in relation to the extent that they have the freedom to do things, regard themselves as being more capable of doing things, and are more appreciated by others for what they do.
- Monitor the different aspects of reading comprehension (technical reading ability, vocabulary, background knowledge, strategic knowledge and motivation).
- Provide differentiation: read texts with different levels of content and difficulty.

What should you not do?

If children have difficulties with reading comprehension, teachers and parents sometimes think that the solution is to make the texts simpler. If you adopt this approach, make sure that you do not remove important learning elements from the texts, such as the anaphora. Removing these elements would deprive the reading child of the possibility to see important learning connections.

It is also not a good idea to make the introductory phase before the reading of the text too long, so that you actually reveal much of the text's content before a single word has been read. Activating prior knowledge is certainly important, as we shall see in the chapter on learning, but keep this introduction short and to the point.

There is more than just reading

With the huge amount of attention that is currently being devoted to reading comprehension, it is sometimes easy to forget that there are other linguistic skills that are just as important, such as writing, speaking and listening. With these last two skills, we do not of course mean the naturally acquired aptitudes for speaking and listening but the cultural variations of these skills: the ability to formulate a clear story or explanation (verbally or on paper) and the ability to extract the essence from a spoken address. These three skills are often more difficult to test and improving them frequently costs more time, so that they sometimes do not get the attention they deserve. Nevertheless, their importance should not be underestimated. Moreover, all three skills can also help to contribute towards the improvement of reading comprehension.

Endnotes

1. Lyons, 1981.
2. Tomasello, 2006.
3. Chomsky, 1957; Chomsky, 1965; Chomsky, 1968; Pinker, 1994.
4. Dehaene-Lambertz et al, 2006; Newbury et al, 2005; Wade, 2001.
5. Goldberg, 2004; MacWhinney, 1991; Savage-Rumbaugh, et al., 1993.
6. Skinner (1957); Ferster & Skinner, 1957; Skinner, 1975.
7. Rice & Dixon, 1998; Yang, 2006.
8. Al-Namlah et al., 2012; McGonigle-Chalmers et al., 2014 ; Winsler et al., 2006.
9. Apperly & Robinson, 2003.
10. Akmajian et al., 1984.
11. Van Oosterdorp, 1999.
12. Laghzaoui, 2007; Laghzaoui & Kurvers, 2006.
13. Minagawa-Kawai et al., 2011; Rescorla et al., 2001; Shafto et al., 2012; Tincoff & Jusczyk, 1999.
14. Jackendoff, 2003.
15. Bijeljac-Babic et al., 1993; Gervain et al., 2008.
16. Miller & Eimas, 1995; Chonchaiya et al., 2013; Kuhl et al., 2006; Palmer et al., 2012; Rivera-Gaxiola et al., 2005.
17. Kuhl et al., 2008.
18. Reddy & Barrett, 1999.
19. Masataka, 2003.
20. Trainor et al., 2000.
21. Masataka, 2003.
22. Swingley, 2008.
23. Swingley, 2008.
24. Mervis & Bertrand, 1994.
25. Bloom, 2002.
26. Logan et al., 2019.
27. Hart & Risley, 1995.
28. Sperry et al., 2019.
29. Golinkoff et al., 2019.

30. Pace et al., 2019.
31. McMillan & Saffran, 2016.
32. Reddy & Barrett, 1999.
33. Golinkoff, 1983.
34. Brinton et al., 1986; Garvey & Hogan, 1973.
35. Gallagher, 1981; Ninio et al, 1997; Anaraki et al., 2013.
36. Benelli et al., 2006; Saiegh-Haddad, 2007.
37. Apperly & Robinson, 2003.
38. Graddol, 2004; Hoff & Core, 2013; Shin & Bruno, 2003.
39. Snow & Kang, 2006.
40. Woumans et al., 2016.
41. Morales et al, 2013.
42. Gathercole, 2013.
43. Hoff et al., 2012.
44. See amongst others: Bak, 2016; Gunnerud et al., 2020.
45. Hoff, 2018.
46. Souza et al., 2013.
47. Goodman, 1967.
48. Castles et al., 2018.
49. See amongst others: Chall, 1967; Flesch, 1955.
50. Hoover & Gough, 1990.
51. O'Reilly et al., 2019.
52. Toste et al., 2020.
53. Flack et al., 2018.
54. See amongst others: Kalb & Van Ours, 2014; Murray & Egan, 2014.
55. Noble et al., 2019.
56. Houtveen, 2018.

1.8

PHYSICAL DEVELOPMENT: ENORMOUS CHANGES

What questions does this chapter answer?

1. What is the influence of the environment on physical development?
2. How do the motor functions, senses and body of a child develop?
3. What can you do to help children grow in the best possible way?

It may seem strange in a book about psychology to talk about the physical development of children and young people. The truth is, however, that it is difficult to separate body and mind. For example, we have already repeatedly referred to 'nature' and how the body acquires certain information through genetic transfer, which allows you to further develop as a person through interaction or transaction with your environment.

The influence of the environment before birth

The environment can exercise a huge influence from the moment of conception, when the sperm penetrates the egg cell, right up to the moment of birth. The effect of this influence can often still be seen years later.

Consider, for example, the effect of medicines, drink or drugs taken by the mother during pregnancy.[1] Similarly, if the mother-to-be experiences stress during pregnancy, this too can have a long-term impact on the development and further life of her child. Researchers now suspect that continued and intense stress can influence the brain development of an unborn baby, so that the child will have a greater likelihood of being affected at a later age by behavioural and/or psychological problems.[2] In terms of learning capabilities, stress or negative emotions experienced by the mother during pregnancy can have a negative effect on, for example, the later development of a child's executive functions.[3]

Does the mother's body pave the way for dealing with a difficult future?

We know that stress in the mother-to-be can lead, for example, to more aggressive behaviour in her child at a later age. But is this necessarily bad? Marco Del Giudice suspects that something else is actually going on. He thinks that the baby is, as it were, being prepared to face the challenges of a more difficult environment, in which the child will need to be able to stand up for themself.[4]

Although we now know that listening to classical music before or after the birth will not necessarily make a child more intelligent,[5] any remedies that can reduce stress during pregnancy – and listening to music is potentially one of them – can have a positive effect,[6] which may also have a beneficial impact on attachment.[7]

What is the best approach for dealing with teenage pregnancies?

In recent decades, the number of teenage pregnancies has fallen dramatically.[8] However, this does not mean that they no longer occur. In the following chapter we will look more closely at sexual and relational development but for now we will concentrate on offering advice about how you can best respond as a parent or teacher when a teenage girl becomes pregnant, so that the levels of stress for all concerned are kept to a minimum.

Fara, an organisation that helps girls and women to make pregnancy choices, suggests the following concrete tips:[9]

- Try to ensure that your first reaction is not overly severe or disapproving. News of the pregnancy will undoubtedly come as unexpected, so that you may find yourself briefly in shock. You might also feel bewildered and confused. It doesn't seem real and an initial desire to deny the news is a completely normal response. Some people react emotionally (they cry or become angry); others remain rational, cool and distant.
- Bear in mind that it is not only the teenager but also you and others around you who will need time to come to terms with this unexpected news. Don't rush things or make hasty decisions.

- Listen to the teenager. Do not bombard her with (well-intentioned) possible solutions for the situation. Instead, make sure that you remove any anxiety she might have about possible 'punishment'.
- Accept the teenager's (confused) thoughts and feelings for what they are, without judgement.
- Talk with the teenager about the normal things in life; her pregnancy should not be the only topic of conversation.
- Don't try to do too much: by just being there and listening you are already doing a lot!
- Avoid trying to take over the situation. As far as possible, allow the teenager to decide what happens.
- Bear in mind that arguments and disagreements may become more frequent than normal, because the teenager will be more confused and stressed than normal.
- Protect and maintain your own boundaries: good self-care is a precondition for taking care of others. Don't be afraid to express your feelings.
- Do not hesitate to ask advice from your local GP or other local care services.

Rapid physical evolution during the first two years of life

If you compare human beings with animals, one of the most striking differences is the degree of helplessness of human babies at birth. While a newborn elephant can stand on its legs almost immediately, it takes many months before a newborn child can do the same. According to Gray and Bjorklund, this might be explained by our superior brain development in the long term. Imagine if the human brain needed to perform all its many tasks immediately after the child's birth. The head would need to be so big that it would never be able to pass through the birth canal.[10]

This does not, however, mean that a child is incapable of movement at birth. These innate movements are known as reflexes: unlearnt, unstructured and involuntary reactions or responses that the child automatically performs when prompted by certain stimuli. In this way, for example, the child's search reflex will cause the child three weeks after birth to turn their head in the direction of something that touches their cheek.

But if human babies start from a position of relative helplessness, their subsequent evolution during their first 18 months to two years of life is spectacular. During this period, they quickly acquire a series of important tools, exploring the world with their hands and feet, first crawling and then gradually with increasingly sure-footed steps, as these gross motor developments progress from big and largely uncontrolled movements to increasingly refined and precise ones. This brings great pleasure to the child, not only through the discovery of the new possibilities they possess but also because of the attention it attracts from others in their environment.

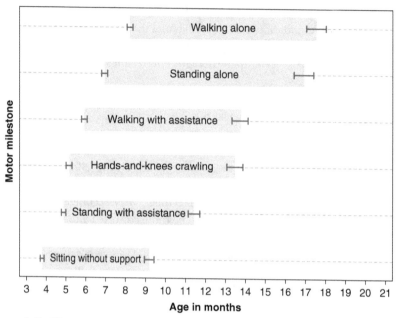

Figure 1.9 The progress a young child makes in physical activities

In this respect, the first steps are often an important landmark. Not all children make developmental progress at the same pace, as can be seen in Figure 1.9, in which ranges of time are given during which a child can be expected to perform certain actions: for example, sitting upright without support, which takes place between the fourth and ninth month after birth.[11]

In addition to these gross motor functions, the child also develops fine motor skills, which are primarily used to allow it to manipulate its environment. These skills are necessary, for example, to raise a spoon with food to your mouth or to pick up your teddy bear and, later on, for writing.

By their nature, these physical and motor developments also have an impact on the child's level of self-confidence and independence, because they become increasingly able to further explore the world in their own personal voyage of discovery.[12]

The evolutions that a child undergoes during the first two years of life are remarkable and can be summarised as follows:

- From the age of two months, the baby gradually gains more control over their environment. You can notice this, for example, by the way they try to shake their rattle or by moving the mobile hanging over their cot.[13]
- During the first three to four months, the baby largely uses their mouth to explore things but gradually progresses to the use of eyes and hands.[14] By the time the baby is five or six months old, this exploration becomes more sophisticated: the baby can pick up toys (but also other things), examine them from different angles, test out what they can do, etc. The child also

becomes curious about the things their carer looks at and will sometimes deliberately turn their head in the same direction.[15] This is an important precursor of crawling.[16]

- Between the ages of seven and ten months, the baby effectively starts to crawl.
- The tendency to look at the same things as the carer becomes more pronounced from the ninth month onwards, so that it is possible to speak of joint attention. The child looks at the things that an adult or older brother or sister indicates.[17]
- From 12 months onwards, the child is also able to point to things or show them to others,[18] and is even able to some degree to make predictions about what might or might not happen. Whereas at an earlier age the child will merely follow the trajectory of the ball if you throw it into the toy box, from this age onwards the child will start to look towards the box before you throw the ball, because they already assume that this is where the ball will end up.[19]
- Now that the child is able to crawl and can explore the world, they become curious to know what their parents think about what they do,[20] and start to do things (which can sometimes seem dangerous) to see how the adults will react.

What can you do to help a young child to develop in the best possible way?

We all want the best for every child but what can you do in concrete terms to help them blossom and grow? Engaging in different forms of interaction is important, so that the child's brain is stimulated in different ways. By cuddling, talking, singing and playing with the child, you not only increase their level of attachment but also challenge the child to make use of their nascent skills. Reading out loud to a child from an early age can also give a significant boost to their development, not only because you exercise their ability to focus when you look at a book together but also because you are engaging a number of different senses at the same time, while also expanding the child's vocabulary.[21]

How do a child's senses evolve during the first two years of life?

In addition to the development of their motor functions, the development of a child's senses is also important for their exploration of the world. In the chapter on perception we will explain why seeing something involves the use of more than just the eyes. You also need a brain to understand what you see. There is a fundamental difference between:

sensations: the physical stimuli that are picked up by the senses, such as light in our eyes, a touch on our skin or a noise in our ear;

and

perception: the ordering, comprehension, analysis and integration of these stimuli by our senses and our brain.

During this early period, the brain is the fastest growing of all the body's many parts,[22] so that not only the child's ability to think but also their ability to move and to perceive develop quickly.

As far as seeing or *visual perception* is concerned, a child's sight is relatively limited at birth but soon improves. At first, the baby only has sharp vision over a distance of 20 centimetres and just a few hours after birth already has a clear preference for looking at the face of their mother. This range of vision gradually increases, so that the child acquires more depth in what they see. By the age of three months, there is a general preference for the faces of people, as opposed to, say, animals.[23] Between the sixth and ninth month of life, the child becomes better able to distinguish between individual faces.[24] And by their first birthday, the child is also able to distinguish between people and zombies (which is always useful).[25]

In comparison, a baby can already hear reasonably well at birth, so that *auditive perception* begins at a very early age. In the first instance, the child can only hear extremely high and extremely low frequencies.[26] Between the ages of six and twelve months, children start to recognise their own mother tongue, which is important for their linguistic development.[27] After nine months, they can also recognise the difference between an up-beat and a down-beat melody.[28]

Other stimuli, such as smell and taste, are also well developed at birth. Some one-year-old children can identify their mother simply by her odour.[29] What children like (or do not like) to eat/taste depends in part on what the mother ate during the pregnancy,[30] although there is also a significant likelihood that they will like sweet things.[31]

Because a baby needs to be able to find their mother's nipple in order to eat and survive, the sense of taste is one of the most highly developed senses in newborn children.[32] Cuddling and massaging with plenty of skin-on-skin contact can positively stimulate the child, which is beneficial for their attachment and later social development.[33] Babies can also feel pain at a very early stage in their life, which can find expression in sweating and/or an increased heart rate.[34] Pain in very young children can have an influence on their later evolution, so that it is possible they may have a greater sensitivity to pain as adolescents or adults.[35]

As adults, we often combine the use of different senses, to create what is called *multi-modal perception*. You don't just eat a bowl of soup; you also smell its aroma, which in turn affects the way it tastes. However, there is still debate about whether very young children can combine the use of their senses in this way.[36]

The physical development of infants

As a result of regular practice through play and also the rapid development of the brain, infants quickly and constantly discover new things that they can do with their body. Moreover, as they get older, their general physical agility and dexterity increase.[37] For example, by the time a child is three years old, they can jump with both feet; by the time they are four years old, they can jump a distance of 70 centimetres; and by the time they are five years old, they can jump a distance of 90 centimetres with a running approach. That being said, there are often large differences between individual children, in which innate temperament and heredity can play a role, as can the relevant degree of encouragement or discouragement in the child's environment.[38]

Differences are also evident between boys and girls, with the former, in general, being stronger and more active than the latter,[39] although girls are generally better at activities that require coordination.[40] Once again – as in almost everything else – there is a clear interaction between nature and nurture. While athletic ability is to a significant degree genetic, it is nurture that determines whether certain skills are more widely practised by boys or girls.[41]

Although it is sometimes already evident in babies, it is usually during infancy that a child's preference for being left-handed or right-handed becomes clear. This preference is hereditary, and therefore exists at birth but in general it only becomes apparent at about the age of five years. Only a very small proportion of children are ambidextrous.[42] Taken as a whole, an average of 90% of children are right-handed. Among the remaining 10%, there are more left-handed boys than girls.

Drawing development

The development of fine motor functions makes it possible for the growing child to draw with increasing skill. At the same time, drawing requires a serious cognitive effort. It is possible to distinguish different phases in the way children draw during their first five years of life:

- From two to roughly four years: the **random scribbling phase**. The child knows how to hold a pencil or crayon in what is known as the 'pincer' grip but the resulting drawings lack form and have little or no meaning.
- At the age of around three years, the scribbling becomes more consistent in terms of form and the child likes to draw circular shapes. This is the **controlled scribbling phase**.
- Towards the end of the third year, the child will gradually combine different forms to make more complex ones, which is known as the **design or pattern phase**.

(Continued)

- In the **pictorial phase**, which takes place between the ages of four and five years, the child draws recognisable objects, in which the 'tadpole' man or woman (just a circular head with legs and arms) is one of the first identifiable figures. Other drawings tend to be of striking things that the child notices. For example, many drawings of girls will have exaggeratedly long hair. It is not (so) important for the child that what they draw is accurate; what counts is that it can be recognised.[43] At this age, colours also start to play a more important role.

When the child starts primary school, their drawing skills will continue to improve, as they learn about perspective and how to apply it. The child will also start to draw more 'scenes', depicting situations in which multiple objects and people interact with each other.

The physical development of primary school children

Primary school children between the ages of six and twelve years continue, of course, to grow but at a much slower rate. The actual rate of physical growth is between 5 and 7 centimetres each year, with girls tending to grow more quickly than boys, because they develop and reach maturity earlier. On average, there is a spurt in growth around the tenth year.

Gross motor functions improve, so that primary school children become better at sports. They can lift more, run faster and jump higher.[44] Before the growth spurt, children aged nine to ten years already have perfect control over their bodies. There is an outdated idea that boys perform better than girls but it now seems that this is not correct.[45]

In primary school significant attention is devoted to the further development of fine motor functions, with the children learning how to write and type. Their drawings also become more refined and more detailed. Having said that, it tends to be the gross motor functions that play the largest role in determining a child's popularity among their peers, especially amongst boys, with those who are physically the strongest also being more popular.[46] This can also play a role with girls but to a lesser degree. The importance of physical performance increases throughout the primary school period but then starts to decline.

Puberty

Puberty is often used in combination with the word 'difficult' but as we saw earlier in the book this is a largely old and outdated idea that doesn't apply to many children and young people. Puberty encompasses the physical changes that children and young people undergo as they develop towards adulthood, including the full development of the sexual organs.

A distinction needs to be made between primary and secondary sexual characteristics. *Primary sexual characteristics* are the result of the development of organs and structures that are directly related to reproduction and procreation. In girls, this involves changes to the vagina and womb. In boys, it involves the growth and enlargement of the penis, scrotum, prostate gland and the testicles. *Secondary sexual characteristics* relate to other visible signs of increasing sexual maturity that have no direct involvement in reproduction and procreation, such as the development of breasts in girls and the growth of pubic hair in both genders.

Puberty starts with a growth spurt, which begins in girls on average around the age of ten years and in boys around the age of twelve years. Throughout this adolescent period both genders will continue to rapidly increase in both height and weight, with boys growing on average some 10.5 centimetres each year and girls almost 9 centimetres.[47] In addition to the differences between the two genders, there can also be significant differences between individuals of the same gender.

Similarly, the age at which girls experience their first menstruation or *menarche* can also vary significantly. This depends in part on the region where you are born and the social class to which you belong, although body weight and/or the proportion of muscle to fat can also have an influence.[48] Playing lots of sport can also delay the menarche.[49] The average age of first menstruation is between eleven and twelve years but the age range is wide, with some girls menstruating at the age of nine years and others having to wait until their sixteenth year. Over time, the average age of menstruation has fluctuated considerably, although in recent years in the western world there has been a trend towards stabilisation or a slight lowering.[50] However, there can still be significant differences between girls from different backgrounds within the same country.[51]

The primary sexual characteristics of boys begin to change around their twelfth year. They reach their full adult size three or four years later. Their first ejaculation (the *spermarche* or *semenarche*) occurs on average at the age of thirteen years. While their semen initially contains relatively few sperm, it would be unwise to assume that intercourse at this age cannot result in pregnancy. Around their twelfth birthday (again on average), boys also start to develop secondary sexual characteristics, such as pubic hair, later followed by armpit and facial hair. Their vocal cords also lengthen and their larynx increases in size, as a result of which their voice deepens.

During this period, a young person's cognitive abilities also continue to improve at an increased rate. In contrast to the first growth spurt during the early years of childhood, adolescents are fully conscious of this second spurt. Their awareness of this development can have an emotional impact, although their reactions are just as likely to be positive as negative.

For example, the menarche and semenarche can have a positive effect on the self-esteem and self-awareness of young people.[52] At the same time, (too) many of them find it difficult to talk about these things in their environment, so that feelings of shame and embarrassment may also result. This is more frequently the case with girls, in whom the growth of fat tissues at this age is sometimes hard to reconcile with unrealistic ideals of what constitutes physical beauty.[53]

What are the possible consequences of early or late maturity?

The age at which boys or girls reach full maturity can have important consequences for their social environment. There is a strong likelihood that this environment will allow itself to be led by what it sees. For example, people will have different expectations of a mature 13-year-old, who looks much older than he/she is, in comparison with their expectations of other young people. This can have both positive and negative effects, although the reality is often far more complex than the simple mechanisms we will now describe.[54]

Boys who mature early are often better at sport, which, as already mentioned, can make them more popular than their other peers. This can also create a more positive self-image but can potentially lead to problems at school (if they neglect their lessons) or to earlier than normal contact with the law (if led astray by older friends).[55] Girls who mature early often have a more difficult time, because they are frequently labelled as being 'different' from their peers. It also needs to be remembered that girls in general mature more quickly than boys, so that an early mature girl can be very young indeed.[56] These girls are often popular with older boys - again based on what the boys see - but this does not mean that the girls are otherwise ready to deal with this attention.[57]

When maturity is delayed, boys can sometimes be less popular with their peers, because they are less good at sport. They often remain smaller than girls until well into their teens. This may (but not necessarily) result in lower self-esteem during adulthood. However, some of these late maturing boys can also be more assertive, because the reactions of others during their puberty required them to stand up for themselves more frequently.[58] Initially, girls who mature late tend to occupy positions lower on the social ladder of popularity but this often evolves positively in later years, when they often conform more closely to societal ideals of beauty.[59]

It needs to be emphasised that in all these cases we are talking about a greater or lesser likelihood that something will occur. Huge differences between individuals are still possible. For example, girls can react in very different ways to the varying speeds of their maturity process: many of them experience no mental problems at all, while others have considerably more difficulty in coming to terms with the changes they are experiencing.[60]

What can you do to help children grow in the best possible way?

1. **Start before the child's life begins.**

    Try to avoid stress as far as possible during pregnancy.

2. **A healthy mind in a healthy body.**

    Provide the necessary conditions that will allow the child to grow up in a healthy environment. Healthy food and plenty of sport/exercise are a good start but don't forget to also consider the way your child feels: physical and mental development have an impact on each other (also see the teacher takeaway on resilience in Chapter 4.1).

3. **Stimulate children to draw.**

    This not only improves fine motor function but also contributes towards cognitive development.

4. **Be alert for possible feelings of shame during puberty.**

    Some young people can feel shame during the period when their primary and secondary sexual characteristics become increasingly more obvious. Give them the support they need, when necessary, underlining that these feelings are perfectly normal and reassuring them that they can always come to you if they need to talk.

Endnotes

1. Galbally et al., 2014.
2. Van den Bergh et al., 2017.
3. See amongst others: Buss et al., 2011; Park et al., 2018.
4. Del Giudice, 2012.
5. De Bruyckere et al., 2015a.
6. Liu et al., 2016.
7. Simpson & Belsky, 2008.
8. Sedgh et al., 2015.
9. These tips come from: Fara (n.d.). *Tips voor ouders van tienerzwangeren en jonge ouders (of andere vertrouwenspersonen)*. www.fara.be/tienerzwangerschap producten/gratis-brochures-over-tienerzwangerschap
10. Gray & Bjorklund, 2018.
11. WHO Multicentre Growth Reference Study Group & de Onis, 2006.
12. Kalkman & Rep, 2017.
13. Watson, 1972.
14. Rochat, 1989.
15. Woodward, 2003.
16. Frankenburg et al., 1992.
17. Tomasello, 2009; Tomasello & Carpenter, 2007.
18. Liszkowski et al., 2006.
19. Falck-Ytter et al., 2006.
20. Walden, 1991.

21. See amongst others: Garlick, 2003; Lafuente et al., 1997.
22. House, 2007; Nihart, 1993.
23. Heron-Delaney et al., 2011.
24. See amongst others: Quinn, 2008; Ramsey-Rennels & Langlois, 2006; Valenti, 2006.
25. Lewkowicz & Ghazanfar, 2012.
26. Fernald, 2001; Werner & Marean, 1996.
27. See amongst others: Chonchaiya et al., 2013; Kuhl et al., 2006; Palmer et al., 2012; Rivera-Gaxiola et al., 2005.
28. Flom et al., 2008.
29. See amongst others: Delaunay-El Allam et al., 2006; Lipsitt & Rovee-Collier, 2012; Mizuno & Ueda, 2004.
30. Mennella et al., 2006.
31. Porges & Lipsitt, 1993; Rosenstein & Oster, 1988; Steiner, 1979.
32. Halth, 1986.
33. Diego & Hernandez-Reif et al., 2009; Gordon et al., 2013; Kersten, 2011.
34. Kohut & Pillai, 2009; Rodkey & Riddell, 2013; Simons et al., 2003; Warnock & Sandrin, 2004.
35. Ozawa et al., 2011; Ruda et al., 2000; Taddio et al., 2002.
36. De Gelder, 2000; Flom & Bahrick, 2007; Lewkowicz, 2002.
37. Planinšec, 2001.
38. Wood et al., 2007.
39. Pellegrini & Smith, 1998; Spessato et al., 2013.
40. Cratty, 1979.
41. Shala & Bahtiri, 2011; Yee & Brown, 1994.
42. Bryden et al., 2011; Marschik et al., 2008; Boller et al., 2003.
43. Breeuwsma et al., 2005; Winner, 1990.
44. Cratty, 1979.
45. Jürimäe & Saar, 2003.
46. Branta et al., 1996; Pintner et al., 1937.
47. Caino et al., 2004; Cratty, 1986.
48. Morris et al., 2011.
49. Sanchez-Garrido & Tena-Sempere, 2013; Woelfle et al., 2007.
50. Papadimitriou, 2016.
51. Deardorff et al., 2021.
52. Johnson et al., 1999; Matlin, 2003; Wilkosz et al., 2011; Yuan, 2012.
53. Cotrufo et al., 2007; McCabe & Ricciardelli, 2006; Crawford & Unger, 2004.
54. Hubley & Arım, 2012; Mendle et al., 2007; Strice, 2003.
55. Costello et al., 2007; Lynne et al., 2007; Taga et al., 2006; Van Jaarsveld et al., 2007.
56. Mendle et al., 2007; Olivardia & Pope, 2002; Franko & Striegel-Moore, 2002.
57. Galvao et al., 2014; Kaltiala-Heino et al., 2003.
58. Benoit et al., 2013; Kaltiala-Heino et al., 2003.
59. Kaminaga, 2007; Leen-Feldner, 2008.
60. Deardorff et al., 2021.

1.9

LET'S TALK ABOUT SEX(UAL DEVELOPMENT)

What questions does this chapter answer?

1. What is the difference between sex, gender identity and gender expression?
2. How do children develop sexually and what impact does this have on them?
3. What does all this mean in terms of practice?

Running parallel with their physical development, children and young people also develop sexually as they grow towards adulthood. This does not mean that they already understand sexuality as an adult does, although an important evolution in this direction does take place.

Words and letters

When we talk about sexuality, many words are often used interchangeably, even though they actually have different meanings. In education worldwide, the *gender-bread person* is frequently used to indicate the difference between sex, gender and gender identity. The following paragraphs are based on the fourth version of the genderbread person.[1]

The first point to make is that gender is not binary. In other words, it is not simply a question of either male or female. To a greater or lesser degree, it is usually a question of both. Keep this in the back of your mind as you read the following concepts.

Gender identity is the term used to indicate how a person experiences and describes their own gender. This is based on the extent to which you recognise yourself in certain characteristics or modes of behaviour that you regard as being male or female. Sounds confusing? In practice, it essentially means that you probably view certain characteristics, certain activities, certain roles, certain expectations, etc. as being more typical of men than women, or vice versa. If you see in your own life more characteristics, activities, roles and expectations that you associate as being typically male, you will probably also see yourself as being more male than anything else. That is your gender identity.

Gender expression is the manner in which you demonstrate your gender to the outside world. What style of clothes, hair, manners, etc. do you adopt to show to others what you feel and how they should regard you?

Sex refers to a person's physical characteristics at birth, which can either be male, female or intersexual. This is your SAAB: sex assigned at birth. The SAAB is not permanent and can be changed in later life. The various primary and secondary gender characteristics that we discussed in the chapter on physical development are all elements of a person's sex. Genetically, the only difference between the sexes is that women have two X chromosomes instead of the XY combination found in men.

Sexual or romantic interest relates to the extent to which a person feels sexually and/or romantically attached to men, women, or to another person's masculine or feminine nature.

By separating these concepts in this way, it becomes possible to form a number of different combinations. For example, it is perfectly possible that someone describes their gender identity as male, feels attracted primarily to women but also adopts feminine forms of expression, and this is irrespective of that person's sex.

As a result of all the possible nuances that exist, a number of letters and letter combinations have been assigned to describe the various possibilities, to which a plus sign (+) has sometimes been added in an attempt to ensure that the descriptions are all-inclusive.[2] The letter combinations and their meanings can vary depending on when, where and who is using them. Consequently, the following letters and meanings, although frequently used, do not form a definitive list:[3]

L: lesbian: as a woman, you are romantically and/or sexually attracted to other women.

G: gay/homosexual: you are sexually and/or emotionally attracted to people with the same gender identity. The term is generally used for men who are attracted to other men.

B: bisexual or bi+: you are romantically and/or sexually attracted to people of more than one gender identity. The gender identities to which you are attracted can vary over time and in intensity. In the past, 'bisexual' was most commonly used as a term to describe a person who felt attracted to both men and women. The definition of bi+ is broader and more gender-inclusive.

T: transgender: your sex assigned at birth does not correspond with your gender identity. If you were born with female sexual characteristics but do not feel yourself to be a woman, you are transgender. If your birth sex and gender identity correspond, you are cisgender.

I: intersexual: your sexual characteristics at birth do not correspond to the classic male/female definitions.

Q: queer or questioning: you are still searching to find your correct position in the LGBTIQ+ spectrum.

A: asexual/aromantic: you are asexual if you seldom or never feel sexually attracted to others. This term is used to describe people who are seldom sexually excited or seldom have a desire for sex with a partner. You are aromantic or 'aro' if you seldom or never feel romantically attracted to others. This does not mean that aromantic people are not capable of building up deep emotional connections with others. In fact, they often do feel love for others but not romantic love.

P: pansexual: you do not regard gender identity as an important factor when seeking a potential partner.

While your sex assigned at birth is more or less clear-cut, all the other characteristics that we have so far mentioned can develop and change over time.

Sexual and gender development during childhood

From almost immediately after their birth, boys and girls are treated differently by the environment around them,[4] so that the same behaviour in both sexes is interpreted differently.[5]

By the time of their first birthday, babies can distinguish between men and women. In general, girls play more with dolls than boys but this may be a result of the kind of toys that are offered to them.[6] This type of 'gender-defined' behaviour can increase with age under the influence of the environment; for example, if a girl is encouraged to play a caring role for a doll.[7] Conversely, it is also possible that the people in the environment might become concerned if a boy shows more interest in playing with so-called 'girl's' toys.

By the age of two years, boys are becoming slightly more independent than girls, which in part may again be attributed to the way that they are both treated by their parents,[8] although the environment cannot be held wholly responsible.[9] From this age onwards, young children clearly identify themselves and others as male or female.[10]

As far as gender identity is concerned, by the time they are four or five years old most children have learnt the stereotypical activities and behaviour that are appropriate to the various gender roles in their culture. They recognise themselves as one of these genders[11] and adjust their gender expression accordingly.[12] Young children often have a tendency to over-emphasise or over-generalise gender differences. If, for example, they notice that a boy likes a particular song, they will assume that all boys like this song.[13] During this phase of their development, children often play more with playmates of the same gender. This self-imposed gender segregation – boys playing with boys, girls playing with girls – reaches its pinnacle between the ages of eight and ten years.[14] Children (more often boys than girls) who do not wish to conform to this segregation run the risk of being bullied or excluded.[15] It is also around this age that an attraction for the same sex can develop,[16] although in some cases this realisation only dawns during adolescence or even in much later life. For example, some women only come to this realisation after years of heterosexual relations and/or motherhood.[17]

Love and sex in adolescence

In the chapter on physical development, we described how the bodies of adolescents change in different ways as they gradually progress towards adulthood. Running parallel with the development of primary and secondary gender characteristics, there are also significant changes in an adolescent's sexual development.[18] A first important observation is that adolescents in the western world nowadays have their first experience of sexual intercourse (with penetration) slightly later than in the past, and not earlier, as many people suppose.[19] As we shall presently see, this does not mean that they do not take their first preliminary steps towards intercourse at an earlier age, although intercourse itself is still seen by many as a milestone event. In the discussion that follows, it also needs to be borne in mind that much of the relevant research has so far been carried out predominantly in western countries, so that much still remains to be learnt.

Kissing between couples is regarded as something normal by 13- to 15-year-olds in the western world, in many cases without there being any other sexual activity at this stage.[20] This does not mean that there are no sexual thoughts at this age. The maturing of the sexual organs often first leads to the performing of sexual acts on their own person and to erotic thoughts, both of which can consume much of their attention.[21] Masturbation is often the first form of sexual experience. Initially, boys masturbate much more than girls but then gradually reduce in frequency. Girls on average tend to start more slowly and then work their way up.[22]

While the act of sexual intercourse is still regarded as the apotheosis of sexual development, there are many intermediate forms of sexual experience that can be attempted before reaching this point. After or in addition to solo-masturbation, it is also possible to engage in mutual or dual masturbation, tribidism (where the sexual organs are rubbed against each other), oral satisfaction and anal satisfaction.[23]

The establishing and exploration of adolescent relationships can differ widely from region to region and culture to culture. While a significant proportion of the initial exploration of mutual interests and the first attempts at seduction nowadays take place online, research suggests that the classic 'date' is still the most dominant intermediary step that is likely to lead to intimacy between adolescents.[24] By forming a couple, young people learn how to build up an intimate and long-term relationship, often with all the instructive ups and downs that this can involve. As well as being fun and enjoyable, this kind of relationship can also have an influence on the partners' status with their peers and has a direct impact on their identity development, as we saw when discussing the theories of Erikson.[25] Not all cultures are open to dating and relationships of this kind. In particular, parents of non-western origin tend to be conservative in their thinking on these matters, which can sometimes lead to conflict.[26]

The forms of intimacy with each other also undergo a certain evolution. If adolescents become sexually active at an early age, the intimacy is often restricted to physical interaction. There is much less psychological intimacy, in which the partners share the joys and sorrows of life with each other.[27] As their age increases, adolescents gradually come to see these mental aspects of a relationship as being increasingly important.

How 'normal' are couples?

If we look at the nature of (love) relationships throughout history, it becomes clear that human beings are creatures that are torn between two relational forms: monogamy (a marital relationship with a single partner) and polygamy (in which one person is married to two or more people at the same time).[28] If we look at the evolution of these matters over time, it can be seen that it was primarily western cultures that introduced pure monogamy as the norm to various parts of the world. Even where polygamy is still accepted, monogamy remains the most common form of relationship.[29]

During the adolescent phase, some young people discover for themselves and sometimes reveal to others that they feel attracted to people of the same gender. This 'coming out of the closet' frequently takes place during late adolescence (17 to 19 years of age), which is later than the actual emergence of the feelings, which (as already mentioned) can develop much earlier. This revelatory process usually takes place in various stages, with brothers, sisters and friends being the first to be informed, followed by the parents, usually starting with the mother.

'Coming out of the closet' can (also) often lead to the loss of heterosexual friends, the disappointment of parents and even to physical and verbal violence at the hands of peers. In some cases, this can result in physical and psychological health problems,[30] especially in some ethnic or religious communities that are less open for non-heterosexual relationships.[31] The more the revelation of homosexuality is accepted by the (wider) environment, the better it is for the psychological development of the young people concerned,[32] since this makes them better prepared to deal with the disapproval with which they may be confronted in society.

These different rites of passage to adulthood do not always pass smoothly for everyone. In particular, there is a risk that boys may display dangerous and antisocial behaviour in order to improve their status and – so they think – make themselves more attractive to the opposite sex: the so-called 'young male' syndrome.[33] That being said, some girls can also behave violently to protect their status.[34]

What does all this mean in terms of practice?

1. **The 'youth of today' do not start earlier with sex.**

   This is contrary to what many people think and is perhaps a mental error induced by the availability heuristic (see Chapter 4.3). Because much is written and discussed about sex and sexuality on social media and elsewhere, the idea of young people and sex attracts a disproportionate amount of our attention, so that it seems as though it is already fact. But it is not. In other words, there is no real need to worry on this score.

2. **Be aware that sexual development often goes hand in hand with powerful emotions.**

   The physical changes of adolescence, in combination with the search to discover who you are, together form an emotional process in which young people experiment and learn about themselves and their position in life in relation to others. If this search deviates from the norm, this can result in deep anxiety, shame and sorrow. Support the young person as they struggle with these matters. Let them know that they can always come to you if they need to talk. Failing this, help them to find someone else to whom they can tell their story. If things look like they are being difficult for a long time, seek professional help before the situation threatens to get out of hand.

3. **Provide unconditional support.**

   Sexual development is a complex process for your child, in which they need your support. Ensure that you are always there for them and give this support unconditionally. Demonstrate this in your own way: by listening, by giving them an occasional hug, etc. If you find it difficult to talk with your child on these matters, encourage them to talk with friends or someone else.

— Teacher takeaways —

How to deal with all those screens and social media

As time passes, the names of the different platforms change - after Facebook came Instagram, Snapchat, TikTok and others- but social media have become an indispensable and irreplaceable part of the world of most young people (and older ones as well). But although social media are here to stay, their popularity and success cause anxiety in some quarters and raise a number of questions.

What is the effect of...

Much research has already been carried out into the length of total screen time. Hattie, in his updated study completed in June 2019, reported that watching too much television has a negative effect on learning of -.18. Other studies have also demonstrated a correlation.[35] For example, it seems that a link with a low SES is possible, although sometimes things are more straightforward: children who are not really interested in learning and education choose other ways to spend their time, which makes it more difficult to establish cause and effect.[36] To make the situation even more complex, it is also necessary to take account of the material that is watched on the various screens that surround us in our daily life. The content of what we watch can influence us in different ways. For example, television can actually help to improve linguistic development and vocabulary.[37] And if all this is not already complicated enough, the situation becomes even more confused when the factors of social media and other technologies are added.

Do social media and, by extension, smartphones make young people more narcissistic, more prone to depression, etc.? Some researchers do indeed suggest that this is the case,[38] but most of the studies so far completed show no more than a correlation with no clear causal relationships.[39] A long-term study, during which 500 young people aged between 13 and 20 were followed for eight years, reached a similar conclusion: there was no link between the number of hours spent on social media and their mental state.[40] Research to establish whether a temporary break from social media could help to make young people feel better likewise concluded that this had no effect on their general mood and attitude.[41]

In a similar vein, the relationship between social media and school performance is one that also needs to be viewed with a significant degree of nuance. On the basis of a meta-analysis conducted in 2018, the researchers concluded:

1. Pupils who use social media to talk about school generally perform better at school.
2. Pupils who use tools like Instagram during their studies and homework perform less well than their fellow pupils who do not use these tools.

(Continued)

3.   There is a very small negative effect if pupils use social media excessively.

4.   Pupils who spend a lot of time on social media do not spend less time on their studies. In other words, social media do not 'steal' time from school.[42]

There are also studies that have demonstrated the important positive role that social media can play in the lives of young people. For example, social media make it possible for young people to meet each other, experiment with different roles and exchange different opinions.[43]

So, are there no problems with screens and social media?

Once again, the situation is far from simple. There are various recommendations relating to screen time. Among the most frequently cited are the recommendations of the American Academy of Pediatrics,[44] which in general err on the side of caution:

- Children younger than 18 months should not make use of screens, except to chat via video.
- For children aged between 18 and 24 months, the parents should choose high quality programmes that should be watched together, so that the parent can clarify and explain what is seen.
- For children aged between two and five years, the recommended maximum screen time is one hour per day, focusing again on high quality programmes that are watched together.
- From the age of six years onwards, screen time should still be limited, in order to ensure that children get sufficient exercise and sleep.

Given this final recommendation, in general it is a good idea for adults to set fixed rules for the screen time of their offspring. Such rules nearly always ensure that less (rather than more) time is spent watching television and other screens but, even more importantly, it has the knock-on effect of encouraging children to become more physically active; for example, by playing more sport.[45] It is also advisable to agree on places and moments where and when screens are not allowed; for example, during the evening meal and in the child's bedroom.

Not using your mobile phone during mealtimes is related to another challenge faced by people of all ages. Most of us, particularly nowadays, have a tendency to multi-task. However, research has shown that human beings are not well suited to doing more than one thing at the same time. We perform better when we focus our attention on a single task. This means that constant interruption - by screens of whatever kind - when children are trying to learn is not a good thing.[46] Supervising and managing when technology can and cannot be used during periods of learning is crucial and is something that needs to be learnt, preferably by the adults setting a good example.

As if this were not bad enough, there are still other dangers, as listed in 2009 by the EU Kids project. Many of their warnings still apply:

Table 1.1 An overview of possible online dangers adapted from the EU Kids project[47]

		CONTENT Child as recipient	CONTACT Child as participant	BEHAVIOUR Child as actor
RISKS	Commerce	Advertising, spam, sponsorship	Tracking/ harvesting personal information	Gambling, illegal downloads, hacking
	Aggressive	Violent/ gruesome/ hateful content	Being bullied, harassed or stalked	Bullying or harassing another
	Sexual	Pornographic/ harmful sexual content	Meeting strangers, being groomed	Creating/ uploading pornographic material
	Values	Racist/biased info/advice (e.g. about drugs)	Self-harm, unwelcome persuasion	Providing advice (e.g. suicide, pro-anorexia)

Cyberbullying will be discussed in the teacher takeaway in Chapter 2.3. For now, suffice it to say that the same general response guidelines remain valid: maintain open communication with your children and make clear that everyone must be treated with respect, both online and offline. As adults, also show interest in what your children are doing online. This positive interest (not spying!) will increase the likelihood that they will come to you if they encounter problems.

It is an illusion to think that you can shield your children from these dangers and problems. Sooner or later, they will be confronted by them. It is therefore better to prepare your children to deal with them, letting them know that you are also there to help, where and when necessary.[48]

Listening to Aretha

(You'd better) think are song lyrics by Aretha Franklin. The word 'think' actually forms a useful acronym that lists a set of simple guidelines for using social media. Before you post something online, ask yourself is it:

- True?
- Helpful?
- Inspirational?

(Continued)

- Necessary?
- Kind?

Just imagine if everyone would think more before they started to type on their smartphone or other device! The world would be a different - and almost certainly a better - place.

The positive side of screens and social media?

Research (involving one of the present authors) established that games and other screens help to improve the users' knowledge of English to a level that is reasonably good, even before they receive formal instruction on the subject in school.[49] This is just one of the advantages to which social media and other screens can contribute. But there are also a number of others:

- Children and young people often find it easier to talk about difficult topics via chat, rather than face-to-face.
- Digital technology can help to bring families closer together (for example, via video chat platforms like Skype), even from a very early age.[50]
- eBooks and other digital media can help to prepare children for school, by facilitating 'correct' forms of parent–child interaction, such as reading aloud, where the emphasis is placed on the story and the understanding of words, rather than on the keyboard and screen.[51]
- Perhaps it sounds strange but digital technology can also help parents to spend more time actively engaging with their children. Think, for example, of father-and-son gaming, which is something that fathers now do much more frequently than in the past, when these technological possibilities were not available.[52]

Sexting?

Something that parents, teachers and other caregivers often worry about is sexting. Sexting is a contraction formed by the words 'sex' and 'texting' and involves the sending and sharing of nude photographs, piquant videos and erotic messages via social media. Sexting is not necessarily a problem and can be a relatively safe way for young people to experiment with sexuality,[53] at least if it occurs without pressure and with the mutual consent of those involved. It is a different matter if you receive photos and videos unsolicited or if your photos and videos are shared with others for whom they were never intended. Eliminating and/or correcting these abuses is not easy. Listening and providing support to its victims is the best response.

Endnotes

1. Killermann, 2017.
2. Although the + can also have another meaning.
3. For the definitions of these letters, we have paraphrased the definitions that you can find in the word list drawn up by Çavaria, https://cavaria.be/woor denlijst, in which this defender of the interests of LGBTI people commented that the meanings can vary with the passage of time, this being the version currently applicable in January 2021.
4. Bridges, 1993; Coltrane & Adams, 1997; Serbin et al., 2001; Clearfield & Nelson, 2006; Laflamme et al., 2002; Parke, 2007.
5. Condry & Condry, 1976.
6. Alexander et al., 2009; Cherney et al., 2003; Serbin et al., 2001.
7. Hill & Flom, 2007; Martin et al., 2002; Schmalz & Kerstetter, 2006.
8. Kuczynski & Kochanska, 1990; Laemmle, 2013; Poulin-Dubois et al., 2002.
9. Levine et al., 1999; Mealey, 2000; Servin et al., 2003.
10. Campbell et al., 2004; Raag, 2003.
11. Kohlberg, 1966.
12. Martin & Ruble, 2004.
13. Bauer & Coyne, 1997.
14. Gray & Feldman, 1997; Whiting et al., 1988.
15. Petitpas & Champagne, 2000; Thorne, 1993.
16. Savin-Williams, 1998.
17. D'Augelli et al., 2001.
18. Kar et al., 2015.
19. See amongst others: Dierckens et al., 2019; de Graaf et al., 2017; Twenge & Park, 2019.
20. Mullinax et al., 2017.
21. Kelly, 2001; Ponton, 1999.
22. See amongst others: Hyde & DeLamater, 2008; Mullinax et al., 2017.
23. Mullinax et al., 2017.
24. Bogle, 2008; Denizet-Lewis, 2004; Manning et al., 2006.
25. Erikson, 1968; Adams & Williams, 2011; Friedlander et al., 2007; Paludi, 2012; Zimmer-Gembeck & Gallaty, 2006.
26. Hamon & Ingoldsby, 2003; Hoelter et al., 2004; Kibria, 2003; Lau et al., 2009.
27. Collins, 2003; Furman & Shaffer, 2003.
28. Dewsbury, 1988.
29. Marlowe, 2000; Murdock, 1981.
30. Lick et al., 2013.
31. D'Augelli, 2005.
32. D'Augelli, 2005.
33. Daly & Wilson, 1990.
34. Campbell, 1995; Campbell, 2013.

35. Even in this case: Johnson et al., 2007.
36. Hancox et al., 2005.
37. Ribner et al., 2017.
38. Twenge, 2017.
39. See amongst others: Odgers & Jensen, 2020; Orben, 2020.
40. Coyne et al., 2020.
41. Hall et al., 2021.
42. Marker et al., 2018.
43. Boyd, 2014.
44. American Academy of Pediatrics, 2016.
45. Carlson et al., 2010.
46. Kirschner & De Bruyckere, 2017.
47. Livingstone & Haddon, 2009
48. Valkenburg, 2014.
49. De Wilde, 2017.
50. McClure & Barr, 2017.
51. Guernsey & Levine, 2016.
52. Livingstone et al., 2018.
53. Van Ouytsel et al., 2014.

1.10

THE DEVELOPMENT OF PLAYING: NOT JUST A GAME

What questions does this chapter answer?

1. What is playing and what kinds of playing are there?
2. How do the different kinds of playing develop in children?
3. What can you do to stimulate the development of play?

A number of the developments that we have discussed so far, such as physical development and linguistic development, contribute towards a further kind of development that involves one of the most important things that children do: playing.

The characteristics of playing

Perhaps it sounds slightly strange to hear playing described in such important terms but it is one of the most crucial factors in physical, motor, cognitive and social development.[1] It is not without good reason that the right to play is included in the Convention on the Rights of the Child.[2]

Playing is not only important for the development of the individual child but also the development of society as a whole!

As early as 1938, the Dutch scientist Johan Huizinga described how communities can develop through play.[3] The reasons for this become clear when you look at the characteristics he attributed to playing:

1. Playing is a free activity and is therefore equivalent to freedom. In play, everything is possible, thanks to the use of fantasy.

2.   Playing is not part of ordinary or everyday life. Even when children are playing 'families', they know it is not real.
3.   Playing is different from ordinary life in both location and duration. The passage of time when you are playing is very different from the way time passes in real life. Or do you think that you can actually get rich in real life as quickly as you can when you are playing Monopoly?
4.   Playing creates order. In fact, playing is order. If you wish to play together, (strict) rules are necessary.
5.   Playing does not serve material interests. Nobody profits from it.

These five characteristics raise some interesting points. Bearing in mind the last point, it is clear that gambling and the practice of sport professionally cannot be regarded as playing in the true sense of the word. It is also worth noting that at first glance the first and the fourth points apparently seem to contradict each other. How can play be freedom, whilst at the same time bring order through the imposition of rules? The answer is simple: you are free to determine the rules within the game. In fact, on many school playgrounds more time is spent on agreeing the rules than on actually playing the game! That being said, the first and fourth characteristics also relate to a distinction that is often made in the literature: the difference between free playing and structured playing.

In *free playing*, children invest all their energy in self-chosen, unstructured and enjoyable activities.[4] This kind of playing is usually voluntary and its main aim is to have immediate fun. In other words, it contains a significant degree of intrinsic motivation (also see Chapter 4.2 on motivation later in the book).[5] *Structured playing* is a planned activity and the activity in question is consciously designed to practise or learn certain things.[6]

We can explain this by using a well-known make of plastic building blocks from Denmark as an example. If you buy a building kit from Lego®, there is usually a building plan that you can use to build the house, car or whatever else is shown on the packet. In this way, while you are playing you learn new techniques by carefully following the plan. This is structured playing.

In free playing, you use the same blocks again – sometimes to the dismay of your parents – but this time you make whatever your imagination inspires you to make. But it is not only the blocks you reuse but also the skills that you acquired during your structured play.

Which of these two forms of playing is the most important? That is a meaningless question. You need them both: structured playing to learn new rules and skills; free playing to explore the boundaries of those rules and to practise both old and new skills.

Play itself is not unique to the human species but there is one aspect of playing that seems to be unique to us, and that is our possibility to engage in *symbolic playing*. We can pretend. We can use our fantasy. Moreover, this symbolic playing develops over time. The more we know and the better our abstract thinking skills become, the more and better we are able to fantasise.[7] In addition, this symbolic playing can be used in both structured and free play.

Parents and playing

A child's first playmates are their parents. Mothers and fathers both play with their offspring but in different ways. In general, fathers play relatively more than mothers, often while the mothers are performing relatively more of the 'care' tasks. The nature of their respective playing is also different. It almost sounds like a cliché and there are certainly exceptions but on average fathers play the 'wilder' and more physical games with their children, while mothers play the calmer, more traditional and more verbal games.[8] It is also the case (cliché or not) that fathers generally tend to play more with boys and mothers play more with girls. As a result, boys and girls are often offered a different range of play and games.[9] Perhaps this is one of the reasons why both genders play differently.[10]

Throughout the development of playing, we see that the parents – even after the stage when they no longer actively play with the children themselves – continue to have a significant influence. For example, the parents' assumption that the neighbourhood in which they live is a dangerous one might mean that they allow their children to play less, at least outdoors and with others.[11] Similarly, parents who are traditional in their opinions and convictions may also prevent their daughters in particular from playing sport.[12]

The development of different kinds of playing

Different kinds of playing develop throughout the years of a child's life. If we look at the purpose of playing, we can distinguish the following types:

- **Functional playing**

  These are **simple activities, often repeated**. The children perform these activities simply to be active with something. They can do this with objects such as rattles, dolls or whatever else is put into their hands and mouths. The activity has no purpose, other than the desire to play.[13] This type of playing starts during early childhood and continues throughout the first years of infancy.
- **Constructive playing**

  This type of playing starts around the fourth year of life, when children begin to **manipulate objects in order to make or build something**. These 'constructions' are repeatedly demolished and rebuilt. Playing of this kind allows children to develop their cognitive and physical skills, such as the exercising and practising of their fine motor functions. Just think about what you actually need to build something. You must know how objects fit together, you need to be able to think about the right order of assembly, and you need to envisage how the finished construction will look. For larger 'projects', you might even need to work together with others.[14]

This latter point – interaction with others during playing – is crucial at all levels of play development:

- Toddlers and infants often start with **parallel playing**, where they play alongside each other but without any real (or much) interaction.[15]
- These toddlers and infants can then evolve to **onlooking playing**, which – as the name suggests – involves watching how others play, without actively taking part. Sometimes this happens in silence but sometimes the watchers give comments and advice on what they see, or even offer support.
- At the end of infancy, two other types of playing emerge. In **associative playing**, the children still do not really play with each other but there is now at least a kind of interaction; for example, they may exchange toys. At the same time, the manner of play that a child sees in another child might inspire his or her own way of playing.
- The second form is **cooperative playing**, in which children do now actually play with each other, sometimes taking turns in a game (also see Chapter 4.1 on executive functions) and sometimes competing with others in races and activities.

Play continues to develop after infancy, with *symbolic playing* becoming increasingly important. Between the ages of three and four years, children start to play different roles with each other. The better the children get to know each other, the more complex this role playing becomes.[16] This kind of playing can also be a training school for the development of friendship. If a child engages in relatively little of such playing, it may lead to a slowing down of its cognitive and linguistic development,[17] with cause and effect probably overlapping.

A special and more sophisticated form of this *pretend play* is the imaginary friend. This is a playmate who does not actually exist but who can nevertheless seem very real to the child concerned. Somewhere between one in two and one in four of all children between the ages of three and eight years create an imaginary friend, who has usually disappeared by the time the child reaches the age of ten years.[18]

Do aggressive games and playing lead to more aggression in children?

This popular idea is much older than the development of violent computer games like *Grand Theft Auto*. Is it possible that this kind of violent game can prompt the development of aggression in those who play them? Much research has been carried out into this matter,[19] with some of the reasoning dating back to the Bobo doll research carried out by Bandura, which we will discuss later in the book. For now, suffice it to say that a large-scale randomised and controlled trial involving hundreds of children and young people to establish whether or not there was any difference between playing a violent computer game, an innocent computer game or no game at all, came to the conclusion that there was... no difference in effect whatsoever.[20]

Endnotes

1. Holmes & Romeo, 2013; McGinnis, 2012; Whitebread et al., 2009.
2. Lester & Russell, 2010.
3. Huizinga, 1938.
4. Truelove et al., 2017.
5. Côté et al., 2007.
6. Tortella et al., 2019.
7. Carlson et al., 2014; Lillard, 2015.
8. Paquette et al., 2003.
9. Clearfield & Nelson, 2006; Laflamme et al., 2002; Parke, 2007.
10. Göncü et al., 2002.
11. Veitch et al., 2011.
12. Heinze et al., 2017.
13. Bober et al., 2001; Kantrowitz & Evans, 2004.
14. Edwards, 2000; Love & Burns, 2006; Shi, 2003.
15. Parten, 1932.
16. Howes, 1994.
17. Smilansky, 1968.
18. Taylor et al., 1993.
19. Schreier, 2013.
20. Kühn et al., 2019.

2
OTHERS

In the previous chapter, we touched briefly but regularly on the role of others, because (with very few exceptions) no child grows up in complete isolation. In fact, throughout every stage of the child and young person's development, the number of people who have an influence on that development continues to grow. In this section, the first chapter will discuss the theories of Bronfenbrenner, which provide a useful framework for better understanding the child's surrounding environment.

After that, we will look at groups – Bronfenbrenner referred to them as microsystems – that certainly have an important impact on a child's development. The first others that a child sees are usually their parents. But how can these parents best deal with their child and what do we know about the different ways in which a child can be raised, more generally known as parenting styles? We will discuss these different styles and also examine what this means for the educational style adopted by teachers, another group who clearly play a leading role in a child's life.

As the child gets older, the influence of their peers increases in importance, often resulting in close friendships. This will be the subject of the final chapter in this section.

2.1

THE BIO-ECOLOGICAL MODEL OF BRONFENBRENNER

(OR HOW YOU NEED A WHOLE VILLAGE TO RAISE A CHILD)

─What questions does this chapter answer?─

1. What systems have an influence on your development as a person?
2. How do the different environmental influences interact during your development?
3. What is a broad-based or community school?
4. What is collective teacher efficacy?

Who helped to make you the person you are today? Your parents, obviously but what about your friends? Your grandparents? Your first boss at work? The longer you think about it, the more you will be able to name a growing list of people who all had an impact on your life. There is an old African saying, which claims that you need a whole village to raise a child.[1] One of the developmental theories that has attempted to summarise and incorporate this wisdom is Bronfenbrenner's bio-ecological system model. In Chapter 1.1 on nature and nurture, in addition to interaction we also discussed the idea of transaction, during which the influence of nature and nurture constantly interact on each other throughout the development of the child. Bronfenbrenner tried to map these different environmental factors in a transactional model that incorporated the mutual influencing of different systems, which can be seen as an onion with five layers that move around the child. Originally, Bronfenbrenner described it as an ecological model,[2] but in order to explain matters such as the interaction between the characteristics of the child derived

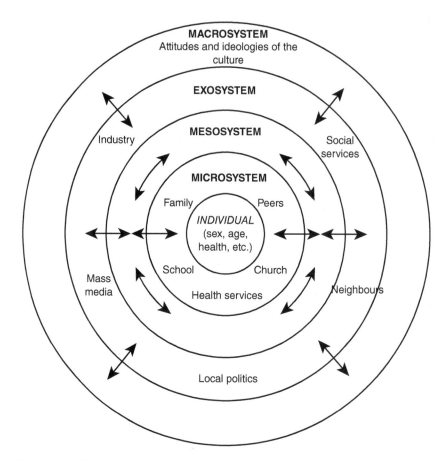

Figure 2.1 Bronfenbrenner's bio-ecological model

(Source: Bronfenbrenner, U., 1977. Toward an experimental ecology of human development. *American Psychologist, 32*(7), p.513–531. Copyright © 1977, American Psychological Association)

from, for example, heredity and the environment, it eventually came to be regarded as (and called) a bio-ecological model (see Figure 2.1).[3]

According to Bronfenbrenner, there are different *microsystems* to be found around each child and young person. Examples of such microsystems include the family, school, friends, etc. These are the people and the places in the life of a child with whom and with which the child regularly comes into direct contact, as a result of which they all help to shape the child as a person.

The different systems and the manner in which they interact with each other result in the creation of a *mesosystem*. This interaction between the different microsystems and the extent to which they all point in the same direction are crucial for the child's formation and development. Imagine, for example, that your parents, your school and your friends all say that studying is important. In that case, you will have a stimulating learning and living environment. However, Bronfenbrenner warns that alienation may occur if the different microsystems do not mutually strengthen each other. Imagine now that your parents and your school say that studying is important but your friends say that studying is a waste of time. When that happens, you are forced to choose between the different microsystems to which you would like to be loyal but this is not possible, so you end up finding yourself isolated and alone. Another example? Dealing with the 'school' microsystem might also be difficult if the family in which the child is growing up does not function properly, so that the child does not get proper study support or is even sent off to school with an empty stomach and an equally empty sandwich box.

Bronfenbrenner and radicalisation

Bronfenbrenner's bio-ecological development model is also used to map out how young people become radicalised.[4] The model makes it possible to chart all the different influences that can have an effect on radicalisation, such as the economic situation and the convictions that exist with certain groups and sub-cultures, as well as identifying the wedges that can be driven between different microsystems.

The next layer of the model's 'onion' outside the mesosystem is the *exosystem*. This contains more general influences, like the local media, the education system, the church (or mosque or synagogue), etc. The child or young person watches films and listens to music, which can also be influenced by parents and friends. Likewise, the quality of the school he/she attends will also determine to a significant degree the quality of that child or young person's learning opportunities. More indirectly, the local economy can also have an impact on the life of a child. Imagine, for example, that the factory in which both the child's parents are working is closed down, making them both unemployed. The effect on the family and on the child can be potentially devastating.

Bronfenbrenner's fourth layer is the *macrosystem*. This relates to the general ideas and convictions that permeate the society in which the child or young person lives. In other words, it is the level of the cultures and sub-cultures to which the child or young person belongs. Consequently, these elements are yet another step further removed from direct contact with the child or young person and therefore seem more abstract. Even so, they are still capable of having a powerful formative effect on the child or young person's development. Consider, for example, the 'one-child' policy that was introduced in China in 1979, which meant that families were unable to have more than one child, unless they wished to risk a serious financial penalty. This legislation, particularly in a society that places a higher value on boys than girls as a way of ensuring familial care and comfort in old age, led to a situation where even today, long after the relevant laws have been repealed, there are still far more boys/men than girls/women, a societal phenomenon that makes itself felt in the lives of many millions of Chinese each day.[5] These large-scale phenomena can often have a knock-on effect throughout the different levels of the model. Imagine that the globalisation of the world economy (macrosystem) leads to the closure of the company (exosystem) for which a child's father works. This puts greater stress on both parents (microsystem), so that they offer the child less encouragement and support for the child's school studies (microsystem). The end result is a living environment (mesosystem) that is much less stimulating for that child.

The final, outer layer of Bronfenbrenner's onion is perhaps more conceptually difficult to understand. It is known as the *chronosystem* and deals with the element of time, both in relation to the development of the child themselves and in relation to the historical events that can shape the life of the child and the nature of all the other systems that surround them. In other, words, the chronosystem – time – interacts not only with the microsystems but also with the mesosystem and the macrosystem. Viewed in these terms, the chronosystem contains both a child's first kiss as a teenager and that child's reaction to the traumatic experience of the 9/11 attacks in New York or the COVID-pandemic worldwide.[6]

Bronfenbrenner and stress in young children

Shonkoff and colleagues have described how being subjected to 'toxic' stress at an early age can have a huge influence on a child's later learning and functioning as an adult.[7] This toxic and infectious stress can already be picked up by a child from their parents (microsystem) while still very young, so that the child's development can be slowed down significantly.[8] To counteract this stress, it is therefore not only necessary to look at the child but also at the microsystem formed by the parents, in the hope of improving their relationship with the exosystem.[9] This might be done, for example, by arranging for the rent on their social accommodation to be reduced, in order to give them more financial breathing space. Sounds far-fetched? Not at all. A study has already shown that this kind of reduction in the family rent can lead to a child's better performance at school.[10]

The most important added value offered by Bronfenbrenner's model is that as a teacher, caregiver or researcher it gives you a language and a framework to examine the complex situation surrounding a child. For example, in the event of a child behaving negatively it automatically makes you aware of the multiple influences that might be in play and therefore helps to prevent you from jumping to conclusions, by directly assuming that this or that must be the cause. For this reason, the bio-ecological model is also used to better understand bullying behaviour,[11] by mapping out the different elements that can trigger bullying, based on Bronfenbrenner's different systems. For example:

- At the level of the microsystem, to what extent does the child feel connected to the school? Does the child have relatively few friends, so that the likelihood of bullying is increased?

- At the level of the mesosystem, what effects do the interactions between the teacher and the child have on the interaction of the child with other pupils? A child that gets on well with a teacher can sometimes be a thorn in the side of other pupils, whose relationship with the teacher is not so good.
- At the level of the exosystem, to what extent do wider external factors have an influence on bullying; for example, advances in technology that make cyberbullying much easier than it was in the past.
- As far as the macrosystem is concerned, a review by Hong and colleagues suggests that to date relatively little research has been carried out in this field, although they did point out that, for example, a culture's attitude towards girls may encourage bullying behaviour in some communities.
- Research into the chronosystem has shown that important events and changes in a child's life – moving to a new house, a death in the family, etc. – can increase the likelihood of that child being bullied.

Criticism of the Bronfenbrenner model

The original criticism of Bronfenbrenner's model was that the child at the centre of it remained more or less passive and simply allowed all the various influences to wash over them. The idea of resilience or resistance was lacking, by which the child might stand up for themselves and work against some of the elements in the different systems. It was also pointed out that although the individual child and all the influences affecting that child are central in the model, it nevertheless overlooks the fact that groups can also develop.[12] Be that as it may, one factor that speaks in favour of Bronfenbrenner was his willingness to regularly amend his theories to reflect criticism and the findings of new research. This can be seen, for example, from the changing evolution of the model from ecological to bio-ecological and also in the way his thinking about the chronosystem changed over time.

How Bronfenbrenner can help to make broad-based or community schools possible

The idea that all the microsystems around a child should ideally all be pointing in the same direction later inspired the concept of the broad-based or community school. What is a community school? It is a collaboration between different elements and sectors in society, in which one or more schools and, for example, the local music school, art academy, sports club, local authority, etc. work together to create a broad-based living and learning environment in both a child's time at school and their free time, with the objective of providing maximum developmental opportunities for all children and young people.[13] By bringing all these different microsystems together at a single location, it becomes possible to reduce the threshold for, say, sport and culture for children who might otherwise not come into contact with these and other life-enhancing activities.

However, most community schools not only seek to lower thresholds for their children and young people but also to increase the involvement of parents by creating more opportunities for them to meet.[14] It is this series of formal and informal contacts between parents and the school that can engender an increase in mutual confidence and trust, which at the same time improves the learning and living environments for the school's pupils.[15]

How everyone pulling in the same direction can improve schools: collective teacher efficacy

In 2017, John Hattie published an update of his list detailing the effect sizes of all the factors that can play a role in the influencing of a child's learning. According to him, the most important effect through which you can improve the learning of children via a specific approach is collective teacher efficacy.[16] Bandura was one of the first to show that the self-confidence that a group of people has in its own ability is an important factor for the success of a team.[17] It was Rachel Eells who demonstrated the added value of this idea for learning in her meta-analysis.[18]

In broad terms, the concept of collective teacher efficacy states that the confidence held by a group of teachers in their power to change the lives of their pupils for the better is greater and more important than the confidence of individual teachers to achieve that same aim. In essence, for the pupils it is the difference between 'we believe in you' and 'I believe in you'.

If you look at the ways in which you can improve collective teacher efficacy in a school, one of the most important aspects relates back to the core point of ensuring that everyone is working in the same direction. Relevant factors in this respect include:[19]

- The extent to which the teachers can influence school policy: are they able to influence decisions about the daily running of the school?
- The extent to which the teachers know about each other's work: teachers have more confidence in the ability of their colleagues to have an impact on pupil learning if they have knowledge about the lesson practices of those colleagues; for example, by being given the opportunity to observe each other's classroom work.[20]
- Team cohesion: the extent to which teachers agree on points of fundamental educational principle and policy.

- Responsive leadership: the extent to which school leaders are responsive, demonstrate care and respect for their team, and protect their teachers from matters that can distract them from their core task of teaching.
- Effective educational interventions: the extent to which use is made of effective didactic approaches, so that all pupils can be successful and perform well.
- Goal consensus: the extent to which the team is in agreement about the goal that they wish to achieve together; such agreement not only enhances collective efficiency but also has a direct, measurable and beneficial effect on the learning performance of your pupils.[21]

Of course, all this involves a lot of work and cannot be achieved overnight. Even so, it is well worth making the necessary effort. It is a pity that the pupils who could most benefit from collective teacher efficacy – the pupils from families with a low SES – more frequently find themselves in schools where less collective teacher efficacy is present.[22] These are the schools that most need support to improve in this important area.

What does all this mean in terms of practice?

1. **Be aware that the negative behaviour of a child is the result of a complex interplay of different factors.**

   If a child is being difficult at home or in class, always try to find out why. Never attribute this behaviour simply to the child's 'bad character'. That being said, attempting to find an explanation for negative behaviour does not mean that in the meantime you have to tolerate that behaviour. You can explain to the child that you know or realise why they are behaving in this manner but it is important that your response to this behaviour is consistent.

2. **Stimulate a broad-based school approach.**

   It is not just the schools that should seek to involve parents more; parents should also seek to become more connected with their children's places of learning. In addition, the neighbourhood and wider local community can also help to create an environment of harmony and unity. The greater the level of connectedness and the more all concerned are working together in the same direction, the clearer and better the situation will become for the pupils at such schools.

3. **Seek as a school to achieve collective teacher efficacy.**

   There is nothing more beneficial for pupils than one team of teachers all working towards the same goal and all believing that together they can make a difference to their school's performance and their pupils' lives.

─ Teacher takeaways ─

The dynamics of a group

How can you best deal with a group of children? Or a group of young people? Or a class of pupils or students? In this practical teacher takeaway, we will look at what group dynamics can teach us.

What is a group?

As soon as two people come together, you have a group. There are many other definitions, in which more and more people are added and where emphases are placed to stress something about the nature of the people involved: people who belong to the same class, people who interact with each other, people who influence each other, people who have a shared identity, people who together form a system, etc. What all these different definitions have in common is the fact that a mutual relationship exists between the different members of the group.[23]

Viewed in these terms, a group can be a school class, a sports club or a parents' association. But it can just as easily be a few people chatting on a bench in the park. In contrast, it is more difficult to see children in a nursery or playground as a group. If there is interaction between them, that is one thing. But if the children do not know each other, do not play with each other or do not even talk to each other, so that essentially they just happen to be in the same place at the same time, this cannot really be called a group.

The terms 'group' (even though it is essentially a neutral word), 'band' and 'gang' are often seen as something negative. A team is a more positive word for a group of people that are connected and work together for a specific purpose.

The characteristics of a group

Whether or not groups are a good or bad thing has been a subject of heated discussion for decades. As far as education is concerned, it has been clear for a long time that things can sometimes go badly wrong for an individual child or young person, depending on the group to which that individual belongs. Even at an early age, it is possible for pressure to be applied and for stress to develop within a class group; for example, when a child is urged by peers to deliberately score poorly in a test.[24] At a later age, similar pressure and stress may be exerted by a group wanting to force a young person to take part in sexting.[25] At the same time, not belonging to a group can also be painful through the feeling of being excluded.

On the other hand, being part of a supportive group or environment can lead to better performance:[26] think back to what we wrote in this chapter on Bronfenbrenner and his ideas; recently both De Bruyckere and Hattie et al. proposed to discuss *collective student efficacy*.[27] In this respect, there is also a link to the size of the group. It is easier to interact with a group of three or four than with a group of 50. In a group consisting of 50 members, a total of more than 1,200 relationships quickly need to be formed and it is precisely these relationships that determine the overall quality of the group.

In the event of optimal relations within the group, you often get:

- Common objectives: the different members of the group are in agreement about what they wish to achieve or for what they wish to work.
- Mutual dependence: everybody realises that everyone is necessary to achieve the common objective.
- Structures that make possible different roles for the group members: these are the expectations that the group members have of each other; for example, this one is a leader, this one is critical, this one is funny, etc.
- Shared norms and values: group members are not only aware of the direction in which they must travel because of structures and roles but also because of shared knowledge about what is possible and what is not possible within the group, on pain of exclusion if certain limits are exceeded.
- Togetherness or cohesion: the group has a certain unity and solidarity, thanks to the different relationships between its members, and is experienced as being coherent by the outside world.

All these different elements interact with each other and, as a result, create a group dynamic. This was the term that Kurt Lewin used in the 1950s to describe how groups and individuals within groups react to changing circumstances.[28]

No, there is no such thing as telepathy between group members

A popular idea in recent decades was that the members of groups shared something that could be described as 'group think', as a result of which group members could intuitively sense each other's needs and thoughts, a process that perhaps (according to some) extended as far as a shared consciousness. In reality, this is an example of the so-called 'group fallacy', whereby characteristics are attributed to a group that can only properly be attributed to individuals. In other words, groups do not have a will of their own; people do.

How does a group function?

If we look at the definitions mentioned earlier, it should be clear that groups can take many different forms: families, colleagues, groups of members of the public, crowds, etc. It would be wrong to think that these groups all have the same structure

(Continued)

and history. In the literature, five steps are described in the group development process, as originally expounded by Tuckman:[29]

- Orientation or the formation of the group, during which information is exchanged between the different group members.
- Conflict or storming, during which discussion arises and the leadership and structure of the group are questioned.
- Structuring or norming: the shared elements within the group take form. Everyone is in agreement about the roles, structures and norms.
- Performing or collaboration: decisions are taken, tasks are performed, and group members work together.

Later, following further research with Jensen, Tuckman added a final phase:

- Termination or dissolution: members leave the group; their level of mutual dependence diminishes and there is a degree of regret or nostalgia for the past.[30]

Although these phases are still often referred to in the literature, they are also the subject of much criticism, with several alternatives being suggested.[31] The most important critique is that it is wrong to think that all groups must go through all the stages in the order specified by Tuckman. In reality, these stages are more like examples of dynamic moments that a group can encounter at some point in its history.

So how do you actually deal with groups?

If we look back at our definitions of what constitutes a group, we can see that relationships between group members play an important role. For example, a disturbed relationship between two pupils can weigh heavily on the entire class. It is therefore crucial to create a positive climate and to do everything possible to ensure that all relationships within the group are as good as they possibly can be, not only between the individual group members - for example, the pupils - but also with the group leader - for example, the teacher.

If we take the need to work at relationships as our starting point, the following actions can help to support groups in an educational context:

- Do not always speak to children and young people as a group. Talk to them sometimes as individuals, so that you build up a relationship with each of them. Teachers in some countries even shake hands with their pupils every day as they enter the class!
- Make sure that children and young people are given a voice, by providing them with opportunities to express themselves. There are lots of different ways you can do this: encouraging them to keep a diary, class discussions,

participation in the student council or other participative bodies, etc. Away from school, youth organisations and sports clubs can offer similar opportunities.

- Observe what is happening in the group and respond accordingly to tensions, friendships, relationships, etc. Be aware that all these aspects of the group dynamic are constantly evolving and therefore constantly changing.
- Try to deal quickly and appropriately with group members who display disruptive behaviour and threaten the natural process of storming, as described by Tuckman. It is crucial that you also build up an individual relationship with these disruptive elements.
- Dealing with disruptive influences is necessary to ensure that children and young people feel safe within the group. Respond in an adult manner to whoever or whatever is threatening them, attacking them, making them feel insecure, bullying them, etc.

Endnotes

1. Goldberg, 2018.
2. See amongst others: Bronfenbrenner, 1994; Bronfenbrenner & Morris, 2007.
3. Rosa & Tudge, 2013.
4. See amongst others International Centre for the Prevention of Crime (ICPC), 2015.
5. Phillips, 2015.
6. Rosa & Tudge, 2013.
7. Shonkoff et al., 2012.
8. See amongst others: Suor et al., 2015; Skoe et al., 2013.
9. Swick & Williams, 2006.
10. Newman & Holupka, 2015.
11. See amongst others: Espelage, 2014; Hong & Espelage, 2012; Swearer & Espelage, 2004.
12. Christensen, 2016.
13. Blaton & Van Avermaet, 2015.
14. Doornenbal, 2014.
15. See amongst others: Coleman, 1987; Hoy & Tschannen-Moran, 1999.
16. You will see that one other thing scored higher on the list, which you can consult on visible-learning.org/backup-hattie-ranking-256-effects-2017/: namely, the extent to which teachers can assess the school performance of pupils and students. However, this high effect score does not refer to something that can be applied but simply shows that it is something that teachers are generally good at. See www.visiblelearningmetax.com for the current overview.

17. Bandura, 1997.
18. Eells, 2011.
19. Donohoo, 2017.
20. Burgess et al., 2019.
21. See amongst others: Robinson et al., 2009; Kurz & Knight, 2004.
22. Belfi et al., 2015.
23. Forsyth, 2018.
24. Killen et al., 2013.
25. Vanden Abeele et al., 2014.
26. Dokuka et al., 2015.
27. See De Bruyckere, 2021; Hattie et al., 2021.
28. Lewin, 1951.
29. Bonebright, 2010.
30. Tuckman & Jensen, 1977.
31. See amongst others: Cassidy, 2007; Maples, 1988.

2.2

WHICH PARENTING OR TEACHING STYLE SHOULD YOU ADOPT?

What questions does this chapter answer?

1. What are the different parenting styles and teaching styles?
2. What effect will these different styles have on my child, pupil or student?
3. What does all this mean in terms of educational practice?

The way you were brought up by your parents will continue to have an impact on you and be evident to others many years after you have left home. It helps to determine your level of self-esteem,[1] the likelihood that you will suffer depression as an adult,[2] and even the likelihood that you will one day end up in court.[3] But which methods of parenting have what effects? And is it not also true that to some extent children also educate their parents?

The different parenting styles

The most frequently used classification of parenting styles dates back to the research carried out in the 1960s by Diane Baumrind. Initially, she identified and described three different styles, which she linked directly to the behaviour of the

32 children she observed in a nursery class.[4] In addition to watching the children, she also investigated their home situations. It became clear that the children who behaved assertively in the class were raised differently from both the children who had low self-esteem or little self-control and from the children who were withdrawn or unhappy.

Maccoby and Martin[5] saw two different dimensions in Baumrind's work: the dimension of involvement, warmth or responsiveness and the dimension of control, power or demandingness. In this way, they arrived at a total of four parenting styles:

1.   Authoritative (also sometimes known as democratic)

     -> scores high for warmth or involvement and also for control.

2.   Authoritarian

     -> scores low for warmth or involvement and high for control.

3.   Indulgent (also sometimes known as permissive, after Baumrind)

     -> scores high for warmth or involvement but low for control.

4.   Uninvolved (also sometimes known as laissez-faire)

     -> scores low for warmth or involvement and also for control.

These four styles can be presented schematically (Figure 2.2).

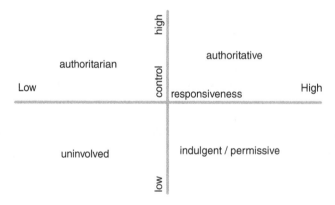

Figure 2.2   The four parenting styles

In her third study Baumrind also came to the conclusion that there was a fourth style, in keeping with what Maccoby and Martin had described.[6] She also discovered some further subcategories – for example, depending on the level of strictness and control used in the authoritarian style – but in most later research carried out by others it was usually the four styles mentioned above that recurred.[7] It therefore seems relevant to look at each of these four styles in more detail.

How universal are the four parenting styles?

Most research into parenting styles was carried out in western countries, which naturally leads to the question of how universal (or not) these styles might be.[8] The scales that were used for the research certainly raise a number of issues[9] and it is certain that more research is needed.[10]

It is probably easiest to understand the differences between the four parenting styles by way of an example that every parent will be familiar with: what do you do when a child does not want to eat what is on their plate?

- With authoritative parents, the child will be told that they must eat but a compromise will usually be sought: 'Eat so much of your greens, so much of your potatoes, etc.'
- With authoritarian parents, there is no discussion and no choice: the child is told to finish the meal and perhaps even threatened with a reprisal (or the return of the same food for the next meal) if the child fails to comply.
- With indulgent parents, it is likely that the child will more quickly get their own way or be offered an alternative that is more acceptable. 'After all, he/she has to eat something..!'
- With neglectful parents, the child will not be forced or even encouraged to finish the meal. This child can simply do what they want.

Authoritarian parents give no explanation for the rules they impose: 'You will do it because we say that you have to!' Authoritative parents react more responsively, explaining their rules and being tolerant of mistakes and errors, where necessary.

On the basis of the above example, you might think that the authoritative or democratic style of parenting is best but the situation is more complex than that. To complicate matters still further, the majority of parents frequently adopt different styles – for example, the father authoritarian and the mother indulgent – in part because the amount of time that the respective parents spend with their child can differ significantly.[11] In addition, the style of parenting often changes as time passes and everyone gets older. For example, often the amount of punishment declines, while the amount of control increases.[12]

Who raises who?

Much of the research into parenting style is correlational. It is ethically difficult to organise experiments that impose a particular style on parents for any length of time. Consequently, it is possible that other factors help to determine the behaviour of both children and

(Continued)

parents. In the meantime, we now also know that our genes can have an influence. Some-where between 23 and 40% of the warmth, level of control and negativity of parents has a genetic basis.[13] Nor should we forget the children's role in all of this. Parents respond to the behaviour of their offspring and, because children are all different, parents will also react differently. So yes, in part children do raise their parents!

What is the effect of the different parenting styles?

As Baumrind already indicated in the conclusions to her first research study, there is a link between parenting style and the behaviour of children and young people. This is a theme that has recurred repeatedly in subsequent research from the 1960s onwards. Bearing in mind that behaviour is never determined by just a single fac-tor, here is a short summary of some of the most important research findings.

Parenting style and alcohol/drug use

Many researchers have established a connection between the neglectful parenting style and the increased likelihood of drug use. In their review of these studies, Becoña and colleagues concluded that no clear link has been demonstrated with other parenting styles.[14] The negative correlation between a neglectful parenting style and the use of alcohol has also been established in, amongst others, a longitu-dinal study involving Spanish teenagers.[15]

Parenting style and delinquency

If both parents adopt a neglectful parenting style, the likelihood of delinquent behaviour – and possible problems with the law – increases in boys. For girls, this seems to be the case with the permissive parenting style. Having at least one authoritative parent in the family results in the least likelihood of delinquency, irre-spective of the child's gender. Delinquent behaviour becomes increasingly likely for each child if both the parents are neglectful in their parenting approach.[16]

Parenting style and school performance

The extent to which parents respond with warmth to their children and give them sufficient autonomy – in other words, the more they adopt an authoritative par-enting style – corresponds with a superior performance of those children at school.

However, the majority of studies in this area have concluded that the correlation is statistically small. Authoritarian, neglectful and permissive parenting styles are associated with poorer school performance, although again the correlation is small.[17]

Parenting style and the personality of children and young people

The children of authoritarian parents often grow up to be more obedient and more highly motivated but score less well for matters such as happiness, social competencies and self-esteem. The children of permissive parents also seem in general to be less happy and score even worse for self-regulation. These children will also be more likely to have problems with authority. The least fortunate children are those who are raised by neglectful parents. There is a much increased likelihood that they will lack self-control and have low self-esteem. In fact, they score poorer for almost every aspect. The children of authoritative parents are usually happier and more successful.[18]

Parenting style and bullying

The likelihood of being either the victim or the perpetrator of bullying can both be linked to parenting style.[19] A permissive style seems to make both possibilities more likely,[20] although the likelihood of becoming a victim is greater.[21]

Parenting style and psychological problems

There is also a small correlation between the manner in which you are raised by your parents and the likelihood of psychological problems in later life.[22] This is not illogical, since the neglectful, permissive and authoritarian parenting styles can all be linked to less responsive parenting and can therefore have an effect on the safe attachment or otherwise of a child. A recent meta-analysis has shown that there is a clear link between parenting style and the likelihood of anxiety disorders, somatic complaints and social isolation. An analysis of the results of some 1,015 studies revealed that warmer parenting, with more control and more autonomy – in other words, an authoritative style – is linked with a lower incidence of such problems. These problems are more likely to be experienced by the children of neglectful or authoritarian parents. Once again, the correlations are statistically small.[23]

Conclusion?

It would seem that authoritative parents score best and that, above all, neglectful parenting should be avoided. However, it needs to be repeated: most of the relevant correlations are statistically small. In other words, there are links but casual relationships are difficult to demonstrate and some negative consequences of parenting are also in part genetic.

Another broad conclusion is the positive effect of giving children the necessary degree of autonomy at the appropriate time – check also the section on self-determination theory in Chapter 4.2 – although to the outside world this can sometimes seem like a neglectful or laissez-faire approach. The essential difference resides in the fact that the granting of autonomy is a conscious decision taken at the right time for the child, and not the result of indifference. For example, giving your toddler the choice between carrots and broccoli (autonomy) is something completely different from not being interested in the child's diet and letting them eat sweets and crisps every day (laissez-faire).

At the same time, some situations need a firm and disciplined approach, which may seem authoritarian. If you are crossing a busy road with your toddler, this is not the moment for a democratic discussion about whether to cross when the light is green or red! Once again, this is the conscious choice of the parent, who seeks to make the difference by adopting a particular style of parenting at the right moment. Similarly, a number of long-term choices can also seem to be authoritarian ('I don't want you to give up on music school. You will thank me later on!') but sometimes this can be necessary, because children and young people are less capable of long-term thought.

Modern parents: tiger mothers, helicopter parents and curling parents

In recent years, a number of new kinds of parent have emerged. In essence, they are variants of the existing parenting styles but with a greater emphasis on control, which can take several different forms; sometimes these forms are described as types of 'overparenting'.

Tiger mothers

In 2011, Amy Chua published *Battle Hymn of the Tiger Mother*,[24] a book in which she attempted to explain why Asiatic children perform better than their American contemporaries. In particular, she described a number of behavioural rules. The list of things that she would never allow her daughters to do includes:

- Stay overnight at a friend's house;
- Play with friends;
- Take part in a play;
- Complain because they can never take part in a play;

- Watch TV or play computer games;
- Choose their own out-of-school activities;
- Get a lower score than an A;
- Not be the best student in every subject, apart from gym and drama;
- Play any other instrument than piano or violin;
- Not play the piano or violin.

Described in this way, Asiatic tiger mothers would seem to adopt an extreme form of the authoritarian parenting style. However, research involving Chinese-American children has revealed that this kind of parenting actually leads on average to poorer results at school, an increased likelihood of psychological problems, and a greater chance of becoming alienated from the rest of the family. Fortunately, this does not seem to be the typical Chinese way to raise children.[25]

Helicopter parents

Helicopter parents have the best interests of their child at heart but think that the best way to achieve this is to hover over them, watching and controlling everything they do. As with tiger mothers, this form of 'overparenting' can actually often lead to poorer performance; for example, if their interference in the children's homework deprives them of important learning opportunities.[26] At the same time, helicopter parenting also produces results similar to those of authoritarian parenting; namely, a larger correlation with depression and a lower level of social competencies.[27]

Curling parents

Curling parents are exponents of another form of over-protective parenting. This form of parenting gets its name from the winter sport, in which the players attempt to protect the stone and move it into the right position by surrounding it and brushing furiously to remove any obstacles in its way. This kind of parenting is a strange combination of control and permissiveness. On the one hand, curling parents seek to control the environment around their children as much as possible. On the other hand, they often allow their children the freedom to do more or less what they like and have difficulty in setting boundaries.[28] Although this concept of parenting has been seen in Scandinavian countries for quite some time, very little research has been carried out into its effects.

Parenting styles and teaching styles

It is not just parents who raise children. Teachers also play an important role in the process. Moreover, it seems that there is a significant overlap between how you can best raise your child as a parent and the manner in which you should deal with your pupils as a teacher.

Douglas Bernstein[29] has summarised what the four parenting styles mean when translated into teaching practice:

- Neglectful teaching does no more than the basic minimum for the pupils. These teachers give the same lessons year after year, discourage their pupils from asking questions and seek to have as little real contact with them as possible, seeing them more as a threat than anything else. They make very little effort to keep order in the classroom and ignore negative behaviour as far as they possibly can.
- Authoritarian teachers also display very little commitment towards their pupils but in contrast to their neglectful colleagues place a heavy emphasis on order and discipline. The rules are the rules and there is little or no room for discussion and possible exemptions. These teachers expect very good performance from their pupils as the norm and reward it with high marks. Weaknesses are ignored, so that poorer performance is seldom improved.
- Permissive teachers are almost overly concerned about the nature of the lessons they give. They want to remove all possible obstacles and stress that can hinder the personal growth of their pupils. Consequently, they often focus on the weaker pupils, as a result of which the others are insufficiently challenged, because the bar is set so low that everyone can achieve a pass grade. These teachers will do everything they can to vary and brighten up their lessons, making them as pleasant and as 'entertaining' as possible.
- Authoritative teachers combine the necessary commitment towards their pupils with a fair form of discipline. They care about both the lessons they give and their pupils' development but reward results and not just effort. They provide good feedback and show understanding when the circumstances (often unforeseen) require it. They think carefully about what they teach (the curriculum) and the rules to apply in the classroom. They communicate these matters in advance and explain the 'why' behind their behaviour, which is consistent at all times.

Adopting an authoritative approach as a teacher is associated with feeling good at school and with good study performance. However, this performance is more likely to be achieved if the teacher has the necessary high expectations of their pupils.[30]

What does all this mean in terms of practice?

1. **Provide the necessary degree of autonomy and involvement.**

   You can do this, for example, by explaining why you are stricter in certain situations and by acting consistently, so that children know what to expect from your behaviour. Set boundaries, where necessary but allow children to experiment freely within those boundaries. You can compare it with exploring freely within a safe and clearly defined playground. Show sufficient attention and involvement, so that the children know that you are still there and still interested in what they do.

2. **Seek to adopt positive elements from different parenting and teaching styles.**

There is no such thing as a single parenting style that is 'perfect' in all respects. Depending on the circumstances, different elements from different styles will produce the best results. Many of these elements can be seen in the authoritative style but in some situations a more authoritarian approach is called for. Fortunately, the raising of children is a matter where many different roads lead to Rome. Parents (and teachers) are human, and as such we make mistakes. But if you take love as your starting point and provide safe attachment for the children under your care, you will not go far wrong.

Teacher takeaways

How do you keep control of a group of children or young people?

No matter how much we like children and young people, they can sometimes make life difficult for us and each other, especially if they are in a group. So, what can we do in these circumstances to make sure that the situation does not get out of hand?

The English Education Endowment Foundation published an extensive report about the different elements that can work successfully in the field of behaviour management at school. By extension, a number of these concrete tips can also be useful in situations outside of a school context.[31] The following matters are particularly relevant:

* Prevention is better than cure.
* Establishing good relationships is crucial.
* Being consistent (individually and as a team) is also crucial (see the sections on collective teacher efficacy (p. 134) and Bronfenbrenner (p. 129) in Chapter 2.1).
* At the same time, adopting specific measures for specific children is equally important.

(Continued)

What is the basis for behaviour in school?

In their model, Ellis and Tod[32] demonstrated that the behaviour of a child at school is caused by a combination of three direct elements:

- How does the child view themselves?
- What is the nature of the child's relations with others?
- How does the ability of the child relate to the curriculum or what needs to be learnt?

These different elements interact on each other, as the following examples make clear:

- If a pupil has a problem with the material to be learnt because they find it too difficult, this can have a negative impact on the child's self-image and motivation, as a result of which the child's relations with others can also deteriorate.
- If the child is being bullied by other pupils, the child will be less inclined to pay attention in class.
- Children can make themselves popular by showing off or by behaving with bravado towards the teacher.

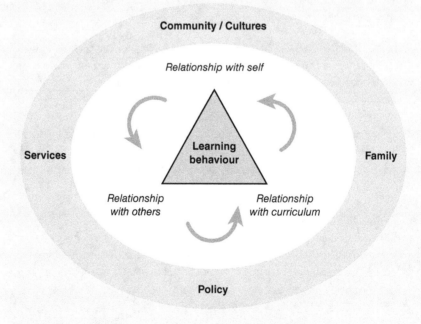

Figure 2.3 The behaviour model by Ellis and Tod (2018)

In keeping with what Bronfenbrenner discussed in his theory and as illustrated in Figure 2.3, the three key determining factors for behaviour can be influenced significantly not only by the family situation but also by the school culture, school policy, the level of support offered, etc.

Bearing in mind these matters, what concrete recommendations is it possible to make?

1. **Know and understand the children and young people in your care and be aware of the factors that can influence them.**

   After reading this book, you will understand that the same behaviour in children and young people can be the result of different causes, most often even a combination of different causes. Sometimes you can do something to influence these causes; sometimes you cannot. To react effectively to the behaviour of a child (or group of children), you must have insight into the possible reasons for that behaviour. To identify these causes and to search together for possible solutions, it is essential to have a supportive relationship with the child or young person. At school, every pupil must have that kind of relationship with at least one member of the school team.

2. **Managing negative behaviour must go hand in hand with teaching good behaviour.**

   What constitutes good behaviour can be set by example but it also needs to be taught explicitly. The following elements can have a positive effect:[33]

   a. Giving recognition to desirable and/or appropriate behaviour.
   b. Setting and teaching class and/or group rules.
   c. Giving feedback about inappropriate behaviour.
   d. Encouraging good behaviour through verbal compliments.
   e. Reinforcing good behaviour through rewards.

   It is also important to stimulate children and young people to think about and reflect on their own behaviour.

3. **Effective class management can make the difference.**

   How the teacher (or, by extension, a group leader) manages a lesson or session can have a significant impact on how children or young people behave. As the adult in the room, it is important that you do a regular mental check to assess how things are progressing, so that you can take corrective action, where necessary. The use of reward systems, if fair and equitable, can help you in this respect; for example, something similar to the token economy system in behavioural therapy.

   (Continued)

4. **Be consistent in your own behaviour and in your treatment of theirs.**

    Dealing with the behaviour of children and young people in a consistent and logical manner can help to improve that behaviour. Consistency involves, amongst other things, clear agreements and rules, clear routines and a clear understanding of the consequences for good or bad behaviour. This helps the child or young person to know exactly where they stand. It is additionally useful if these rules, agreements, routines and rewards are consistent throughout the school.

5. **Be aware of individual needs.**

    This may seem to run contrary to the previous point about the need for consistency but a consistent general approach will not be sufficient by itself to achieve the desired behavioural results, simply because the needs of children and young people can sometimes be very different. Particularly with children and young people whose behaviour is challenging, it is essential to consider their specific requirements, which may involve the need for outside help.

Endnotes

1. Orth, 2018.
2. Pinquart, 2017.
3. Hoeve et al., 2011.
4. Baumrind, 1967.
5. Maccoby & Martin, 1983.
6. Baumrind, 1971.
7. Power, 2013.
8. Sorkhabi & Mandara, 2013.
9. Stewart & Bond, 2002.
10. Huang & Gove, 2015.
11. Hoeve et al., 2011.
12. Loeber et al., 2000.
13. Klahr & Burt, 2014.
14. Becoña et al., 2012.
15. Martínez-Loredo et al., 2016.
16. Hoeve et al., 2011.
17. Pinquart, 2016.
18. Power, 2013.
19. Charalampous et al., 2018.
20. Gómez-Ortiz et al., 2014.
21. Baldry & Farrington, 2007.
22. Lopes et al., 2015.

23. Pinquart, 2017.
24. Chua, 2011.
25. Kim, S. et al., 2013.
26. Locke et al., 2016.
27. Moilanen & Manuel, 2019.
28. Widding & Berge, 2014.
29. Bernstein, 2013.
30. Wentzel, 2002.
31. Rhodes et al., 2019.
32. Ellis & Tod, 2018.
33. Flower et al., 2014.

2.3

FRIENDS AND OTHER RELATIONSHIPS

— What questions does this chapter answer? —

1. How do friendships develop?
2. What factors have an influence on the development of friendships?
3. What does all this mean in terms of practice?

In addition to their parents and their teachers, children and young people come into contact with many other people, a significant number of whom are age contemporaries, generally designated by the term 'peers'. Children and young people meet each other at school, in their local neighbourhood, in youth and sports clubs, etc. Their interaction with these peers can differ considerably in terms of quality and depth. Some will become friends and some may even fall in love, while others might bully them or lead them astray, or even into criminality.

In this chapter we will look in more detail at these different types of others, starting with the development of friendships, before moving on to how you can best deal with groups of people.

The development of friendships

During the early years of life

As we described in Chapter 2.2 and in Chapter 1.3 on attachment, the people with whom the newborn baby has most contact during its first months of life are its parents or its caregivers. However, babies can also soon come into contact with other children, in the form of older brothers and/or sisters or other babies and infants in the nursery or crèche. Even at best, the baby will only have a limited form of interaction with these others, probably no more than a brief smile and a few gurgling noises.[1] At this age, and in addition to their parents, babies have a preference for people who they see frequently and can clearly recognise, such as their other caregivers and siblings. Gradually, as they gain movement, their level of social intercourse increases. From the age of nine months onwards, these young children can exchange toys, play games of 'peek-a-boo' and crawl after each other. Some of these things, like crawling, come naturally; others, like the sharing of toys, need to be learnt, which is not always easy.[2]

Although all these things might seem very simple, they can be very important for the child's later development, because they create a first basis (whose significance should not be underestimated) for subsequent social relationships. In particular, children learn how to generate reactions in others and also how they should themselves react in a growing number of situations.[3] This alternation of roles during play is something that you can also see in the development of language and of executive functions.

By the time they are 14 months old, children start to copy the behaviour of people they know well.[4] This happens after the child has learnt how to imitate, because its own behaviour was imitated by others. As time passes, the child will start to observe other babies and will acquire and use the skills they possess, again through imitation.[5]

Yet while there is considerable interaction between the child and the ever-expanding environment, it is still too early to speak of friendships and the child's parents and wider family will continue to play the most important role in their young life.

Infancy

The first forms of friendship develop at around the age of three years. Whereas children previously saw their age contemporaries as playmates with whom they could do things, they now come to see their fellow toddlers as individuals who can be different from each other and, for that reason, acquire greater worth. As they continue to get older, their image of friendship will evolve in parallel, until it reaches the stage when it is increasingly regarded as something more permanent.[6] At the same time, children will start to attach more abstract concepts to their nascent idea of friendship, such as trust and loyalty to each other. As already mentioned elsewhere, the act of playing will further help to change the nature of this relationship[7] and the play and the friendship will mutually influence each other. Children who engage in a greater number of social interactions will also see the nature of their play evolve more quickly,[8] while those who only develop increased social interactions at a later stage will continue to be followers and onlookers for longer.[9] In some cases, they may even be excluded, because they possess fewer social skills or because they have difficulty in assessing what is allowed (or not) during the play process.[10]

This evolution is difficult to separate from some of the concepts we discussed in Chapter 1.4 on moral development and, in particular, theory of mind, which we defined as the possibility of reading the thoughts of others. To be able to do this, you need to correctly sense and interpret emotions, intentions and ideas in both yourself and others. This in turn requires the possession of the necessary cognitive capabilities but also (and equally crucially) the necessary social interactions with others. This explains why social interaction and playing are so important during this phase of a child's life.[11] It further explains why theory of mind determines how popular a child is with their peers.[12]

Friendships in primary school

As children reach primary school age, friendship assumes an increasingly important and more central position in their thinking and doing. Damon[13] has identified the following stages or evolutions:

Stage 1, between the ages of four and seven years: friendship based on the behaviour of others.

- In this case, a friend is another child that likes me. They share their toys with me and I do the same. In other words, friendships develop between children who spend a lot of time with each other and do a lot of activities together.
- At this stage, the friendship has little connection with the personal characteristics of the children involved. Above all, it is what the children do – their behaviour – that is the key determining factor.

Stage 2, between the ages of eight and ten years: friendship based on trust.

- For this second stage in the development of friendship trust becomes increasingly central. If the trust between friends at this age is broken – for example, by sharing a secret with others[14] – this can have serious consequences for the future of that friendship. The damage can only be repaired, if at all, by sincere apologies.
- In contrast to the previous stage, personal characteristics start to play a more important role and now add a kind of 'bonus' to the behaviour that other children display.

Stage 3, from the age of 11 years and throughout adolescence: friendship based on psychological compatibility.

- As the end of primary school approaches, a new vision of friendship develops, which also helps to shape further relationships throughout adolescence.
- During this stage, (psychological) closeness and mutual loyalty are central. A friend is someone with whom you can share all your ups and downs

and who accepts you as you are. This kind of psychological compatibility requires complete openness on both sides.

- In this way, friendships become more intense and more exclusive. At the same time, young people during this stage do fewer and fewer things together, in part because of their increasingly busy personal agendas but this is now less important in comparison with the more psychological benefits they are now seeking.
- At this point, teenagers also have a clear picture of the kind of behaviour that they find acceptable and value in others, and also what is unacceptable.

In summary: as a child progresses from infancy to adolescence, the key criterion for forming friendships shifts from the behaviour of others to the personal characteristics and qualities of others. But what does this involve exactly? And why is one child more popular than another?

Where you sit in class helps to determine your popularity

Teachers can unintentionally have an impact on the popularity of certain pupils with their classmates, according to the Dutch researchers Yvonne van den Berg and Antonius Cillessen.[15] Their study revealed that 11-year-old children who were positioned at the edges of the classroom by their teacher during their first term were, in general, regarded as being less fun than the children who were positioned closer to the middle of the room. There is also a tendency to have more liking for fellow pupils who sit near to you in comparison with those who sit further away. Of course, this second conclusion also helps to partially explain the first one: children in the middle of the class have more other pupils sitting near to them. It is worth noting that this effect was still in evidence after a period of six months, even if the classroom positions had been changed in the interim.

This kind of research is often carried out by making use of sociograms, which are visual representations of the interpersonal relations within a group; for example, a class.[16]

Some of the elements in Damon's stages can help to provide an explanation. Popular children tend to share a number of common characteristics. Qualities such as reciprocity and social understanding are particularly important. In general, more popular children are also helpful, work together with others more easily, and dare to take leadership in a positive manner, although this is slightly more the case for girls than for boys.[17] These more popular children are also often funny and have a good sense of humour.[18] This is another area where reciprocity plays a role, because popular children also appreciate the jokes of others. Whereas less popular children frequently find it harder to read and understand the emotions of people in their environment (in keeping with theory of mind), their more popular peers will experience no such difficulty, which allows them to better adjust their behaviour to match the circumstances.[19]

In case you were thinking that this explanation runs contrary to almost every youth series or film you have ever seen on television or in the cinema, honesty compels us to admit that, yes, it is indeed also possible for children and young people to become popular through negative behaviour. Children often look up to their peers who behave in a bold, reckless or even aggressive manner. They dare to do things that the admiring child would never dream of doing.[20] In fact, amongst teenagers it is those who walk the fine line between empathy and aggression who are the most popular of all with their peers.[21] Fortunately, it is equally true that there is a strong link between social skills and popularity, with the added plus point that these skills are only partially innate, so that they can also in part be learnt.[22]

Various researchers, including Wentzel and Asher, have pointed out that a straightforward division between 'popular' and 'not popular' takes too simple an approach to a more complex situation. For example, in addition to popular children who are generally well liked by more or less everyone, there are also controversial children who are regarded as popular by some but by no means everyone. With regard to the children who are unpopular, a distinction needs to be made between those who are liked by no one in the group, so that they are rejected and excluded, and those who are simply ignored and therefore tolerated indifferently by the group, which regards them (if it regards them at all) as being neither good nor bad.[23]

Helping children with social skills processing theory

Dodge and colleagues distinguished five different steps in the way that children deal with peers of their own age:[24]

1.   The reception and decoding of incoming information.

      What is the child with whom you are talking or playing actually doing?

2.   Interpreting what the other child is doing.

      What does the child think are the intentions of the child with whom they are playing?

3.   Searching for responses.

      What are the possible responses to what the other child is doing?

4.   Evaluating and selecting a response.

      Which is the best of those different possible reactions?

5.   Implementing the reaction.

The child reacts.

These five steps can be helpful to analyse what can go wrong when children are playing or otherwise interacting. Perhaps the child fails to notice some of the incoming information (step 1), or fails to interpret the intentions behind this information correctly (step 2), or has a repertoire of reactions that is too limited to respond effectively (step 3), which then makes the following two steps no longer possible.[25]

So, what are the causes of a child not being accepted or being ignored in a (class) group? In this respect, we saw previously that the level of social skills already plays a role with toddlers and that it continues to have an impact for a long time during the primary school years. This leads to a vicious circle, because excluding a child from play for a lack of social skills deprives them of the chance to practise precisely those key skills. As a result, these children often go to play in smaller groups or with less popular peers.[26] By the time a child reaches Damon's third stage, the role of behaviour and play is diminishing, so that the cause of being unpopular now shifts above all to being too aggressive or (the worst of all crimes) dishonest.

Why is friendship so important?

It sounds like stating the obvious to say that friendships play an important role in the development of children, and even more so of young people. But what does this mean, exactly? We have already seen how social skills and interactions can be practised with friends. Likewise, that one very special best friend with whom you can share everything is also a training ground for the development of mental intimacy. But there is more to it than that. Throughout the years of primary and secondary education, the key source of emotional support for a child shifts from parents in the case of young children to friends in the case of young adolescents.[27] You need at least one good friend to avoid feeling lonely and to enjoy the emotional support that everyone needs. In the absence of this support, a child or young person's feelings of competence and self-esteem are put under pressure, which might be a precursor to poor mental health in later life.[28] Research has demonstrated that friendship can help to ward off depression, particularly in girls,[29] as well as other psychological conditions during adulthood.[30]

Studies have also shown that adolescents with friends on average enjoy a higher sense of well-being than those without friends.[31] Such friendships can also play a role in helping to compensate for the harmful effects of a young person's unfavourable domestic situation.[32]

Can you be friends with someone of the opposite gender?

Most adults would probably (and spontaneously) answer positively to this question. In particular, men in later life admit that there is a certain attraction.[33] So yes, it is possible. However, during the developmental years of children and young people friendships often tend to be segregated. Perhaps you have seen it for yourself when observing children at school or in the playground: while children of three years or younger pay little or no attention to the gender of the child they are playing with, from that age onwards there is a growing tendency for boys to play with boys and girls with girls. Amongst infants (five years of age and older), the likelihood that a child plays with another child of the same gender is nine times greater than the likelihood that they will play with a child of a different gender.[34] In fact, children of the opposite gender are often deliberately avoided at school,[35] with segregation reaching its peak between the ages of eight and ten years.[36] Children who play with the 'other group' can sometimes be bullied, with this being more common among boys than girls.[37] If there is contact between children of different genders, this can often be interpreted by the environment as being romantic. And as children get older, so that inter-gender contact and friendships become more frequent and more 'normal', for example in friendship clubs,[38] romantic interests can indeed start to play a role.[39] It is these relationships that mark the end of adolescence.

Before groups and clubs of different genders are formed, the nature and the quality of the friendships of boys and girls can differ markedly. Boys tend to be closer and spend more time together, as well as being more exclusive, in the sense of being more reluctant to admit newcomers to their circle. There is also a greater degree of hierarchy among boys, often with a more obvious leader.[40] Groups of friends amongst boys are generally bigger than those amongst girls.[41]

And the others?

Of course, it is not possible to be friends with everyone. Even so, these others, the children and young people with whom you are not friends, still have an influence on you. Between the ages of 10 and 14 years, children and young teenagers reach a peak of adjusting their behaviour in an effort to belong to a group.[42] This is not necessarily bad, because in some cases this form of peer pressure can help to encourage good habits,[43] although it can also lead to more dubious or even dangerous behaviour.[44] In particular, it is clear that adolescents are sensitive to the influence of their peers in matters like music, TV series, films, clothes, etc. As they get older, this desire to conform with others in order to belong gradually diminishes.

During early adolescence it is not uncommon for smaller groups or cliques to develop within the larger groups of peers. These cliques tend to be formed around certain themes, sports or shared hobbies and it is primarily in this setting that new friendships tend to be formed.

Not being accepted by a group can come as a serious blow to the child or young person concerned. The reason for the rejection might be inappropriate behaviour, linked to imperfectly developed social skills (see above), but that is not always the case. Non-acceptance of this kind can lead to a fall-off in school performance[45] or degenerate into bullying. However, it is worth noting that even children who have no problems with their social skills, as well as those who are more reserved, can be bullied.[46]

Brothers and sisters?

A special group of other children and young people who can play an important role in your life and development but who nevertheless have a position very different from that of friends, are brothers and sisters (if, of course, you have any). The closer that siblings are in terms of age and interests, the greater this influence becomes.[47] An older brother or sister can stimulate the cognitive development of a child, although in general it will be the child's parents who continue to do this most.[48] Jealousy can occur between brothers and sisters - for example, if a new baby arrives in the family - but as a rule the relationship is one of interest and affection.[49] Does this mean that an only child is missing out on important learning experiences that only siblings can provide? Fortunately not. In terms of self-image, feelings of loneliness and quality of friendships there is no difference between the two groups. It seems that only children simply find other ways to learn the same skills.[50]

What does all this mean in terms of practice?

1. **Allow your child to play and experiment with other children as early as possible.**

    In this way, the child starts to learn social skills from an early age, skills that form an important basis for friendships later on.

2. **Be alert for bullying behaviour.**

    We have collected together a number of tips on this subject in a separate teacher takeaway (see below).

3. **Avoid stereotyping and preconceptions.**

    Resist the temptation to make easy (and often false) generalisations, for example, about only children.

─ Teacher takeaways ─

Bullying

That bullying is a serious and as yet unresolved problem, generating numerous negative psychological effects in both the short and the long term, is something that hardly needs to be emphasised. Children and young people of all ages and in all types of education are confronted with this highly unpleasant phenomenon. However, there is good news: with the right approach, bullying can be reduced! This was the conclusion of a large-scale study carried out in the Netherlands in 2018,[51] which examined in detail 10 promising anti-bullying programmes used widely in primary education.

What is bullying and what is the difference with teasing?

Bullying is the display of systematic physical and/or verbal aggression towards the victim, with the aim of harming or damaging that person in some way. This, of course, is just one of the many definitions of bullying, although many of the same elements frequently recur:[52]

1. Bullying involves some kind of physical, verbal or psychological attack or intimidation.
2. The perpetrator is - or is regarded as being - more powerful than the victim.
3. The perpetrator intends to make the victim frightened or to harm them in some way.
4. Bullying is not provoked by the victim.
5. Bullying is regularly repeated.
6. Bullying generally achieves its desired effect.

Bullying is therefore not the same as teasing, which does not seek to cause harm. Sometimes it is possible for the more subtle forms of bullying to seem like teasing to outsiders ('Come on, I was only joking!') but the victim knows all too well that this behaviour will be repeated in the future, even though they have repeatedly indicated that they do not like it and want it to stop. This is clearly still bullying.

Bullying can be *direct* or *indirect*. Direct bullying tends to involve the physical or verbal attacking of the victim or the damage/removal of their property. But gossiping about, excluding or bad-mouthing the victim is also bullying, albeit in a more indirect form. Because the victim is not present at the time, they only learn about this indirect bullying later on. This does not make it any less painful or harmful.

Why do people bully others? Research has demonstrated that one of the main reasons is that the perpetrator wants to appear 'cool' and be popular, so that they can increase their own position, power and influence within a group. It is also often a way to conceal their own weaknesses.[53]

Is bullying part of the natural development of a child?

Bullying occurs most commonly between the ages of 10 and 16 years. It is sometimes suggested that this is a natural part of every child's development, a kind of conflict phase through which every young person has to pass. This is not true. If bullying was a natural phase in a person's development from childhood to adulthood, then:

1. Adults would no longer bully (sadly, this is not the case: think of the many instances of bullying at work).
2. All children would have to go through this phase but that is not what happens.

Moreover, the extent to which bullying occurs in schools can differ significantly from place to place. An international study[54] concluded that there is substantially more bullying in some countries than in others (from 41% in Lithuania to 6% in Sweden). This again suggests that bullying is not wholly 'natural' and that nurture also plays an important role. Other key factors include school culture and the wider environment (parenting, friends, etc.). With this in mind, some research into anti-bullying programmes[55] suggests that the problem goes much further than schools alone (think of the influence of family and peers outside of the school context), so that interventions confined to within the school walls probably do not go far enough.

Is bullying ingrained in our genes?

Yes, to some degree. In fact, to quite a large degree, according to one study[56] of more than 8,000 children, which concluded that 70% of the explanation for why you might become a bully is to be found in your genes. This is primarily related to your innate personality: the way you deal with power, how impressionable you are, your attitude and response towards aggression, etc. Think back to the Big Five dimensions of personality we referred to earlier in the book. Is your behaviour antisocial/aggressive or are you by nature more tolerant?

Is working to improve the assertiveness and resilience of the victim the answer?

Working to improve the assertiveness and resilience of the victim as part of the solution can help to reduce the effect of some of the symptoms of bullying but does nothing to tackle the fundamental cause of the problem, which is a conflict in the social interaction between the bully, the victim and the bystanders. Moreover, simply focusing on the victim's resilience sends out the wrong signal, to the effect that it is the individual responsibility of the victim to resolve the situation. Once the bullying has ended, it can certainly benefit the victim to follow therapy as a means to strengthening their self-confidence. Once again, this is not the solution to bullying but it can help to heal some of the scars.

(Continued)

What can you do if you know that someone is being bullied?

What can you do as a parent/teacher?[57]

Step 1: Listen to the child and take them seriously

First and foremost, it is important to listen to the child carefully before taking any action. The child needs to feel safe to tell their story. Show interest and concern for what the child has to say, without judging or criticising the child or others.

Be aware that you are only hearing one version of the story. There may be things that are not being said or elements that are twisted for effect. However, that is not important at this stage: what counts is the child's experience of the situation. Even so, do not accept the truth of everything the child says and bear this in mind during the following stages.

Step 2: Search together with the child for possible solutions

As so often in parenting and education, there is no 'one size fits all' solution. Every child is different and every bullying situation is different. For this reason, the input of the child is so important. Involve the child in the solution process and search together for the right answer. Give the following clear message: 'If we do nothing, it will happen again.'

Possible guidelines for yourself: What does the child want me to do? What kind of solution is the child comfortable with? What is important for the child to tell the class, school, sports club, etc.?

Step 3: Taking action

Following on from the previous step, it is important to keep the promises you have made to the child and take the action that you have agreed together. The child may or may not be involved in this actioning process, as seems most appropriate.

Based on our primeval survival instincts, we generally react in one of two ways to danger situations: *fight* or *flight*. Freezing is also a reaction but this does nothing to change the situation and the problem (in this case, bullying) remains. So which is better? Fight or flight?

- *Fight*: With the agreement of the child (step 2), notify the problem to the responsible person in the organisation where the bullying is taking place. This will often be the school (in which case you will need to speak to the teacher, headteacher, care coordinator, etc.) but it may also be a sports club (trainer) or a youth club (leader). Discuss the situation and try to find a solution together, bearing the following matters in mind:

- ○ The first golden rule, according to bullying expert Gie Deboutte, is to ask the school or club to do nothing in the first instance. Taking immediate action raises the danger that the victim will be seen as a tell-tale and will be treated accordingly by the group.
- ○ Share the information you possess (cf. step 2).
- ○ Ask for the situation to be more closely monitored, with action to be taken when the situation threatens to get out of hand, so that the bullying can be brought to an end.
- ○ Ask to be kept informed of developments and agree how this will be done.

- *Flight*: If the bullying continues and nothing (or not enough) is done to prevent it by those responsible for the relevant environment, so that the risk of harmful consequences for the victim persists, 'flight' is often the only remaining solution. Stop your child from attending the (sport, youth, etc.) club in question or arrange for them to change schools. Be aware that the scars caused by the bullying will not disappear immediately and that your child's vulnerability will continue for some time, even in a new school or environment.

What should you not do?

1. **Do not minimise the situation.** (*'It is not as bad as you think', or 'It could be much worse', or 'You are making it out to be worse than it is'.*)

   Comments of this kind are often well-intended, with the aim of comforting the child or supposedly helping them to see the situation 'more realistically'. Following on from the bullying itself, this often comes as a second blow for the child: 'I am not being taken seriously', 'I am making things up', 'I am exaggerating', 'I am a drama queen...'. Each child experiences difficult situations differently and, consequently, their impact will also differ. In the first instance, it is not down to you as 'the adult' in the conversation to decide how serious the situation really is.

   What can you do? Listen without judging, take the child seriously, show understanding, say that it is okay to feel bad in this kind of situation and that it is normal for it to hurt.

2. **Do not fail to listen careful and do not make hurtful comments.** (*'Don't worry, it will pass', 'Don't think about it too much', 'You are just seeking attention'.*)

   Once again, the child will feel that it is being ignored and fobbed off with meaningless words. If you do this, the likelihood that the child will feel inclined to discuss the situation with you again in the future is pretty small. Why should they? After all, you haven't really been listening.

   (Continued)

What can you do? If children are not feeling good about things, it is important to listen attentively to their story. This not only applies for bullying but for all psychological difficulties that a child might experience.

3. **Do not offer well-intentioned but compelling advice.** *('Don't let yourself be pushed around', 'You have to learn to stand up for yourself more', 'You just have to ignore it!')*

In this way, the victim will feel that everything is their fault and that they are not strong enough to react as they should. This increases the victim's feelings of guilt and has a negative impact on their self-image.

What can you do? This kind of advice about being more assertive is often made from the best of motives, in the hope of leading to a quick solution to the situation but it should only be made once the victim has given signs that this kind of approach might help. Once again, first and foremost you should just listen to what the child has to say.

4. **Do not attempt to immediately take the matter in hand and do not approach the bully.**

As a parent, it is only normal to be furious when you learn that your child is being bullied. Your first reaction is to do something about it, which often means confronting the bully the very next day. Once again, this is well intentioned but it often serves simply to make things worse. Sometimes, you will not be aware of the whole truth, so that you may not actually tackle the 'main' bully. More importantly, as a parent you have insufficient power and influence over a group for which you have no formal responsibility. For this reason, it is always better to speak to the person who is responsible for the environment in question (school, youth movement, art academy, sports club, etc.). They are the only people who can effectively put a stop to the bullying, because they have insight into and influence over what happens in the group. If, as a parent, you confront the bully, your child will be even more afraid (once you have left the scene) to stand up to their tormentor, who is probably now angrier than ever before! When this happens, your child will think twice before talking to you again about their problems. So don't do it!

What can you do? Bullying expert Gie Deboutte advises you to think first about the following matters before acting:

• To what extent are you respecting what your child actually wants? A child will take account of three key factors:

1. Will I be safer after my parent's intervention?
2. Will I belong to the group again?
3. Will I be able to make new friends?

- Do you know the full truth? Is the situation actually as it has been explained to you?
- Do you have influence over the group? No? In that case, speak to someone who has the necessary authority.

What can you do if you know that someone is bullying or helping to bully?

There are two golden rules. (1) Once again, listen carefully to what they have to say. (2) But also set a boundary: 'I have listened carefully to your story and I am not going to judge you but what is happening is not okay and the bullying has to stop.'

What can you do as a school?

1. **Monitor the bullying.**

   The first important action to be taken as part of any anti-bullying policy is to establish the facts and their seriousness.[58] Who exactly is involved? How much bullying is there? How much is still under the radar? A large-scale study of various anti-bullying programmes in the Netherlands[59] concluded that there is actually much more bullying taking place than children are prepared to admit. A monitoring system that maps out and follows up incidents of bullying is a necessary first step, not only to gain insight into the overall situation but also to assess if your anti-bullying policy is working. This allows you to adjust your approach, so that your policy can offer a workable and sustainable solution for your school, your pupils and your teaching staff.

2. **Anti-bullying programmes.**

   Many experiments have been carried out in the educational world to find an effective approach to combat bullying. The good news is that some of these approaches work! The 'bad' news is that there is once again no 'one size fits all' solution. However, the following list details a number of the most common 'success' ingredients:

   - Adopt a systematic approach (operating at different levels for the bully, the victim, peers, the school team, parents, the school culture, the environment).
   - Attitude change must also apply to teachers and the school team; if they refuse to change their way of thinking, why should the pupils change theirs?
   - Provide clear leadership within the school (to anchor the change and make it last).
   - Involve parents.

(Continued)

- Introduce better monitoring and supervision.
- Make use of intensive programmes.
- Draw up and implement an effective and uncompromising disciplinary code for bullying, which makes it hard for the practice to continue.
- Work at both the school and class level.
- Focus on the crucial role of the teacher (which does not mean that the teacher needs to solve everything alone!).

In the Benelux region, programmes like KiVa and PRIMA have already proven their worth. Taakspel for young children and Kanjertraining for classes with multiple conflicts have also been shown to have a positive effect. Equivalents are available in most western countries. Much depends on the extent to which the programmes can be translated and embedded for the long term into the specific culture of your school. Research[60] has confirmed the importance of adjusting anti-bullying policies to reflect the context of the school, with monitoring systems that can regularly evaluate and update the policy, where necessary. Once again, there is no such thing as a 'one size fits all' approach.

What about cyberbullying?

Nowadays, this is often an extension of 'ordinary' bullying. For this reason, most of the standard responses as outlined above continue to apply. The main difference is that cyberbullying can increase the overall impact of the bullying as a whole, because it does not stop at the school gates. Moreover, cyberbullying is often harder to detect, so that it is more difficult (but not impossible!) to take effective action.

Endnotes

1. Mueller & Brenner, 1977.
2. Hay & Ross, 1982.
3. Eckerman & Peterman, 2001; Endo, 1992.
4. Ray & Heyes, 2011.
5. Meltzoff, 2002; Meltzoff & Moore, 1994; Meltzoff & Moore, 1999a; Meltzoff & Moore, 1999b; Meltzoff et al., 2012.
6. Hay et al., 2004; Proulx & Poulin, 2013.
7. Kawabata & Crick, 2011; Park et al., 1993.
8. Brownell et al., 2006; Dyer & Moneta, 2006; Trawick-Smith & Dziurgot, 2011.
9. Linsey & Colwell, 2003.
10. Dodge et al., 1983.

11. McAlister & Peterson, 2006; Müller et al., 2012; Nelson et al., 2008.
12. Slaughter et al., 2015.
13. Damon & Hart, 1991.
14. Liberman, 2020.
15. Van den Berg & Cillessen, 2015.
16. Coie et al., 1982.
17. Lansu & Cillessen, 2015.
18. Laursen et al., 2020.
19. Rinaldi, 2002; Rose & Asher, 1999.
20. Meisinger et al., 2007; Schonert-Reichl et al., 2012; Woods, 2009.
21. Hartl et al., 2020.
22. Asher & Rose, 1997; Bierman, 2004.
23. Wentzel & Asher, 1995.
24. See amongst others: Dodge et al., 1986; Dodge & Rabiner, 2004.
25. Crick & Dodge, 1994.
26. Ladd, 1983.
27. Furman & Buhrmester, 1992.
28. Sullivan, 1953.
29. Brendgen et al., 2013.
30. Bagwell et al., 1998.
31. Newcomb & Bagwell, 1996.
32. Gauze et al., 1996.
33. Bleske-Rechek et al., 2012.
34. Neal et al., 2014.
35. McHale et al., 2003; Mehta & Strough, 2009; Rancourt et al., 2013.
36. Gray & Feldman, 1997; Edwards & Whiting, 1988.
37. Petitpas & Champagne, 2000; Thorne, 1993.
38. Richards et al., 1998.
39. Beal, 1994.
40. Beal, 1994; Pedersen et al., 2007.
41. Beal, 1994; Pedersen et al., 2007.
42. Steinberg & Monahan, 2007.
43. Steinberg, 2015.
44. Steinberg, 2008.
45. Wentzel & Asher, 1995.
46. Ahmed & Braithwaite, 2004; Katzer et al., 2009.
47. Harris, 1998.
48. Lewis et al., 1996.
49. Dunn & Kendrick, 1982.
50. Falbo, 2012.
51. Baar et al., 2018.
52. Juvonen et al., 2003.
53. Juvonen et al., 2003; former website https://web.archive.org/
web/20160607084322/http://www.ooitalzogereageerd.be/(which no longer
exists); www.4voor12.be/hoe-kan-je-helpen

54. Due et al., 2005.
55. Swearer et al., 2010.
56. Veldkamp et al., 2019.
57. Audiosource: amended from podcast 'Groeimee: expert aan het woord (Gie Deboutte)' [Be part of growing: the expert speaks] – Aflevering 5: Pesten, consulted via https://soundcloud.com/user-215608879/groeimee-podcast-aflevering-5-pesten
58. Kyriakides et al., 2014.
59. Baar et al., 2018.
60. Kyriakides et al., 2014.

3

LEARNING

In recent years, much attention has been devoted to cognitive psychology in education. Insights into how children learn can also be useful for parents and other caregivers. However – and in keeping with the guiding principles of this book – we also want to look a little further. Learning starts with perception but even with something so seemingly simple things can still go wrong. For that reason, we begin this third section with a chapter on the nature of perception, followed by an overview of the most important current insights into learning, and ending with a summary of the methods most appropriate for building up expertise.

3.1

EVERYTHING STARTS WITH PERCEPTION

── What questions does this chapter answer? ──

1. Do we see what we think we see?
2. What do the laws of perception tell us about the way our brain thinks?
3. Which cognitive errors or distortions do we make during perception?
4. What does all this mean in terms of practice?

If you want to learn or acquire knowledge, you first need to be able to perceive. Perception occurs via the senses and therefore takes different forms: listening, touching, looking, tasting, smelling. Perception is so crucial for human learning, development and action that a separate branch of psychology has been devoted to it, known (unsurprisingly) as perception psychology. As a result, no general introduction to psychology as a whole can fail to have a chapter on perception. In fact, it is usually the first subject to be discussed. The reason for this is historical. During the 19th century, perception psychology formed the basis for experimental psychology, which at that time was referred to as psychophysics. The German Gustav Fechner was one of the first scientists to investigate the relationship between the objective properties of a stimulus (for example, the mass of a block of iron) and its perceived properties. He discovered that this is not a one-to-one relationship. For example, if you give a person a block of iron weighing 1 kilogram and then give them a block of iron weighing 2 kilograms, the difference is clear and easily perceptible. However, if you first give them a block weighing 10 kilograms and then a block weighing 11 kilograms, the difference is now much less perceptible, even though the actual weight difference remains the same in both cases: 1 kilogram. If you make similar comparisons for other weights and chart the results in a graphic, you will soon see that there is a smooth (logarithmical) progression between the stimulus intensity and the perceived sensation. This is known as the Weber–Fechner Law. Experiments of this kind in psychophysics gave support to the idea that the human psyche could also be approached in a similarly scientific manner, which until then had been seriously doubted. In other words, it is possible to contend that the study of all psychology began in a certain sense with the study of perception psychology. And it is certainly indisputable (at least nowadays) that any attempt to understand learning and instruction first requires an understanding of perception. Or as the educational psychologist Ronald Marx commented in 1983: 'Any rendering of how students learn in school that is derived from theories of cognitive psychology will have to include a discussion of perceptual phenomena.'[1]

There is nothing that we humans are more certain about than the accuracy of what we see. A good example of this is the hype surrounding 'the dress',[2] a photograph that amused (and bemused) the world back in 2015. Some people thought the dress had blue and black stripes; others were equally convinced that the stripes were gold and white! How is it possible that something as simple as the pattern of stripes on a dress can be perceived in two such different ways? And what should we conclude from the fact that we are so certain about the accuracy of our own perception and therefore equally certain about the fallacy of other people's? Moreover, this kind of perceptual ambiguity is not confined to the sense of sight alone. In 2018, there was a similar international furore about a short sound fragment in which the name of either Yanni or Laurel (depending on your perceptual point of view) was heard.[3] Once again, opinions were passionately divided, although it later transpired that the reason for the difference was a question of age: the older you get, the less able you are to hear high frequencies. As a result, young people heard Yanni; older people heard Laurel.

Phenomena of this kind are, of course, entertaining but they actually conceal a much deeper significance. They make clear that we do not all seem to perceive the world in the same way. Various factors have an influence on the manner in which we perceive the things around us. In the case of Yanni and Laurel, that factor was age but there are many other factors that can have equally intriguing effects. For example, the place where you grow up determines your cultural background, and this in turn determines the way you look at things. In an experiment by Masuda and colleagues, a group of American and Japanese test subjects were asked to assess the facial expressions in a series of cartoons they were shown (for example, a happy face followed by a sad face). The main figure in the cartoon displayed the desired emotion but was surrounded by others who displayed either the same or a different emotion. The assessment of emotions differs very little worldwide but the experiment showed that to reach their conclusions the Japanese focused on the people surrounding the central figure, while the Americans concentrated on the central figure alone.[4] In other words, the Japanese use different information from the Americans to perceive what they see. Similarly, the way in which we organise information into different categories also varies from culture to culture. In our western culture, we regard dogs as household pets, almost as members of the family. In some other cultures, dogs are no more than guard dogs at best and a dangerous nuisance at worst. This means, for example, that people from these different cultures would react to a stray dog in a very different way.

The context in which something happens is also important. This can help to determine whether you notice something or not. In terms of visual perception, this can relate to all different kinds of perceptual characteristics: shape, colour, size, orientation, etc. But the same effect can also be experienced in relation to auditory perception. If you are talking to someone at a party where there is lots of ambient noise, you sometimes think that you can hear your name being spoken by someone in the background. This is known as the 'cocktail party' effect and is caused by sounds from different sources being mixed before reaching your ears. Similar contextual effects can also play a role in the classroom.

But perhaps the single most important factor for determining how we perceive the world is prior knowledge. Prior knowledge not only determines what you see but also what you notice. Consequently, you could also explain cultural differences in perception as being the result of the different kinds of acquired knowledge that people have gained since birth in their respective cultures.

Bottom-up versus top-down

In order to understand why context and prior knowledge are so important for perception, it is first necessary to make a distinction between the 'bottom-up' and 'top-down' processing of information. In Gibson's theory of direct (visual) processing, the bottom-up approach is central.[5] 'Bottom-up' means the one-directional processing of raw input from the senses, designated by Gibson as 'sensation' and defined as every stimulus received from one of the senses. This is a continuous process but one of which we are not aware for most of the time. This awareness only occurs when we deliberately focus our attention on sensations. For example, if you carefully listen to all the sounds around you, it is only then that you will hear all the individual components – birdsong, a passing car, etc. – that you previously absorbed as unregistered sensations.

In contrast, attention is a top-down process. Via the application of attention, your knowledge, experience and expectations influence if or how sensations reach you and how you subsequently interpret them. This also means that the things to which you pay no attention scarcely penetrate your consciousness (or fail to penetrate it all), even if you are looking at them directly. A classic example of this 'inattentional blindness' was demonstrated in an experiment conducted in 1999 by Simons and Chabris.[6] The participants were asked to watch a film in which two groups of people were throwing a basketball to each other. The participants' task was to count the number of times the ball was thrown. While the film was running, a man dressed in a gorilla suit ran into the middle of the scene, beat his hands on his chest Tarzan-like, and then ran off again. Afterwards, more than half the participants correctly reported the number of times the ball was thrown but could not recall having seen the gorilla-man! This is the selective power of attention. What you consciously perceive is, to a large extent, what you expect to perceive. And you perceive it at the expense of all the other things you are not expecting to see and on which you therefore focus no attention. According to Gregory's theory of perception,[7] most of the impressions and information directed at us are lost during our processes of physical perception. In fact, he suspects that as much as 90% of all sensations are not consciously perceived, so that our brain has to fill in all the resulting 'gaps'. In other words, the brain makes a construction of reality, by linking together the things we do perceive with 'bridges' created by our prior knowledge, which replace the sensations we did not perceive. As a result of this 'patchwork' approach, our perception can often be wide of the mark, so that it becomes necessary to regularly check that we are seeing and hearing what we think we are seeing and hearing.

How do children develop their perception?

If prior knowledge plays such an important part in perception, how is it possible for babies to perceive? A newborn child has virtually no knowledge of the world that surrounds them. The child hears noises in the mother's womb and these noises can already exercise an important influence on the child (although there is no proof for the so-called 'Mozart' effect[8]). However, immediately after the birth, the baby is subjected to a multitude of new sensations, amongst which the visual stimuli are especially prominent. If a child is born into the world as a blank sheet of paper, a tabula rasa, does this mean that Gregory's theory must be wrong? This is what Piaget,[9] but also a number of other respected scientists,[10] have assumed. However, more recent research has shown that although a child has very little knowledge at the time of their birth, they acquire knowledge at a much faster speed than has previously been supposed. As we saw in Chapter 1.8 on physical development, babies are very quickly able to recognise faces and, more importantly, to distinguish the faces of their parents from the rest. Understandably, it is very difficult to investigate these kinds of phenomena with extremely young children but thanks to several ingenious studies in recent years researchers are now suggesting that newborn infants are very soon able to recognise the correct form of a face in comparison with images in which the faces are not anatomically correct (because the nose or mouth are in the wrong place).[11] One study has even concluded that this ability exists from as early as the second month of life.[12] Research into how quickly a baby can recognise their mother's face on a video (so that the baby cannot recognise her by smell) has recorded that on the day after their birth the child already looks longer at images of their mother than at images of other women.[13] In other words, children do not come into the world as a blank sheet of paper. They also seem to have a preference for faces that are also regarded as being more attractive by adults.[14] This all suggests that we humans are born with a kind of prototype in our head of what a face should look like or else that we have an innate mechanism in the brain that can quickly assemble this prototype face from all the faces that we see shortly after our birth. Moreover, this is not a purely visual phenomenon. Studies have shown that a baby can distinguish their mother's voice from the voice of other women within a couple of days of arrival in the world,[15] while other research has concluded that a preference for the child's mother tongue also develops with similar speed,[16] although this may be associated with the hearing and learning of words while still in the womb.[17] By the age of four months, children can even add up and subtract! In one study, the researchers showed the child a ball. The ball was then hidden behind a screen, with the child still watching. The child was then shown a second ball, which was also placed behind the screen. When the screen was removed, only a single ball was left (the other having been surreptitiously removed), which prompted a reaction of amazement from the child. This amazement indicates that the child understands that what they are seeing is not logical. It also confirms that very young children possess something known as object permanence. This is the realisation that things continue to exist, even if we can no longer see them.[18] Last but not least, newborn babies can also imitate behaviour that they witness in others.[19] Taken together, all these indications suggest an explanation for at least part of the way in which human beings learn and continue to develop. Yet even if newborn children are capable of much more than has previously been thought, they still have an awful lot of learning left to do!

I recognise that sentence!

DeCasper and Spence[20] asked mothers to regularly read aloud a piece of text during the final six weeks of their pregnancy. Following the birth, the newborn babies were read a number of texts by the mother, including the one that she had recited during the previous weeks. The babies had a clear preference for the text that they had already heard while they were in the womb. Of course, this does not mean that they understood the text but it does show that even before they are born children are capable of listening to and recognising certain elements of what they hear, such as rhythm and intonation.

Laws of perception

Whether innate or not, we all seem to share a number of basic laws of perception. These phenomena are the subject of so-called Gestalt psychology or gestaltism, a branch of the psychological sciences that emerged at the start of the 20th century as a result of the work of German scientists like Max Wertheimer, Wolfgang Kohler and Kurt Koffka.[21] Roughly translated, Gestalt means 'organised form' or 'whole form' and it therefore looks at the human mind and human behaviour as a whole.

The theory has received a certain amount of criticism over the years, primarily because it is largely descriptive in nature and does not, in contrast to the theories of Gregory, attempt to give an explanation. Nevertheless, this field of study has led to the formulation of a number of Gestalt or organisational laws that govern how we perceive things. These laws (or principles) assist the functioning of the visual memory and even today still have an influence on the work of designers, photographers and social psychologists.[22]

Here is a summary of the most well-known of these laws:[23]

- **The law of proximity**

   We see things that are close to each other as a group. In Figure 3.1 on the left, we see the 36 dots as a single group. On the right of the figure, we see the same 36 dots as three groups of 12.

Figure 3.1   The law of proximity

- **The law of similarity**

   We are more likely to place objects that are similar to each other in the same group. With regard to the 36 dots in Figure 3.2, this means that we are likely to group the darker dots and the lighter dots together in separate groups.

Figure 3.2   The law of similarity

- **The law of closure**

  Shapes that are not complete will nonetheless be experienced as being complete. In other words, the dotted lines in Figure 3.3 will be perceived as a circle and a rectangle, respectively.

Figure 3.3 The law of closure

- **The law of continuity**

  Closely related to the law of closure, this law states that elements that are positioned on what seems to be a continuous line will be perceived as such. As a result, the diagram in Figure 3.4 is perceived as two intersecting lines rather than as two inverted 'V's or as a random arrangement of dots.

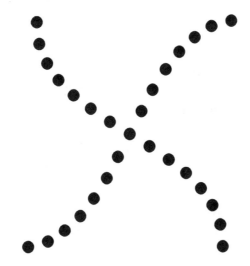

Figure 3.4 The law of continuity

- **The law of figure and ground**

  This law states that people instinctively perceive objects as either being in the foreground or the background. They either stand out prominently in front (figure) or recede into the distance (ground). But as the drawing in Figure 3.5 indicates, this can be relative. Are we looking at a vase or two faces?

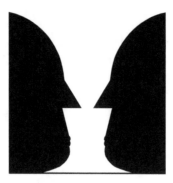

Figure 3.5　The law of figure and ground

The order of perception

You usually give more attention to the things that you first perceive or have most recently perceived, as a result of which you are more likely to remember them. These phenomena are known respectively as the primacy effect and the recency effect or, when taken together, the serial position effect. If you listen to a series of words, you will best remember the first four and the last eight words.[24] For this reason, it is important, for example, to begin any presentation by setting out a clear structure and to end with a summary of your most important insights. The final things that you say are the things that will be best remembered by your listeners.[25]

The primacy effect during studying

The primacy effect also has an impact on studying, although this has less to do with perception and more to do with organisation and time management. Students will more frequently read and re-read first chapters than last chapters, so that they generally know the former better than the latter.[26] For this reason, it is a good idea to regularly change the order of what you study; a principle that is known as interleaving.[27]

Perception and reasoning

In addition to the Gestalt laws, there are also a number of other perceptual principles that can lead to errors in thinking. A single characteristic or attribute of a person – for example, his or her attractiveness – can sometimes determine the overall impression we have of that person. Back in the 1920s, Edward Thorndike referred to this as the 'halo' effect.[28] Subsequent research has confirmed that teachers can indeed sometimes be influenced by the physical appearance of pupils and students when judging their performance.[29] A distinction also needs to be made between the halo effect, whereby one aspect of a person creates a positive image, and the horn effect, whereby one aspect of a person creates a negative image in the observer. Studies have shown, for example, that over-active and unruly behaviour, such as is commonly found in children with attention deficit hyperactivity disorder, or ADHD, can negatively influence the image a teacher has of such children.[30]

Similarly, (unconscious) expectations can also play a misleading role in our reasoning. Various heuristics in our thinking create 'biases' that influence our opinions and actions. We will look at this in more detail in Chapter 4.3 on behavioural economics.

Errors of perception in making assessments

We often need to assess others. Teachers assess students and their work every day. Employers assess the people who apply for jobs. Bosses must assess the performance of their subordinates. And the Tripadvisors and Yelps of the world encourage us all to assess where we have been and what we have done. Many of the matters that we have discussed in this chapter can affect these assessments. The order in which the teacher corrects the pupils' work; the order and appearance of the candidates for an oral examination; the order and appearance of competitors in a beauty competition or witnesses in a court of law: these are all things that can have an impact on what people decide.[31] It seems that there is even a recency effect at work in the Eurovision Song Contest: the results over the years suggest that it is better to sing near the end.[32] Similarly, it can make a difference where you sit in a classroom or lecture hall. Students who sit at the front are perceived as being more active and more involved than the students who prefer to sit at the back.[33] The halo and horn effects can also play a role, even across a number of different students, whereby a negative experience with one student in a group can influence the assessment of one or more other students in that same group.[34] Being aware of all these possibilities is the first step to limiting their impact.

The combination of errors in our perception and our reasoning can have important consequences for the way in which we deal with stereotyping and prejudices in our day-to-day lives.[35] It means, for example, that we group people together on the basis of a certain (physical) characteristic, such as the colour of their skin, to which we then link certain associations. Or to express it in slightly different terms: we group people together on the basis of a common characteristic (according to the laws of perception) and then use this single characteristic as a further basis for attributing to those people certain other characteristics (according to the logic of the halo and horn effects). In concrete terms, this results in our frequently overestimating the extent of the correlations between some human characteristics. One disadvantage of this is that it can create a self-reinforcing effect. In this way, for example, a teacher's expectations of a pupil's performance can help to determine the outcome of that performance.[36] This type of effect is also often associated with the phenomenon of the so-called self-fulfilling prophecy, a term first introduced by Merton in 1948.[37] Nowadays, it is better known as the Pygmalion effect (after the legendary sculptor in Greek mythology, who carved a statue so perfectly beautiful that he wished it could be brought to life, a wish that was granted by Aphrodite, the goddess of love), although it is sometimes also referred to as the Rosenthal effect (after the researcher who, together with Leonore Jacobson, first established empirically the existence of the effect in education).[38] The Pygmalion effect refers to the interaction between positive expectations and positive effects, which was the purpose of Merton's original research. However, it can also be described in the opposite terms – negative expectations leading to negative effects – in which case it is known as the Golem effect.[39]

The Pygmalion effect has less impact than some people think. A study by Jussim and Harber of 35 research projects investigating the effect in education concluded that its influence is actually limited and seems likely to disappear over time.[40] However, if you examine the way in which a teacher looks at a class as a whole, the impact of expectations then appears to be significantly greater.[41] For example, what teachers think about the performance of a whole group with a particular ethnic background can be linked to better or worse school recommendations. This applies equally to socio-economic status.[42]

Conclusion

In this chapter, we have looked at various aspects of perception. We started with perception as a purely sensory phenomenon. It immediately became clear that neutral or objective perception is impossible. Working top-down, your brain adds all different kinds of information to what you perceive, based on prior knowledge, attention and expectation. This often works well, because it is ultimately the way in which we give meaning to the mass of information and sensations with which we are bombarded. However, sometimes it can also lead to errors in perception and flawed interpretations. The more you are aware of this latter possibility, the more easily you will be able to avoid making the mistakes it often entails. Perhaps our human perception is not always correct but a knowledge of perception psychology can at least help to prevent us from being deluded too frequently by our own brain and senses.

What does all this mean in terms of practice?

1. **There is no such thing as objective perception.**

    Our brains are coloured by our past, our previous experiences and our prior knowledge, as a result of which our perception is subjective. Errors in reasoning further add to this subjectivity. The brain 'fills in' the gaps in what we see or what we have forgotten but sometimes these gaps are filled in incorrectly. Consequently, it is not a good idea to blindly trust what people say (for example, in relation to bullying at school) but it is also important to be aware that your own coloured perception might influence the way you look at a situation.

2. **Be aware of how our brains perceive things.**

   The fact that we view people who are close to each other as a group rather than as individuals is a classic example of the way in which the laws of perception programme our brains to analyse situations in terms of 'us-and-them' thinking. Using a series of mental tricks and short-cuts (heuristics), the brain attempts to assess reality in a faster and more manageable manner, so that we can react and anticipate more quickly.

3. **Start and end your lessons with the most important matters.**

   As a result of the recency and primacy effects, we now know that the things we hear first and last are also the things that stay longest in our memory. It is therefore a good idea to start a lesson by outlining a clear structure (with headlines) and to finish with a short summary of the most important points.

4. **Be aware of the existence of the self-fulfilling prophecy.**

   Our brains are clever and make use of all kinds of tricks and short-cuts that allow us to analyse reality more easily and react to it more quickly. Unfortunately, this sometimes has a downside, since it results in flawed thinking and stereotypical generalisations that are not always correct. We can do nothing to alter the way our brains work: being aware of the possibility of this kind of misinformation and viewing it critically is all that we can do to limit or avoid its misleading effects.

Teacher takeaways

How to deal with preconceptions

Preconceptions and stereotypes can help us to assess a situation quickly. They are a kind of unconscious mental short-cut that allows us to make fast decisions. Both terms are often used interchangeably but they do not mean the same thing. Stereotypes can best be regarded as broad generalisations, ideas and images about people and groups. For example, lorry drivers are macho, overweight people are jolly, etc. A preconception (or, more negatively, a prejudice or bias) adds an emotional element. For example, you are afraid of lorry drivers because they are macho. Or you like overweight people because they are so jolly.

(Continued)

Unfortunately, these short-cuts (both stereotypes and preconceptions) can lead to errors of judgement and discrimination. You will never judge a situation or a person correctly if you base your overall assessment on just a single factor, such as age, gender, skin colour, stuttering, over-activeness, etc. As a result, you may end up unconsciously favouring one person and unfairly disadvantaging another.

In recent years, much research has been conducted to find ways in which the negative processes associated with preconceptions, prejudices and biases can be counteracted. The starting point for this research is often the theory that the more people come into contact with each other and the better they get to know each other, the more likely that preconceptions can be invalidated and eliminated.[43]

This sounds encouraging but in reality the results of studies conducted on this basis have been neither uniformly clear nor transferable. This lack of transferability means, for example, that contact with people from a migration background might well help to reduce prejudice and increase acceptance with regard to this particular group but this will not necessarily be the case for other groups, such as the elderly. It is possible, however, that contact with one group of people may lead to greater tolerance for other groups of a similar nature, such as political refugees, most of whom also have a migration background.[44]

In the field of education, recent research has suggested that there is a possible positive effect if pupils and students are brought into contact with a wide diversity of people rather than with people confined to just a few specific groups.[45]

What can we do?

The Anne Frank Foundation has drawn up a series of practical tips that can be used to help children and young people deal with possible preconceptions and prejudice:[46]

- **Make the subject more personal and more concrete.**

  Words and concepts like stereotypes, preconceptions and even racism or discrimination can seem far too abstract for children and young people. As a result, it is a good idea to let them find out for themselves what stereotypes and generalisations they use. Becoming aware of these things is a first important step towards dealing with them. These examples can then be used to make clear why stereotypes and preconceptions exist and why, in some circumstances, they can be harmful or even dangerous.

- **Explain the difference between stereotypes and preconceptions.**
- **Always discuss preconceptions and their possible link to discrimination.**

  Be aware that this kind of discussion can sometimes provoke strong emotional reactions in children and young people. In some cases, they may have already been the victims of prejudice and/or discrimination. In other cases, perhaps they are still being bullied or excluded in your school. Some teachers see this as a reason for avoiding such discussions but this is often a mistake. These are matters that are best aired and discussed openly. In order to do so, it is essential to allow enough time and to create a safe atmosphere in which everyone feels able to talk about their own experiences. If this results in strong emotions, so be it. That is not necessarily a bad thing. The most important thing, however, is that everyone is listened to and, with the right feedback and the right guidance, can move forward together.

Endnotes

1. Marx, 1983.
2. See, for example, NOS, 27 February 2015. https://nos.nl/op3/artikel/2021672-thedress-meerderheid-ziet-blauw-zwart.html
3. See, for example, NOS, 16 May 2018. Mei 16. https://nos.nl/op3/artikel/2232059-dit-zegt-de-wetenschap-over-dat-gekke-laurel-of-yanny-fragmentje.html
4. Masuda et al., 2008.
5. Gibson, 1966; Gibson, 1972.
6. Simons & Chabris, 1999.
7. Gregory, 1970.
8. See *Urban Myths about Learning and Education*, neuro-myth 7 (De Bruyckere et al., 2015a).
9. Egan, 2004.
10. Pinker, 2003.
11. Fantz, 1961.
12. Maurer & Barrera, 1981.
13. Walton et al., 1992.
14. Slater et al., 1998.
15. DeCasper & Fifer, 1980.
16. Moon et al., 1993.
17. DeCasper & Spence, 1986.
18. Readers who once learnt about Piaget or are familiar with his works will perhaps be amazed to read this. Piaget situated object permanence around the eighth month of life, which now seems to be wrong. Examples of the experiments mentioned can be found in: Wynn (2000).
19. See amongst others: Meltzoff & Moore, 1977; Meltzoff & Moore, 1983.
20. DeCasper & Spence, 1986.
21. Rock & Palmer, 1990.
22. Peterson & Berryhill, 2013.
23. Spielman et al., 2014.
24. Murdock, 1962.

25. Miller & Campbell, 1959.
26. Tan & Ward, 2000.
27. Rohrer, 2012.
28. Thorndike, 1920.
29. Rasmussen, 2008.
30. See amongst others: Abikoff et al., 1993; Stevens & Quittner, 1998.
31. See amongst others: De Bruin, 2005; Glejser & Heyndels, 2001; Steiner & Rain, 1989.
32. See amongst others: De Bruin, 2005; De Bruin & Keren, 2003.
33. McGowan et al., 2017.
34. Borman, 1975.
35. See amongst others: Hamilton & Sherman, 1989; Schmader, 2012.
36. De Boer et al., 2018.
37. Merton, 1948.
38. Rosenthal & Jacobson, 1968.
39. Babad et al., 1982.
40. Jussim & Harber, 2005.
41. This was mentioned by Hattie (2009) but more recent research seems to confirm it. See amongst others: Rubie-Davies et al., 2015.
42. See amongst others: Boone & Van Houtte, 2013; Rubie-Davies et al., 2006; Turner et al., 2015.
43. Allport, 1954.
44. Harwood et al., 2011.
45. Vasiljevic & Crisp, 2013.
46. Anne Frank Stichting. (2018). *Omgaan met vooroordelen en discriminatie in de klas*. Consulted via www.annefrank.org/nl/educatie/tips-voor-docenten/omgaan-met-vooroordelen-en-discriminatie-de-klas

3.2

LEARNING

What questions does this chapter answer?

1. What is learning?
2. How do we learn according to the theories of behaviourism and cognitivism?
3. What does all this mean in terms of practice?

Learning is without doubt one of the central elements in human psychology. Yet despite this central role, in many general reference works on psychology the subject seldom merits a separate chapter of its own.[1] The reason for this is that the many different elements of psychology – development, perception, memory, motivations, etc. (to name but a few) – are all connected to a greater or lesser degree with learning. These subjects and their interaction with learning are all discussed at varying length elsewhere in this book. Even so, it seemed important to also devote a separate chapter to the psychology of learning itself. This allows us to bring together all the different perspectives on learning and to cherry-pick from the huge amount of research on this subject the most useful tips and pieces of information that can best help parents, caregivers and teachers.

Learning is a condition for survival. But what exactly is learning?

For all living organisms the capacity to learn is essential for survival. And no other organism is better suited for this purpose than we humans, not only in terms of adjusting with extreme flexibility to our surrounding environment but also in terms of furthering our own cultural and scientific improvement. Both these qualities are based on and dependent upon our ability to learn.

There are countless different definitions of learning but in general we can speak of learning when a person is able to master a new pattern of behaviour or adjust an existing one. An additional condition is that this adjustment must be perceivable, since it is otherwise not possible to establish with certainty that something has been learnt.

Learning is therefore change. It takes place if someone alters their existing behaviour or displays a new kind of behaviour. It does not include reflexive behaviour, such as the contraction of the pupils in our eyes when we look at a bright light. This type of behaviour is innate, and therefore not learnt. As we have already seen, this is one of the central issues in psychology: which aspects of human behaviour are inborn and which are acquired through the subsequent experience of our environment? In other words, are these aspects the result of nature or nurture, and, if so, to what extent? These questions are also important for the psychology of learning, if for no other reason than the fact that innate behaviour does not need to be explicitly learnt. The way in which we seem to 'automatically' learn our mother tongue is a good example of this kind of inborn skill. Thanks to the complex workings of evolution, we have been biologically programmed over many thousands of years to be able to speak our native language at an early age without the need for active effort. We pick up the features and characteristics of this language by an instinctive process that is known as *informal learning*.

Is this the way we learn all aspects of language? Sadly not! In order to be able to read and write, instruction and active practice are a necessary condition, as part of what is known as *formal learning*.

The developmental psychologist David Geary refers to this as the difference between primary knowledge – the knowledge with which you are born and do not need to learn (or, according to Geary, is impossible for you to learn via instruction) – and secondary knowledge – culturally acquired knowledge that is deemed to be important for normal functioning and which can only be learnt via explicit instruction.[2]

There is no straightforward and generally accepted view about which knowledge is primary and which is secondary. Tricot and Sweller argue that various generic skills, such as communicating with others and the use of heuristics (including means-ends analysis) to solve problems, are examples of primary knowledge.[3] As a result, there is no point in trying to learn these skills, because it cannot be done. This has implications for the teaching of so-called '21st century skills', a concept that has been popular in educational circles for many years. These 21st century skills also include generic skills like communication, problem-solving and creative thinking, so that one wonders just how 'teachable' they are.

Some educational theorists still believe that it is useful to include these general skills in the school curriculum. There are even some who believe that the teaching of these skills is more important than the acquisition of domain knowledge (that is, knowledge about a specific topic). Geary's theory casts serious doubt on these propositions and suggests that focusing on '12th century skills' rather than '21st century skills' may be wiser and more effective in the long run. Or as Oscar Wilde once said: 'It is well to remember from time to time that nothing that is worth knowing can be taught.'[4]

Because of the central role that learning plays in our everyday functioning, the psychology of learning is one of the central pillars in general psychology as a whole. Having a good knowledge of learning and how it operates is important for all teachers who want to provide a more pleasant, more efficient and more effective way of learning for their pupils.[5] In many respects, however, this knowledge is even more important for the learners themselves. Like many other aspects of psychology, most people know something about learning. After all, nearly everyone spent the best part of the first two decades of their life in an institution of learning of one kind or another. Some of these basic ideas about learning, notwithstanding their popularity, have no valid scientific foundation. In our book *Urban Myths about Learning and Education* we tried to deal with a number of such ideas and relegated some of them to the status of educational myth. Among the most important myths to be debunked in this way was the concept of learning styles (the idea that everyone learns in a different way – for example, thinkers, dreamers, doers, etc. – and that teachers must adjust their lessons to reflect this)[6] and the concept of the learning pyramid (the idea that listening to a teacher only allows you to acquire 10% of the knowledge you need, whereas explaining something to someone else allows you to acquire up to 80 or 90%, or some other equally ridiculous percentages).[7]

Perspectives on learning

Like other aspects of psychology, you can only hope to understand learning properly if you study it from a number of different perspectives. And in the case of learning, the range of these perspectives is wide and varied, and includes:

- behaviourist
- cognitivist
- cognitive loading
- biological
- social
- ...

To complicate matters still further, a number of these perspectives can be combined; for example, embodied cognition combines the biological and cognitivist perspectives. In this chapter we will examine a number of the perspectives that we think are most relevant for teachers, caregivers and parents.

Behaviourism

No text about the psychology of learning can avoid consideration of the behaviourist perspective. Although this perspective has been around for decades, its influence is still relevant today. The central tenet of behaviourism is that behaviour should be made visible and (experimentally) controllable. It is a theory of learning based on the idea that all behaviours are acquired through conditioning, which occurs through interaction with the environment.

At the start of the 20th century, it was thought that the only way for psychology to acquire the same scientific status as the natural sciences was to study observable behaviour, with the aim of explaining as much of learning behaviour as possible with the fewest possible rules. In this respect, behaviourism can be regarded as a 'black box' theory. You can observe someone for hours but you cannot really know what is going on inside that person's head. The only thing you can know for certain is what you can see or perceive.

The systematic experiments in conditioning carried out by the Russian physiologist Ivan Pavlov (1849–1936) formed the ideal platform for pursuing behaviourist ideas further. Pavlov and his team carried out a rigorous series of experiments on dogs, as a result of which they discovered the basic principles of associative learning: the conditioning of a neutral stimulus, the generalisation of a conditioned stimulus, discriminating between two stimuli, second and higher order conditioning, etc.

Classic conditioning involves making a link or association between an innate reflex and a new stimulus. Imagine that during the first week of school you give a sweet to every pupil every day as soon as the bell for the morning break sounds. You can be fairly certain that by the start of the second week the mouths of those pupils will start to water in anticipation as soon as they hear that bell! A previously neutral stimulus (the bell) is now regarded by the pupils as a conditioned stimulus, as a result of which they exhibit a specific type of behaviour (conditioned response) when the stimulus is applied. This kind of approach is still used today; for example, to help children and young people to stop biting their nails. The revolting photographs nowadays displayed on packets of cigarettes are designed to have the same conditioning effect.

By using higher order conditioning, it is possible to construct complex associations but the process is far from simple. Part of the difficulty is that people are also subject to other processes at the same time, so that identifying a purely reflexive explanation for the conditioned response is a complicated matter. It could be said that nothing new is learnt – it is all a matter of reflexes – but it could equally be said that what is learnt is how to give a certain aspect of behaviour a different trigger. One could state that it's not about learning something new, but applying something you were already able to do as a reflex as a reaction to a new cause.

In addition to classic conditioning, there is also another form of associative learning: *operant conditioning*. Edward Thorndike and B. F. Skinner were the pioneers of a method of learning based on the reward or non-reward of behaviour, which goes much further than the reflex approach. Skinner's experiments in the mid-20th century demonstrated that the behaviour of both animals and humans can be influenced and shaped, depending on the situation in which those animals and humans find themselves. Via 'shaping' – the step-by-step learning of complex behaviour by reinforcing (= rewarding) behaviour that moves in the right direction – and the use of reinforcement schedules – which determine the manner in which certain behaviour is rewarded on some occasions and on others not – you can make behaviour manageable and controllable.

You can see these same principles at work in, for example, computer games but also in more serious contexts, such as the encouragement of healthy behaviour (for which the term 'nudging ' is often used: see Chapter 4.3 on behavioural economics).

Token economy or how loyalty systems also work in the school

You probably have a number of customer loyalty cards in your wallet or on your smartphone: cards that record how much you have spent in a particular shop or store, with the aim of giving you a discount on future purchases once you reach a certain amount. This is an approach that was developed on the basis of behaviourist theory and it seems that it works on people of all ages. In much the same way that shops are unable or unwilling to reward you after every visit but prefer to see you come back time after time to spend and save more, likewise at school (but also at home) it is often not possible or desirable to reward a child after every act of good behaviour with a present, a sweet, the playing of a game, etc. For this reason, it is useful in both cases to work with a system of 'tokens'. Tokens are symbols or objects that have no value of their own (a mark on a board, a stamp or sticker on a card, a scribbled signature, etc.) but which can be exchanged by the learner or shopper for something that does have a value (an ice-cream, a game, a discount) as soon as you have saved enough of them. This mechanism is now known as a *token economy*. Today, this mechanism is also evident in so-called gamification, which is the use of elements from games as a tool in education (and elsewhere). Computer games or apps like DuoLingo make use of different forms of reward until the learner has mastered a particular skill.

A number of behaviourist principles can still be seen in education today, particularly in the field of classroom management. However, the behaviourist perspective in general is regarded as being too limited or inappropriate for full-scale use in the modern educational system. For example, the principles of operant conditioning presuppose that motivation is a process that can be externally regulated in its entirety. Behaviourists do not deny the existence of internal motivational drivers but they do tend to ignore them, simply because they cannot be observed and researched, which is a main prerequisite of behavioural theory. At the same time, it should be evident that we do not learn everything though conditioning alone. You can also learn, for example, by observing (role) models. At some point in our youth, most of us will have watched our heroes – favourite footballer, coolest pop star, perhaps even our parents! – and tried to imitate them. Or we will see how someone is punished for throwing away an empty crisp packet and will consciously try to avoid the same (clearly undesirable) behaviour in order to avoid receiving the same punishment. Many other actions are also learnt by first observing and then copying: from how to cross the road when the light is green to how to stir the spaghetti the same way as mum...

This raises the central question about behaviourist theory. Do we really need to be rewarded or punished before we adjust our behaviour? Is it not also possible to learn much of what we need to learn through observation and imitation? A classic study conducted by Bandura in 1965, which eventually led to the elaboration of the social-cognitive theory of learning, seemed to suggest that we do learn significantly from what others around us do.[8] Bandura's experiment divided up 66 children into three separate groups. Each group was allowed to watch a video in which an adult picked up a doll – the Bobo doll – and (mis)treated it harshly, with punching, kicking, pinching, etc. However, the three groups were each shown a different ending to the scene:

- The control group only saw the adult's aggressive behaviour towards the doll.
- The first experimental group saw how the adult was subsequently rewarded for their aggressive behaviour towards the doll.
- The second experimental group saw how the adult was subsequently punished for their aggressive behaviour towards the doll.

Later on, the children were placed in a room with the same doll to see how they would react. Both the control group and the first experimental group (which had seen the adult rewarded for their behaviour) were aggressive towards the doll, imitating the behaviour they had witnessed in the video. This was much less the case with the second experimental group, which had seen how the adult had been punished for their behaviour.

In this way, Bandura demonstrated that the behaviourists' schedules of reinforcement needed to be supplemented by other learning methods, which led him to the conclusion that a person processes external stimuli and then chooses appropriate reactions to those stimuli, either consciously or unconsciously. Consequently, Bandura's theory concentrates more on the way in which people deal with the information they receive. As a result, the influence of attention, memory and motivation is recognised and the learner's black box is opened just a little bit more. This theory of social-cognitive learning can be regarded as a link between behaviourism and cognitivism.

Imitating is not child's play!

It seems like the simplest thing that a young baby can do: laughing back at your smiling face. The child sees you laughing and imitates what they see. Throughout our lives we make much use of this kind of imitation, from practical demonstrations in the classroom to standing behind others in the queue at the supermarket.

Having said that, the processes involved in imitating someone or something are far from simple. Tim Faber has explained it in the following terms:

> When you see behavior displayed by somebody else (e.g., your mother smiling at you), you will see this behavior from a flipped perspective (as displayed by the mother) and you will only see the visual effects of the displayed behavior. At the same time, producing behavior yourself (e.g., smiling; moving your hand), is determined by a motor command which directs muscle movements that subsequently provide visual feedback from a first person perspective (or no feedback at all).[9]

In his research, Faber contends that imitation is probably not something innate but is a form of learnt behaviour. It seems that babies may begin to imitate because they themselves are also often imitated; for example, by their doting parents. This has put a serious dent in the popular idea that imitation is an inborn skill, a theory that emerged several years ago following the discovery of mirror neurones. Mirror neurones do, of course, exist but much research still needs to be done to establish their precise function and mode of operation. The work currently in progress tends to support the idea that these matters are learnt.[10]

What do we not yet know?

Punishing, rewarding and ignoring (operant conditioning) cannot explain why there are so many behavioural differences between children. Consider, for example, the task of tidying up your room. Why is it that one child learns the desired behaviour (tidying up) through a process of reward and punishment, while another child does not (or perhaps more slowly).

Similarly, the theory does not explain why children learn some things independently through their own effort, without there being any question of punishment or reward. Children have a natural urge to explore and to discover new things and, in this way, constantly push forward their own development.

As soon as we start to discuss the acquisition and application of knowledge (in other words, complex learning behaviour), behaviourism and social-cognitive learning theory have very few answers to offer.

The cognitive perspective: learning and memory

Over many years, the study of the philosophy of education produced countless speculative ideas about effective and ineffective ways of learning. One of the reasons for this was that it was long thought that the mental life of human beings could not be properly researched. This finally changed in the second half of the 19th century, thanks to the work of a number of German scientists. Gustav Fechner (1801–1887), for example, demonstrated the relationship between the intensity of an applied stimulus and the intensity with which that stimulus is perceived (as previously mentioned with the kilogram experiment on p. 173).

Fechner's experimental approach to the mind paved the way for Hermann Ebbinghaus (1850–1909), who studied the relationship between learning, remembering and forgetting in a systematic manner.[11] Ebbinghaus's work[12] and findings led to a revolution in the psychology of memory and learning, which even today still influences the way we think about the learning process, even though he was the only test subject in his own experiments! One of his many discoveries was the forgetting curve, which charts the speed at which we forget what we have learnt if we do not repeat it (see Figure 3.6).[13]

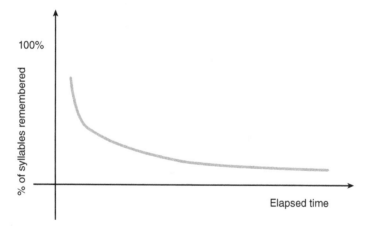

Figure 3.6   Ebbinghaus's forgetting curve that inspired spaced practice

Taken from WikiCommons.[14]

Ebbinghaus also established the effect of overlearning: even if you have repeatedly learnt a list of words until you know it perfectly, further repetition is still beneficial, if this level of perfection is to be retained. In other words, repetition makes it easier to remember even the things you thought you had mastered completely.[15] In a similar vein, he concluded that learning spread over time – spaced practice – is more effective than trying to learn something all at once – massed practice – and also that the learning effect is to a significant extent dependent on whether or not the material being learnt is meaningful for the learner.

The principles elaborated by Ebbinghaus have stood the test of time well and many later theories of learning have made grateful use of his ideas. Even today, *The Learning Scientists* website still displays posters on which his various principles are explained and illustrated, using contemporary applications.[16] In this way, applications from cognitive psychology can sometimes improve modern educational methods with relatively simple but often far-reaching interventions.[17] However, such interventions are not always easy to introduce and research has shown that pupils often fail to recognise and value useful leaning strategies, no matter how effective they are.[18]

Cognitive load

One of the theories most widely embraced in educational science circles, which seeks to explain the mechanisms behind the processing of instruction and the effect that the presentational style and content of that instruction can have on the processing operation, is the cognitive load theory, which was first formulated by the Australian John Sweller.[19] Cognitive load theory takes as its starting point the ideas that (1) our working memory has only a limited capacity and that (2) the processing of information places a burden or load on that memory. If the information to be processed is too complex or if the presentation of that information places too heavy a demand on the working memory, this will lead to an overload, as a result of which nothing is actually learnt or remembered. It is clear that the starting points of Sweller's theory have a number of important implications for both teaching (instruction) and learning.

A pupil who is still a beginner in a particular field of learning benefits from plentiful explanation and concrete examples of the material to be learnt. For a more advanced pupil, who can rely on a degree of prior knowledge and for whom new knowledge will be less likely to place an excessive strain on their working memory, it is more useful to provide a series of open learning tasks. This is known as the expertise reversal effect: the effectiveness of a method of learning is determined by its ability to lead the pupil to a higher level of independent leaning as their knowledge and experience increase. However, this theory is not without its problems,[20] not in the least because a number of new and sometimes seemingly contradictory principles have emerged in recent years.[21] Even so, the basic idea continues to be useful for all teachers.

Without proper guidance, discovery learning is doomed to failure. In 2004, the American educational scientist Richard Mayer[22] questioned the merits of the idea that pupils learn more effectively if they are allowed to discover the content of the material to be learnt for themselves. This idea had been propagated and tested in the educational world on numerous occasions over the years and had consistently led to disappointment. Cognitive load theory offered one explanation for why this might be the case: inexperienced pupils confronted with new learning material need to make use of all their cognitive reserves to make sense of the discovery-based learning task they have been given. When the reserves are not equal to the task, overload results and nothing is learnt.

Mayer's reservations were followed in 2006 by the publication of one of the most frequently cited educational articles of all time. Written by Paul Kirschner, John Sweller and Richard Clark, it concluded that discovery learning without proper guidance will never be effective, because it is a logical impossibility: the idea is simply not compatible with the way our cognitive information processing system works.[23]

Social-constructivism

The behaviourist and cognitive perspectives both focus primarily on the way in which individuals learn. According to some theorists, this view of knowledge acquisition is too limited.[24] In contrast, the social-constructivist perspective focuses on the importance of social interaction in the construction of knowledge. The development of knowledge does not take place in a vacuum but always in relation to others and always within the context of a specific culture. Social-constructivism therefore rejects the idea that knowledge can be localised in the brain of just a single person. Instead, the theory views learning as a social activity, which makes use of cultural tools. These tools can be 'physical' (for example, the use of the smartphone as a teaching/learning aid) but the language you speak is also such a tool.[25] This idea – that everyone creates their own reality through interaction with others and by using tools that offer a specific form of cultural information – implies that there is no such thing as absolute truth, because knowledge by this definition is a social construction. We call something 'a metre' because that is what we have agreed, whereas in other places other people may have agreed to use different distances of measurement.

This is what makes the description and analysis of social-constructivism so difficult: it is not just one concept but multiple concepts.[26] That interaction with others via language helps to shape learning is patently self-evident and beyond dispute but the idea that knowledge is a personal construction that does not stand in direct relation to the outside world is much more open to question.[27] For this reason, social-constructivism can best be viewed as a theory of knowledge rather than as a theory of learning. In this respect, the basic tenets of the social-constructivist perspective are closer to philosophy than to psychology.

Nevertheless, social-constructivist ideas can still be found in the world of education and in recent decades have played an important role in the classroom. The fact that we often refer to a learning environment is a direct reference to the theory. If it is not possible to teach anyone anything directly, because all knowledge is a personal construction, the task of the 'teacher' becomes the creation of an environment in which the child or young person can build up their own knowledge independently. So how do you then arrive at shared knowledge? Through working together: hence the idea of social-constructivism.

Another example of social-constructivism in education is the theory of situated cognition. This argues that, assuming all learning takes place in a social, cultural and physical context, the best way to learn is by implementing actions of your own in an (authentic) context.[28] This equates (more or less) to learning by doing. Authentic learning tasks must therefore ask the pupil to use their knowledge, skills and attitude in combination, in a manner that should lead to a better integrated form of knowledge. For example, in the Four Components of Instructional Design model (4C/ID)[29], which is focused on the learning of complex cognitive skills, authentic learning tasks form a central element.

A number of cognitivist thinkers have criticised some of the claims made by the social-constructivists.[30] These critics have argued that leaning does not always have to take place in a specific context. Nor is it the case that learning in a specific context per se leads to greater knowledge transfer than if there is no such context. Admittedly, learning in a social context can be useful but the individual learning and the training of skills also has a value.

In short, the different perspectives of learning all have something to offer but in the final analysis it is impossible to circumvent the principles that govern the human processing of information (as previously described). Unassisted discovery learning might very well be learning in an authentic context but the high cognitive load it places on the working memory means that it is not effective and, consequently, should be avoided.

A many-sided discipline

As the previous pages will have made clear, there are many different facets to the psychology of learning. It is rather like an octopus that stretches out its tentacles into every other aspect of the psychological discipline. In much the same manner, it influences education and teaching in a number of different ways. For this reason, a knowledge of the philosophy of learning is essential for every teacher. The behaviourist approach places the emphasis on small changes in the environment that can help to shape behaviour. However, it is not possible to learn everything using this method. For that reason, the cognitive approach focuses on the manner in which our brains work or, more accurately, the manner in which we process and store information (and sometimes forget it). In addition, and as we saw in Chapter 3.1 on the psychology of perception, it is vital as a teacher to take account of the prior knowledge of your pupils. This not only determines whether or not the pupils will understand what you are trying to teach them but also indicates the method of instruction that will be best suited to the pupils in question, with the aim of progressing from a formal learning structure with concrete examples to an approach that allows more freedom and self-exploration.

What does all this mean in terms of practice?

1. **As a teacher (caregiver or parent) you have an exemplary role.**

   Bullying, racism, other forms of discrimination... How do you react to these things? If you fail to react at all, children will learn that this kind of behaviour can be practised without incurring either sanction or disapproval.

2. **Repetition is crucial for learning.**

   Have we mentioned this already? Even so, it is worth repeating again.

3. **Prior knowledge is an important starting point for learning.**

   It is a child's level of prior knowledge that will determine how effectively that child can learn something. At first, this learning process needs to be assisted, especially when dealing with basic knowledge and basic skills.

Teacher takeaways

Effective studying methods

How can you study something effectively? Bearing in mind the precepts of the cognitive load theory, it is important to realise that you need to practise strengthening the link between your working memory and your long-term memory, as illustrated in a model devised by Daniel Willingham (Figure 3.7).[31]

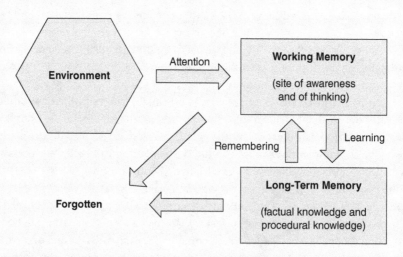

Figure 3.7 Willingham's memories model (Willingham (2009). Copyright © 2009, John Wiley & Sons – Books)

This 'memory model' underlines that if you want to learn something, you:

- need to think and focus your attention to actively process knowledge in the working memory; and
- need to repeat the learning process to fix knowledge in the long-term memory and to ensure that you can both recall it and do not forget it.

In 2013, Dunlosky and colleagues[32] compiled a classification table of the best and worst studying methods. Willingham's memory model helps us to understand why some of these methods work and why others don't:

- What things do not work (or work very little) because you often do them without active thought?
    - o   Underlining or marking with a marker pen (some studies suggest that this can even have a negative effect).
    - o   Just re-reading the same text over and over again.
    - o   Making summary texts with full sentences (not as bad as underlining but still largely ineffective).
- What things work because they involve active thinking and repetition?
    - o   Spaced learning instead of one long marathon session (see the earlier section on learning and the theories of Ebbinghaus). Also make use of interleaving: change subjects regularly, so that you give yourself time to forget, before you recall the same material again.
    - o   Retrieval practice: put your study material to one side and write down (or sketch out) everything that you can remember about it. Do this as carefully as possible. Afterwards, check to see how accurate and complete your recall was.
    - o   Practice testing: make and complete small test exercises, not to be marked for points but simply to recall and refresh the relevant learning material. Making and using flash cards can also help.
    - o   Explaining key ideas, preferably in detail.
    - o   Thinking about concrete examples to allow better understanding of abstract concepts.
    - o   Dual coding. This refers to the fact that there are seemingly two channels in our working memory: one for words and one for images. Combining these channels makes it easier to store information in your long-term memory. You can achieve this by searching for images in your study material. When you see these images, you automatically think about their content and how this relates to what is written about the same content.

The posters illustrating these principles on *The Learning Scientists* website have been translated into many languages and build further on this research, offering a handy summary of all the most relevant points.

Endnotes

1. Hothersall, 2004.
2. See Geary, 2008; Sweller, 2008.
3. Tricot & Sweller, 2014.
4. In *Intentions* (1891), 'The Critic as Artist', part 1.; Ratcliffe, S. (2017).
5. Child, 2007. See also Ormrod, 2020; Mazur, 2016.
6. Visser, 2017.
7. See our earlier books on these matters: De Bruyckere et al., 2015a; De Bruyckere et al., 2019.
8. Bandura, 1965.
9. Faber, 2017, p 182.
10. Heyes & Catmur, 2021.
11. Roediger, 1985.
12. Ebbinghaus made use of self-devised nonsense syllables, three-letter combinations that consisted of a random consonant, then a vowel and then another random consonant. Ebbinghaus's biographers suggest that he got the idea from reading the poem 'Jabberwocky' in Lewis Carroll's *Through the Looking-Glass*.
13. Schimanke et al., 2013.
14. https://commons.wikimedia.org/wiki/Category:Hermann_Ebbinghaus#/media/File:Ebbinghaus_Forgetting_Curve.jpg
15. This idea was far from being unknown. Francis Bacon had already noted in his work *Novum Organum* from 1620: 'If you read a piece of text through twenty times, you will not learn it by heart so easily as if you read it ten times while attempting to recite from time to time and consulting the text when your memory fails' (Bacon, 1620).
16. The Learning Scientists, 4 March 2020.
17. Roediger & Pyc, 2012. For practical tips, see also Kirschner et al., 2018.
18. Deslauriers et al., 2019.
19. Sweller, 1988.
20. Hulshof & Bokhove, 2020.
21. Sweller et al., 2019.
22. Mayer, 2004.
23. Kirschner et al., 2006.
24. See for example Simons, 1999.
25. Palincsar, 1998.
26. See Boudry & Buekens, 2011, for a critical assessment, in which the authors argue that 'strict' social-constructivism opens the door for pseudoscience (citing as an example Freud's psychoanalytical theory).
27. This latter concept is known as epistemological relativism.
28. Lave & Wenger, 1991.
29. Van Merriënboer & Kirschner, 2017.
30. See for example Anderson et al., 1996.
31. Willingham, 2009.
32. Dunlosky et al., 2013.

3.3

WHAT IS THE DIFFERENCE BETWEEN A BEGINNER AND AN EXPERT?

What questions does this chapter answer?

1. In what ways are beginners and experts different?
2. How do you develop expertise?
3. What are the disadvantages of expertise?

Through learning you build up knowledge and expertise but what is the difference between knowing a little and knowing a lot? Between being able to do very little or a great deal? And at what point do you become an expert?

The difference between beginners and experts

A simple but nevertheless not unimportant question that you can ask about expertise is this: what actually makes an expert? People who study a particular subject for a long time eventually acquire a great deal of information about that subject. They know much more about it than others know. In the previous chapter, on the psychology of learning, we saw that the difference between beginners and experts has an influence on the style of instruction that is best for them: experts learn in a different way from beginners.[1] Our knowledge about the difference between experts and beginners also teaches us how we can improve the level of expertise in beginners.

An expert is *not* someone who knows more than others about a subject in purely quantitative terms. Research suggests that there is also a qualitative difference: the knowledge of an expert is organised differently from the knowledge of a beginner. One of the first studies in which the importance of knowledge organisation was demonstrated was A. D. de Groot's classic study of chess players.[2] If you show chess grandmasters a position on a chess board for just a few seconds, they are capable of reproducing that position with considerable accuracy. This accuracy is much greater than the accuracy of people who have little or no chess experience. A grandmaster can position more than 20 pieces on the right squares, in comparison with the beginner's eight pieces. However, it seems that this difference in performance disappears if the pieces do not represent a meaningful position in a chess game. If the pieces are arranged randomly, the performance of the experts and the beginners is similar. In other words, the experts have more knowledge than others but this knowledge is organised in such a way that it can only find expression in the recognition and remembrance of meaningful patterns.

In another classic experiment, Michelene Chi and colleagues investigated how a group of relative beginners (novices) and experts differed in the categorisation of physics problems. The results showed that the experts had a different way of categorising things than the beginners. The experts recognised the underlying characteristics of the problems and categorised accordingly, while the novices were more inclined to organise the problems on the basis of their superficial characteristics.[3] This is another example of how prior knowledge so often makes a difference.

Another characteristic of expertise is the way in which the expertise of experts is largely confined to the domain in which their knowledge is acquired. In a further experiment, Chi compared the memory performance of 10-year-old chess experts with that of adults with no chess experience. As in de Groot's experiment, the expert children performed better than the adults in remembering chess pieces when they were meaningfully positioned but the results were reversed dramatically when the pieces were positioned randomly: now it was the adults who performed significantly better than the children.[4]

The picture is clear: in their domain of expertise experts are more easily able than beginners to distinguish between meaningful and non-meaningful patterns. A research study carried out among teachers further supports this conclusion. A group of experienced teachers and a group of starter teachers were asked to watch a video that simultaneously displayed three different images of different parts of a classroom that was full of activity. Afterwards, the experienced teachers were easily able to recognise what was happening in the three situations, whereas the novice teachers where confused by the multiplicity of images and actions.

In short, expertise makes it possible for relevant patterns of behaviour to be recognised as such. Equally as important, patterns of behaviour that are not relevant are ignored. John Sweller's theory of cognitive load, which we discussed in the previous chapter, explains why beginners – like the novice teachers in the previous example – soon experience cognitive overload. Beginners are not able to make use of their long-term memory for the processing of new information. This means that everything the beginner perceives must be processed by the short-term memory but this only has a limited capacity. This in turn means that it is impossible for a beginner to notice and take in everything that is happening. The cognitive load theory therefore implies that if a beginner wishes to successfully acquire expertise, it is essential not to overload them with too much information at an early stage.[5]

The careful build-up and gradual expansion of learning situations may seem like a slow method but in the long run it is also much more effective. However, the cognitive load theory also teaches us another important lesson: the manner in which you learn must not be allowed to hinder what you are trying to learn. Attempting to understand a method of instruction also makes demands on the limited capacity of the short-term memory. As a result, instruction methods for beginners need to be kept as simple as possible. Throwing them in at the deep end, as it were, as is the case, for example, with discovery learning, is therefore not a good idea. Why? Because the mechanisms of the method impose too heavy a burden on the short-term memory, so that little or no capacity is left over to process and acquire new knowledge and skills. This, for example, is often the fate of new teachers, when they are required to stand in front of a class of real, live pupils for the very first time... Conversely, research has also shown that this kind of 'throw them in at the deep end' method is appropriate and even useful for experts, since their level of prior knowledge allows them to swim rather than sink. This is the phenomenon we referred to in the previous chapter as the expertise reversal effect.

Imposter syndrome

Do you sometimes feel afraid? Afraid that someone will suddenly tap you on the shoulder and say that they know that you are only pretending to be what you are. Pretending to be good at everything. Pretending to know everything. But they have seen through you. They know that you are just a fraud... If this happens, there are just two possibilities: either they are right or else (and more likely) you are suffering from imposter syndrome. The good news? You are not alone. This syndrome often occurs in the early stages of a person's career[6] and can frequently be linked to a certain kind of perfectionism. More good news? With the right degree of support its effects can be reduced or nullified.[7] The literature sometimes suggests that women are more prone to the syndrome than men but in part this probably has something to do with the fact that more research has been carried out on women. A recent review study concluded that there is probably no significant gender difference.[8]

Acquiring expertise

You don't just become an expert by magic; you need to make a serious effort. There are different theories to explain the progress from beginner to expert (and beyond) and almost all of them see this as a process over time in which a number of different stages need to be distinguished.

One of the oldest and most influential theories about the acquisition of expertise is the model developed by Fitts and Posner, which focused on the acquisition of motor skills.[9] Fitts and Posner identified three stages to this acquisition:

- the cognitive stage;
- the associative stage;
- the autonomous stage.

Imagine that someone is trying to learn how to use a smartphone or some other electrical device for the very first time. The first thing you need to learn is what functions the device is capable of performing and which button or key does what. The gathering of information of this kind is central to the *cognitive stage*. During this stage, the learner needs plenty of verbal explanation and often it is also necessary to give practical demonstrations of the skills involved. For many learners this is a difficult stage, in which rapid progress alternates with mistakes and confusion. Gradually, however, the performance of some of the tasks becomes easier. During the *associative stage*, the rate of progress slows down but by now there is not as much new knowledge that still needs to be acquired. This is the stage in which you learn to combine various actions through a process of trial and error. In this way, consciously learnt declarative knowledge – knowing what something is – is converted into procedural knowledge – knowing how to use something. A tennis player who wishes to develop a good first serve takes a series of verbally learnt and subsequently practised movements and attempts to transform them into a single, supple and automatic action. Once this stage of fluency has been reached, the learner has arrived at the *autonomous stage*, so that the tennis player now no longer really needs to think before serving.

For the acquisition of knowledge (rather than skills) another useful model is the one devised by Patricia Alexander. Like Fitts and Posner, she argues that this is a three-stage process:[10]

- the acclimation stage;
- the competence stage;
- the proficiency stage.

The *acclimation stage* is characterised by the gaining of increased familiarity with the new domain of knowledge. During this stage, many pieces of loose information are acquired, which have no real connection with each other. Think, for example, of pupils who often know lots of little bits of information but are unable to see the overall 'big' picture. People who remain locked in this stage will probably soon forget the knowledge they have learnt, because it is not organised or linked in any way with their long-term memory. This is also the stage in which misconceptions about the domain can arise, simply because the learner's knowledge of the domain is purely superficial, so that a deeper understanding is lacking. This superficiality might also mean that at this stage the learner shows little interest in the subject. For this reason, it is important to make use of striking and thought-provoking examples that can generate interest and capture the learner's attention.

After a time (the length of which should not be underestimated), the learner will gradually enter the *competence stage*. During this stage, it is no longer the case that everything is 'new', as a result of which additional information falls more easily into place. The learner is now better and more easily able to see through the superficial characteristics of the domain and can identify its underlying structures. The number of misconceptions also starts to decrease significantly. This was also noticeable in the previously described experiment carried out by Chi and colleagues relating to the classification of physics problems: the experts classified the problems on the basis of their underlying characteristics (the fundamental physical principles involved), whereas the novices made their classification based on the wording of the questions, which only sketched the superficial aspects of the problems. During the competence stage, the subject becomes more and more interesting for the learner, because now not every additional aspect is completely new: some elements already feel 'familiar'. In many knowledge domains, this point of competence is only reached after years of study. Consequently, for many people the stage of competence is also the final stage.

For those who achieve it, the third stage of *proficiency* (or expertise) is characterised by full mastery of the knowledge domain, combined with the ability to think flexibly about the subject and even to contribute new information to it. The Japanese researchers Hatano and Inagaki argue that in this stage the ability to deal with the subject flexibly and to adjust your thinking makes it possible to distinguish between routine expertise and adaptive expertise.[11]

A major advantage of the acquisition of knowledge is the resulting 'automatisation' of component skills. Gaining greater expertise makes it easier to carry out some tasks without the need to consciously think about them. Simple examples include the reading of words and the identification of colours, tasks in which most of us are relatively expert. However, both these processes are so automatic that we have difficulty pronouncing the word RED when it is printed in blue letters. This is known as the Stroop effect, after its discoverer. In one sense, the Stroop effect demonstrates that expertise can also have its disadvantages; namely, that it can lead to the automatic and 'mindless' implementation of certain actions without thought. This is sometimes also referred to as 'surfing on intuition'. In this context, the American psychologist and Nobel Prize winner Daniel Kahneman contends that we have two different systems of thought: an automatic, fast and unconscious system and a premeditated, slow and conscious system.[12] Because experts make use of their intuition, their judgement is not always taken seriously. Why? Because the speed at which they make their unconscious decisions makes it difficult for them to explain the underlying rationale. In short, they sometimes find it hard to explain why they do what they do. For this reason, an expert in a domain is not necessarily a good teacher in that domain. That being said, research has confirmed that the decisions of experts, intuitive or not, are still generally more accurate than those of others.

Anders Ericsson: the importance of deliberate practice

So far in this discussion about the acquisition of expertise, the role of practice has been emphasised. Over the years, however, many commentators have been inclined to ask whether or not (unique) talent actually has a greater defining impact. A similar discussion has also been raging in scientific circles for decades about the extent to which innate skills (another way to describe talent) are the most important factor in developing expertise: this is the crux of the nature versus nurture debate. One of the leading figures in this debate is the American professor Anders Ericsson, who believes that acquisition of expertise is a process of long-term and focused practice, which he refers to as deliberate practice.[13] In his view, inborn talent plays no role (or at best a marginal one).[14] How long is long-term? Opinions on this differ significantly.

No, there is no such thing as the 10,000 hour rule

Thanks in part to the publicity given by journalist Malcolm Gladwell,[15] Ericsson's ideas have become popularly known as the '10,000 hours' rule. This is the idea that you need to practise an activity for a minimum of 10,000 hours to become an expert. In our book *More Urban Myths about Learning and Education* we debunked this idea as a myth, since the figure of 10,000 is just a convenient round number to describe what, in effect, is a very rough average. The actual number of practice hours needed to become an expert can be significantly less or significantly more than this average.[16]

Studies to determine the minimum amount of practice you need to become a superstar in a particular discipline are often difficult to compare, because they require different ways of practising deliberately. According to Ericsson, simply performing or repeating an action is not sufficient: this is no more than what might be called 'ordinary' practice. Having said that, a large-scale meta-analysis study carried out by Macnamara and colleagues concluded that the effect of deliberate practice in general should not be exaggerated.[17] For sports the effect is very clearly demonstrable but for other disciplines the position is less clear-cut. Differences between individuals and also differences in the types of task to be practised seem to have a greater role in explaining variations in performance levels than Ericsson initially believed.

Conclusion

The route leading from beginner to expert is a long and complex one, full of twists, turns, pitfalls and dead ends. Ericsson notwithstanding, practice alone is not enough: it needs to be accompanied by good guidance and advice. Innate skills and talents seem to play a less important role than was once thought but this (sadly) does not mean that everyone can become an expert in everything. Other factors still play a role, factors that are covered in more depth in the chapters on personality development (Chapter 1.2), intelligence (1.5) and motivation (4.2).

─── Teacher takeaways ───

What is creativity? And can you learn it?

Test yourself. Take a pen and something to write on. Choose one of the following objects:

- a paper clip
- a piece of paper
- a chair

Now try to think of as many possible ways to use the object that you have chosen.

This is known as the alternative uses task or test. It was originally devised by Guilford in 1967 for the purpose of assessing people's creativity.[18] The test became more widely known after it was used by Sir Ken Robinson in his popular TED talk *Do schools kill creativity?*

Perhaps your paper was not big enough to note down all your ideas? If so, great! Perhaps you are a creative genius in the making. Or perhaps not. The test measures the quantity of your ideas but not their quality. So don't give up the day job just yet. One thing, however, is certain, because research has proved it: intelligence and creativity are not the same thing.[19]

It does indeed seem at first glance as though this test measures creativity as an easily transferable, general skill. However, David Didau and Nick Rose[20] argue that all attempts to measure creativity suffer from the same lack of validity and reliability.

(Continued)

So let's ask another question. Of the following two options, who do you think will come up with the most (qualitatively) creative solutions for fixing a leaking sink?

a.   a musician
b.   a plumber

The answer seems obvious: the plumber. But who would be most creative when it comes to writing a song? Probably the musician. Just because the plumber is creative at finding solutions for leaking sinks, this does not mean that they are automatically creative in other fields. Creativity takes many different forms in many different domains, and experience and expertise in a domain can always strengthen a person's creative abilities.

In other words, creativity is not a general, overarching skill. In fact, creativity is not really a skill at all but is more a human quality or 'trait', which cannot be learnt to any significant degree, in contrast to the more influenceable 'states', which are personality characteristics that remain relatively stable over time. But if creativity is very difficult to learn, this does not mean that the creativity a person already possesses cannot be stimulated by organising the best possible environment (see Chapter 1.1 on nature and nurture).

Smith and Firth[21] have offered the following definition of creativity as: 'The ability to create something, ideally something that is useful or entertaining in some way. Typically, this is going to involve a rearrangement of existing parts or concepts (words, musical notes, mathematical notation, etc.) rather than making something completely new and unrecognisable.' In other words, creativity is about making new and useable combinations of existing information.

Viewed in this way, creativity cannot be seen in isolation from domain-specific knowledge and skills. We have already seen this with the musician: great at writing songs, sometimes rubbish at fixing sinks. Education plays a huge and important role in developing the necessary knowledge and skills that allow creativity to express itself.

Some more examples?

- Finding a creative solution during a game of chess is easier for an expert than a beginner.
- Finding a creative solution during a home renovation project is easier for someone who has a good knowledge of tools and techniques.
- In the classroom: suggesting creative solutions for environmental problems will be easier for pupils who have a better background knowledge on this subject.
- If you play a musical instrument, you will write and play more creatively if you have a knowledge of notes and chords than if you have no such knowledge.
- You can be perfectly creative on a football field and in the kitchen but have no creativity whatsoever when it comes to mathematics, languages, etc.

Put simply: 'Creativity is intelligence having fun' (Albert Einstein).

Can we learn and grow creativity?

Short answer: no, but we can stimulate it and bring it to the surface by creating the right conditions.

Long answer: the good news is that most research has confirmed that we become more creative as we get older. This is only logical, since by then we have acquired much more domain-specific knowledge, which is what you need to be qualitatively creative. Does this mean that basic knowledge is less important and that we no longer need it? Far from it! This is a major misconception: we still need schools to teach this crucial domain knowledge to our children and young people. It is the first important step on the way to improving their creativity in the long run.

In summary (and based on a broad vision of creativity):[22] without knowledge there can be no creativity (probably).

How can this knowledge best be imparted to our children and young people? In most cases, it is unlikely that they will acquire this crucial basic knowledge through discovery-based learning. Consequently, it is better to use a more structured and controlled approach with a teacher, as is the case, for example, with direct instruction. However, as soon as the pupils possess the necessary basic knowledge, they can be stimulated to develop more creative 'out-of-the-box' thinking under the right conditions. This is a matter for which there is still room for improvement in many schools. What is needed is the creation of a safe learning climate in which pupils do not need to be afraid of making mistakes, being laughed at or criticised. In short, they need a place where they can be themselves, a place of autonomy (see Chapter 4.2 on motivation) where they can have the courage to experiment and take risks.

How can creativity be stimulated?

In addition to developing your pupils' basic knowledge and constructing a safe environment in which they can dare to be imaginative, clever, artistic, original, inventive, inspired, etc., you can also help to stimulate their creativity by using the following tips:

Do's

1. Work at improving their domain-specific knowledge (expertise).
   - As soon as pupils have a sound basis of knowledge, they can be encouraged to question assumptions, view situations critically and develop qualitatively creative solutions.
2. Stimulate pupils to make connections between different domains of knowledge.
   - On the basis of a good basic knowledge of different domains, encourage pupils to creatively translate thoughts or solutions from one domain into a different domain.

(Continued)

3.   Create a psychologically safe learning climate.

- Pupils must feel confident to experiment and think 'out of the box' without the possibility of being criticised or laughed at by their teachers and classmates. They must have the courage to take risks, make mistakes and be themselves.
- One way to do this is to ensure that creative tasks are not marked with points or grades. Stress to 'perform' can limit a creative spirit.
- As a teacher, also ensure that pupils are not harshly criticised or ridiculed by their classmates. They must be free to exchange ideas, however seemingly bizarre, without fear. Establish an atmosphere in which out-of-the-box thinking is valued and appreciated.

4.   Invest in 'away time'.

- Our minds need a certain amount of away time, time when we do not need to concentrate or be attentive. Make sure that your pupils have sufficient time to be 'unaware' or 'absent'. This kind of 'time-out' is not only useful for allowing our brains to relax, for processing emotions and for putting things in perspective but also helps to bring our creative inspiration to the surface.
- Creative ideas often emerge when you least expect it: under the shower, during a walk, tidying up your room, just doing nothing... Free time is not wasted time.
- With this in mind, allow your pupils sufficient (coffee) breaks, quiet moments, chat time, etc. It is an illusion to think that children and young people can concentrate non-stop throughout a 50-minute lesson.

5.   Encourage daydreaming or mind-wandering.[23]

- During periods of away time, encourage pupils to clear their heads and let their minds wander. This kind of random and fragmentary thinking stimulates creativity.

6.   Encourage sufficient sleep.

- This is not always easy with children and young people but it is a crucial factor. After your REM sleep (the dream phase), you reach a kind of hyper-associative state in which your thoughts are given free rein, some of which resurface in your waking hours. Like daydreaming, night-time dreaming is also good for your creativity.[24]

7.   Encourage plan making.

- This is something else that is not always easy with children and young people. Even so, planning and structure promote mental rest, which in turn is necessary to allow your brain to get into the right kind of 'mind-flow' that can lead to interesting mental connections and good ideas.

- Good planning, good structure and a degree of automatic thinking help to create the mental bandwidth that gives our brains the space to be creative. Think of the scarcity model devised by Mullainathan and Shafir.[25]
- It may sound contradictory to claim that planning and structure can lead to creativity but the reasoning is simple. Without planning, you will always be trying to catch up with all the things you still have to do and therefore will be continually under pressure. Your brain reminds you constantly of all these uncompleted tasks, which also take up much of its own available capacity. As a result, your mind will never be at rest and it is precisely these moments of rest that you need to develop creative ideas.
- Good planning does not mean over-planning.[26] Trying to 'programme' an hour or two of 'creativity' into your busy schedule simply will not work. Most of us will have had moments in the classroom or during a meeting when we need to find a creative solution but are simply unable to do it, because we are too busy thinking about what we have already done today and what we still have to do before we can go home!

8. Develop routines and habits.

- Developing an automatic approach to certain tasks (like your morning routine or cooking a meal that you have cooked a hundred times before) means that you no longer have to think about them consciously, so that you once again free up capacity in your brain for the kind of thinking that can lead to creativity.[27]

9. Make time for creativity.

- Do not expect pupils to dream up creative ideas in fixed periods of 30 minutes or an hour. Creative thought takes time and requires a different kind of concentration. Switching continually from one task to another (sometimes known as multi-tasking[28]) costs time and, above all, mental energy. If you want to work creatively, you need to give it time. Creativity cannot be forced; it will come when it is ready.
- Make sure that pupils are not disturbed during their creative work. Teach them that distractions and interruptions are not beneficial for the in-depth creative thinking process. It is well known that after an interruption it can take quite some time for children and young people to refocus their thoughts on their tasks.[29]

Don'ts

10. Do not organise brainstorming sessions.[30]

- Decades of research have consistently shown that brainstorming in groups produces fewer ideas than when the same number of people first

(Continued)

work alone and only subsequently come together to explain their ideas to each other.

- It is much better to transform brainstorming sessions into debating sessions, during which solutions are freely discussed and critically assessed in a group context.

11. Do not try to force yourself to come up with a creative idea at a specific moment.

    - It is simply not possible to say: 'I am going to be creative now!' Good ideas come when they are ready, often 'out of the blue'. Something in your brain clicks, often when you least expect it, and you get a sudden insight, the well-known 'aha' experience, perhaps when you are in the shower or out walking. Our brains cannot be ordered to be creative, no matter how hard you try.

12. Do not set broad and highly open creative tasks.

    - This can lead to cognitive overload. If a task is too open and wide-ranging, so that pupils have no clear idea of what the teacher wants, their brains are forced to stumble around blindly, which is not good for creativity.
    - David Didau and Nick Rose stated that you cannot make pupils creative just by setting them 'creative tasks'.[31] A supposedly creative task will not necessarily lead pupils to formulate creative ideas.
    - A viable alternative? Set well-structured tasks with clear limits and clear problems that need to be addressed and overcome. You can see it as the difference between renovating an existing house and building a new one from scratch. The former is a challenging yet feasible task with clear limits, while the latter is so complex that it is likely to lead to cognitive overload. Unless, of course, you are an architect!

13. Do not create situations that result in pressure, stress, tension and anxiety.

    - Make sure that the pupils do not feel pressured to perform or are afraid of suggesting a 'wrong' solution. The pupils must feel safe and at ease.
    - Create a safe learning environment in which creativity is both possible and allowed!

Endnotes

1. Kalyuga et al., 2003.
2. de Groot, 1965.
3. Chi et al., 1981.
4. Chi, 1978.
5. Sweller et al., 1998.
6. Legassie et al., 2008.
7. Vergauwe et al., 2015.
8. Bravata et al., 2020
9. Fitts & Posner, 1967.
10. Alexander & Judith, 1988. See also Alexander, 2003.
11. Hatano & Inagaki, 1986.
12. Kahneman, 2003. For a criticism of the dual-process models of information processing, see Glöckner & Witteman, 2010.
13. Ericsson et al., 2009.
14. Ericsson, 2007.
15. Gladwell, 2008.
16. De Bruyckere et al., 2019.
17. Macnamara et al., 2014.
18. De Bruyckere et al., 2015a; De Bruyckere et al., 2019.
19. Sawyer, 2011.
20. Didau & Rose, 2016.
21. Smith & Firth, 2018, p.116.
22. Sawyer, 2011.
23. Geraerts, 2015.
24. Smith & Firth, 2018.
25. Mullanaithan & Shafir, 2013.
26. Pastoor, 2019.
27. De Bruyckere, 2018.
28. De Bruyckere et al., 2015a.
29. Kraft & Monti-Nussbaum, 2020.
30. De Bruyckere et al., 2015a.
31. Didau & Rose, 2016.

4

BEHAVIOUR

In this final section the actions and behaviour of children and young people are central. Perhaps you have had experience of children who find it hard to concentrate or have difficulty with planning? As a parent, teacher or caregiver, you will almost certainly have experienced how challenging it can be to motivate children and young people. And not necessarily for 'serious' matters. Perhaps all you want them to do is to turn out the light when they leave the room or maybe learn to eat a little more healthily? These are the kinds of themes that will be discussed during this last chapter. Our actions and behaviour are controlled by our executive functions. These functions help us to focus and to plan, two aspects of life for which children and young people are not always renowned. So what can you do as an adult to help? We will look at how children and young people can be motivated, examining both intrinsic and extrinsic motivation, as well as the important grey area in between. Finally, we will show that there are ways in which behaviour can actually be influenced and how our own mental fallacies can be used to give children and young people (and adults!) a 'push' in the right direction. This is the domain of behavioural economics.

4.1

EVERYTHING UNDER THE CONTROL OF OUR EXECUTIVE FUNCTIONS

What questions does this chapter answer?

1. What exactly are our executive functions?
2. How do executive functions develop?
3. To what extent and in what ways can you work to improve and support executive functions?

A young boy is sitting in a room. He is watching a marshmallow intently. He is alone in the room and he does not know that he is being filmed. He looks around furtively. You can see that he is struggling to control himself. He wants to eat that marshmallow, so badly! But if he can wait until that nice research person comes back, he has been promised that he will get two...

This boy is taking part in the famous Stanford marshmallow experiment devised by Walter Mischel,[1] which was carried out at the university over a number of years during the 1960s and 1970s. The purpose of the experiment was to establish the extent to which young children have self-control. Would children between the ages of three and six years be able to resist the temptation of a marshmallow? Years later, in a follow-up experiment, Mischel and his fellow researchers discovered a number of remarkable correlations: the children who had been better able to control themselves during the experiment when they were young later went on to perform better than average at school,[2] achieve a higher than average level of qualifications[3] and have a lower than average body mass index (BMI).[4] Before you rush off to start experimenting on your child, your pupils or even your partner, you need to remember that this research only showed a correlation, not a causal link. It will become clear in the course of this chapter that the extent to which these correlating phenomena are the result of nature and/or nurture is a very difficult question to answer.

Inhibition, or the ability to control yourself, is one of the human body's executive functions. So what exactly are these functions? That is another question that is far from simple to answer. You could describe the executive functions as the process by which a person's behaviour is directed and controlled for the purpose of achieving a specific goal. This is the definition offered by Slater and Bremner.[5] You can compare your executive functions with a kind of command centre in your head that helps to ensure that you can concentrate, plan things and react flexibly to unexpected circumstances. As soon as you can no longer do things on automatic pilot, you need your executive functions.[6]

Executive functions, behavioural economics and that one favourite purchase!

As we already mentioned in the section on expertise, Daniel Kahneman believes that we have two systems or channels of thought in our brains: a fast and intuitive system (our automatic pilot) and a slow and rational system (our command centre or cockpit; in short, our executive functions).[7] Imagine that during the winter sales you see the pair of shoes (or piece of furniture or hard-to-find CD) that you have been looking for at a knock-down discount price. Clearly an opportunity too good to miss! But was this purchase well considered? Did you think consciously and rationally about what you were doing before you opened your wallet or purse? Or did you simply give in to the temptation of your fast and intuitive system? Which system gained the upper hand? It is in situations of this kind that we need our executive functions, to prevent us from buying everything in the shop! In the section on behavioural economics we will look more closely at these two systems of thought and how they can sometimes mislead us, so that we fail to make conscious and rational choices. At this stage, suffice it to say that you don't need to be too hard on yourself if you occasionally succumb to bargain buys, a bag of chips or an extra glass of wine at your favourite bar! The good news is that there are ways to make yourself aware of when you are more susceptible to the influence of your intuitive system and can rely less on your rational system.

During the writing of this book, we have consulted various sources but it is not really possible to give a clear definition of human executive functions, because there is no consensus about the different dimensions they contain and perhaps still conceal.[8] The best we can do is to look at what some of the leading researchers in the field have concluded.

Two of the most popular authors on this subject are Dawson and Guare. They have provided the following list of executive functions, which they actually regard as skills:

- Response inhibition: the extent to which you think before you do something or say something.
- Emotional control: the extent to which you are able to hold your feelings in check, in order to achieve a goal or to complete a task.
- Sustained attention: the extent to which you are able to maintain focus, irrespective of distraction, tiredness or boredom.
- Task initiation: the extent to which you are able to start and complete tasks on time, without delay.
- Flexibility: the extent to which you are able to adjust your plans to take account of setbacks, obstacles, new information, mistakes, etc.
- Goal-directed persistence: the extent to which you can persevere to achieve a goal without being distracted by other needs or questions.[9]

In earlier editions of their book – for example, the edition published in 2009 – metacognition was also listed as an executive function but it was no longer included in the 2018 edition.

Adele Diamond's list is shorter, perhaps because she refers to 'core' executive functions:

- Inhibition: the extent to which you have the necessary self-control to resist temptation and protect yourself from impulsive behaviour.
- Interference control: the extent to which you can focus your attention and not allow yourself to be distracted.
- Your working memory.
- Cognitive flexibility: the extent to which you are able to see things from different perspectives (this relates to your ability to think creatively out of the box and your ability to adjust quickly and flexibly to changing circumstances).[10]

You will note that certain aspects of this list correspond with Dawson and Guare's list but even when use is made of the same words, like 'flexibility', it is still possible that they do not necessarily mean the same thing.

One of the very first writers to discuss executive functions was the Russian scientist Alexander Luria. His list was very different from what we have seen so far:

- Anticipation: having realistic expectations and understanding the consequences of choices.
- Planning: being able to organise things.
- Execution: being flexible while remaining focused on the goal.
- Self-monitoring: being able to keep your feelings under control, while also recognising mistakes you might make while implementing a task.[11]

One of the few things that everyone seems to agree about is that executive functions are important. Adele Diamond argues that they are an even more important predictor for success in life than intelligence. However, because this is still a relatively young branch of research, there is currently less consensus about what these functions involve. Even so, this has not prevented researchers from looking at the possible role of executive functions in the raising and education of children and young people.

Yet another theory about autism: the lack of executive functions

There are different theories about what autism actually might be, most of which supplement or nuance each other. This theme goes beyond the scope of this book but here is a summary of the most important theories, the first of which we have already touched upon in earlier chapters:

- The theory of mind hypothesis: this hypothesis suggests that people with autism have difficulty in understanding other people's thoughts and convictions.
- The central coherence hypothesis: this hypothesis suggests that autism is related to an inability to see the coherence and interconnectedness of things, pointing to the difficulty that people with autism experience in integrating information, tending instead to perceive this information as separate elements. A variant of this hypothesis is the concept of context blindness, as a result of which names, faces and content are linked to specific situations, which makes it difficult to recall or recognise them again in a different situation.[12]
- A third hypothesis relates specifically to executive functions. This executive function hypothesis suggests that autism is caused by the reduced functioning of executive functions like inhibition, planning and mental flexibility. Consequently, children and young people who are positioned somewhere within the autistic spectrum find it harder to direct their own actions independently. Consider, for example, the seemingly straightforward task of filling a bookcase. While this is a relatively simple task for most children and young people, it can require considerably more effort from people with autistic spectrum disorder (ASD), because it involves planning and foresight: you have to know what you need, what you do not need, and when. Any variation from fixed formats and routines makes this task even harder. However, it is important to note that this hypothesis, if correct, only explains part of an autistic person's behaviour but by no means all of it.[13]

How do executive functions develop?

Whichever classification of executive functions you use, it is clear that the impulse control of a baby is very different from the impulse control of a primary school child or teenager. Thanks to brain research (amongst other things), we know that the various executive functions are activated at different moments during the child or young person's development. It also seems that these functions are closely related to the frontal part of the brain, known as the prefrontal cortex. This part of the brain reaches optimal functionality around 23 years of age, when it is best capable of offering effective resistance to stronger emotional systems in a young person's brain. This explains (but only in part!) the greater propensity for risk behaviour among adolescents and teenagers, as expressed in their greater willingness to experiment with sex, drugs and (in some cases) even vandalism. This development of inhibition actually takes place during infancy but this does not mean that typically 'infantile' behaviour cannot occur at a later stage, such as emotional decision-taking, impulsive reactions and the seeking out of dangerous situations.[14]

The ability to plan becomes evident in primary school children around the time of their eighth birthday but can experience decline again during the years of adolescence.

Which functions at what age?

Diana Smidts has summarised the broad age ranges at which the various executive functions become active, although it needs to be borne in mind that this can vary from child to child and that the progression is not always as linear or as harmonious as she suggests, and that periods of regression may be possible:

- 0-3 years: motor impulse control (more control over bodily movements), activation of the working memory (being able to remember one or two things at the same time).
- 3-6 years: verbal impulse control (waiting your turn before saying something), flexibility in thinking and doing (seeing things from someone else's perspective), further development of the working memory (being able to remember two or three things at the same time).
- 6-9 years: awareness of time, planning (looking further ahead than 'now'), emotional impulse regulation.
- 9-13 years: more detailed planning, self-evaluation (insight into your own behaviour).[15]

Nature and/or nurture

Are executive functions something that you get from your genes or are they shaped through interaction with your environment? This is not an easy question to answer, because the answer can vary, depending on the definition or the list of executive functions that you use. For, example, the fact that research has demonstrated that the level of a child's ability to focus their attention at the age of three years is a good predictor for that child's level of ability to focus their attention at the age of five years certainly suggests a strong genetic element.[16] This same conclusion can also be deduced from one of the shortcomings in Walter Mischel's original research. Most of the children who took part in the original marshmallow test came from comfortable backgrounds, which meant that the children had been raised in almost optimal conditions. The fact that differences in their impulse control were not only noted but also reflected in their later level of school performance again seems to point to a hereditary component in executive function skills.

But... (there is always a but) ... there are also a number of environmental factors that can help to ensure that your executive functions do not develop properl and/or perform well. Stress during the early phases of life can hinder general brain development, which in turn has a negative impact on various executive functions.[17] This also helps to explain why poverty can impede the development of certain cognitive skills.[18] In a similar way, experiencing money problems in later life can make it harder to keep your emotions under control.[19] Even the performance of the working memory of children as young as 12 years of age can be affected by the income of their parents,[20] with the relevant research concluding that a subsequent rise in the parents' income can reduce the effect previously caused by a significantly lower income.

Drink can also have a negative effect on executive functions but perhaps that is something you have already seen or experienced for yourself. It is not without good reason that alcohol has a reputation for removing inhibitions. But it also has much more serious effects than that. Alcohol intake by the mother during pregnancy – even in relatively small amounts – can be associated with reduced executive functions and poorer levels of attention in children by the time they are five years old.[21] Likewise, alcohol can reduce the performance of executive functions in the drinkers themselves,[22] while reduced executive functions also make it harder to keep the amount you drink under control.[23]

Perhaps you have noticed that you find it more difficult to concentrate when you are tired? No, you are not imagining things. Tiredness can also have a negative influence on the performance of executive functions.[24]

Executive functions and ADHD

Perhaps when reading the above paragraphs your thoughts turned automatically to children with ADHD. ADHD stands for attention deficit hyperactivity disorder – and the condition is well named. Amongst others, Barkley describes ADHD as the imperfect functioning of key executive functions, such as the working memory and self-regulation (impulse control).[25] That being said, more recent research has concluded that it would be wrong to define ADHD purely on this basis.[26]

Can you work to improve executive functions?

Once again, the answer is yes and no. And once again, it depends on the list and the definitions of executive functions that you use. We know, for example, that working to improve the metacognition of children – in other words, the way they learn – can have a major positive effect.[27] But there is also a difference between effects in the short term and effects in the long term. Similarly, various research studies have shown that working to improve executive functions can also have an immediate positive effect. Sadly, however, there is no evidence to show that this effect is lasting.[28] Nor is it the case that if you are able to improve a specific executive function, such as inhibition control, that the other executive functions will also automatically improve.[29]

Nevertheless, perhaps it is still worth working to improve children's executive functions, even if only for the short term, providing this makes it possible for them to learn more during the temporary period when their functions are improved.

Promising?

If you examine recent studies that suggest that a lasting positive effect on executive functions might be possible, you will often see that they emphasise the importance of rituals and ritual learning. One of these studies was based on the condition that the test children had to copy as closely as possible everything that the teacher did or told them. The study - details of which were published in *Child Development* - was conducted to the highest professional standards, with double pre-tests and post-tests. A number of seven- and eight-year-old children were divided randomly into three groups and the research was conducted at two different locations in widely different contexts: Slovakia and Vanuatu (close to Fiji).

The 210 children were divided into three groups of 70 children each:

1. The control group;
2. A group in which the children had to copy everything the teacher did or told them but were also given an explanation about the value of what they were doing;
3. A group in which the children had to copy everything the teacher did or told them but were not given an explanation about the value of what they were doing.

The purpose of the third group in particular was to explore the possibilities presented by ritual learning. What did the results show? The performance of groups 2 and 3 were better in the post-tests than in the pre-tests, with group 3 doing even better than group 2. What is so special about this approach, and why is it important? The approach is actually a highly

(Continued)

classical and traditional method of teaching/learning, in which the pupils are given no explanation about the 'why' of what they are doing, which runs contrary to many modern pedagogic recommendations.[30] These results are interesting, even promising, but much further research still needs to be done, since it is possible that some rituals work better than others in this respect.

Practical examples of how you can work to improve executive functions

Harvard University has published a useful oversight of activities that have proven their worth – in the short term – for helping to improve the executive functions of children and young people, depending on their age (from babies to adolescents).[31] These are concrete and worthwhile tips, although some of them are probably things that you already do:

For children aged between 6 and 18 months:

- **Peek-a-boo games** or **hiding things** and making them appear again help to exercise the child's working memory. With very young children you need to make this as simple as possible but as they get older you can make it more difficult, by making them look for what you have hidden. 'Warm, warmer... oh no, now you are cold.' By the time they are 18 months, you can play the well-known game with a ball or object under one of three cups, which you move all the time.
- As soon as the child is old enough, it is a good idea to play **hide-and-seek**.
- Using **rhymes** to match what you do with the child or what they do themselves also helps to stimulate the working memory.
- Young children like to imitate. Stimulating this can help to prevent distraction and can encourage greater self-control. Giving them **toy versions of the things they see adults using** – for example, a brush – can also be useful.
- **Finger or hand games**, preferably with appropriate accompanying songs, also teach young children how to copy and are beneficial for both the working memory and linguistic development.
- It is very important to **talk enough** to young children, not only to fix their attention but also to improve their working memory and self-control.

For children aged between 18 and 36 months:

- **Active running, imitation and singing games** help to train children's working memory by requiring them to follow simple 'rules'. Think of games like 'hands, knees and boomps-a-daisy', where children need to focus their attention on the words of the song. Older children in this phase can start to play running games like 'freeze dance' or 'Simon says'. These games encourage the focusing of attention and the control of other impulses (inhibition).

- **Finger or hand games** with appropriate accompanying songs continue to be useful as a means of challenging children to focus their attention.
- In **conversations** with the child, you can now start to ask questions like 'Why did you do that?' or 'What did you think of the birthday party?' or 'What are you going to do next?' This not only encourages the child to think about past actions but also to think about planning their follow-up actions, which can become rooted in the working memory. **Talking about feelings** is also important for stimulating the regulation of emotions.
- **Sort-and-match games** and **simple puzzles** help to train the child's working memory and to focus their attention. With matching and sorting, only use a single criterion (colour, shape, size, etc.). With puzzles, use two criteria (form and colour).
- The child's impulse to imitate can now gradually be converted into **'let's pretend' games**, like 'playing house', in which ideally the child should determine the role of the adult who is playing along, since this encourages seeing things from someone else's perspective but is also a first step towards giving instructions and regulating others. As the adult, make sure that you ask enough questions and that there are enough different things to play with.

For children from 3 to 5 years:

- General: At this age, the executive functions develop very quickly. This needs careful and appropriate guidance, which should gradually be scaled down to zero, so that children can develop their regulatory skills independently.
- **'Pretend' games** become more complex and evolve into cooperative games with age peers, in which they often regulate each other's behaviour. This is a basis for regulating their own behaviour later on. If you want to elevate these games to a higher level:
  - Once again, provide enough realistic toys and playing material. Later on, let them choose these materials themselves. The reuse of familiar objects (for example, using the tube of a kitchen role as a telescope) stimulates their cognitive flexibility.
  - Provide them with rich experiences that they can copy by reading to them from books, using videos and taking them to visit interesting places.
  - Let children plan their play and even put it down on paper, either alone or in a group. This teaches them how to plan and how to keep other impulses under control (inhibition), while also improving language and social problem-solving skills.

- Stimulate **storytelling** as much as possible by asking them to write down, draw or play their own stories. One interesting way to do this is the co-creation of stories in a group: one child starts, the next one continues, and so on. This not only requires all the children to be attentive but also to remember previous changes in the plot in their working memory and to adjust their own thinking to reflect them, which all demands a significant degree of self-control.
- **Song-and-dance games** help to focus attention and encourage the suppression of other impulses by requiring the children to follow patterns and rules (for example, rhythm, synchronised singing and dancing, freeze games, fast-slow dancing, looking for a dancing partner when the music starts, etc.). Songs that involve continuous repetition (for example, 'Ten green bottles') help to train the working memory.
- New physical challenges during **movement games** at school or in the playground (for example, obstacle courses, climbing frames, etc.) teach children to evaluate and adjust their actions, as well as emphasising the need to persevere to achieve a goal. Also provide **calmer activities** (for example, balancing games, yoga, etc.) that teach them to reduce the number of stimuli and to focus their attention.
- Cognitive flexibility can continue to be trained in **'sort-and-match' games**, which at this age can be made more complex by using a mix of different rules. A good example is a lotto or bingo game in which the child is not asked to indicate the matching word or number but its opposite (for example, the picture showing 'day' if the card for 'night' is drawn). This teaches them to suppress certain responses and trains the working memory.
- **Cooking with your child** is a good way to teach them how to focus (for example, on the weighing of ingredients) and also how to hold impulses in check until they receive new instructions.

For children from 5 to 7 years:

- Challenging but feasible **board games** are an ideal way to further develop the executive functions of children of this age. Memory games train the working memory, while games like *UNO* stimulate cognitive flexibility, by requiring the children to adjust their strategy to the cards that are played. A game like *Jungle Speed* – in which each child tries to grab the totem first when the symbol on their card matches someone else's – encourages concentration and attention but also inhibition and self-control, when your card is not a match. Every board game that involves strategy is good for the working memory (remembering different steps and moves), flexibility (reacting to changing situations) and inhibition (holding in your excitement or disappointment at a good or bad move or card).

- **Physical games** like musical chairs, cat-and-mouse tag and freeze dance train fast responses in some situations and the holding in of responses in other situations.
  - ○ **Fast ball games** like dodge ball train skills that include rapid decision-taking, self-control, continuous monitoring and compliance with rules.
- **Complex clapping songs** like 'Pat-A-Cake' demand cognitive flexibility and stimulate both inhibition and the working memory. **Songs with continuous repetition** should now become more complex at this age (for example, 'Old McDonald had a farm'), with the aim of further challenging the working memory. **Repetitious memory games** like 'I go on holiday and take with me...' have a similar effect.
- **Brainteasers** (labyrinths, simple word puzzles, matching games, etc.), **logical reasoning games** like *Mastermind Junior* and *Who Am I?* train problem-solving skills that require the use of both the working memory and cognitive flexibility.
- **Search games** are also popular at this age. This can start with relatively simple versions, such as 'I spy with my little eye something beginning with...' or with books like *Where's Wally?* As the children get older, **search books with picture puzzles** (like 'Spot the difference') become more appropriate, since they encourage the selective focusing of attention on the right objects.

For children between 7 and 12 years:

- **Increasingly complex card and board games** now pose even more serious challenges for the working memory, cognitive flexibility and planning, particularly if the games are strategy-based. Examples include hearts, patience and even (for older children) poker, rummy or chess. Card games like Old Maid train attention and speed of decision-making.
- The popular computer game *Minecraft* and the board game *Dungeons and Dragons* are examples of **complex fantasy games** that challenge children to remember and deal with complex information, rules and strategies for the purpose of achieving specific goals.
- At this age, **brainteasers** can now include crossword puzzles, sudoku, a Rubik's cube, etc., all of which are excellent ways to train the working memory and cognitive flexibility, providing the level of complexity is adjusted to reflect the child's age.
- **Physical games** can now also be taken to a higher level:
  - ○ **Organised sports** become increasingly popular. Sports that are based on rules and strategies, like basketball, train the working memory (to remember the rules and strategies) but also require the monitoring of your own and the other player's actions, the taking of quick decisions

and flexible responses to changing situations. Coordination sports, like football, self-evidently stimulate all the executive functions.

○   **Rope skipping games** with particular rules and rhythms, often accompanied by rhymes or songs, are also popular. They are good for the working memory, learning to focus and controlling attention.

○   Laser games or games like paintball help to improve selective attention, monitoring and inhibition, since they require the constant scanning of the environment and rapid responses to potential 'threats'.

•   **Making music, singing and dancing**, often in a more organised way, also become increasingly popular at this age and are all beneficial for the working memory, cognitive flexibility and self-control. The playing of a musical instrument stimulates all the executive functions, since it requires simultaneous coordination of these functions with the movements of your hands.

For adolescents:

•   Adolescents are expected to be able to exercise **self-control** in a number of different environments (school, social activities, etc.). This involves setting goals, making both short-term and long-term plans, the monitoring of these plans and the adjustment of their behaviour, where necessary. It is necessary to give guidance to adolescents about how best to train these skills. Here are a few tips:

○   Stimulate adolescents to plan for specific objectives in the short term (for example, getting their driving licence, saving up enough money for a guitar or a special trip/event). It is only after this short-term approach that you can later teach them how to plan for the long term.

○   Give them advice about the various intermediary steps that may be necessary to reach their objective. For example, what exactly do you need to do to get a driving licence (lessons, theoretical exam, practical exam, etc.)? How are they going to plan and practise for these things? What problems might they encounter along the way?

○   Remind them to systematically monitor their own behaviour and planning. Is everything going the way they envisaged? Has anything changed? In this way, adolescents can learn to identify counterproductive habits and impulsive actions, whilst at the same time remaining focused on and in control of their end objective.

•   Various tools and methods are available to encourage self-monitoring:

○   **Self-talk** is a powerful way to increase self-awareness. Talking yourself through a difficult task step by step in your head helps to put things in perspective and also teaches you to identify problematic patterns of thought and behaviour that can result in strongly negative emotions or can prevent you from reaching your objective. Encourage positive self-talk that is focused on growth in the future and not on failure in the past. What went wrong? How can you do things better next time? These self-reflections can also be written down in a **personal diary**, in which feelings, thoughts, actions, convictions and decisions can be recorded and analysed.

o   Help adolescents to be aware of and **deal with constant interruptions and distractions**, which is so important in our society where mails, smartphones and social media are constantly demanding our attention. It has long been known that multi-tasking is not effective, so teach them to set priorities and to plan accordingly, if two tasks demand their attention at the same time.

o   Encourage young people to learn about other people's motivations and drivers, even if they are different from their own. In this way, they learn to think about alternative scenarios that take account of others.

• The following activities all help to train various self-regulatory skills. It is important to strive for continuing improvement and an increasing level of difficulty.

o   In **competitive sports** young people learn how to monitor their own and other people's behaviour, as well as how to respond flexibly and take quick decisions.

o   **Yoga and meditation** are an excellent way to learn how to maintain your focus of attention. They also reduce stress and teach young people to make more aware decisions, instead of behaving impulsively.

o   **Making music, singing and dancing** continue to be popular among adolescents. From this age onwards, more complicated pieces with more sophisticated rhythms can provide new challenges that will further aid self-regulation.

o   **Drama and acting** are also good for training the working memory and attention.

o   **Logical puzzles and strategy games** should become increasingly complex. **Computer games** can also be beneficial, providing a time limit is set on their use. Games of any kind help to train selective attention, monitoring and inhibition. Games that involve complex fantasy worlds stretch the limits of the working memory.

• Adolescents need to be able to work in a more independent and more organised way, in order to deal with the increasing challenges of studying. Study skills make demands on all the executive functions and the following tips will help young people to cope with these demands successfully:

o   Divide a project or (study) task into easier-to-manage sections.

o   Draw up a feasible plan with intermediate deadlines for each section.

o   Monitor yourself while you are completing each section. Use a timer, check that you understand what is required, and make sure that you are sufficiently focused (for example, that you are not too distracted by your smartphone). If there is something you do not understand or if you do indeed find yourself being distracted, try to establish the causes and take action to put things right, certainly for next time. How and where can you find more help? How can you prevent distractions? Set a number of key moments for self-monitoring; for example, when you leave home, when you submit a task, etc.

o   Minimise distractions. Be aware of the crucial moments when you most need to focus. Turn off your smartphone and find a quiet and stimulus-free room in which to work.

o   Use memory aids for the organising of your tasks, for example, a to-do list.

o   Keep a checklist (either digital or analogue) of your deadlines.

o   After completing the task, reflect on what worked and what did not work. Make a list of the things that helped you to organise properly and to focus your attention. Also draw the right conclusions from tasks that did not go well. What were the reasons and how can you avoid the same problems next time?

Teacher takeaways

How can you work to improve your resilience?[32]

Because it seldom happens that people are never confronted with setbacks in life, it is a good idea to try and make our children and young people as resilient as possible, so that they are better able to deal with these difficult moments when they arrive. But how can you actually improve your resilience? Sadly, science does not have a magical recipe that is guaranteed to work every time, because children, young people and the contexts in which they find themselves are all different. However, there are a number of things that we can be reasonably confident will help to move us in the right direction.

What are the different components of resilience?

The literature distinguishes between a number of different components that together make up resilience. These components are:

• Self-awareness: this allows you to recognise your own emotions, whilst also providing you with a clear self-image and sufficient self-esteem, as well as the ability to reflect on these things.

• Self-management: this provides you with the necessary self-discipline to express emotions appropriately, to set and follow up objectives, to show initiative, and to work independently.

- Social awareness: this provides you with the necessary degree of empathy, allowing you to recognise and appreciate the perspectives of others, to contribute meaningfully to society, to help others, and to understand relationships.
- Social management: this allows you to communicate, collaborate, take decisions, arbitrate conflicts, reach solutions, build up and maintain relationships, and play a leadership role, if necessary.[33]

The sounds like quite a lot and it is certainly the case that some people will have a greater predisposition for some components than others, just as it is also possible to show more resilience in some kinds of situations than in others.[34]

What resilience is not

Being resilient does not mean that a child or young person will never again feel stress or be upset by setbacks. Such feelings are normal and at some point, the child or young person is almost certain to be affected by them. Resilience is what allows you to bounce back from these disappointments and to carry on as before. This quality is not per se innate, although this differs from person to person, but it is certainly something you can work at improving.[35]

How can you work at your resilience?

The libraries are full of self-help books that offer you tips about how to deal with stress and how to improve your resilience. On the basis of the recommendations issued by the American Psychology Association (APA), here is some advice that it may be useful for parents, caregivers and teachers to bear in mind:

The importance of the collective

The concept of collectivity, as described in the theories of Bronfenbrenner earlier in the book (see Chapter 2.1), also seems to have a positive influence on the development of resilience in children and young people. The more that everyone in the child or young person's environment is on the same wave length and working in the same direction, the greater the likelihood that the child or young person will develop reserves of resilience.[36] In line with the principles of collective teacher efficacy, also described earlier in Chapter 2.1, it is therefore better for a school to have a single policy for social-emotional learning than for each teacher to develop their own approach.[37]

The importance of that one all-important friend

Having a good friend can work wonders for a child or young person's resilience.[38] A British study (amongst others) has confirmed that youngsters who have genuine

(Continued)

and qualitative bonds of friendship with an age peer find it easier to deal with difficult situations and crises. The researchers noted that such friendships help to develop the coping mechanisms that make it possible to come to terms with setbacks and disappointments. Particularly beneficial in this respect is the way in which such friendships open up avenues for expressing deep emotions.

The importance of these key friendships is a factor that the 'village' around the children and young people should also take into account and seek to promote. You cannot 'force' children and young people to become friends but there are a number of things that you can do as a parent, caregiver or teacher to encourage it. For example, when setbacks occur or crisis situations arise, you can give priority to stimulating contacts with those who you know are close friends and others who might give support. Similarly, you can monitor how friendships are developing (in the classroom, in the neighbourhood, in the sports club, etc.) and also highlight the importance of mutual support in various projects, activities and events.

The importance of that one all-important adult

Having a good relationship with an adult can also help to build up a child or young person's resilience. Above all in crisis situations, having an adult on whom the child or young person can rely for appropriate guidance, explanation and understanding is hugely beneficial.[39]

The importance of the group

In addition to the importance of the collective in the wider sense, membership of a group at a more prosaic level can also sometimes stimulate the development of a child or young person's resilience. This can apply to groups of many different kinds: for a hobby, for a sport, riding to school on the same bus each day, etc.[40]

Having the courage to ask for help

Perhaps one of the most important lessons that a child or young person needs to learn is that there is nothing wrong in asking for help if you are finding things difficult. Once again, this is something where your friends and the people around you can play an important role. In education, reference is sometimes made to the zero-line in the number of help lines that are available to a pupil, this being the line of friends and classmates, who are often the first ones to notice that something is wrong. However, it is also important that there are good formal lines of support to which a child or young person in need can turn for help. Make sure that children and young people know that this support exists and where it can be found. It is also worth pointing out that helping others is also a good way to build up your own resilience.

Taking good care of yourself

Mens sana in corpore sano: a healthy body in a health mind. This saying has existed since ancient times, and it contains an important core of truth. Keeping your body fit and healthy can help you to deal with setbacks. This means, of course, that when things go wrong it is not a good idea to turn to alcohol or comfort food for solace.[41]

Setting realistic objectives

Having objectives in your life helps you to look forward to the future, rather than remaining trapped in the present and the past. It can be a great help to children and young people if you teach them how to set and to follow up realistic goals. Unrealistic goals can actually have a negative effect on resilience, as can having a passion that is too all-consuming.[42] Being passionate in the pursuit of your goals is fine but it needs to be tempered by a sense of perspective that makes it easier to bounce back if setbacks are encountered. This is a process of trial and error that can be learnt with the assistance of parents, teachers and caregivers, for example, through the giving of constructive feedback.

Learn how to recognise fallacies and wrong thinking

As will be discussed in Chapter 4.3 on behavioural economics, we all make errors of reasoning and we are all capable of thinking and acting irrationally. No, there is no ghost in the cupboard at the top of the stairs. No, there is almost no chance that the plane taking us on holiday to Spain will crash. Helping children and young people to see where they are making errors of reasoning of this kind can help to make them more resilient. If a child thinks that they are constantly failing, discuss the matter openly and honestly, with the necessary degree of understanding. Yes, of course, people fail from time to time. But failing all the time...? No, there are times when we all do things right... So, focus on them!

Endnotes

1. Mischel, 2014.
2. Mischel et al., 1989.
3. Ayduk et al., 2000.
4. Schlam et al., 2013.
5. Slater & Bremner, 2017.
6. Norman & Shallice, 1986.
7. Kahneman, 2011.
8. Lehto et al., 2003.

9. Dawson & Guare, 2018.
10. Diamond, 2013.
11. Luria, 1966.
12. Pijnacker et al., 2010.
13. Slater & Bremner, 2017.
14. See amongst others: Diamond, 2002; Crone & Dahl, 2012.
15. Smidts, 2007.
16. Kraybill et al., 2019.
17. Fareri & Tottenham, 2016.
18. Kim P. et al., 2013.
19. Mani et al., 2013.
20. Finn et al., 2017.
21. Kesmodel et al., 2012.
22. Montgomery et al., 2012.
23. Blume et al., 2005.
24. Dahl, 1996.
25. Barkley, 1997.
26. Castellanos et al., 2006.
27. See amongst others: Hattie, 2009; Quigley et al., 2018.
28. Jacob & Parkinson, 2015.
29. Kassai et al., 2019.
30. Rybanska et al., 2018. See also: Tian et al., 2018.
31. Bowne, 2015.
32. This section appeared previously in De Bruyckere, 2020.
33. This list is based on: Australian Curriculum Assessment and Reporting Authority (ACARA), 2012; Mansfield et al., 2016.
34. Shonkoff et al., 2015.
35. American Psychological Association (APA) Help Center, 2012.
36. There is considerable evidence for this, a summary of which can be found in Cahill et al., 2014.
37. See also: Ashdown & Bernard, 2012; Durlak et al., 2011.
38. Graber et al., 2016.
39. Shonkoff et al., 2015.
40. Denovan & Macaskill, 2017.
41. APA Help Center, 2012.
42. O'Keefe et al., 2018.

4.2

MOTIVATION

── What questions does this chapter answer? ──

1. What different kinds of motivation can we distinguish?
2. Why is more motivation not necessarily always better?
3. How can we improve the motivation of teachers and pupils?

Motivation and learning viewed differently

In the section on behaviourism in Chapter 3.2 (p. 190), we saw how children can learn and unlearn something by:

1. The repeated linking of a neutral stimulus (for example, a sweet) to a specific situation (for example, the sounding of the school bell) (= classic conditioning).
2. Being punished, rewarded or ignored (= operant conditioning).
3. Seeing a role model punished, rewarded or ignored (= social learning).
4. Observing and copying a role model (= social learning).

In other words, behaviourism assumes that children learn by being conditioned, punished, rewarded or ignored (or by seeing punishments and rewards being given to others). *Classic conditioning, operant conditioning* and *social learning* can indeed explain much of children's learning behaviour but not all of it. We can all sense that children have the ability to spontaneously learn something without the need for punishment or reward. Natural curiosity and the urge to explore were already recognised by Aristotle,[1] who wrote that 'all men by nature desire to know'.[2] Think, for example, of the inquisitiveness of babies, who instinctively put all kinds of different things in their mouths and look on in wonder at everything around them that moves (or doesn't move). White[3] described this as the need of infants and pupils to master their environment.

It was in this context that Deci and Ryan[4] investigated people's *intrinsic motivation* to perform and persevere in certain aspects of their behaviour. By this they meant the activities that we do of our own free will and out of interest, for which we require no reward or no other resulting consequence. In other words, activities that we do for the activity's own sake. In short: you do the activity because you regard it as fun, interesting or satisfying. You study history because history fascinates you, not because you get good marks at school or because, at the end of the road, will get a diploma. These latter aspects are known as *extrinsic motivation*.

Based on their earlier research into intrinsic motivation,[5] Deci and Ryan gradually developed their *self-determination theory* (SDT), which was further researched and elaborated by, amongst others, Vansteenkiste and Soenens.[6] As a result of their studies, we now know that the simple distinction between intrinsic and extrinsic motivation is much more complex than was originally thought.

Other theories about motivation?

In this book, we will examine the self-determination theory at length but it is by no means the only theory that seeks to explain the nature of motivation. Artino and Cook analysed five of the leading theories relating to learning motivation:

- Self-determination theory
- Expectancy-value theory
- Attribution theory
- Goal orientation theories
- Social-cognitive theories

One of the interesting things to note is that these different motivation theories have a number of points in common:

1. Competence and feasibility: the difficulty of a challenge and the likelihood (or not) of being able to complete it successfully can influence the motivation of the learner. Note the use of 'can' rather than 'does': it depends on how the learner experiences the challenge.
2. Value: how important is the activity for the learner? Is the task useful, beneficial, interesting or good for the self-image or reputation of the learner? Or does the learner expect to be made happy, satisfied, proud, etc., if the task is completed successfully? The learner becomes less motivated if there is the possibility of a loss of face or if they are afraid of failing or regard the task as worthless.
3. Control: how much control does the learner have over the different component elements of the task? Learners perform better if they are convinced that their effort can influence the successful implementation of the task; that they can (help to) make the difference and are not just handed everything on a plate, as it were.

4. Cognitive analysis: all five of the theories accept that cognitive processes influence motivation, and not feelings and emotions (at least not in the first instance).

5. Social aspects: motivation is strongly influenced by the interactions of learners with others, not only in the past but also during the implementation of the task and equally with an eye to its effects on their social interactions in the future.

Notwithstanding these common elements, the five theories differ significantly on other matters and in particular on how they are interdependent on each other.[7]

From intrinsic and extrinsic motivation to autonomous and controlled motivation[8]

Whereas in the past a distinction was only made between *intrinsic motivation* (your own internal motivation) and *extrinsic motivation* (motivation generated by some exterior agency), the self-determination theory classifies motivation as running from a total absence of motivation (amotivation) through to intrinsic motivation, with three types of extrinsic motivation in between, which differ depending on the extent of the psychological freedom or autonomy they allow (see Table 4.1).

Table 4.1 Summary of the different kinds of motivation according to the SDT

	Amotivation = 'I can't'	Controlled motivation = 'I must'		Autonomous motivation = 'I want to!'	
Type of motivation		Extrinsic	Extrinsic	Extrinsic	Intrinsic
Type of regulation	No regulation	External regulation	Introjected regulation	Identified regulation	Intrinsic regulation
Motivational drive	Lack of belief or self-confidence	Expectations, reward, punishment	Guilt, shame, fear, internal pressure	Personal value/ purpose	Pleasure, interest, passion
Underlying emotions	Discouragement, fear of failure	Stress, pressure, obligation	Stress, pressure, obligation	Voluntary, (psychological) freedom	Voluntary, (psychological) freedom
Internalisation	None	None	Partial	Full	Not necessary

Adapted from Deci and Ryan (2000).

These different forms of motivation differ in four key areas:

- Regulation: does the motivation come from inside or outside the person concerned?
- Motivational drive: what are the different kinds of reasons that make a person motivated?
- Underlying emotions: what emotions are connected with the person's motivation?
- Internalisation: to what extent does the person internalise or identify with the actions for which motivation is required?

What are the four different forms of regulation?

- **External regulation**

  We have already encountered this type of extrinsic motivation. It is based on punishments and rewards (operant conditioning). Children or young people at school are motivated by the awarding of good grades (reward) or by the desire to avoid detention (punishment). In other words, their behaviour is driven or regulated by external expectations. For example, a pupil might behave well in class simply to avoid getting black marks on their disciplinary record. In other words, their behaviour is dictated by external pressure and is not an act of their own initiative. The pupil feels, as it were, an external obligation to conform to what is expected of them. But as soon as the punishment (or, in other circumstances, reward) is removed, it is open to question whether or not the pupil will continue to display the same behaviour. Remember what we said earlier about the awarding of points for in-class tests.

- **Introjected regulation**

  There is a second type of extrinsic motivation for which the pressure can also come from an outside source. Think, for example, of children and young people who set the bar very high for themselves, as a result of which they place themselves under a kind of internal pressure to perform (during routine class tests, end-of-year exams, etc.). They are motivated to experience feelings of pride (if they score well) or to avoid feelings of guilt and shame (if they score badly). This kind of motivation is also found in the world of competitive sport, in which the high level of performance and expectation that children impose on themselves in their desire to win can lead to serious stress. In both cases – school and sport – the children's self-imposed pressure is often associated with additional pressure from parents, trainers, supporters, etc.

  This explains, for example, why one child needs to be motivated by the parents to study, while another child finds that studying comes naturally. The first child needs external pressure before acting; the second child imposes pressure on themself. Another example? When you were at school, do you remember feeling guilty when you watched your favourite television programme during the middle of the exam period? This feeling of guilt (probably) gave you the motivation to get back to your studying and redouble your efforts as soon as the programme was finished. In instances of this kind, the regulation of behaviour comes from inside your own person, in contrast to external regulation, when your behaviour is a response to exterior factors, like punishment and reward. Hence the use of the term 'introjected regulation': you unconsciously accept the ideas of others and make them your own.

- **Identified regulation**

  Here is another example you might recognise. Putting the dustbins out each week, tidying up your room, repetitive exercises during your sports training, learning to write without making 'i before e except after c' errors, etc.: these are probably activities that you do not regard as being 'fun' but which you nonetheless take it upon yourself to do because you recognise that they are personally important or useful. It is much the same with school rules. It is difficult to motivate pupils intrinsically to abide by these rules but they can still appreciate that they serve a useful function and, consequently, agree to follow them of their own free will. And the same thing applies with showing respect for other people's property. When children or young people can see the personal importance or usefulness of a certain kind of behaviour, they will be motivated from within themselves to perform that behaviour, and not because of any feelings of stress or obligation. They identify with the personal value of the behaviour in question.

  When children or young people make this value (respect) their own, they internalise the regulatory process. Or to express it in slightly different terms: whereas in the past your parents and teachers needed to point out to you the importance of having respect for your own and other people's things, you now understand that this is indeed something important and useful, so that henceforth you identify with that value of your own volition.

- **Intrinsic regulation**[9]

  This is the most well-known form of motivation. It relates to everything that you like to do, everything that is 'fun': playing sports at the weekend, looking forward to your holidays, studying history simply because it fascinates you, etc. In other words, you are motivated because the activity in question pleases, amuses, satisfies or entertains you. You do it because you want to do it of your own free will and without the need for any reward or subsequent beneficial consequence. You go running simply because you enjoy running. It has intrinsic value for you. This is a different kind of motivation from running to get fit or to improve your physical condition, which are both forms of identified motivation.

On the basis of these different systems of regulation, drives, emotion and the extent to which internalisation takes place, it is possible to make a distinction between controlled and autonomous motivation.

- **Controlled motivation**

  Because external and introjected regulation both involve a degree of stress and obligation, these two types of motivation are known as forms of controlled motivation. Based on Vansteenkiste we could describe this as 'must-ivation', emphasising the mandatory or compelling nature of this kind of motivation. Children or young people feel no psychological freedom with regard to the actions involved: they do them because they have to do them and not because they want to do them, as a result of which their motivation will be qualitatively less good.

- **Autonomous motivation**

  Because intrinsic motivation (intrinsic regulation) and identified regulation involve psychological freedom of mind and a voluntary willingness to perform a certain act of behaviour, both these types of motivation are known as forms of autonomous motivation. The person – or pupil – in question does not feel obliged to implement the act but does so because they want to, and therefore they do it with enthusiasm.

Quality versus quantity in motivation

To summarise: the classification of motivation as either extrinsic or intrinsic was gradually superseded by a new distinction between autonomous and controlled motivation. Moreover, whereas in the past it was customary only to talk about the quantity of motivation, it is now more usual to also refer to the quality (or type) of that motivation. In other words, it used to be said: 'the more motivation, the better'; nowadays, it is more a question of: 'is more motivation by definition better?' Numerous research studies have confirmed that autonomous motivation can be associated with psychological well-being in general and positive school outcomes and attitudes in particular, including deeper learning, more independent learning, greater perseverance, better performance, better results, better use of metacognitive strategies (for example, planning) and better transfer of study behaviour.[10]

In contrast, it seems that controlled motivation can be associated with various negative learning outcomes, such as poorer school results, more fear of exams, more fear of failure, an increased inability to deal with failure in a reasoned and respectful manner, superficial processing strategies, less effective use of strategies for concentration and time management, more delay behaviour and a greater risk of drop-out.

The motivation profiles of pupils[11]

Based on the division between autonomous and controlled motivation, Sierens and Vansteenkiste drew up a schedule in which they identified four distinct motivation profiles for pupils (see Table 4.2).

Table 4.2   Schematic summary of motivation profiles

		Autonomous motivation	
		High	Low
Controlled motivation	High	Quantitatively well motivated pupils	Qualitatively weak motivated pupils
	Low	Qualitatively well motivated pupils	Quantitatively weak motivated pupils

From Sierens and Vansteenkiste (2009).

Qualitatively well motivated pupils are pupils who experience little or no pressure and who study primarily because they want to study and enjoy it. It is their own choice. This group displays the most well-adapted methods of learning and performance: they show initiative, actively participate in class, can plan well, study in appropriate surroundings, are determined, etc. This is reflected in deep learning processes and excellent school results.

Qualitatively weak motivated pupils are motivated primarily in a controlled manner. They feel compelled to study, as a result of which they experience external and/or internal pressure and, consequently, stress. They find study tiresome and boring, often engage in procrastination, and seldom adapt their learning processes, which are therefore often superficial. This is the group that contains the most cheats and copycats, which, together with the many other aspects of their negative approach to their studies, is reflected in poor school results.

Quantitatively well motivated pupils display high levels of both controlled and autonomous motivation. On the one hand, they study voluntarily (autonomous) but they also study because they feel a sense of obligation to do so (controlled). These are pupils who like to study but still feel the internal and/or external pressure of tests, exams, etc. As a group, such pupils come across as being very well motivated, in part perhaps because of the (performance) pressure they regularly feel. They tend to follow a strict and rigid planning process, study and revise thoroughly, adjust their learning processes where necessary, and do not easily give up.

Quantitatively weak motivated pupils display, in contrast, low levels of both controlled and autonomous motivation. They feel under no pressure to study but also fail to take the initiative to study voluntarily. When both autonomous and controlled motivation are absent in this manner, we can speak of a situation of amotivation (see Table 4.1). The researchers suggest that these are possibly the pupils who 'breeze through their studies and their school career in a carefree way, and with complete indifference'. They are procrastinators, copycats and sometimes even truants, which is reflected in their poor school results.

Of course, the above profiles can find expression in different pupils in differing degrees. In particular differences can arise:

- Over time: not everyone is qualitatively well motivated all the time.
- From subject to subject: pupils are often better at some subjects than others and there can even be variations within the same subject; for example, good at geometry but poor at algebra.

Should we no longer reward pupils?

Behaviourism has shown (according to the behaviourists) that rewards (or punishments) only work if you apply them consistently and immediately. This is the only way for the 'carrot and stick' method to be effective.

This is hardly a whole-hearted endorsement but the self-determination theory takes an even dimmer view of rewards and punishments, regarding them as a threat to autonomous motivation and a stimulus for controlled motivation. Put simply, the more you reward a pupil, the less that pupil will find motivation from within their own self to display certain types of learning behaviour and will become increasingly driven by the external (extrinsic) prospect of reward and/or the avoidance of punishment. This principle has been demonstrated in an experimental study involving infants, in which they were asked to make a puzzle. Let's imagine that at first they regard this as 'fun'; they are intrinsically motivated to do it. Now imagine that they are given a sweet every time they complete the puzzle correctly. After the fourth or fifth time, they come to expect the sweet automatically. Result? When the researcher stops handing out the sweets, the children stop making the puzzle. Their motivation has been transformed from pleasure (intrinsic regulation) to reward (extrinsic regulation). As discussed earlier, it is equally possible to question the extent to which pupils would continue to study if their efforts were no longer rewarded with good marks. Or is it more the case that the education system is crushing their intrinsic inquisitiveness with its reward-based system of percentages and 'points out of ten'?

As so often, the answer lies somewhere in the middle. When the advocates of SDT talk about the need to limit rewards as much as possible, they are talking primarily about *controlling material rewards*: things like money, sweets, points, medals, stickers, etc.

What exactly does this kind of controlling reward (or punishment) involve?

1. It is a reward that is promised before the desired behaviour has been displayed, in other words, a conditional reward. This might be extra pocket

money if you get ten out of ten in maths, or a bar of chocolate if you have been good all day, or watching your favourite series once you have finished your homework, etc.

2. It is a reward that must be given as promised, once the desired behaviour has been displayed.

3. It is a reward that is material in nature and has a controlling or directive effect.

The issuing of this kind of performance reward does more to undermine autonomy than a task-related reward.

In contrast, an *informative reward* (for example, a social reward like positive feedback) tends to encourage competence and stimulate autonomous motivation, whereas an evaluating or controlling reward tends to promote controlled motivation.

In summary, we can say that punishments and rewards of a certain kind (operant conditioning) do explain certain types of controlled learning behaviour. But rewards and punishments are varied and cannot all be viewed in the same light. It is the type of reward and punishment you give that determines the type of motivation you stimulate. A meta-analysis by Cameron and Pierce[12] has shown that verbal rewards do not have a negative impact on intrinsic motivation in the same way that a material reward does.

That being said, reality is never so clear-cut and in practice it is often the case that a combination of 'good' and 'bad 'rewards (in other words, social rewards and material rewards) is necessary. In the world of professional sport, for example, rewarding a football player after a victorious game with exclusively material rewards (points, prizes, money, etc.) need not automatically damage the player's motivation, providing they are also autonomously motivated to play simply for 'the love of the game'. Viewed in these terms, perhaps the question we should be asking is this: when and in what circumstances do controlling rewards (and therefore controlling motivation) risk gaining the upper hand over autonomous motivation?

A second reason for not completely abandoning rewards and punishments is connected to the age-related development processes of children. While young children certainly need and benefit from external rewards and regulation, as they get older, they increasingly internalise various aspects of their behaviour.[13] Imagine, for example, that a young child is punished for hitting another child. At such a young age, perhaps the child does not yet realise that this kind of behaviour is undesirable, whereas the punishment will serve to make this clear. However, it is important as a parent or caregiver to explain why the punishment is being given. At a later age, this 'reason why I shouldn't do this' will have been internalised and the child will refrain from hitting others of their own volition, because the importance of not doing so is now self-evident. In other words, as the child gets older, an earlier form of external regulation is internalised and converted into identified regulation. Consequently, the use of rewards and punishments with young children does work in circumstances where they still have too little affinity with certain norms and values.

A third reason for persisting with rewards and punishments is when they can be used to help children who are simply unable to motivate themselves; for example, in instances of amotivation. At a more adult level, consider (by way of illustration) your own approach to the COVID-19 measures introduced by various governments. How motivated were you to follow those regulations during the first, second and then third lockdown? From the perspective of the government, it needs to be accepted that no one will regard these regulations as being 'fun'. Consequently, people's motivation to continue following the regulations is likely to be greater if their usefulness is emphasised and everyone can be made to understand their importance to society as a whole. In this way, people can be encouraged to respect the rules, even when they are not under supervision by the authorities, with their powers to punish. That being said, people are, of course, all different, as the section on the Big Five earlier in the book (Chapter 1.2, p. 32) clearly illustrated. In this respect, your personality also helps to determine your motivation. For example, one person will follow the regulations with greater care and from a greater sense of civic duty (in other words, through internal pressure created by fear, social solidarity, feelings of guilt, etc.) than their neighbour next door. The continuum between service-mindedness and self-interest also plays a role in the extent to which you interpret the regulations as being 'useful'. The more you are willing to put yourself at the service of others, the better motivated you will be to keep the rules, sometimes even to your own detriment. However, this also means that there are some people who you cannot motivate by seeking to exploit the 'in your own interests' argument. They simply fail to see the value of the corona measures and respond to them accordingly. For them, punishment awaits, if caught. In other words, it continues to be more sustainable and more effective to focus on autonomous motivation where possible but when this fails to work rewards and punishment are the only remaining tools capable of securing the desired behaviour, even though everyone knows that this behaviour will cease from the moment when the rewards and punishments no longer apply.

Which comes first: motivation or learning?

As has already been seen in this chapter, the link between motivation and learning is complex. But which comes first? Tuong-Va Vu and colleagues concluded in their review study that when we talk about motivation and learning we are actually talking about a cycle on which we can exert influence on both aspects from the outside; for example, through the quality of the instruction and the level of autonomy we give.[14] In contrast to the age-old chicken and egg discussion, this means that it is perfectly possible for motivation - for example, in the form of an urge to explore - to precede learning, whereas it is equally possible that a successful learning moment will create new curiosity and motivation.

The ABC of basic needs

We know that autonomous motivation is a more qualitative form of motivation. Consequently, as teacher, parent or caregiver we wish to stimulate this form as much as possible, so that our children and young people can be better motivated for their studies at school. But how exactly can we do this? The self-determination theory takes as its starting point the assumption that every human being is born with three innate and fundamental psychological needs: autonomy, belonging and competence. When these three basic needs are satisfied, the likelihood is greater that people (and pupils!) will be qualitatively motivated, feel ownership of their behaviour, and perform better. In other words, they promote self-determined or self-regulated behaviour. However, a word of caution is needed. We have deliberately used the words 'likelihood is greater', because the satisfaction of the three basic needs is not an absolute guarantee that autonomously motivated behaviour will result. Likewise, autonomously motivated behaviour is not stimulated exclusively by satisfaction of the three basic needs. There are other ways it can be stimulated.[15]

Leaving this to one side, what do the three basic needs – sometimes referred to as the ABC of the self-determination theory – actually involve?

Autonomy: The need for autonomy finds expression in the experiencing of psychological freedom and choice in relation to a particular form of behaviour.[16] When this need is satisfied, a child or young person feels that they are the owner of their actions, thoughts and feelings, and also feel that they are allowed and able to be their own selves.

Belonging: The need for belonging[17] (or relational connectedness) finds expression in the establishing of good and close relations with others. Children and young people who have the feeling that they can care for others and that others – for example, their teachers and fellow pupils – care for and appreciate them will generally experience a high level of relational connectedness. We can then speak of a warm and safe learning climate.

Competence: The need for competence[18] finds expression in the feeling of a child or young person that they can carry out an activity with success. This is also known as (self-) effectiveness. Pupils feel competent, for example, if they are able to correctly and independently solve a maths problem that they were not able to solve the day before.

How can you work at the ABC of basic needs with children?

A	B	C
Autonomy	Belonging	Competence
Experiencing freedom of choice Being involved in setting the basis for actions	Feeling connected with fellow pupils and the teacher	Feeling capable Being able to achieve goals
BEING ALLOWED AND ABLE TO BE YOURSELF	HAVING GOOD AND CLOSE RELATIONS	GETTING BETTER AND BETTER

How can the teacher improve things?		
Autonomy-supportive style of teaching	Commitment, a warm and safe teaching environment	Structured teacher actions and behaviour

How can the teacher undermine things?		
Controlling style of teaching	Cold learning environment	Chaotic teacher actions and behaviour

Figure 4.1   The ABC of the self-determination theory[19]

How can you work at autonomy?

The central pillar of an *autonomy-supportive style of teaching*[20] is the stimulation of the autonomous functioning of pupils. This must give the pupils the feeling that they are allowed and able to be themselves, so that they can further feel that they are responsible for setting the basis for their own actions and behaviours.

Research has shown that the following teacher actions and behaviours can contribute towards the supportive development of autonomy:

• **Identifying the interests and personal values** of the pupils. This involves attempting to pin-point the inner drivers of the pupils, either by explicitly asking them or else by simply talking and listening to them, so that it is possible to learn more about them indirectly. Pupils need to have the feeling that they are respected and that their opinion counts. So, allow pupils to have their say and take what they say seriously.

- Once identified, it is important to **encourage and nurture the interests and personal values** of the pupils. As a teacher, this can be achieved by allowing them time and options for independent work. When the teacher gives feedback, it is important that it is autonomy-supportive (not 'you must work faster' but 'try to work a bit faster, so that you can finish before the morning break starts') and informative ('why not try this strategy, it might help you to find the answer more quickly?').
- The **encouragement and development of new interests and personal values** is also necessary. Pupils do not regard everything that they are required to learn or do as being fun or useful. For this reason, providing meaningful explanations is crucial for helping pupils to see and understand the personal importance of these matters, so that they will hopefully feel able to identify with the values of the task or behaviour in question.

Table 4.3, based on research by Vansteenkiste and colleagues,[21] takes a deeper look at these three types of autonomy-supportive behaviour, providing a number of examples from and for classroom practice.

Table 4.3 Autonomy-supportive teacher behaviour

A. Identifying interests and personal values		
1. Listening time	Listening carefully to the pupils.	E.g. Walking around the class during group work, informal chats before and after lessons, etc.
2. Talking time (for the pupils)	Giving the pupils the opportunity to express their opinions.	E.g. During roundtable or class discussions, group work, school trips, before or after lessons, etc.
3. Asking what the pupils want	Trying to discover the pupils' interests and values.	E g. Via fill-in forms, by asking for opinions or allowing input for tasks/book lists/weekly themes, in the class/pupil council, etc.
4. Allowing the pupils to participate in decision-making	Trying to discover the pupils' opinions, values and preferences.	E.g. Over deadlines for tasks/tests, themes for investigation/discussion, compilation of the lesson roster/year plan, etc.
5. Expressing empathy	Showing understanding for the pupils' perspectives.	E.g. When a pupil fails to do their homework or scores badly during a test, when dividing up the teams for group work, etc.

(Continued)

Table 4.3   (Continued)

B. Encouraging and nurturing interests and personal values		
6. Allowing time for independent work	Letting pupils work alone to solve problems and complete tasks.	E.g. Independent work with guidance, project work, corner work, etc.
7. Giving pupils their own responsibilities	Generating trust and confidence, allowing the pupils to take independent action to participate in decision-making.	E.g. Allowing the pupils to organise a school trip within certain parameters or to suggest new ideas and initiatives, etc.
8. Providing positive feedback	Giving pupils genuine and unconditionally positive comments.	E.g. 'Nice job!', 'You did that really well', 'Better luck next time', etc.
9. Providing informational tips	Providing supportive information when pupils are experiencing difficulties.	E.g. 'Why not try it this way?', 'Perhaps you should turn it the other way around', etc.
10. Identifying points for improvement in an informational manner	Suggesting supportive ways to perform better.	E.g. 'Perhaps you should analyse this type of problem more thoroughly before you start', 'Next time try consulting this source for a deeper understanding', etc.
11. Offering unconditional encouragement	Motivating pupils to persevere.	E.g. 'Come on, you can do it', 'Just hang in there, it will be easier next time', etc.
12. Offering choices	Giving options that allow pupils to realise their own interests and values.	E.g. Working alone or in pairs, oral or written tests, book choices, task programming, discussion themes, etc. = differentiation on the basis of interests and learning preferences.
13. Using autonomy-supportive (instead of controlling) language	Using 'can' and 'would like' instead of 'must' and 'expect' and using 'I' messages.	E.g. 'I would like you to complete task 10 by the end of the week' and not 'You must complete task 10 by the end of the week' or 'I have the feeling that you haven't really revised enough for this test' and not 'It is obvious that you haven't revised enough for this test'.

14. Avoiding a focus on performance and competition	Placing the focus on individual progress rather than on comparison with other members of the class.	E.g. Avoid ladder competitions but encourage pupils to challenge themselves.
C. Encouraging and developing new interests and personal values		
15. Offering reasons and explanations	Giving specific and meaningful reasons for the completion of tasks.	E.g. 'It is important to make summaries because they help you to remember', etc.
16. Connecting pupils with the learning material	Explaining the use and value of the learning material and the possibility of transfer to other contexts.	E.g. 'Calculating surface areas will be useful later on when you need to know how much paint to buy for painting a wall', 'There are also lots of texts to read in biology, so predictive reading is important in that subject as well', etc.

Based on Vansteenkiste et al. (2007a).

The opposite of an autonomy-supportive style of teaching is a *controlling style of teaching*, in which the pupils are instructed to perform certain tasks that are imposed by the teacher. Perhaps some of you in the teaching profession are thinking: 'What do you expect? We have an obligation to follow a specific learning programme and to achieve certain attainment targets!' This is true but an autonomy-supportive approach does *not* mean that pupils are free to choose and do whatever they like. As we shall see in the section on competence, a certain degree of structure is always necessary. Moreover, it is perfectly possible for teachers to set tasks in an autonomy supportive as opposed to a controlling manner. In both cases the tasks need to be set but with an autonomy-supportive approach it is possible to allow a degree of input from the pupils with regard to matters like the order of completion, the date of submission, etc. The controlling approach allows much less flexibility of this kind; instead, the teacher decides everything and 'enforces' their decisions with the possibility of various rewards and punishments.

Within a controlling style of teaching, it is possible to distinguish two main elements:

- **Controlling behaviour**, in which the teacher prefers to remain in control of all aspects of the learning process and criticises pupils if they do not behave/perform in the manner expected of them.
- **Controlling or compelling use of language**, in which imperative (commanding) forms are used, such as 'must' and 'expect'. The use of this kind of language can induce guilt and shame ('I am disappointed that you have understood nothing'), generate anxiety ('If you don't pass the exam

this time, you will never pass'), and negatively impact on pupils' self-esteem ('This is something we already covered last year and I expected much better results'), all of which can lead to feelings of incompetence and have a harmful effect on self-image and self-confidence.

Table 4.4 takes a deeper look at these two aspects of a controlling teaching style, providing a number of (bad) examples from classroom practice.

Table 4.4   Controlling teacher behaviour

A. Controlling behaviour		
1. Giving solutions and moving on without further explanation	...so that pupils are not given the opportunity to discover or analyse things for themselves.	E.g. Always organising tests in the classical manner, failing to give pupils sufficient thinking time, focusing on outcomes rather than the reasons for those outcomes, etc.
2. Giving criticism	...because the pupils have not performed/behaved as expected.	E.g. 'That is not the right way to tackle that problem, that is not what I taught you.'
3. Placing the emphasis on results	Prioritising good exam/ test results and classroom performance at the expense of individual progress.	E.g. Reading out the scores for exams/tests in class, stressing the importance of a good end-of-year report: 'These things are important!'
B. Controlling language		
4. Giving orders	Instructing or commanding pupils to do things.	E.g. 'Turn to page 46 in your textbooks and do it now!'
5. Using imperative verbs like 'must'	Using phrases like 'You must...' and 'I expect you to...', instead of 'Could you...' and 'I would like you to...'.	E.g. 'You must clean up that mess and you must do it now!', 'I expect you to have completed task 10 by tomorrow', 'You have got to obey me, you have no choice!'
6. Using controlling questions	Asking questions in a compelling and derogatory tone.	E.g. 'Do you actually think you can get it right this time?', 'When are you finally going to behave the way I expect?'
7. Using controlling encouragement	Encouraging pupils but in a peremptory manner.	E.g. 'Come on, one last effort, because everyone is expecting you to do it.'

8. Giving guidance but in a controlling manner	Offering tips but again with a peremptory tone.	E.g. 'You must try a different strategy, if you ever want to succeed.'
9. Giving conditional positive feedback	Only offering encouragement or positive confirmation after satisfactory compliance with a condition or expectation.	E.g. 'Good girl! That's exactly how I told you to do it!'
10. Indicating points for improvement in a controlling manner	Pointing out where improvement must be made but often linked to a threat.	E.g. 'If you ever want to succeed, you are going to have to work a lot harder.'
11. Using guilt-inducing language	Playing on the feelings of guilt and shame felt by pupils.	E.g. 'You have disappointed me', 'I expected better of you', 'You should have been able to do that last time', 'It is time you learnt to stand on your own two feet', 'You will understand later why I am saying this now.'
12. Using language that casts aspersions on the pupils' self-esteem	Playing on the pupils' sense of duty.	E.g. 'In our day...', 'Your generation...'
13. Using deadline statements	Putting the pupils under time pressure.	E.g. 'I expect your project to be finished by next week', 'You must have those exercises completed by tomorrow.'

Based on Vansteenkiste et al. (2007, pp. 17–18).

How can you work at belonging?

Having good and close relationships is important for belonging. The more you feel you belong and the more you feel connected to others, the more motivated you will feel from within yourself to do something and to persevere. This applies equally to pupils at school and adults at work. Having good friends at school improves your motivation to learn and having good colleagues at work makes working more fun and helps you to keep at it for longer.

If you wish to promote a feeling of mutual connectedness between pupils and also with their teachers, it is first necessary to foster a warm and safe classroom environment. To achieve this, it is essential for both the school and its teachers to create as many opportunities as possible to connect. This 'teambuilding' process can take a few lesson hours at the start of the school year but it more than rewards the effort as that year progresses.

Table 4.5 gives some examples of how you can stimulate connectedness and a feeling of belonging at school.

Table 4.5   Tips for creating a greater sense of belonging in the classroom

A. Maintaining positive relationships		
1. Invest in getting to know each other and teambuilding	Not only at the start of the school year but throughout all three terms. Don't forget latecomers and new arrivals.	E.g. Teambuilding and sports days at the start of the year, introductory sessions in the classroom (which can often easily be linked to learning material), round-robin discussions, etc.
2. Get to know your pupils individually	Ask about their personal lives in a friendly and non-intrusive way and do not be afraid to tell them something about your personal life as well.	E.g. Ask about their hobbies, where they live, their wider interests. In return, tell them something about your life – your own hobbies, your first girlfriend/boyfriend, etc. – but set and maintain your own boundaries.
3. Address your pupils personally	Welcome your pupils at the start of the school year and learn their names as quickly as possible.	E.g. Stand by the door as your pupils enter the class and welcome them. Never address a pupil as 'you there in the red pullover' but always use their first name (they will often be pleasantly surprised to discover you know it!).
4. Be physically present in the classroom	Make use of the physical space in the classroom and move regularly between your pupils' desks. Arrange the desks so that this is possible.	E.g. Do not remain seated at your own desk when the pupils are completing exercises but walk through the classroom. If you are using a PowerPoint, you can stand at the back of the class to give your explanation. Position the pupils strategically in the classroom, with nervous or difficult pupils near the front, where you can see and reach them more easily.

5. Believe in your pupils	Demonstrate to your pupils that you believe unconditionally in their ability to grow.	E.g. Even if pupils have performed badly or done something wrong, continue to encourage them and show that you have confidence in them.

B. A warm, positive and safe learning environment

6. Create a safe and positive learning climate	Reassure pupils and treat them with understanding. Respect their opinions.	E.g. Give your pupils enough listening and talking time. Ensure that they can dare to express their opinions and emotions, for example, during class discussions or evaluation moments.
7. Stop bullying before it starts	Act quickly to stop bullying as soon as you become aware of it, at both class and school level (see the teacher takeaway on bullying, p. 162).	E.g. In addition to preventative awareness campaigns, take repressive action to stamp out bullying, if or when it occurs. Ensure that there is an effective bullying policy, tailored to the context of your school.
8. Be enthusiastic	Show that you are also interested in the material they have to learn, using humour wherever possible.	E.g. Giving lessons in a passionate and enthusiastic manner is infectious. The pupils can feel your positivity. Making jokes always helps.
9. Involve the pupils actively in the lessons	Let the pupils have their say.	E.g. Give the pupils ample opportunity to speak, both during classical learning moments and in group work. If some pupils start to dominate these opportunities, find a way to get everyone involved (for example, by choosing random names, using placemats, etc.).
10. Allow failure	Ensure that you create a classroom climate in which pupils feel safe to experiment and make mistakes.	E.g. Do not allow the strongest pupils, who usually know the right answers, to dominate classroom proceedings. This creates too high a threshold for less confident pupils to answer.
11. Avoid creating a stressful and competitive climate	Do not place an exaggerated focus on competition and performance.	E.g. Never read out exam or test scores in the classroom and try to prevent pupils from comparing their performances with each other. Consider *not* awarding points for certain tasks.

(Continued)

Table 4.5 (Continued)

12. Give pupils the opportunity to get to know each other	At classroom level, encourage the pupils to interact with each other. At school level, ensure a degree of continuity in class composition.	E.g. When the pupils do not yet know each other, they feel safer if the teacher decides on group formation. Alternatively, you can use a 'speed-date' session to find good matches. Make sure that pupils do not always sit next to different pupils for lessons in different subjects. A degree of change is fine but make sure that an overall balance is maintained.
13. Let the pupils work together	Plan enough collaborative tasks and lessons, with groups of changing composition.	E.g. Use cooperative work forms (share-share exchanges, placemat, etc.) and other methods to divide the pupils randomly into groups (e.g. playing cards: all the hearts together, online tools, etc.).
14. Adopt an open and positive attitude towards the pupils	Accept every pupil as a unique person and treat them with sincerity, honesty and authenticity.	E.g. Make sure that you always listen to the pupils attentively during difficult conversations (without looking at your watch every 30 seconds!).
15. Be a role model	Behave as you want the pupils to behave, both to you and to others.	E.g. React to discriminatory, racist or other inappropriate comments.
16. Let the pupils evaluate your own behaviour	Ask pupils what they thought of the lesson. Do not be afraid to make yourself vulnerable and show a willingness to listen to their opinions.	E.g. Use exit tickets to find out what your pupils thought of a lesson. What did they understand? What did they not understand? What would they like to have seen explained in a different way? How could the lesson have been improved?

How can you work at competence?

Providing structure for pupils improves their competence, which in turn improves their autonomous motivation. These structure-enhancing teacher practices[22] give your pupils something solid and recognisable to hold on to in the classroom environment, helping them to feel more competent and to become better at what they are learning. As the teacher, you know what exercises and other support you can offer to your pupils by erecting scaffolding in their zone of proximal learning.[23] This will allow them to achieve their goals and to grow in confidence and competence.

You can offer structure to pupils in two different dimensions:

- First, there is the **disciplinary dimension**. This means that as the teacher you must draw up and apply a set of clear and consistent rules, agreements and expectations. Think back to the kind of firm but fair teacher that all of us had in our youth! This approach provides the necessary degree of calm and predictability in the classroom, in contrast to a more chaotic, laissez-faire approach, where things are allowed on one occasion but not on another. This latter kind of arbitrary behaviour is confusing and frustrating for pupils.
- Second, it is also possible to offer structure within the **learning process**. This involves giving good lessons and supporting the pupils in their efforts to learn, so that they can feel more competent and more able: for example, using exercises that are not too difficult but also not too easy, providing help and guidance where necessary, giving additional explanation and remediation for the pupils who need it, differentiating between levels of ability, etc. The list of possibilities in this dimension is long.

Are autonomy and structure compatible?

At first glance, autonomy and structure may seem like opposites but in the classroom they actually go hand in hand. Autonomy in an educational context is not complete independence to do whatever you like. You can compare it with the difference between being forced by your parents to go and live on your own in the big bad world and being encouraged by your parents to voluntarily live on your own in a protected setting (like, say, a university). Autonomy in a structured environment means 'being yourself' and 'making your own choices' but within a framework that offers safety and security. Parents, trainers and caregivers all provide such frameworks. So too must teachers. Some examples? Every pupil knows that they must sit a final exam (structure) but as a teacher you can be flexible about the date and time, thereby offering the pupils involvement and choice in the process (autonomy). Similarly, as a trainer you can set up the gym so that there are exercises of different difficulty in each of the four corners (structure), from which the pupils can choose (autonomy), progressing from one to the other as their confidence (competence) improves under your continued and unconditional guidance and encouragement.

Table 4.6 takes a deeper look at the two dimensions of structure, providing a number of tips and examples for classroom practice.

Table 4.6 Structure-enhancing teacher practices

A. The disciplinary dimension		
1. Set out clear expectations	Communicate clearly about rules, norms and agreements that need to be respected in the classroom.	Ideally, it is a good idea to draw up a class charter with the pupils at the start of the school year, detailing the rules to be followed and the consequences for not doing so (input = autonomy). Some rules are not open for discussion (no phones in class, no dropping of litter, etc.), so make this clear in advance. Do not assume that the pupils will automatically know what is acceptable and what is not.
2. Follow the agreed guidelines consistently	What has been agreed in principle must always be honoured in practice.	Honesty and consistency are crucial. Always do what you have said/promised. What will you do if a pupil uses their phone in class? Communicate clearly the consequences of not following the agreed rules. Better still, agree these consequences with the pupils. That way, there is a greater likelihood that they will accept them without complaint.
B. The learning process		
3. Draw up a step-by-step plan	Indicate the intermediary steps that will lead to the attainment of the final goal.	E.g. Divide up the pupils' end-of-year project into smaller elements that are more manageable. Or introduce new learning material gradually, perhaps through a series of progressive exercises.
4. Give positive feedback	Offer encouragement and support whenever possible: not only for good performance but also for effort, social skills, etc.	E.g. Sometimes a pupil will simply not be good at, say, maths, so find other ways to give them encouragement: for their perseverance, concentration, collaboration with others, etc. Avoid person-oriented feedback ('you are clever').
5. Engender confidence	Do not be afraid to give praise: a word of appreciation, a pat on the back, etc.	It is important to show pupils that you believe in them. You can do this both verbally and non-verbally. Sometimes a look is enough.

6. Offer help by giving tips	Do not give pupils solutions but offer guidance that will allow them to find the solutions for themselves.	E.g. Use prompts ('If we compare A with C, what can we see?') and hints ('Try not to interpret the text too literally').
7. Suggest points for improvement	Make clear in a constructive way where things could be better and offer tips to make this possible.	E.g. 'Your essay lacks coherence and the transfer between paragraphs is not as fluent as it should be. Try using the signal words we learnt about last week.'
8. Set optimally challenging tasks	Exercises should be in the zone of proximal learning, just outside the pupils' comfort zone.	E.g. Do not make exercises too difficult or too easy. Differentiate between the different levels of your pupils' ability and offer support (scaffolding), where necessary. This is important for giving all pupils success experiences!
9. Develop rituals and habits	This is possible through a clear lesson structure, and the use of recurrent and predictable elements, and the clear setting of lesson targets ('What are we going to learn today?').	E.g. End every lesson that involved new learning material with an exit ticket. End every series of lessons with a class discussion. Never give unannounced tests but always give tests at the end of each series of lessons. In all of these instances, pupils will know what to expect (predictability).

Based on Vansteenkiste et al. (2007a).

What do we not yet know?

A first caveat that needs to be pointed out is that the self-determination theory is often incorrectly seen as a learning theory and not as a motivation theory.[24] This can lead to the misconception that if a pupil is motivated, they will also learn.

In other words, there is a difference between learning something and being motivated to learn something. These two elements are not necessarily mutually exclusive, and much research has been carried out to show that there can indeed be a connection between them. Motivation can lead to better learning performance and therefore to better learning but there is no absolute guarantee that this will be the case. Put simply, no causal relationship has been established: just because you are (autonomously) motivated, this does not mean that you will always learn better.[25] For example, I might be highly and voluntarily motivated to learn how to kite surf but without the right context (equipment, guidance, weather conditions, etc.) and without being able to satisfy the right basic requirements (physical fitness, no fear of heights, etc.) I am unlikely to get very far. The question I need to ask myself is therefore this: where can I find kite surfing lessons that are organised in precisely the right way, so that I can learn what I need to learn, and learn it effectively?

Motivation (and therefore the exploitation of autonomy, belonging and competence) is just a single element in the creation of a powerful learning environment. True, it is an important element but it is by no means the only one!

Endnotes

1. Barnes, 2014.
2. This is the opening sentence from his *Metaphysics*.
3. White, 1959.
4. Deci & Ryan, 2000.
5. Deci, 1975.
6. Vansteenkiste & Soenens, 2015.
7. Cook & Artino, 2016.
8. Vansteenkiste et al., 2007a.
9. Deci & Ryan, 2000.
10. Vansteenkiste et al., 2007b.
11. See amongst others: Sierens & Vansteenkiste, 2009; Vansteenkiste et al., 2007b.
12. Cameron & Pierce, 1994.
13. Vansteenkiste & Soenens, 2015.
14. Vu et al., 2021
15. Deci & Ryan, 2000.
16. Deci & Ryan, 2000.
17. Deci & Ryan, 2000.
18. White, 1959; Deci, 1975.
19. Amended from Aelterman et al., 2017.
20. See amongst others: Reeve & Jang, 2006; Vansteenkiste et al., 2005; Vansteenkiste & Soenens, 2015.
21. Vansteenkiste et al., 2007a.
22. See amongst others: Reeve & Jang, 2006; Vansteenkiste et al., 2005; Vansteenkiste & Soenens, 2015.
23. See Chapter 1.6 on cognitive development, in which we explain why we do not use the term 'zone of proximal development'.
24. De Meester, 2007.
25. De Bruyckere et al., 2019.

4.3

BEHAVIOURAL ECONOMICS: HOW TO GIVE PEOPLE A PUSH IN THE RIGHT DIRECTION

— What questions does this chapter answer?—

1. Why is it that our reasoning is so often faulty?
2. What are the different kinds of errors of thought?
3. How can you encourage children and others in the right direction?

May we introduce you to Linda? Linda is 32 years old, studied philosophy at university and loves reading poetry. Given what you now know about her, which of the following two comments do you think is most likely to apply to Linda?

A. Linda works in a bank.
B. Linda works in a bank and is a women's rights activist.

In practice, the majority of people choose answer B. And that is wrong. Of all the 32-year-old Lindas in the world who studied philosophy and love poetry, only relatively few will be fervent advocates of women's rights. Even so, many people think that they have enough with those three bits of information to conclude: 'We know Linda's type, and she would never work in a bank unless she was also a supporter of women's rights!'

This example is taken from the work of Daniel Kahneman and Amos Tversky and was described by Kahneman in his book *Thinking, Fast and Slow*.[1] Together with Amos Tversky (amongst others), he is one of the pioneers of behavioural economics. This relatively young branch of scientific research combines the disciplines of psychology and economics to investigate how people make their decisions and how this can lead to errors of reasoning. In this respect, the 'Linda' exercise can be described as an example of confirmation bias or, to put it another way, of people seeing and hearing what they want to see and hear. This chapter will first look at the origins of the theory behind behavioural economics and its most important precepts, before moving on to look at the most important errors of reasoning that people commonly make.

The study of behavioural economics is particularly useful because of the number of practical applications it has yielded. Based on the theory's principles of false reasoning, Richard Thaler has devised the concept of 'nudging'. This involves using the errors of thought that people make in order to change their behaviour. A final section will look at some concrete examples that can be used on children and young people; for instance, to help them eat more healthily!

An alternative for classic economic thinking?

Are human beings rational creatures that make well-considered choices? If you look at some of the members of your family and friends, perhaps you might be in two minds about the answer to this question! Be that as it may, until recently many of the classic theories in economics were based on the idea of 'homo economicus'. Homo economicus is a rational being who takes rational decisions about what he buys, how he spends his time and how he satisfies his needs (of course, this 'he' can also be a 'she'). These decisions are based on what is most efficient, costs the least, and takes best account of possible risks and alternatives.[2]

Perhaps this would not be applicable to an individual who makes an impulse buy at the check-out in a supermarket but if you view everyone in society as a whole, then the average person – according to classic economic theory – is a reasonably rational thinking being.[3] It was this argument that Tversky and Kahneman sought to challenge, using new insights derived from research in the field of cognitive psychology carried out in the 1960s. This research investigated the mechanisms behind the way in which people make their decisions and used the resulting conclusions to put forward new economic models. And so, the science of behavioural economics was born.

How do errors of reasoning occur?

In his 2011 book, Kahneman explains errors of reasoning – which he refers to as fallacies – in the following terms:

Every person has two systems of thought, which determine everything we do:

- System 1 is the fast system. It works quickly and more or less automatically on the basis of what we see, sudden impulses, emotions and needs. Because of its speed of operation and by avoiding the need for too much reflection, this system costs us very little effort or bother. At the same time, its impulsive nature makes it difficult to keep under control.
- System 2 is the slow system. It works consciously, rationally and with a great deal of attention, which in turn requires the use of a great deal of energy. In other words, System 2 costs much more effort than System 1 but it is also necessary to keep System 1 under control.

The more work System 2 is required to process, the faster System 1 is able to escape from its control and take over. It can often happen, for example, that the children in your class have been concentrating on their lessons all morning (System 2 working hard) but as lunchtime approaches, they become increasingly boisterous (System 1 taking over). Emotions can also take over in a similar way. Imagine that you have just had a major disappointment and decide to turn to crisps, chocolate, alcohol, etc. for comfort, even though you know it is not really a good idea. This is another instance of System 1 gaining the upper hand over System 2.

But don't let these examples give you the wrong idea: you can make errors of reasoning in both System 1 and System 2 but these errors will have a different basis. Even if you think about something deeply using System 2, you can still come to the wrong decision. And people with lots of experience in a particular field can still sometimes make rapid and correct decisions using System 1. When this happens, we often say that the person concerned has used their intuition but in fact a whole different set of mechanisms are at play!

Is your intuition correct?

The head of the local fire brigade is standing in front of a burning building. They suddenly give a signal that all the fire-fighters should withdraw. Just as the final fire-fighter emerges, the building collapses. It seems as if the commander's intuition has saved the fire-fighters from disaster...

However, this is not an example of intuition; it is an example of experience. In his autobiography, Herbert Simon[4] wrote that intuition is nothing more than the recognition of a situation based on experience. The head of the fire brigade had already seen countless fires and perhaps recognised, unconsciously or not, a certain sound or smell or movement that made them believe that the building was likely to collapse – and so they ordered the fire-fighters to come out while there was still time. It was the commander's experience, gained over many years, that allowed them in this situation to trust their gut feeling or 'intuition'.

(Continued)

In essence, this is an instance of transfer: applying what you have learnt in one situation in a different situation.[5] We have already seen how difficult this is and, according to Kahneman, the acquisition of this kind of intuitive expertise is only possible if:

1.   The experiences are sufficiently regular to be predictable; or, to put it another way, to be sufficiently comparable.
2.   You have been able to practise making use of these regular experiences often enough and over a sufficient length of time.

At the very top of the most recent list of effect sizes in education published by John Hattie[6] stands the ability of teachers to accurately assess their pupils. However, Hattie himself concluded that this is not the result of teachers being 'trained' in this kind of assessment but is actually the result of years of experience that allow teachers to evaluate the knowledge, skills and personalities of their pupils with precision. In other words, they have seen countless other pupils in the same circumstances.

Viewed in these terms, intuition is an example of System 1 at work. But whether the intuitive decision is right or wrong is not a matter of which system is being used but is more a question of the degree of experience that the person making the decision possesses.

A summary of errors of reasoning

There are many different and important errors of reasoning that people can make. Often, they are examples of what are known as heuristics, which are a kind of fast mental short-cut that System 1 uses to avoid the need to think too much. You will probably (and irritatingly!) recognise some of these heuristics in your own thinking. But at least that proves that you are human! Or perhaps you think that you can see more of these mental pitfalls in the behaviour of those around you, errors from which you are immune? Don't be so sure: perhaps that is just an example of a blind spot...

1.   **The anchor or reference effect.**

You see a pair of shoes you want in the shop window. You check the price and see that they cost 150 euros. You then notice that they are currently for sale with a discount of 40%. In comparison with 150 euros, 90 euros for a pair of shoes doesn't seem like very much, you think, and so you rush into the shop and buy them. This is an example of the anchor or reference effect, where the first information you receive – the anchor – has an influence on everything that follows. For example, the first version of a song that you hear and come to like will often sound better than the original song on which that version was based. Perhaps more problematical, the first impression a child makes on a teacher can sometimes colour that teacher's further perception.

2. **The availability heuristic.**

We have already mentioned in an earlier chapter the largely baseless fear that some people have when it comes to plane crashes but there are countless other examples of the availability heuristic. You may not believe that cigarettes can cause cancer, because your Granny smoked 40 a day and lived to be 100 years old. The availability heuristic makes use of information that you already possess – and can therefore be recalled quickly and without much mental effort – to determine what you think about a new subject or situation. You were planning to go on a sea voyage but have recently watched the film *Titanic*, so that you are now thinking of cancelling.

Salience bias is another mental fallacy related to the availability heuristic, although in this case you make your deductions about people, things and situations based on their most striking (salient) characteristic, such as a person who is overweight (and therefore greedy) or a car with a big dent in the side (which must have a bad driver). Other less noticeable characteristics are pushed into the background.

3. **The bandwagon effect.**

The greater the number of people who believe in the same idea, the more seemingly credible that idea becomes. In the supermarket you will frequently see advertising like 'The world's best-selling brand!' Is it? Who knows but it often persuades new customers to buy. The manager of Elvis Presley once thought up the slogan '50,000,000 Elvis fans can't be wrong', following which the singer's popularity increased still more. A Belgian supermarket chain took this same idea to come up with the slogan 'Two million customers a day is something you need to earn!' The effect can also be used for more social purposes: speed devils can hopefully be influenced by messages like '90% of drivers stick to the speed limit here'.

4. **The blind spot effect.**

Just as our eyes and the rear-view mirrors of our cars have a blind spot, so people can also have a blind spot when it comes to their own behaviour. This is the tendency – mentioned in the introduction to this section – to see mental fallacies in others, combined with a failure to recognise the same fallacies in yourself. You see that your friends overpraise their child as though the child is going to be the next Albert Einstein but you fail to see that you do exactly the same with your own child. Or you think that your colleague is too easily led by first impressions, whereas in reality you are just as bad.

5. **Choice-supportive bias.**

The alternative name for this mental lapse – post-purchase rationalisation – perhaps makes clearer how it works. After you have bought something on the spur of the moment, you can explain perfectly why it was such a good idea.

That new guitar for 500 euros? It was a bargain! You conveniently forget that you already have 20 or so guitars at home (a situation not unknown to one of our authors). The explanation usually only occurs to you *after* you have made the purchase. The reason for this is that people wish to avoid a feeling known as cognitive dissonance. This is the feeling that your behaviour is not consistent with your convictions. You know you have 20 guitars, and you know that 500 euros is a lot of money... but it was a bargain! Wasn't it? In theory, rational thinking people do not make bad or unnecessary purchases. Choice-supportive bias helps them to justify their actions when they do.

6.   **The clustering illusion.**

As already touched upon in Chapter 3.1 on perception, people like to see patterns in random sequences and events. If you have just won at roulette three times in row by betting on red, you will probably do the same for a fourth time, even though you know that the outcome is dictated entirely by chance. In other words, you see a connection where no real connection exists.

7.   **Confirmation bias.**

Imagine, contrary to all scientific evidence, that you are convinced that the world is flat. You will automatically focus on every 'fact' and every scrap of information that seems to confirm your conviction, ignoring the mass of indications that seem to suggest something else. In other words, you hear, see and read what you want to hear, see and read. People are not easily or quickly inclined to change their opinions. The colleague you so dislike is suddenly being friendly towards you? That can't be right: they must be after something! You receive new information ('my colleague is being friendly') but you interpret it in such a manner ('they must be after something') that you do not need to change your opinion ('I still dislike them'). Another example? The difficult pupil who always scores badly in math tests suddenly gets 9 out of 10. Is the pupil trying harder? Or are they cheating? Probably the latter. After all, that pupil has always been difficult...

Confirmation bias of this kind is closely related to conservatism bias, which is the difficulty of accepting new information that seems to contradict existing information. In medieval times, even intelligent men and women had trouble accepting that the world was round and was not the centre of the universe.

8.   **The information fallacy.**

It may sound strange but getting more and more information is not necessarily a good thing. People will sometimes look for extra reasons... not to do something. They search for additional information to postpone the implementation of a decision. As a result, this fallacy is also known as the equivocation fallacy. We really wanted to publish this book last year but waited to see if new research might prove that this fallacy does not exist… You, see? No one is immune!

9. **The ostrich effect.**

   Ignoring bad news or information that does not suit your purposes is like the behaviour of an ostrich, which supposedly buries its head in the sand whenever it feels scared or threatened.[7]

10. **Outcome bias.**

    Outcome bias, as the name suggests, involves assessing the quality of a decision on the basis of its outcome, rather than on the basis of the considerations that preceded the decision. Imagine that it is decided that a child should re-sit a year at school, rather than moving on to the next class. During the re-sit year, the child's performance improves significantly. As a result, the parents and the school think: 'The decision we took was a good one'. But it is far from certain that the improved performance was a consequence of the decision to re-sit. Many other and more important factors may be at play.

11. **Overconfidence bias.**

    People often have a tendency to overestimate their own ability. Individuals who think they are good at reading maps will refuse to open Google maps, even when they[8] lose their way. Hattie and Yates[9] have also described how children and young people consistently underestimate the time they need to make something or complete a particular task. They think that they can do things faster than they actually can. But be careful: adults – and even experts – are not immune from the same thing.

The Dunning-Kruger effect

This mental fallacy is often described as a counterpart of overconfidence bias but at the opposite end of the spectrum. It relates to people who know nothing about a particular subject or situation and whose incompetence or lack of knowledge is so great that they are unable to see or admit that some of their choices and conclusions about the said subject or situation are clearly wrong.[10] An example? Anyone who works in education will no doubt have been at family gatherings where aged aunts, uncles and grandparents explain at great length precisely 'what is wrong' with today's educational system, with a degree of certainty that even the Minister of Education would not claim!

12. **The placebo effect.**

Believing that something can have an effect is sometimes sufficient to create that effect. Most of us will have heard of medical research in which some patients are given a false non-medicine that has no effect, known as a placebo but which nevertheless succeeds in improving the patients' condition. The opposite effect also exists and is known as the nocebo effect. In this case, a person with authority in a given field – for example, a priest or a doctor – can create negative expectations in someone by giving an unfavourable diagnosis (which may or may not be accurate).

A third variant is placebo by proxy, which can affect parents, children and even animals. This occurs when a patient's (or pet's) response to therapy is affected by the response of people who know that the therapy is taking place. A parent (or pet owner) who is optimistic about the outcome of the therapy can 'pass on' this optimism to the therapy's recipient, which can have a positive impact on the progress of the illness.[11]

13. **The recency effect.**

This is the effect, already encountered in Chapter 3.1 on perception psychology, which gives paramountcy to new information over old information. In part, this is because the most recent information in your memory is easier to recall than what went before. For example, most of us will remember the last names in a list better than the first names. Once again, there is a counterpart to this effect: the so-called primacy effect. The first things that we see, hear or read are perhaps not as well remembered as the last things but are still significantly better remembered than the things in the middle. This effect is related to both confirmation bias and the availability heuristic, which were mentioned earlier in this section.

14. **Survival bias.**

This logical error has even led to the publication of a series of books that seek to discover the 'secret' of successful people. You can read tips about how Mark Zuckerberg and Bill Gates both dropped out of college but still went on to be billionaires, although nothing is said about the countless others who did the same and were not successful at all. That is the point about survival bias: it concentrates on people or things that made it past some kind of selection process, while overlooking those that did not, typically because of their lack of visibility. This can lead to false conclusions.

There are still many other forms of fallacy, logical error and faulty reasoning that we have not mentioned but we would like to finish with one last example – long live the recency effect! – that underlines an important central concept. This is the concept of loss aversion, or the fear of losing something.[12] This concept means (amongst other things) that the feeling of disappointment when you lose 100 euros is greater than the feeling of happiness when you win 100 euros. This was the conclusion of a research study based on the following two scenarios:

- Scenario 1: you are guaranteed to win 900 euros, or you take a 90% chance of winning €1,000 euros.
- Scenario 2: you are guaranteed to lose 900 euros, or you take a 90% chance of losing €1,000 euros.

The results showed that in the first scenario there is a greater likelihood that you will take the guaranteed 900 euros, giving up the riskier possibility of gaining a further 100 euros. In the second scenario – even though the difference is that same 100 euros – you will be more inclined to take a 90% risk in order to minimise your losses. Why? Because we hate losing more than we love winning. People will often not be willing to accept a bet where there is as much as a 50% chance of winning, because there is also a 50% chance of losing. This is not logical but in our minds the possibility of losing outweighs the possibility of winning.

Marketing people understand this all too well and exploit it frequently. If you try to book a hotel on a well-known online booking site, you will soon see advisory messages that there are only a few rooms left at the offered price. They are hoping (often with good reason) that your fear of losing the room will force you into a quick decision, without looking anywhere else. However, a recent review study has added a degree of nuance to the impact of this phenomenon, arguing that such decisions are significantly influenced by the context: the size of the amount, the wealth of the person making the decision, etc.[13]

Nudging: errors of reasoning as a push in the right direction?

How can you ensure that people take the lift more than they take the stairs? Or eat more salad than chips in the work canteen? Or pay their taxes on time, like a good citizen should?

Let's start with the final example. In 2016, the Belgian tax office experimented with nine different kinds of reminder letter for people who were late in paying. It became clear that even relatively minor changes in the wording can have a major impact. In addition to addressing people by name and simplifying the use of language wherever possible, the other key changes included:

- An indication of how many people (the vast majority) had paid their taxes on time.
- A clear indication of the penalty (fine) that would be levied in the event of further delay.
- A clear indication of the purposes for which the collected tax would be used, such as education, health care, etc.

Two of these three amendments actually contain logical errors of thinking. Have another look and see if you can identify what they are. You can find the answers in the following endnote.[14]

Believe it or not, these small changes raised an extra 18 million euros for the Belgian Treasury.[15] They are examples of what since 2008 have been known as 'nudges', a term that became popular following the publication of the book *Nudge: Improving Decisions About Health, Wealth, and Happiness* by Richard Thaler and Cass Sunstein.[16] A nudge is a small adjustment that can give people a gentle push (which, of course, is what 'nudge' means) in the right direction. Many of these nudges, like in the tax examples above, are based on fallacies, which 'trick' people into taking a course of action that they might not otherwise have taken.

Is this kind of manipulation ethical?

One of the most important criticisms of nudging relates to it ethicality. No matter how you look at it, a nudge is intended to manipulate people. True, this manipulation is often with the best of intentions but do the ends justify the means? Others regard nudges as a form of state paternalism or (to put it more crudely) unwarranted interference by the powers that be into the lives of ordinary people.[17] The advocates of nudges say that this is not a valid argument because we are all influenced (and influence others) each and every day. They talk instead about the creation of a 'choice architecture'. They are not suggesting that chips and other unhealthy junk foods should be banned but they believe that when choices are being made about what to eat it is important that the healthier options are made more visible (on the principle of the salience effect) and will therefore perhaps be chosen more often.[18]

Concrete examples of nudging:

- People in Brussels being encouraged to take the stairs by making the individual steps musical (they also look like piano keys);
- Encouraging people only to sit in groups or 'bubbles' of four during the COVID-19 crisis by painting circles on the ground (see Figure 4.2) or using nudging to keep a distance or to convince to take a vaccine (see Figure 4.3).

How can you encourage children to eat more healthily at school? Here are some tips from gezondevoeding.nl, a leading Dutch site about healthy eating:[19]

- If you are offering sandwiches, only use wholemeal bread, so that the pupils need to ask specifically if they want white bread.
- As far as drinks are concerned, offer tap water as standard. Only put water and 'light' variants of soft drinks in the fridge, so that once again the pupils need to ask specifically for alternatives.
- Offer 'small' portions of products as standard, so that those who want 'medium' or 'large' portions will have to ask for them.
- Does your school sell warm meals? Make small portion sizes standard. If large portion sizes are also sold, make sure that the price per gram remains the same (so that they are not relatively cheaper).

Be aware that nudging is not a miracle remedy. One of its most damning criticisms is that there is very little evidence that its effects are long-lasting.[20]

Figure 4.2 Nudging circles in the park in Ghent, Belgium

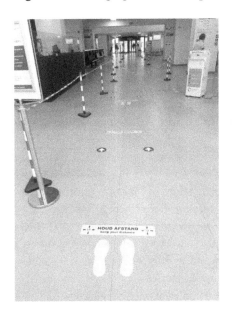

Figure 4.3 Two examples of nudging during the COVID-19 pandemic in a hospital: feet marks to keep a distance and a '97% have already been vaccinated' sign

Behavioural economics and nudging at school

Education is also a domain in which many choices need to be made. Many of these choices also involve errors of reasoning, so nudging and behavioural economics can also play a role.

What can go wrong when choosing what course of studies to follow?

Research has shown that there are specific causes that can negatively influence both parents and children when it comes to choosing what course and subjects to follow at school:

- Having a tendency towards short-term thinking;
- Sticking too rigidly to the familiar;
- Focusing too strongly on negative self-images;
- The availability of too many choice options, combined with too little information about them.[21]

Of course, these errors are present in differing degrees (or not at all), depending on the nature of the pupils and families concerned. Age, gender and socio-economic status can all play a role.[22]

Examples of successful nudging experiments in and around education

Let's begin with the youngest children of pre-school age. We know that the linguistic development of children benefits from there being sufficient linguistic interaction with the parents. A project in California sent text messages with language tips over an eight-month period to the young parents of four-year-olds. At the end of this period, a positive effect was noted on the language skills of the children concerned.[23]

Parental input was also the subject of a different study, in which the effect was monitored of sending a weekly one-sentence text message from teachers to parents, who then interacted with their children on the basis of the message content.[24] This was shown to be a cheap and effective approach that succeeded in reducing the number of children who failed to earn course credits, as well as improving the general communication between the parents and their offspring. In particular, it seems that messages about how to improve the behaviour of the children were the most effective.

Text messages were also used to encourage students in American universities to increase their participation in peer tutoring sessions that would improve their study skills. One-off reminder messages resulted in a significant rise in the number of students taking part in the sessions.[25]

These and similar techniques can also play a role in the classroom. Arie de Wild, a lecturer at the Rotterdam University of Applied Sciences, has described a number of approaches used by teachers to improve pupil behaviour and/or performance:[26]

- **You want your pupils to arrive more punctually.**

  Nudge: Organise a competition amongst the pupils or between two different classes. Every pupil who arrives on time scores a point for themselves or their team. Bearing in mind the principles of token economy (see the section on behaviourism, p. 190), it is a good idea to make the points visible: marbles in a jar, stickers on a chart, etc.

  However, you can also turn this concept around and organise a competition based on loss aversion. This time, every pupil starts with the same number of marbles, stickers, etc. but loses one each time that they are late. Dylan Wiliam did something similar in the 2010 BBC documentary *The Classroom Experiment* with his Secret Student, which involved one pupil being monitored and assessed each day by their teachers without the pupil knowing it. If the pupil did nothing wrong, the class scored a point. When a class had collected enough points, they were eligible for an upgrade on the next school trip.

- **You want your pupils to perform better.**

  Nudge: Arie de Wild suggests using a subject for which tests are frequent. Ask the children in advance (by filling in a form) to estimate how many points they think they will score in the next test. Will they get more or less than an 8? And how much study time will they need for the test? These are then the anchors, because this approach seeks to make use of the anchor (or reference) effect. The anchors set a kind of minimum standard that the pupil will at least want to equal and, hopefully, better. The process can be repeated periodically.

- **You want a litter-free playground.**

  Nudge: Let the pupils vote using rubbish bins. Place at least two bins next to each other. By throwing their rubbish into one of the two (or three or four) bins, they can vote for, say, the music they want to hear next week on the school PA system during the lunchtime break. The bin with the most rubbish at the end of the week wins.

But hang on a minute...

A review study into nudging in education, conducted in 2018,[27] added a number of important nuances that need to be borne in mind. The researchers concluded that very few nudging interventions have a positive effect on all children. Some approaches will be more inclined to change the behaviour of children from families with a high SES, while other approaches – such as those based on text messages for language improvement, reminders or goal setting – are more effective on children from families with a low SES. For this reason, the researchers recommend close monitoring of all nudges, to ensure that the gulf between rich and poor is not increased still further.

─ Teacher takeaways ─

Growing up in a world of addictions

Are my children addicted to gaming? Or perhaps to food? Or social media? Will they later succumb to the addictive temptation of drink, drugs or sex? Or maybe even laughing gas (one of the more recent options). Or will gambling (an older classic) be their chosen form of dependency?

As a parent, caregiver or teacher, you can worry a lot about these things as children get older. Although there has been a positive downward turn in addiction to drinking and drugs in both Belgium and the Netherlands during the past decade, the most recent figures suggest a possible reversal in this trend.[28]

What exactly is an addiction?

An addiction is a form of compulsive dependency on a substance or an activity, in which the dependent person's desire for the substance or activity systematically increases and becomes more intense, irrespective of the harm it might cause. A distinction needs to be made between biological addiction and psychological addiction. *Biological addiction* involves dependency on a substance (coffee, alcohol, drugs, etc.) to which the body becomes so accustomed that it can no longer function properly without it.[29] *Psychological addiction* is a dependency in which the dependent person uses a substance or an activity (like gambling) as a kind of coping or escape mechanism, so that they no longer need to think about the cause of the stress or the problems that they are experiencing. Of course, this does nothing to deal with the root of the stress or problems; on the contrary, it only makes things worse. It seems that emotions like sorrow and grief are most likely to reduce the threshold for the use of addictive agents.[30]

Why do young people use addictive substances?

There can be various reasons why young people are attracted to addictive substances, in addition to the obvious reason that they help to anaesthetise the mental pain of serious problem situations. The most common of these secondary reasons are:

- As an aid to having fun or relaxing;
- Because it is daring and exciting;
- Because it might improve performance at school;[31]
- To copy famous celebrity examples;
- Because of pressure exerted by peers and friends;[32]
- Because some people seemingly have a genetic predisposition that increases the likelihood of substance abuse.[33]

Is there a link between behavioural economics and addiction?

Earlier in this chapter, we described how Kahneman identified two operating systems in the brain for the processing of information: a fast, spontaneous system and a slower, more aware system. With addiction, many of the associated processes surrounding substance abuse become automatic. The substance is taken without much prior thought and the act is therefore largely controlled by the spontaneous system, which Kahneman referred to as System 1. Perhaps the user would like to be less dependent on whisky or cannabis but by now the spontaneous system has a firm control over the user's actions and this control cannot be wrestled from its grip by the more aware system. You can compare it with a runaway horse (System 1) galloping out of control with a helpless rider (System 2).[34] Breaking through these automatic responses is a serious challenge. The first crucial step for an addict is to become aware that such responses are indeed automatic. Do you still open the fridge for a beer as soon as you get home at night? Do you light up a cigarette without thinking as soon as you get out of the office?

Becoming more aware of the physical and psychological effect of your addiction can also help. You start to notice how much stress you are feeling or how your craving is becoming increasingly intense and troublesome. This awareness is good but the phenomena themselves are not good, because stress and tiredness make it easier for the unconscious System 1 to dictate your thoughts and actions. However, there is hope. Research into coffee drinkers - one of the safer and less harmful addictions - has established that while serious coffee drinkers certainly experience a craving for coffee this does not mean that they think coffee is particularly tasty.[35] Promising research is currently taking place to investigate how this process of increasing awareness can be used to help people to resist their addiction.[36]

(Continued)

How can you recognise an addiction?

Alcohol is the most common addiction in many countries, primarily because it can be obtained cheaply, easily and legally. One of the most worrying problems among young people is the phenomenon of binge drinking, during which huge quantities of alcohol are consumed in a short space of time. This can have far-reaching consequences, including aggression, alcohol poisoning and even cardiac arrest.[37] Other 'popular' addictive substances include tobacco and drugs.

Concrete indications that someone may be developing a problem in relation to a particular substance or activity are:

- Using alcohol or drugs to relax or to get into a good mood;
- Using more alcohol or drugs more often and more quickly;
- Using subterfuge to camouflage the problem (using mints to hide the smell of alcohol, turning your computer off when you hear your parents coming upstairs, etc.);
- Failure to keep promises to stop or reduce consumption;
- The appearance of withdrawal symptoms, such as anxiety, sweating, shaking, excessive tension (when not drinking, smoking, gambling, etc.);
- Gradual changes in personality (not to be confused with temporary periods of indisposition);
- (In cases of gaming or gambling addiction) the abandonment of other hobbies.

In the above, we have deliberately referred to the problematic use of a substance or activity, because addiction is something that should be properly diagnosed by a professional. However, if a sufficient number of the above indications are present, it is always a good idea to recommend that the (young) person concerned should seek advice from a mental health care specialist. This is the reason why we do not consider it appropriate for us to offer 'tips' about how you can best deal with the situation.

Endnotes

1. See also: Tversky & Kahneman, 1983; Kahneman, 2011.
2. This line of reasoning is thought to date back to John Stuart Mill, although he never described it as such. One of the other sources is Edgeworth, 1881. See also: O'Boyle, 2009; Persky, 1995.
3. Sen, 1977.
4. Simon, 1996.

5. See also: De Bruyckere et al., 2019.
6. You can keep track of the ongoing collection of meta-analysis via https://www.visiblelearningmetax.com
7. For Dutch readers, you can recognise this bias in the Kids for Kids song *Als ik de baas zou zijn (van het Journaal)* (If I was in charge of the news), when the children sing that if they were running the news people would be more friendly, more positive and the world a better place.
8. Or she, although he is probably more common. Or is this yet another example of flawed reasoning?
9. Hattie & Yates, 2013.
10. Kruger & Dunning, 1999.
11. Whalley & Hyland, 2013.
12. Tversky & Kahneman, 1991.
13. Gal & Rucker, 2018.
14. By referring to everyone who has already paid their taxes, the tax office hopes to exploit the bandwagon effect. The explicit reference to the fine plays on the concept of loss aversion.
15. See amongst others: Sokol, 31 October 2016. www.vrt.be/vrtnws/nl/2016/10/31/directere_aanmaningsbrieflevertfiscus18miljoeneu-roop-1-2807919/
16. Thaler & Sunstein, 2009.
17. Hausman & Welch, 2010.
18. See amongst others: Mills, 2013; Sunstein, 2014.
19. De Gezonde Schoolkantine, n.d. *Leerlingen verleiden gezond te eten.* Voedinsgscentrum. www.gezondeschool.nl/voortgezet-onderwijs/gezondheidsthemas-en-criteria-vignet/schoolomgeving-voeding
20. Marchiori et al., 2017.
21. Lavecchia et al., 2016.
22. Kahneman, 2013.
23. York et al., 2019.
24. Kraft & Rogers, 2015.
25. Pugatch & Wilson, 2018.
26. https://issuu.com/klasse.be/docs/kma_009_issuu
27. Damgaard & Nielsen, 2018.
28. For a summary, see De Bruyckere, 2020.
29. Cami & Farré, 2003; Munzar et al., 2003.
30. Dorison et al., 2020.
31. Schwarz et al., 2012.
32. Nation & Heflinger, 2006; Urberg et al., 2003; Young et al., 2006.
33. Clarke et al., 2008; Edwards & Kendler, 2013; Mares et al., 2011.
34. This comparison was inspired by Geeraerts et al., 2019.
35. Koranyi et al., 2020.
36. Veling et al., 2014.
37. Van de Wiel et al., 2002.

NOW WHAT...?

The writing of this book took four years. Because science never stands still, we continued to add new insights and nuances right until the very end. Science speaks with the voice of today, not with the voice of yesterday. But now this book is finally finished, and we need to let it go, at least in part.

It is a bit like raising and educating a child or young person. Throughout the development and learning process, whether as a parent, a teacher or a caregiver, you constantly need to give and let go. Sometimes this can be a difficult process but it is a necessary one. After all, at the end of the day we want them to be able to stand on their own two feet, don't we?

Well, that is also what we now want for this book. Of course, in the years ahead we will no doubt check to see how it is progressing, asking ourselves, like all good parents should, whether or not there are any little pieces of good advice we can still give or minor adjustments that we can still make.

REFERENCES

Abikoff, H., Courtney, M., Pelham, W. E., & Koplewicz, H. S. (1993). Teachers' ratings of disruptive behaviors: The influence of halo effects. *Journal of Abnormal Child Psychology, 21*(5), 519–533.

Adams, H. L., & Williams, L. R. (2011). Advice from teens to teens about dating: Implications for healthy relationships. *Children and Youth Services Review, 33*(2), 254–264.

Aelterman, N., De Muynck, G., Haerens, L., & Vande Broek, G. (2017). *Motiverend coachen in de sport.* Acco.

Ahmed, E., & Braithwaite, V. (2004). Bullying and victimization: Cause for concern for both families and schools. *Social Psychology of Education, 7*(1), 35–54.

Ainsworth, M. D. S., & Bell, S. M. (1970). Attachment, exploration, and separation: Illustrated by the behaviour of one-year-olds in a strange situation. *Child Development, 41*, 49–67.

Ainsworth, M. D. S., Bell, S. M., & Stayton, D. F. (1974). Infant–mother attachment and social development: Socialization as a product of reciprocal responsiveness to signals. In M. Richards (Ed.), *The integration of the child into the social world.* Cambridge University Press.

Ainsworth, M. D. S., Blehar, M. C., Waters, E., & Wall, S. N. (2015). *Patterns of attachment: A psychological study of the strange situation.* Psychology Press.

Akmajian, A., Demers, R. A., & Harnish, R. M. (1984). *Linguistics.* MIT Press.

Alexander, G. M., Wilcox, T., & Woods, R. (2009). Sex differences in infants' visual interest in toys. *Archives of Sexual Behavior, 38*(3), 427–433.

Alexander, P. A. (2003). The development of expertise: The journey from acclimation to proficiency. *Educational Researcher, 32*(8), 10–14. https://doi.org/10.3102/0013189x032008010

Alexander, P. A., & Judith, E. (1988). The interaction of domain-specific and strategic knowledge in academic performance. *Review of Educational Research, 58*(4), 375–404. https://doi.org/10.3102/00346543058004375.

Allport, G. W. (1954). *The nature of prejudice.* Addison-Wesley.

Allport, G. W., & Odbert, H. S. (1936). Trait-names: A psycho-lexical study. *Psychological Monographs, 47*(1), i–171. doi:10.1037/h0093360

Al-Namlah, A. S., Meins, E., & Fernyhough, C. (2012). Self-regulatory private speech relates to children's recall and organization of autobiographical memories. *Early Childhood Research Quarterly, 27*(3), 441–446.

American Academy of Pediatrics. (2016). *American Academy of Pediatrics announces new recommendations for children's media use.* Retrieved from www.aap.org/en/news-room/news-releases/aap/2016/aap-announces-new-recommendations-for-media-use/

American Psychological Association [APA] Help Center. (2012). *Building your resilience.* www.apa.org/topics/resilience

Anaraki, Z. G., Ghasisin, L., Bakhtiari, B. M., Fallah, A., Salehi, F., & Parishan, E. (2013). Conversational repair strategies in 3 and 5 year old normal Persian-speaking children in Ahwaz, Iran. *Audiology, 22*(1), 25–31.

Anastasi, A., & Urbina, S. (1997). *Psychological testing* (7th ed., p. 413). Prentice-Hall.

Anderson, J. R., Reder, L. M., & Simon, H. A. (1996). Situated learning and education. *Educational Researcher, 25*(4), 5–11. https://doi.org/10.3102/0013189X025004005

Anne Frank Stichting. (2018). *Omgaan met vooroordelen en discriminatie in de klas.* www.annefrank.org/nl/themas/vooroordelen-en-stereotypen/wat-kun-je-doen-tegen-vooroordelen

Apperly, I. A., & Robinson, E. J. (2003). When can children handle referential opacity? Evidence for systematic variation in 5-and 6-year-old children's reasoning about beliefs and belief reports. *Journal of Experimental Child Psychology, 85*(4), 297–311.

Arnett, J. J. (2004) *Emerging adulthood: The winding road from the late teens through the twenties.* Oxford University Press.

Arnett, J. J. (2007). Suffering, selfish, slackers? Myths and reality about emerging adults. *Journal of Youth and Adolescence, 36*(1), 23–29.

Arnold, M. L. (2000). Stage, sequence, and sequels: Changing conceptions of morality, post-Kohlberg. *Educational Psychology Review, 12*(4), 365–383.

Ashdown, D. M., & Bernard, M. E. (2012). Can explicit instruction in social and emotional learning skills benefit the social-emotional development, well-being, and academic achievement of young children? *Early Childhood Education Journal, 39*(6), 397–405.

Asher, S. R., & Rose, A. J. (1997). Promoting children's social-emotional adjustment with peers. In P. Salovey & D. J. Sluyter (Eds.), *Emotional development and emotional intelligence: Educational implications* (pp. 196–230). Basic Books.

Australian Curriculum, Assessment and Reporting Authority [ACARA]. (2012). *General capabilities in the Australian Curriculum.*

Ausubel, D. P., Novak, J. D., & Hanesian, H. (1968). *Educational psychology: A cognitive view.* Holt, Rinehart, & Winston.

Ayduk, O., Mendoza-Denton, R., Mischel, W., Downey, G., Peake, P. K., & Rodriguez, M. (2000). Regulating the interpersonal self: Strategic self-regulation for coping with rejection sensitivity. *Journal of Personality and Social Psychology, 79*(5), 776–792. https://doi.org/10.1037/0022-3514.79.5.776

Baar, P., Goosens, F., Kocken, P. L., Meulen, M., & Wienke, D. (2018). *Effecten van anti-pestprogramma's: beoordeling van de resultaten van het empirisch effectonderzoek 2016/2017 naar tien anti-pestprogramma's. Commissie Anti-pestprogramma's.* https://repository.tno.nl//islandora/object/uuid:1ab38188-b9da-4a1b-8a4a-b432b0dd33e5

Babad, E. Y., Inbar, J., & Rosenthal, R. (1982). Pygmalion, Galatea, and the Golem: Investigations of biased and unbiased teachers. *Journal of Educational Psychology, 74*(4), 459–474. https://doi.org/10.1037/0022-0663.74.4.459

Bacon, F. (1620). *Novum organum.* Clarendon Press.

Bagwell, C. L., Newcomb, A. F., & Bukowski, W. M. (1998). Preadolescent friendship and peer rejection as predictors of adult adjustment. *Child Development, 69*(1), 140–153.

Bak, T. H. (2016). Cooking pasta in La Paz: Bilingualism, bias and the replication crisis. *Linguistic Approaches to Bilingualism, 6*(5), 699–717.

Bakermans-Kranenburg, M. J., & Van IJzendoorn, M. H. (2009). The first 10,000 Adult Attachment Interviews: Distributions of adult attachment representations in clinical and non-clinical groups. *Attachment & Human Development, 11*(3), 223–263.

Baldry, A. C., & Farrington, D. P. (2007). Effectiveness of programs to prevent school bullying. *Victims and Offenders, 2*(2), 183–204.

Bandura, A. (1965). Vicarious processes: A case of no-trial learning. In Berkowitz, L. (Ed). *Advances in experimental social psychology* (Vol. 2, pp. 1–55). Academic Press.

Bandura, A. (1997). *Self-efficacy: The exercise of control.* W. H. Freeman and Company.

Barbaro, N., Boutwell, B. B., Barnes, J. C., & Shackelford, T. K. (2017). Rethinking the Transmission Gap: What behavioral genetics and evolutionary psychology mean for attachment theory: A comment on Verhage et al. (2016). *Psychological Bulletin, 143*(1), 107–113.

Barkley, R. A. (1997). Behavioral inhibition, sustained attention, and executive functions: Constructing a unifying theory of ADHD. *Psychological Bulletin, 121*(1), 65–94. https://doi.org/10.1037/0033-2909.121.1.65

Barnes, J. (Ed.). (2014). *Complete works of Aristotle, volume 1: The revised Oxford translation* (Vol. 1). Princeton University Press.

Baron-Cohen, S. (2012). *The science of evil: On empathy and the origins of cruelty.* Basic Books.

Bashford, A., & Levine, P. (Eds.). (2010). *The Oxford handbook of the history of eugenics.* Oxford University Press.

Bauer, P. J., & Coyne, M. J. (1997). When the name says it all: Preschoolers' recognition and use of the gendered nature of common proper names. *Social Development, 6*(3), 271–291.

Baum, N. L., Ginat, R. S., & Silverman, P. R. (2014). Childhood bereavement and traumatic loss. In R. Pat-Horenczyk, D. Brom, & J. M. Vogel (Eds.), *Helping children cope with trauma* (pp. 66–78). Routledge.

Baumrind, D. (1967). Child care practices anteceding three patterns of preschool behavior. *Genetic Psychology Monographs, 75*(1), 43–88.

Baumrind, D. (1971). Current patterns of parental authority. *Developmental Psychology, 4*(1, Pt.2), 1–103. https://doi.org/10.1037/h0030372

Beal, C. R. (1994). *Boys and girls: The development of gender roles* (pp. 169–173). McGraw-Hill.

Becoña, E., Martínez, Ú., Calafat, A., Juan, M., Fernández-Hermida, J. R., & Secades-Villa, R. (2012). Parental styles and drug use: A review. *Drugs: Education, Prevention and Policy, 19*(1), 1–10.

Beeney, J. E., Wright, A. G., Stepp, S. D., Hallquist, M. N., Lazarus, S. A., Beeney, J. R., ... & Pilkonis, P. A. (2017). Disorganized attachment and personality functioning in adults: A latent class analysis. *Personality Disorders: Theory, Research, and Treatment, 8*(3), 206–216.

Beilin, H. (1992). Piaget's enduring contribution to developmental psychology. *Developmental Psychology, 28*(2), 191–204.

Belfi, B., Gielen, S., De Fraine, B., Verschueren, K., & Meredith, C. (2015). School-based social capital: The missing link between schools' socioeconomic composition and collective teacher efficacy. *Teaching and Teacher Education, 45*, 33–44.

Bell, S. T. (2007). Deep-level composition variables as predictors of team performance: A meta-analysis. *Journal of Applied Psychology, 92*(3), 595–615.

Belsky, J., & Fearon, R. M. P. (2008). Precursors of attachment security. In J. Cassidy & P. R. Shaver (Eds.), *Handbook of attachment* (2nd ed., pp. 295–316). Guilford Press.

Benelli, B., Belacchi, C., Gini, G., & Lucangeli, D. (2006). 'To define means to say what you know about things': The development of definitional skills as metalinguistic acquisition. *Journal of Child Language, 33*(1), 71–97.

Benoit, A., Lacourse, E., & Claes, M. (2013). Pubertal timing and depressive symptoms in late adolescence: The moderating role of individual, peer, and parental factors. *Development and Psychopathology, 25*(2), 455–471.

Benware, J. (2013). Predictors of father–child and mother–child attachment in two-parent families. *All Graduate Theses and Dissertations.* 1734. https://digitalcommons.usu.edu/etd/1734

Benyamin, B., Pourcain, B., Davis, O. S., Davies, G., Hansell, N. K., Brion, M. J., ... & Haworth, C. M. A. (2014). Childhood intelligence is heritable, highly polygenic and associated with FNBP1L. *Molecular Psychiatry, 19*(2), 253–258.

Bernstein, D. A. (2013). Parenting and teaching: What's the connection in our classrooms? *Psychology Teacher Network, 23*(2), 1–6.

Berzonsky, M. D. (2008). Identity formation: The role of identity processing style and cognitive processes. *Personality and individual differences, 44*(3), 645–655.

Bierman, K. L. (2004). *Peer rejection: Developmental processes and intervention strategies.* Guilford Press.

Bijeljac-Babic, R., Bertoncini, J., & Mehler, J. (1993). How do 4-day-old infants categorize multisyllabic utterances? *Developmental Psychology, 29*(4), 711–721.

Blaton, L., & Van Avermaet, P. (2015). *Ouders aan boord van de Brede School: Brede School Ahoy!* Steunpunt Diversiteit & Leren, Universiteit Gent.

Bleske-Rechek, A., Somers, E., Micke, C., Erickson, L., Matteson, L., Stocco, C., ... & Ritchie, L. (2012). Benefit or burden? Attraction in cross-sex friendship. *Journal of Social and Personal Relationships, 29*(5), 569–596.

Bloom, P. (2002). Precis of How children learn the meanings of words. *Behavioral and Brain Sciences, 24*, 1095–1103.

Blume, A. W., Schmaling, K. B., & Marlatt, G. A. (2005). Memory, executive cognitive function, and readiness to change drinking behavior. *Addictive Behaviors, 30*(2), 301–314.

Bober, S. J., Humphry, R., Carswell, H. W., & Core, A. J. (2001). Toddlers' persistence in the emerging occupations of functional play and self-feeding. *American Journal of Occupational Therapy, 55*(4), 369–376.

Bogle, K. A. (2008). 'Hooking up': What educators need to know. *Chronicle of Higher Education, 54*(28), A32–A33.

Boller, F., Grafman, J., Segalowitz, S. J., & Rapin, I. (Eds.). (2003). *Handbook of neuropsychology: Child neuropsychology, Part 1.* Elsevier.

Bonebright, D. A. (2010). 40 years of storming: A historical review of Tuckman's model of small group development. *Human Resource Development International, 13*(1), 111–120.

Boone, S., & Van Houtte, M. (2013). Why are teacher recommendations at the transition from primary to secondary education socially biased? A mixed-methods research. *British Journal of Sociology of Education, 34*(1), 20–38.

Borke, H. (1975). Piaget's mountains revisited: Changes in the egocentric landscape. *Developmental Psychology, 11*(2), 240–243. https://doi.org/10.1037/h0076459

Borman, W. C. (1975). Effects of instructions to avoid halo error on reliability and validity of performance evaluation ratings. *Journal of Applied Psychology, 60*(5), 556–560. https://doi.org/10.1037/0021-9010.60.5.556

Boudry, M., & Buekens, F. (2011). The epistemic predicament of a pseudoscience: Social constructivism confronts Freudian psychoanalysis. *Theoria, 77,* 159–179. https://doi.org/10.1111/j.1755-2567.2011.01098.x

Bowlby, J. (1982). *Attachment and loss: Attachment* (Vol. 1). Basic Books. (Original work published 1969.)

Bowne, J. (2015). *Enhancing and practicing executive function skills with children from infancy to adolescence.* Center on the Developing Child, Harvard University.

Boyd, D. (2014). *It's complicated: The social lives of networked teens.* Yale University Press.

Branta, C. F., Lerner, J. V., & Taylor, C. S. (1996). Physical activity and youth sports: Social and moral issues. *Peace and Conflict: Journal of Peace Psychology, 2*(4), 301–303.

Bravata, D. M., Watts, S. A., Keefer, A. L., Madhusudhan, D. K., Taylor, K. T., Clark, D. M., ... & Hagg, H. K. (2020). Prevalence, predictors, and treatment of impostor syndrome: A systematic review. *Journal of General Internal Medicine, 35*(4), 1252–1275.

Breeuwsma, G., Haanstra, F., Koopman, C., Laarakker, K., Schram, D., & Witte, T. (2005). *Ontwikkelingsstadia in het leren van kunst, literatuur en muziek.* Cultuurnetwerk Nederland.

Brendgen, M., Vitaro, F., Bukowski, W. M., Dionne, G., Tremblay, R. E., & Boivin, M. (2013). Can friends protect genetically vulnerable children from depression? *Development and Psychopathology, 25*(2), 277–289.

Bretherton, I. (1992). The origins of attachment theory: John Bowlby and Mary Ainsworth. *Developmental Psychology, 28*(5), 759–775.

Bridges, J. S. (1993). Pink or blue: Gender-stereotypic perceptions of infants as conveyed by birth congratulations cards. *Psychology of Women Quarterly, 17*(2), 193–205.

Brinton, B., Fujiki, M., Loeb, D. F., & Winkler, E. (1986). Development of conversational repair strategies in response to requests for clarification. *Journal of Speech, Language, and Hearing Research, 29*(1), 75–81.

Bronfenbrenner, U. (1994). Ecological models of human development. *Readings on the Development of Children, 2*(1), 37–43.

Bronfenbrenner, U., & Morris, P. A. (2007). The bioecological model of human development. In Lerner, R. M. (ed). *Handbook of child psychology* (Vol. 1). Wiley.

Brown, G. L., McBride, B. A., Shin, N., & Bost, K. K. (2007). Parenting predictors of father–child attachment security: Interactive effects of father involvement and fathering quality. *Fathering: A Journal of Theory, Research & Practice about Men as Fathers, 5*(3), 197–219.

Brown, R. E. (2016). Hebb and Cattell: The genesis of the theory of fluid and crystallized intelligence. *Frontiers in Human Neuroscience, 10,* 606.

Brownell, C. A., Ramani, G. B., & Zerwas, S. (2006). Becoming a social partner with peers: Cooperation and social understanding in one-and two-year-olds. *Child Development, 77*(4), 803–821.

Brussoni, M. J., Jang, K. L., Livesley, W. J., & MacBeth, T. M. (2000). Genetic and environmental influences on adult attachment styles. *Personal Relationships, 7*(3), 283–289.

Bryden, P. J., Mayer, M., & Roy, E. A. (2011). Influences of task complexity, object location, and object type on hand selection in reaching in left and right-handed children and adults. *Developmental Psychobiology, 53*(1), 47–58.

Buekens, F. (2006). *Freuds Vergissing. De illusie van de psychoanalyse.* Uitgeverij Van Halewyck.

Burgess, S., Rawal, S., & Taylor, E. (2019). *Teacher peer observation and student test scores: Evidence from a field experiment in English secondary schools.* Annenberg Institute/ Brown University.

Burt, C. (1966). The genetic determination of differences in intelligence: A study of monozygotic twins reared together and apart. *British Journal of Psychology, 57*(1–2), 137–153.

Buss, C., Davis, E. P., Hobel, C. J., & Sandman, C. A. (2011). Maternal pregnancy-specific anxiety is associated with child executive function at 6–9 years age. *Stress, 14*(6), 665–676.

Butterworth, G. (2014). *Principles of developmental psychology: An introduction.* Psychology Press.

Cahill, H., Beadle, S., Farrelly, A., Forster, R., & Smith, K. (2014). *Building resilience in children and young people.* The University of Melbourne.

Caino, S., Kelmansky, D., Lejarraga, H., & Adamo, P. (2004). Short-term growth at adolescence in healthy girls. *Annals of Human Biology, 31*(2), 182–195.

Cameron, J., & Pierce, W. D. (1994). Reinforcement, reward, and intrinsic motivation: A meta-analysis. *Review of Educational Research, 64*(3), 363–423.

Cami, J., & Farré, M. (2003). Drug addiction. *New England Journal of Medicine, 349*(10), 975–986.

Campbell, A. (1995). A few good men: Evolutionary psychology and female adolescent aggression. *Ethology and Sociobiology, 16*(2), 99–123.

Campbell, A. (2013). *A mind of her own: The evolutionary psychology of women.* Oxford University Press.

Campbell, A., Shirley, L., & Candy, J. (2004). A longitudinal study of gender-related cognition and behaviour. *Developmental Science, 7*(1), 1–9.

Carlson, S. A., Fulton, J. E., Lee, S. M., Foley, J. T., Heitzler, C., & Huhman, M. (2010). Influence of limit-setting and participation in physical activity on youth screen time. *Pediatrics, 126*(1), e89–e96.

Carlson, S. M., White, R. E., & Davis-Unger, A. C. (2014). Evidence for a relation between executive function and pretense representation in preschool children. *Cognitive Development, 29*, 1–16.

Carpendale, J. (2009). Piaget's theory of moral development. In U. Müller, J. Carpendale, & L. Smith (Eds.), *The Cambridge companion to Piaget* (pp. 270–286). Cambridge University Press.

Carson, R. C. (2019). *Interaction concepts of personality.* Routledge.

Caspi, A. (2003, July 18). Influence of life stress on depression: Moderation by a polymorphism in the 5-HTT gene. *Science, 301*(5631), 386–389.

Cassidy, K. (2007). Tuckman revisited: Proposing a new model of group development for practitioners. *Journal of Experiential Education, 29*(3), 413–417. https://doi.org/10.1177/105382590702900318

Castellanos, F. X., Sonuga-Barke, E. J., Milham, M. P., & Tannock, R. (2006). Characterizing cognition in ADHD: Beyond executive dysfunction. *Trends in Cognitive Sciences, 10*(3), 117–123.

Castles, A., Rastle, K., & Nation, K. (2018). Ending the reading wars: Reading acquisition from novice to expert. *Psychological Science in the Public Interest, 19*(1), 5–51.

Cattell, R. (1949). *Culture free intelligence test, scale 1, handbook.* Institute of Personality and Ability Testing.

Çavaria vzw. (2021, January). *Woordenlijst.* https://cavaria.be/woordenlijst

Chabris, C. F., Lee, J. J., Cesarini, D., Benjamin, D. J., & Laibson, D. I. (2015). The fourth law of behavior genetics. *Current Directions in Psychological Science, 24*(4), 304–312.

Chaiklin, S. (2003). The zone of proximal development in Vygotsky's analysis of learning and instruction. *Vygotsky's Educational Theory in Cultural Context, 1*, 39–64.

Chall, J. S. (1967). *Learning to read: The great debate.* McGraw-Hill.

Charalampous, K., Demetriou, C., Tricha, L., Ioannou, M., Georgiou, S., Nikiforou, M., & Stavrinides, P. (2018). The effect of parental style on bullying and cyber bullying behaviors and the mediating role of peer attachment relationships: A longitudinal study. *Journal of Adolescence, 64*, 109–123.

Cherney, I. D., Kelly-Vance, L., Glover, K. G., Ruane, A., & Ryalls, B. O. (2003). The effects of stereotyped toys and gender on play assessment in children aged 18–47 months. *Educational Psychology, 23*(1), 95–106.

Chi, M. T. H. (1978). Knowledge structures and memory development. In R. Siegler (Ed.), *Children's thinking: What develops?* (pp. 73–96). Erlbaum.

Chi, M. T. H., Feltovich, R., & Glaser, R. (1981). Categorization and representation of physics problems by experts and novices. *Cognitive Science, 5*, 121–152. https://doi.org/10.1207/s15516709cog0502_2

Child, D. (2007). *Psychology and the teacher* (7th ed.). Continuum.

Chitty, C. (2007). *Eugenics, race and intelligence in education.* Bloomsbury Publishing.

Chomsky, N. (1957). *Syntactic structures.* Mouton.

Chomsky, N. (1965). *Aspects of a theory of syntax.* MIT Press.

Chomsky, N. (1968). *Language and mind.* Harcourt Brace Jovanovich.

Chonchaiya, W., Tardif, T., Mai, X., Xu, L., Li, M., Kaciroti, N., ... & Lozoff, B. (2013). Developmental trends in auditory processing can provide early predictions of language acquisition in young infants. *Developmental Science, 16*(2), 159–172.

Chopik, W. J., Edelstein, R. S., & Grimm, K. J. (2019). Longitudinal changes in attachment orientation over a 59-year period. *Journal of Personality and Social Psychology, 116*(4), 598–611.

Christensen, J. (2016). A critical reflection of Bronfenbrenner s development ecology model. *Problems of Education in the 21st Century, 69*, 22–28.

Chua, A. (2011). *Battle hymn of the tiger mother.* Bloomsbury Publishing.

Clarke, T. K., Treutlein, J., Zimmermann, U. S., Kiefer, F., Skowronek, M. H., Rietschel, M., ... & Schumann, G. (2008). HPA-axis activity in alcoholism: Examples for a gene–environment interaction. *Addiction Biology, 13*(1), 1–14.

Clearfield, M. W., & Nelson, N. M. (2006). Sex differences in mothers' speech and play behavior with 6-, 9-, and 14-month-old infants. *Sex Roles, 54*(1), 127–137.

Cloninger, C. R. (2004). *Feeling good: The science of well-being.* Oxford University Press.

Cloninger, C. R., Svrakic, D. M., & Przybeck, T. R. (1993). A psychobiological model of temperament and character. *Archives of General Psychiatry, 50*(12), 975–990.

Coie, J. D., Dodge, K. A., & Coppotelli, H. (1982). Dimensions and types of social status: A cross-age perspective. *Developmental Psychology, 18*(4), 557–570. https://doi.org/10.1037/0012-1649.18.4.557

Coleman, J. S. (1987). Families and schools. *Educational Researcher, 16*(6), 32–38.

Collins, W. A. (2003). More than myth: The developmental significance of romantic relationships during adolescence. *Journal of Research on Adolescence, 13*(1), 1–24.

Colom, R., & Flores-Mendoza, C. E. (2007). Intelligence predicts scholastic achievement irrespective of SES factors: Evidence from Brazil. *Intelligence, 35*(3), 243–251.

Colonnesi, C., Van Polanen, M., Tavecchio, L. W., & Fukkink, R. G. (2017). Mind-mindedness of male and female caregivers in childcare and the relation to sensitivity and attachment: An exploratory study. *Infant Behavior and Development, 48*, 134–146.

Coltrane, S., & Adams, M. (1997). Children and gender. In T. Arendell (Ed.), *Contemporary parenting: Challenges and issues. Understanding families* (Vol. 9, pp. 219–253). Sage.

Condry, J., & Condry, S. (1976). Sex differences: A study of the eye of the beholder. *Child Development, 47*(3), 812–819.

Conger, R. D., Ge, X., Elder Jr, G. H., Lorenz, F. O., & Simons, R. L. (1994). Economic stress, coercive family process, and developmental problems of adolescents. *Child Development, 65*(2), 541–561.

Cook, D., & Artino, J. (2016). Motivation to learn: An overview of contemporary theories. *Medical Education, 50*, 997–1014.

Corr, P. J., & Matthews, G. (Eds.). (2009). *The Cambridge handbook of personality psychology*. Cambridge University Press.

Costello, E. J., Sung, M., Worthman, C., & Angold, A. (2007). Pubertal maturation and the development of alcohol use and abuse. *Drug and Alcohol Dependence, 88*, S50–S59.

Côté, J., Baker, J., & Abernethy, B. (2007). Practice and play in the development of sport expertise. In Tenenbaum, G., & Eklund, R. C. (Eds.). *Handbook of sport psychology*. Wiley (Vol. 3, pp. 184–202).

Cotrufo, P., Cella, S., Cremato, F., & Labella, A. G. (2007). Eating disorder attitude and abnormal eating behaviours in a sample of 11–13-year-old school children: The role of pubertal body transformation. *Eating and Weight Disorders-Studies on Anorexia, Bulimia and Obesity, 12*(4), 154–160.

Coyne, S. M., Rogers, A. A., Zurcher, J. D., Stockdale, L., & Booth, M. (2020). Does time spent using social media impact mental health?: An eight year longitudinal study. *Computers in Human Behavior, 104*, 106160.

Cratty, B. J. (1979). *Perceptual and motor development in infants and young children*. Prentice-Hall.

Cratty, B. J. (1986). *Perceptual and motor development in infants and young children* (3rd ed.). Prentice-Hall.

Crawford, M., & Unger, R. (2004). *Women and gender: A feminist psychology*. McGraw-Hill.

Crews, F. (1996). The verdict on Freud. *Psychological Science, 7*(2), 63–68.

Crick, N. R., & Dodge, K. A. (1994). A review and reformulation of social information-processing mechanisms in children's social adjustment. *Psychological Bulletin, 115*(1), 74–101.

Crone, E. A., & Dahl, R. E. (2012). Understanding adolescence as a period of social–affective engagement and goal flexibility. *Nature Reviews Neuroscience, 13*(9), 636–650.

Cummings, E., & Davies, P. (1994). *Children and marital conflict.* Guilford Press.

Curtiss, S. (1977). *Genie: A psycholinguistic study of a modern-day wild child.* Academic Press.

Dahl, A. (2019). The science of early moral development: On defining, constructing, and studying morality from birth. In J. B Benson (Ed.), *Advances in child development and behavior* (Vol. 56, pp. 1–24). Academic Press.

Dahl, R. E. (1996, March). The impact of inadequate sleep on children's daytime cognitive function. *Seminars in Pediatric Neurology, 3*(1), 44–50.

Daly, M., & Wilson, M. (1990). Killing the competition. *Human Nature, 1*(1), 81–107.

Damgaard, M. T., & Nielsen, H. S. (2018). Nudging in education. *Economics of Education Review, 64*, 313–342.

Damon, W., & Hart, D. (1991). *Self-understanding in childhood and adolescence.* Cambridge University Press.

Darley, J. M., & Latané, B. (1968). Bystander intervention in emergencies: Diffusion of responsibility. *Journal of Personality and Social Psychology, 8*(4, pt. 1), 377–383.

Darwin, C. (1877). A biographical sketch of an infant. *Mind, 2*(7), 285–294.

D'Augelli, A. R. (2005). Stress and adaptation among families of lesbian, gay, and bisexual youth: Research challenges. *Journal of GLBT Family Studies, 1*(2), 115–135.

D'Augelli, A. R., Patterson, C. J., & Patterson, C. (Eds.). (2001). *Lesbian, gay, and bisexual identities and youth: Psychological perspectives.* Oxford University Press.

Davies, G., Tenesa, A., Payton, A., Yang, J., Harris, S. E., Liewald, D., ... & McGhee, K. (2011). Genome-wide association studies establish that human intelligence is highly heritable and polygenic. *Molecular psychiatry, 16*(10), 996–1005.

Davies, P., & Cummings, E. (1994). Marital conflict and child adjustment: An emotional security hypothesis. *Psychological Bulletin, 116*(3), 387–411.

Dawson, P., & Guare, R. (2018). *Executive skills in children and adolescents: A practical guide to assessment and intervention.* Guilford Press.

Deardorff, J., Marceau, K., Johnson, M., Reeves, J. W., Biro, F. M., Kubo, A., ... & Hiatt, R. A. (2021). Girls' pubertal timing and tempo and mental health: A longitudinal examination in an ethnically diverse sample. *Journal of Adolescent Health, 68*(6), 1197–1203.

Deary, I. J., Batty, G. D., & Gale, C. R. (2008). Childhood intelligence predicts voter turnout, voting preferences, and political involvement in adulthood: The 1970 British Cohort Study. *Intelligence, 36*(6), 548–555.

Deary, I. J., Strand, S., Smith, P., & Fernandes, C. (2007). Intelligence and educational achievement. *Intelligence, 35*(1), 13–21.

De Boer, H., Timmermans, A. C., & Van der Werf, M. P. C. (2018). The effects of teacher expectation interventions on teachers' expectations and student achievement: Narrative review and meta-analysis. *Educational Research and Evaluation, 24*(3–5), 180–200. https://doi.org/10.1080/13803611.2018.1550834

De Bruin, W. B. (2005). Save the last dance for me: Unwanted serial position effects in jury evaluations. *Acta Psychologica, 118*(3), 245–260.

De Bruin, W. B., & Keren, G. (2003). Order effects in sequentially judged options due to the direction of comparison. *Organizational Behavior and Human Decision Processes, 92*(1–2), 91–101.

De Bruyckere, P. (2018). *The ingredients for great teaching.* Sage.

De Bruyckere, P. (2020). *Met de Kinderen Alles Goed.* LannooCampus.

De Bruyckere, P. (2021). De kracht van het collectief geloof: Collective student efficacy. In B. Spruyt, E. Coenen, & L. Bradt (Eds.), *Over Leven op School.* Acco.

De Bruyckere, P., Kirschner, P. A., & Hulshof, C. D. (2015a). *Urban myths about learning and education.* Academic Press.

De Bruyckere, P., Kirschner, P., & Hulshof, C. (2019). *More urban myths about learning and education.* Routledge.

De Bruyckere, P., Struyf, E., & Kavadias, D. (2015b). Rousseau en Arendt in de iPad-klas, de oudere wortels van hedendaagse discussies over technologie op school. *Pedagogische Studiën, 92*(3), 202–212.

DeCasper, A. J., & Fifer, W. P. (1980). Of human bonding: New-borns prefer their mothers' voices. *Science, 208*(4448), 1174–1176.

DeCasper, A. J., & Spence, M. J. (1986). Prenatal maternal speech influences new-borns' perception of speech sounds. *Infant Behavior and Development, 9*(2), 133–150.

Deci, E. L. (1975). *Intrinsic motivation.* Plenum Press.

Deci, E. L., & Ryan, R. M. (2000). The 'what' and 'why' of goal pursuits: Human needs and the self-determination of behavior. *Psychological Inquiry, 11*(4), 227–268.

De Gelder, B. (2000). Recognizing emotions by ear and by eye. In R. D. Lane & L. Nadel (Eds.), *Cognitive neuroscience of emotion. Series in affective science* (pp. 84–105). Oxford University Press.

De Gezonde Schoolkantine. (n.d.). *Leerlingen verleiden gezond te eten.* Voedinsgscentrum. https://gezondeschoolkantine.voedingscentrum.nl/nl/inspiratie/leerlingen-verleiden-gezond-te-eten-nudging-.aspx

Degotardi, S., & Sweller, N. (2012). Mind-mindedness in infant child-care: Associations with early childhood practitioner sensitivity and stimulation. *Early Childhood Research Quarterly, 27*(2), 253–265.

De Graaf, H., Van den Borne, M., Nikkelen, S., Twisk, D., & Meijer, S. (2017). *Seks onder je 25e: Seksuele gezondheid van jongeren in Nederland anno 2017.* Eburon.

de Groot, A. D. (1965). *Thought and choice in chess.* Mouton.

Dehaene, S. (2020). *How we learn: The new science of education and the brain.* Penguin.

Dehaene-Lambertz, G., Hertz-Pannier, L., & Dubois, J. (2006). Nature and nurture in language acquisition: Anatomical and functional brain-imaging studies in infants. *Trends in Neurosciences, 29*(7), 367–373.

Delaunay-El Allam, M., Marlier, L., & Schaal, B. (2006). Learning at the breast: Preference formation for an artificial scent and its attraction against the odor of maternal milk. *Infant Behavior and Development, 29*(3), 308–321.

Del Giudice, M. (2012). Fetal programming by maternal stress: Insights from a conflict perspective. *Psychoneuroendocrinology, 37*(10), 1614–1629.

De Meester, E. (2017). Een expert leert anders dan een beginner. *ScienceGuide.* www.scienceguide.nl/2017/06/een-expert-leert-anders-dan-een-beginner/

Denizet-Lewis, B. (2004, May 30). Friends, friends with benefits and the benefits of the local mall. *New York Times Magazine.*

Denovan, A., & Macaskill, A. (2017). Building resilience to stress through leisure activities: A qualitative analysis. *Annals of Leisure Research, 20*(4), 446–466.

Deslauriers, L., McCarty, L., Miller, K., Callaghan, K., & Kestin, G. (2019). Measuring actual learning versus feeling of learning in response to being actively engaged in the classroom. *Proceedings of the National Academy of Sciences of the United States of America, 116*(39), 19251–19257. doi:10.1073/pnas.1821936116

De Wilde, V. (2017). False beginners: beginsituatie voor het vak Engels. Presented at the ORD 2017 – Onderwijs Research Dagen 2017.

De Wolff, M. S., & Van Ijzendoorn, M. H. (1997). Sensitivity and attachment: A meta-analysis on parental antecedents of infant attachment. *Child Development, 68*(4), 571–591.

Dewsbury, D. A. (1988). The comparative psychology of monogamy. In D. W. Leger (Ed.), *Comparative perspectives in modern psychology.* Nebraska Symposium on Motivation, 1987 (Vol. *35*, pp. 1–50). University of Nebraska Press.

Diamond, A. (2002). Normal development of prefrontal cortex from birth to young adulthood: Cognitive functions, anatomy, and biochemistry. In D. Stuss & R. Knight (Eds.), *Principles of frontal lobe function* (pp. 466–503). Oxford University Press.

Diamond, A. (2013). Executive functions. *Annual Review of Psychology, 64*, 135–168.

Didau, D., & Rose, N. (2016). *Psychologie in de klas: Wat iedere leraar moet weten.* Phronese.

Diego, M. A., Field, T., & Hernandez-Reif, M. (2009). Procedural pain heart rate responses in massaged preterm infants. *Infant Behavior and Development, 32*(2), 226–229.

Dierckens, M., De Clercq, B., & Deforche, B. (2019). *Studie Jongeren en Gezondheid, Deel 4: gezondheidsgedrag – Seksuele gezondheid en relaties.* www.jongeren-en-gezondheid. ugent.be/wordpress/wp-content/uploads/2019/09/HBSC201718_Factsheet_ seksualiteit.pdf

Digman, J. M. (1990). Personality structure: Emergence of the five-factor model. *Annual Review of Psychology, 41*, 417–440.

Dodge, K. A., Pettit, G. S., McClaskey, C. L., Brown, M. M., & Gottman, J. M. (1986). Social competence in children. *Monographs of the Society for Research in Child Development, 52*(2), i–85.

Dodge, K. A., & Rabiner, D. L. (2004). Returning to roots: On social information processing and moral development. *Child Development, 75*(4), 1003–1008.

Dodge, K. A., Schlundt, D. C., Schocken, I., & Delugach, J. D. (1983). Social competence and children's sociometric status: The role of peer group entry strategies. *Merrill-Palmer Quarterly, 29*(3), 309–336.

Dokuka, S., Valeeva, D., & Yudkevich, M. (2015). Co-evolution of social networks and student performance. *Educational Studies, 3*, 44–65.

Domingue, B. W., Belsky, D. W., Conley, D., Harris, K. M., & Boardman, J. D. (2015). Polygenic influence on educational attainment: New evidence from the National Longitudinal Study of Adolescent to Adult Health. *AERA Open, 1*(3), 1–13. doi: 10.1177/2332858415599972.

Donohoo, J. (2017). *Collective efficacy: How educators' beliefs impact student learning.* Corwin.

Doornenbal, J. (2014). Samenwerking met ouders aan de randen van het onderwijs. In Oostdam, R., & de Vries, P. (Eds). *Samenwerken aan leren en opvoeden: basisboek over ouders en school* (pp. 227–236). Coutinho.

Doorman, M. (2015). *Rousseau en ik: over de erfzonde van de authenticiteit.* Prometheus.

Dorison, C. A., Wang, K., Rees, V. W., Kawachi, I., Ericson, K. M., & Lerner, J. S. (2020). Sadness but not all negative emotions, heightens addictive substance use. *Proceedings of the National Academy of Sciences, 117*(2), 943–949.

Due, P., Holstein, B. E., Lynch, J., Diderichsen, F., Gabhain, S. N., Scheidt, P., & Currie, C. (2005). Bullying and symptoms among school-aged children: International comparative cross sectional study in 28 countries. *European Journal of Public Health, 15*(2), 128–132.

Dunlosky, J., Rawson, K. A., Marsh, E. J., Nathan, M. J., & Willingham, D. T. (2013). Improving students' learning with effective learning techniques: Promising directions from cognitive and educational psychology. *Psychological Science in the Public Interest, 14*(1), 4–58.

Dunn, J., & Kendrick, C. (1982). *Siblings: Love, envy and understanding.* Basil Blackwell.

Durlak, J. A., Weissberg, R. P., Dymnicki, A. B., Taylor, R. D., & Schellinger, K. B. (2011). The impact of enhancing students' social and emotional learning: A meta-analysis of school-based universal interventions. *Child Development, 82*(1), 405–432.

Duschinsky, R. (2012). Tabula rasa and human nature. *Philosophy, 87*(4), 509–529.

Dutton, E., & Lynn, R. (2013). A negative Flynn effect in Finland, 1997–2009. *Intelligence, 41*(6), 817–820.

Dutton, E., & Lynn, R. (2015). A negative Flynn Effect in France, 1999 to 2008–9. *Intelligence, 51*, 67–70.

Dweck, C. S. (2006). *Mindset: The new psychology of success.* Random House.

Dweck, C. S. (2008). Can personality be changed? The role of beliefs in personality and change. *Current Directions in Psychological Science, 17*(6), 391–394.

Dyer, S., & Moneta, G. B. (2006). Frequency of parallel, associative, and cooperative play in British children of different socioeconomic status. *Social Behavior and Personality: An International Journal, 34*(5), 587–592.

Eckerman, C. O., & Peterman, K. (2001). *Peers and infant social/communicative development.* In G. Bremner & A. Fogel (Eds.), *Handbooks of developmental psychology. Blackwell handbook of infant development* (pp. 326–350). Blackwell.

Edgeworth, F. Y. (1881). *Mathematical psychics: An essay on the application of mathematics to the moral sciences* (Vol. 10). Kegan Paul.

Edwards, A. C., & Kendler, K. S. (2013). Alcohol consumption in men is influenced by qualitatively different genetic factors in adolescence and adulthood. *Psychological Medicine, 43*(9), 1857–1868. https://doi.org/10.1017/S0033291712002917

Edwards, C. P. (2000). Children's play in cross-cultural perspective: A new look at the Six Cultures study. *Cross-Cultural Research, 34*(4), 318–338.

Edwards, C. P., & Whiting, B. (1988). *Children of different worlds: The formation of social behavior.* Harvard University Press.

Eells, R. J. (2011). *Meta-analysis of the relationship between collective teacher efficacy and student achievement* (133). [Dissertation. Loyola University Chicago]. ECommons. https://ecommons.luc.edu/luc_diss/133

Egan, K. (2004). *Getting it wrong from the beginning: Our progressivist inheritance from Herbert Spencer, John Dewey, and Jean Piaget*. Yale University Press.

Ellis, S., & Tod, J. (2018). *Behaviour for learning: Promoting positive relationships in the classroom*. Routledge.

Endo, S. (1992). Infant-infant play from 7 to 12 months of age: An analysis of games in infant-peer triads. *Japanese Journal of Child and Adolescent Psychiatry, 33*(2), 145–162.

Ericsson, K. A. (2007). An expert-performance perspective of research on medical expertise: The study of clinical performance. *Medical Education, 41*(12), 1124–1130. https://doi.org/10.1111/j.1365-2923.2007.02946.x

Ericsson, K. A., Nandagopal, K., & Roring, R. W. (2009). Toward a science of exceptional achievement: Attaining superior performance through deliberate practice. *Annals of the New York Academy of Sciences, 1172*, 199–217. doi:10.1196/annals.1393.001

Erikson, E. H. (1968). *Identity: Youth and crisis* (No. 7). WW Norton & Company.

Espelage, D. L. (2014). Ecological theory: Preventing youth bullying, aggression, and victimization. *Theory into Practice, 53*(4), 257–264.

Faber, T. W. (2017). *When imitation falls short: The case of complementary actions.* [Doctoral dissertation, Universiteit van Amsterdam.]

Falbo, T. (2012). Only children: An updated review. *Journal of Individual Psychology, 68*(1), 38–49.

Falck-Ytter, T., Gredebäck, G., & Von Hofsten, C. (2006). Infants predict other people's action goals. *Nature Neuroscience, 9*(7), 878–879.

Fantz, R. L. (1961). The origin of form perception. *Scientific American, 204*(5), 66–73.

Fara. (n.d.). *Tips voor ouders van tienerzwangeren en jonge ouders (of andere vertrouwens personen)*. www.fara.be/fara-voor-professionals/publicaties-en-producten/gratis-brochures-over-tienerzwangerschap

Fareri, D. S., & Tottenham, N. (2016). Effects of early life stress on amygdala and striatal development. *Developmental Cognitive Neuroscience, 19*, 233–247.

Feldman, R. S. (2012). *Ontwikkelingspsychologie*. Pearson Education.

Fernald, A. (2001). Hearing, listening, and understanding: Auditory development in infancy. In G. Bremner & A. Fogel (Eds.), *Blackwell handbook of infant development* (pp. 35–70). Blackwell.

Ferster, C. B., & Skinner, B. F. (1957). *Schedules of reinforcement*. Appleton-Century-Crofts.

Finn, A. S., Minas, J. E., Leonard, J. A., Mackey, A. P., Salvatore, J., Goetz, C., ... & Gabrieli, J. D. (2017). Functional brain organization of working memory in adolescents varies in relation to family income and academic achievement. *Developmental Science, 20*(5), e12450.

Fitts, P. M., & Posner, M. I. (1967). *Human performance*. Brooks/Cole.

Flack, Z. M., Field, A. P., & Horst, J. S. (2018). The effects of shared storybook reading on word learning: A meta-analysis. *Developmental Psychology, 54*(7), 1334.

Flesch, R. (1955). *Why Johnny can't read: and what you can do about it*. Harper & Brothers.

Flom, R., & Bahrick, L. E. (2007). The development of infant discrimination of affect in multimodal and unimodal stimulation: The role of intersensory redundancy. *Developmental Psychology, 43*(1), 238–252. https://doi.org/10.1037/0012-1649.43.1.238

Flom, R., Gentile, D. A., & Pick, A. D. (2008). Infants' discrimination of happy and sad music. *Infant Behavior and Development, 31*(4), 716–728.

Flower, A., McKenna, J. W., Bunuan, R. L., Muething, C. S., & Vega Jr, R. (2014). Effects of the Good Behavior Game on challenging behaviors in school settings. *Review of Educational Research, 84*(4), 546–571.

Flynn, J. R., & Flynn, J. R. (2012). *Are we getting smarter?: Rising IQ in the twenty-first century*. Cambridge University Press.

Forsyth, D. R. (2018). *Group dynamics*. Cengage Learning.

Fraley, R. C., Roisman, G. I., Booth-LaForce, C., Owen, M. T., & Holland, A. S. (2013). Interpersonal and genetic origins of adult attachment styles: A longitudinal study from infancy to early adulthood. *Journal of Personality and Social Psychology, 104*(5), 817–838.

Frankenburg, W. K., Dodds, J., Archer, P., Bresnick, B., Maschka, P., Edelman, N., & Shapiro, H. (1992). *The Denver II training manual*. Denver Developmental Materials.

Franko, D. L., & Striegel-Moore, R. H. (2002). The role of body dissatisfaction as a risk factor for depression in adolescent girls: Are the differences Black and White? *Journal of Psychosomatic Research, 53*(5), 975–983.

Freedle, R., & Kostin, I. (1997). Predicting Black and White differential item functioning in verbal analogy performance. *Intelligence, 24*, 417–444.

Freedman, M. B., Leary, T. F., Ossorio, A. G., & Goffey, H. S. (1951). The interpersonal dimension of personality 1. *Journal of Personality, 20*(2), 143–161.

Friedlander, L. J., Connolly, J. A., Pepler, D. J., & Craig, W. M. (2007). Biological, familial, and peer influences on dating in early adolescence. *Archives of Sexual Behavior, 36*(6), 821–830.

Friedrich, M., Wilhelm, I., Born, J., & Friederici, A. D. (2015). Generalization of word meanings during infant sleep. *Nature Communications, 6*, 6004.

Fukkink, R. (2017). *Pedagogisch curriculum voor het jonge kind in de kinderopvang*. Bohn Stafleu van Loghum.

Furman, W., & Buhrmester, D. (1992). Age and sex differences in perceptions of networks of personal relationships. *Child Development, 63*(1), 103–115.

Furman, W., & Shaffer, L. (2003). The role of romantic relationships in adolescent development. In P. Florsheim (Ed.), *Adolescent romantic relations and sexual behavior: Theory, research, and practical implications* (pp. 3–22). Erlbaum.

Gal, D., & Rucker, D. D. (2018). The loss of loss aversion: Will it loom larger than its gain? *Journal of Consumer Psychology, 28*(3), 497–516.

Galbally, M., Snellen, M., & Power, J. (2014). Antipsychotic drugs in pregnancy: A review of their maternal and fetal effects. *Therapeutic Advances in Drug Safety, 5*(2), 100–109.

Gallagher, T. M. (1981). Contingent query sequences within adult–child discourse. *Journal of Child Language, 8*(1), 51–62.

Galton, F. (1883). *Inquiries into human faculty and its development*. Macmillan and Company.

Galvao, T. F., Silva, M. T., Zimmermann, I. R., Souza, K. M., Martins, S. S., & Pereira, M. G. (2014). Pubertal timing in girls and depression: A systematic review. *Journal of Affective Disorders, 155*, 13–19.

Gardner, H. (2016). Multiple intelligences: Prelude, theory, and aftermath. In R. J. Sternberg, S. T. Fiske, & D. J. Foss (Eds.), *Scientists making a difference* (pp. 167–170). Cambridge University Press.

Garlick, D. (2003). Integrating brain science research with intelligence research. *Current Directions in Psychological Science, 12*(5), 185–189. https://doi.org/10.1111/1467-8721.01257

Garvey, C., & Hogan, R. (1973). Social speech and social interaction: Egocentrism revisited. *Child Development, 44*(3), 562–568.

Gathercole, V. C. M. (Ed.). (2013). *Issues in the assessment of bilinguals.* Multilingual Matters.

Gauze, C., Bukowski, W. M., Aquan-Assee, J., & Sippola, L. K. (1996). Interactions between family environment and friendship and associations with self-perceived well-being during early adolescence. *Child Development, 67*(5), 2201–2216.

Geary, D. C. (2008). An evolutionary informed education science. *Educational Psychologist, 43*, 179–195. https://doi.org/10.1080/00461520802392133

Geeraerts, G., Claessens, J., & Verstuyf, G. (Eds.). (2019). *Waarom is een verslaving zo moeilijk te doorbreken?* VAD. www.vad.be/assets/verslaving_moeilijk_te_doorbreken_-_twee_systemen

Geraerts, E. (2015). *Mentaal kapitaal.* Uitgeverij Lannoo.

Gervain, J., Macagno, F., Cogoi, S., Peña, M., & Mehler, J. (2008). The neonate brain detects speech structure. *Proceedings of the National Academy of Sciences, 105*(37), 14222–14227.

Gibson, J. J. (1966).*The senses considered as perceptual systems.* Houghton Mifflin.

Gibson, J. J. (1972). A theory of direct visual perception. In J. Royce and W. Rozenboom (Eds.), *The psychology of knowing* (pp. 215–227). Gordon & Breach.

Gilligan, C. (1977). In a different voice: Women's conceptions of self and of morality. *Harvard Educational Review, 47*(4), 481–517.

Gladwell, M. (2008). *Outliers: The story of success.* Little, Brown and Company.

Glejser, H., & Heyndels, B. (2001). Efficiency and inefficiency in the ranking in competitions: The case of the Queen Elisabeth Music Contest. *Journal of Cultural Economics, 25*(2), 109–129.

Glöckner, A., & Witteman, C. (2010). Beyond dual-process models: A categorisation of processes underlying intuitive judgement and decision making. *Thinking and Reasoning, 16*, 1–25. https://doi.org/10.1080/13546780903395748

Goldberg, A. E. (2004). But do we need universal grammar? Comment on Lidz et al. *Cognition, 94*(1), 77–84.

Goldberg, J. (2018). *It takes a village to determine the origins of an African proverb.* NPR.

Golinkoff, R. M. (1983). Infant social cognition: Self, people, and objects. In L. S. Liben (Ed.), *Piaget and the foundations of knowledge* (pp. 179–200). Psychology Press.

Golinkoff, R. M., Hoff, E., Rowe, M. L., Tamis-LeMonda, C. S., & Hirsh-Pasek, K. (2019). Language matters: Denying the existence of the 30-million-word gap has serious consequences. *Child Development, 90*(3), 985–992.

Gómez-Ortiz, O., Del Rey, R., Casas, J. A., & Ortega-Ruiz, R. (2014). Parenting styles and bullying involvement/Estilos parentales e implicación en bullying. *Cultura y Educación, 26*(1), 132–158.

Göncü, A., Patt, M. B., & Kouba, E. (2002). Understanding young children's pretend play in context. In P. K. Smith & C. H. Hart (Eds.), *Blackwell handbook of childhood social development* (pp. 418–437). Blackwell.

Goodman, K. S. (1967). Reading: A psycholinguistic guessing game. *Journal of the Reading Specialist, 6*, 126–135. https://doi.org/10.1080/19388076709556976

Gopnik, A. (2012). Scientific thinking in children: Theoretical advances, empirical research, and policy implications. *Science, 337,* 1623–1627. https://doi.org/10.1126/science.1223416

Gordon, I., Voos, A. C., Bennett, R. H., Bolling, D. Z., Pelphrey, K. A., & Kaiser, M. D. (2013). Brain mechanisms for processing affective touch. *Human Brain Mapping, 34*(4), 914–922.

Gottfredson, L. S., & Deary, I. J. (2004). Intelligence predicts health and longevity but why? *Current Directions in Psychological Science, 13*(1), 1–4.

Gowers, S. (2005). Development in adolescence. *Psychiatry, 4*(6), 6–9.

Graber, R., Turner, R., & Madill, A. (2016). Best friends and better coping: Facilitating psychological resilience through boys' and girls' closest friendships. *British Journal of Psychology, 107*(2), 338–358.

Graddol, D. (2004). The future of language. *Science, 303*(5662), 1329–1331.

Granqvist, P., Sroufe, L. A., Dozier, M., Hesse, E., Steele, M., Van Ijzendoorn, M., … & Steele, H. (2017). Disorganized attachment in infancy: A review of the phenomenon and its implications for clinicians and policy-makers. *Attachment & Human Development, 19*(6), 534–558.

Gray, P., & Bjorklund, D. F. (2018). *Psychology* (8th ed.). Macmillan.

Gray, P., & Feldman, J. (1997). Patterns of age mixing and gender mixing among children and adolescents at an ungraded democratic school. *Merrill-Palmer Quarterly, 43*(1), 67–86.

Gregory, R. (1970). *The intelligent eye.* Weidenfeld and Nicolson.

Gregory, R. L., & Zangwill, O. L. (1987). *The Oxford companion to the mind.* Oxford University Press.

Groeimee: expert (2021). *Groeimee Podcast Aflevering 5 Pesten* (Gie Deboutte) [Audio]. https://soundcloud.com/user-215608879/groeimee-podcast-aflevering-5-pesten

Guernsey, L., & Levine, M. H. (2016). Getting smarter about e-books for children. *YC Young Children, 71*(2), 38–43.

Gunnerud, H. L., Ten Braak, D., Reikerås, E. K. L., Donolato, E., & Melby-Lervåg, M. (2020). Is bilingualism related to a cognitive advantage in children? A systematic review and meta-analysis. *Psychological Bulletin, 146*(12), 1059–1083.

Hall, G. S. (1916). *Adolescence: Its psychology and its relations to physiology, anthropology, sociology, sex, crime, religion and education* (Vol. 2). D. Appleton.

Hall, J. A., Xing, C., Ross, E. M., & Johnson, R. M. (2021). Experimentally manipulating social media abstinence: Results of a four-week diary study. *Media Psychology, 24*(2), 259–275.

Halth, M. M. (1986). Sensory and perceptual processes in early infancy. *The Journal of Pediatrics, 109*(1), 158–171.

Hamilton, D. L., & Sherman, S. J. (1989). Illusory correlations: Implications for stereotype theory and research. In D. Bar-Tal, C. F. Graumann, A. W. Kruglanski, & W. Stroebe (Eds.), *Stereotyping and prejudice* (pp. 59–82). Springer.

Hamon, R. R., & Ingoldsby, B. B. (Eds.). (2003). *Mate selection across cultures.* Sage.

Hancox, R. J., Milne, B. J., & Poulton, R. (2005). Association of television viewing during childhood with poor educational achievement. *Archives of Pediatrics & Adolescent Medicine, 159*(7), 614–618.

Haney, C., Banks, C., & Zimbardo, P. (1972). *Interpersonal dynamics in a simulated prison* (No. ONR-TR-Z-09). Stanford University, California, Department of Psychology.

Harris, J. R. (1998). *The nurture assumption.* Bloomsbury.

Hart, B., & Risley, T. R. (1995). *Meaningful differences in the everyday experience of young American children.* Paul H. Brookes Publishing.

Hart, D., Goel, N., & Atkins, R. (2017). Prosocial tendencies, antisocial behaviour and moral development in childhood. In A. Slater & J. G. Bremner (Eds.), *An introduction to developmental psychology* (pp. 511–539). Wiley.

Hartigan, J., & Wigdor, A. (1989). Fairness in employment testing. *Science (New York, NY), 245*(4913), 14.

Hartl, A. C., Laursen, B., Cantin, S., & Vitaro, F. (2020). A test of the bistrategic control hypothesis of adolescent popularity. *Child Development, 91*(3), e635–e648.

Harwood, J., Paolini, S., Joyce, N., Rubin, M., & Arroyo, A. (2011). Secondary transfer effects from imagined contact: Group similarity affects the generalization gradient. *British Journal of Social Psychology, 50*(1), 180–189.

Hatano, G., & Inagaki, K. (1986). Two courses of expertise. In H. Stevenson, J. Azuma & K. Hakuta (Eds.), *Child development and education in Japan* (pp. 262–272). W. H. Freeman & Co.

Hattie, J. (2009). *Visible learning: A synthesis of over 800 meta-analyses relating to achievement.* Routledge.

Hattie, J., & Yates, G. C. (2013). *Visible learning and the science of how we learn.* Routledge.

Hattie, J., Fisher, D., Frey, N., & Clarke, S. (2021). *Collective student efficacy: Developing independent and inter-dependent learners.* Corwin Teaching Essentials. Corwin.

Hausman, D. M., & Welch, B. (2010). Debate: To nudge or not to nudge. *Journal of Political Philosophy, 18*(1), 123–136.

Haworth, C. M. A., & Plomin, R. (2012). Genetics and education: Toward a genetically sensitive classroom. In K. R. Harris, S. Graham, & T. Urdan (Eds.), *APA educational psychology handbook: Vol. 1. Theories, constructs, and critical issues* (pp. 529–559). American Psychological Association.

Haworth, C. M., Wright, M. J., Luciano, M., Martin, N. G., de Geus, E. J., Van Beijsterveldt, C. E., ... & Kovas, Y. (2010). The heritability of general cognitive ability increases linearly from childhood to young adulthood. *Molecular Psychiatry, 15*(11), 1112–1120.

Hay, D. F., Payne, A., & Chadwick, A. (2004). Peer relations in childhood. *Journal of Child Psychology and Psychiatry, 45*(1), 84–108.

Hay, D. F., & Ross, H. S. (1982). The social nature of early conflict. *Child Development, 53*(1), 105–113.

Hayden, E. C. (2013, October 2). Ethics: Taboo genetics. *Nature, 502,* 26–28. https://doi.org/10.1038/502026a

Heinze, J. E., Heinze, K. L., Davis, M. M., Butchart, A. T., Singer, D. C., & Clark, S. J. (2017). Gender role beliefs and parents' support for athletic participation. *Youth & Society, 49*(5), 634–657.

Heron-Delaney, M., Wirth, S., & Pascalis, O. (2011). Infants' knowledge of their own species. *Philosophical Transactions of the Royal Society B: Biological Sciences, 366*(1571), 1753–1763.

Herrnstein, R. J. (1995). *The bell curve debate: History, documents, opinions.* R. Jacoby & N. Glauberman (Eds.). Times Books.

Herrnstein, R. J., & Murray, C. A. (1994). *The bell curve: Intelligence and class structure in American life*. The Free Press.

Heyes, C., & Catmur, C. (2021). What happened to mirror neurons? *Perspectives on Psychological Science*. Advance online publication. https://doi.org/10.1177/1745691621990638

Hicks, R. D. (Ed.). (2015). *Aristotle de anima*. Cambridge University Press.

Hill, S. E., & Flom, R. (2007). 18-and 24-month-olds' discrimination of gender-consistent and inconsistent activities. *Infant Behavior and Development, 30*(1), 168–173.

Himebauch, A., Arnold, R. M., & May, C. (2008). Grief in children and developmental concepts of death #138. *Journal of Palliative Medicine, 11*(2), 242–244.

Hoelter, L. F., Axinn, W. G., & Ghimire, D. J. (2004). Social change, premarital nonfamily experiences, and marital dynamics. *Journal of Marriage and Family, 66*(5), 1131–1151.

Hoeve, M., Dubas, J. S., Gerris, J. R., Van der Laan, P. H., & Smeenk, W. (2011). Maternal and paternal parenting styles: Unique and combined links to adolescent and early adult delinquency. *Journal of Adolescence, 34*(5), 813–827.

Hoff, E. (2018). Bilingual development in children of immigrant families. *Child Development Perspectives, 12*(2), 80–86.

Hoff, E., & Core, C. (2013, November). Input and language development in bilingually developing children. *Seminars in Speech and Language, 34*(4), 215–226.

Hoff, E., Core, C., Place, S., Rumiche, R., Señor, M., & Parra, M. (2012). Dual language exposure and early bilingual development. *Journal of Child Language, 39*(1), 1–27.

Hoffman, M. L. (2001). *Empathy and moral development: Implications for caring and justice*. Cambridge University Press.

Hofmann, S. G., Doan, S. N., Sprung, M., Wilson, A., Ebesutani, C., Andrews, L. A., ... & Harris, P. L. (2016). Training children's theory-of-mind: A meta-analysis of controlled studies. *Cognition, 150*, 200–212.

Hofstee, W. K., De Raad, B., & Goldberg, L. R. (1992). Integration of the big five and circumplex approaches to trait structure. *Journal of Personality and Social Psychology, 63*(1), 146–163.

Holmes, R. M., & Romeo, L. (2013). Gender, play, language, and creativity in preschoolers. *Early Child Development and Care, 183*(11), 1531–1543.

Hong, J. S., & Espelage, D. L. (2012). A review of research on bullying and peer victimization in school: An ecological system analysis. *Aggression and Violent Behavior, 17*(4), 311–322.

Hoogeveen, S., Sarafoglou, A., & Wagenmakers, E. J. (2020). Laypeople can predict which social-science studies will be replicated successfully. *Advances in Methods and Practices in Psychological Science, 3*(3), 267–285.

Hoover, W. A., & Gough, P. B. (1990). The simple view of reading. *Reading and Writing, 2*(2), 127–160.

Hothersall, D. (2004). *History of psychology* (4th ed.). McGraw-Hill.

House, S. H. (2007). Nurturing the brain nutritionally and emotionally from before conception to late adolescence. *Nutrition and Health, 19*(1–2), 143–161.

Houtveen, A. A. M. (2018). *Goed geletterd: opbrengsten van het Lectoraat Geletterdheid 2006–2018*. Hogeschool Utrecht, Kenniscentrum Leren en Innoveren.

Howes, C. (1994). *Collaborative construction of pretend*. SUNY Press.

Hoy, W. K., & Tschannen-Moran, M. (1999). Five faces of trust: An empirical confirmation in urban elementary schools. *Journal of School Leadership, 9*(3), 184–208.

Huang, G. H., & Gove, M. (2015). Asian parenting styles and academic achievement: Views from eastern and western perspectives. *Education, 135*(3), 389–397.

Hubley, A. M., & Arım, R. G. (2012). Subjective age in early adolescence: Relationships with chronological age, pubertal timing, desired age, and problem behaviors. *Journal of Adolescence, 35*(2), 357–366.

Huizinga, J. (1938). *Homo ludens: proeve fleener bepaling van het spel-element der cultuur.* Tjeenk Willink.

Hulshof, C., & Bokhove, C. (2020). *Cognitive load theory: A more progressing or degenerating programme?* [Manuscript in preparation.]

Hyde, J. S., & DeLamater, J. D. (2008). *Understanding human sexuality.* McGraw-Hill Higher Education.

International Centre for the Prevention of Crime [ICPC] (2015, December). *Preventing radicalization: A systematic review.* Montreal.

Itard, J. (1806). Rapport sur les nouveaux développements de Victor de l'Aveyron. *Paris: de L'imprimerie Imperiale.*

Jackendoff, R. (2003). Précis of foundations of language: Brain, meaning, grammar, evolution. *Behavioral and Brain Sciences, 26*(6), 651–707.

Jacob, R., & Parkinson, J. (2015). The potential for school-based interventions that target executive function to improve academic achievement: A review. *Review of Educational Research, 85*(4), 512–552.

Jensen, A. (1969). How much can we boost IQ and scholastic achievement? *Harvard Educational Review, 39*(1), 1–123.

Johnson, J. G., Cohen, P., Kasen, S., & Brook, J. S. (2007). Extensive television viewing and the development of attention and learning difficulties during adolescence. *Archives of Pediatrics & Adolescent Medicine, 161*(5), 480–486.

Johnson, N. G., Roberts, M. C., & Worell, J. E. (1999). *Beyond appearance: A new look at adolescent girls.* American Psychological Association.

Johnson, S. (2005). *Everything bad is good for you: How today's popular culture is actually making us smarter.* Riverhead Publishing.

Jürimäe, T., & Saar, M. (2003). Self-perceived and actual indicators of motor abilities in children and adolescents. *Perceptual and Motor Skills, 97*(3), 862–866.

Jussim, L., & Harber, K. D. (2005). Teacher expectations and self-fulfilling prophecies: Knowns and unknowns, resolved and unresolved controversies. *Personality and Social Psychology Review, 9*(2), 131–155.

Juvonen, J., Graham, S., & Schuster, M. A. (2003). Bullying among young adolescents: The strong, the weak, and the troubled. *Pediatrics, 112*(6), 1231–1237.

Kahneman, D. (2003). A perspective on judgment and choice: Mapping bounded rationality. *American Psychologist, 58*(9), 697–720. https://doi.org/10.1037/0003-066X.58.9.697

Kahneman, D. (2011). *Thinking, fast and slow.* Macmillan.

Kahneman, D. (2013). Maps of bounded rationality: Psychology for behavioral economics. *American Economic Review, 93*(50), 1449–1475.

Kalb, G., & Van Ours, J. C. (2014). Reading to young children: A head-start in life? *Economics of Education Review, 40*, 1–24.

Kalkman, E., & Rep, M. (2017). Baby's en bewegen. In Kaklkman, E., & Rep, M. (Eds.) *Spelenderwijs bewegen* (pp. 68–75). Bohn Stafleu van Loghum, Houten.

Kaltiala-Heino, R., Kosunen, E., & Rimpelä, M. (2003). Pubertal timing, sexual behaviour and self-reported depression in middle adolescence. *Journal of Adolescence, 26*(5), 531–545.

Kalyuga, S., Ayres, P., Chandler, P., & Sweller, J. (2003). The expertise reversal effect. *Educational Psychologist, 38*, 23–31.

Kaminaga, M. (2007). Pubertal timing and depression in adolescents. *Japanese Journal of Educational Psychology, 55*(3), 370–381. https://doi.org/10.5926/jjep1953.55.3_370

Kan, K. J., Wicherts, J. M., Dolan, C. V., & Van der Maas, H. L. (2013). On the nature and nurture of intelligence and specific cognitive abilities: The more heritable, the more culture dependent. *Psychological Science, 24*(12), 2420–2428.

Kantrowitz, E. J., & Evans, G. W. (2004). The relation between the ratio of children per activity area and off-task behavior and type of play in day care centers. *Environment and Behavior, 36*(4), 541–557.

Kar, S. K., Choudhury, A., & Singh, A. P. (2015). Understanding normal development of adolescent sexuality: A bumpy ride. *Journal of Human Reproductive Sciences, 8*(2), 70–74.

Kassai, R., Futo, J., Demetrovics, Z., & Takacs, Z. K. (2019). A meta-analysis of the experimental evidence on the near- and far-transfer effects among children's executive function skills. *Psychological Bulletin, 145*(2), 165–188. https://doi.org/10.1037/bul0000180

Katzer, C., Fetchenhauer, D., & Belschak, F. (2009). Cyberbullying: Who are the victims? A comparison of victimization in Internet chatrooms and victimization in school. *Journal of Media Psychology, 21*(1), 25–36.

Kaufman, A. S., Zhou, X., Reynolds, M. R., Kaufman, N. L., Green, G. P., & Weiss, L. G. (2014). The possible societal impact of the decrease in US blood lead levels on adult IQ. *Environmental Research, 132*, 413–420.

Kawabata, Y., & Crick, N. R. (2011). The antecedents of friendships in moderately diverse classrooms: Social preference, social impact, and social behavior. *International Journal of Behavioral Development, 35*(1), 48–57.

Keirse, M. (2002). *Kinderen helpen bij verlies. Een boek voor al wie van kinderen houdt.* Lannoo.

Kelly, G. (2001). *Sexuality today: A human perspective* (7th ed.). McGraw-Hill.

Kennisnet. (2016). *Kinderen en terreur op sociale media.* https://www.kennisnet.nl/fileadmin/kennisnet/publicatie/Kinderen_en_terreur_op_sociale_media_po.pdf

Kenny, M. E., & Gallagher, L. A. (2002). Instrumental and social/relational correlates of perceived maternal and paternal attachment in adolescence. *Journal of Adolescence, 25*(2), 203–219.

Kersten, L. E. (2011). *Children of mothers who were postpartum depressed: Early intervention and developmental outcomes in their first school years* [Doctoral Dissertation, Radboud Universiteit Nijmegen]. https://repository.ubn.ru.nl/bitstream/handle/2066/83184/83184.pdf

Kesmodel, U. S., Bertrand, J., Støvring, H., Skarpness, B., Denny, C. H., Mortensen, E. L., & Lifestyle During Pregnancy Study Group. (2012). The effect of different alcohol drinking patterns in early to mid pregnancy on the child's intelligence, attention, and executive function. *BJOG: An International Journal of Obstetrics & Gynaecology, 119*(10), 1180–1190.

Kibria, N. (2003). *Becoming Asian American: Second-generation Chinese and Korean American identities.* Johns Hopkins University Press.

Killen, M., Rutland, A., Abrams, D., Mulvey, K. L., & Hitti, A. (2013). Development of intra- and intergroup judgments in the context of moral and social-conventional norms. *Child Development, 84*(3), 1063–1080.

Killermann, S. (2017). Genderbread Person v4. 0: A teaching tool for breaking the big concept of gender down into bite-sized, digestible pieces. *The Genderbread Person.* Austin.

Kim, P., Evans, G. W., Angstadt, M., Ho, S. S., Sripada, C. S., Swain, J. E., ... & Phan, K. L. (2013). Effects of childhood poverty and chronic stress on emotion regulatory brain function in adulthood. *Proceedings of the National Academy of Sciences, 110*(46), 18442–18447.

Kim, S. Y., Wang, Y., Orozco-Lapray, D., Shen, Y., & Murtuza, M. (2013). Does 'tiger parenting' exist? Parenting profiles of Chinese Americans and adolescent developmental outcomes. *Asian American Journal of Psychology, 4*(1), 7–18.

Kirk, E., Pine, K., Wheatley, L., Howlett, N., Schulz, J., & Fletcher, B. (2015). A longitudinal investigation of the relationship between maternal mind-mindedness and theory of mind. *British Journal of Developmental Psychology, 33*(4), 434–445.

Kirschner, P. A., Claessens, L., & Raaijmakers, S. (2018). *Op de schouders van reuzen. Inspirerende inzichten uit de cognitieve psychologie voor leerkrachten.* Ten Brink Uitgevers.

Kirschner, P. A., & De Bruyckere, P. (2017). The myths of the digital native and the multitasker. *Teaching and Teacher Education, 67,* 135–142.

Kirschner, P. A., Sweller, J., & Clark, R. E. (2006). Why minimal guidance during instruction does not work: An analysis of the failure of constructivist, discovery, problem-based, experiential, and inquiry-based teaching. *Educational Psychologist, 41*(2), 75–86. https://doi.org/10.1207/s15326985ep4102_1

Klahr, A. M., & Burt, S. A. (2014). Elucidating the etiology of individual differences in parenting: A meta-analysis of behavioral genetic research. *Psychological Bulletin, 140*(2), 544–586. https://doi.org/10.1037/a0034205

Klasse. (2015). *Hoe praat je met jongeren over controversiële thema's?* www.klasse. be/29704/hoe-praat-je-met-jongeren-over-controversiele-themas/

Klein, R. A., Vianello, M., Hasselman, F., Adams, B. G., Adams Jr, R. B., Alper, S., ... & Batra, R. (2018). Many Labs 2: Investigating variation in replicability across samples and settings. *Advances in Methods and Practices in Psychological Science, 1*(4), 443–490.

Klemmensen, R., Hatemi, P. K., Hobolt, S. B., Skytthe, A., & Nørgaard, A. S. (2012). Heritability in political interest and efficacy across cultures: Denmark and the United States. *Twin Research and Human Genetics, 15*(1), 15–20.

Kohlberg, L. (1966). A cognitive-developmental analysis of children's sex role concepts and attitudes. In E. E. Maccoby (Ed.), *The development of sex differences* (pp. 82–173). Stanford University Press.

Kohlberg, L. (1976). Moral stages and moralization: The cognitive-development approach. In T. Lickona (Ed.), *Moral development and behavior: Theory research and social issues* (pp. 31–53). Holt, Rinehart, and Winston.

Kohlberg, L. (1981). *Essays on moral development, Vol l. I: The philosophy of moral development.* Harper & Row.

Kohut, S. & Pillai, R. (2008). Does the NFCS discriminate between infants experiencing pain-related and non-pain related distress? Paper presented at the Canadian Pain Society Annual Conference, Victoria, BC, mei 2008. *Pain research and Management,* 12, 120.

Kohut, S. A., & Riddell, R. P. (2009). Does the neonatal facial coding system differentiate between infants experiencing pain-related and non-pain-related distress? *The Journal of Pain, 10*(2), 214–220.

Komada, Y., Adachi, N., Matsuura, N., Mizuno, K., Hirose, K., Aritomi, R., & Shirakawa, S. (2009). Irregular sleep habits of parents are associated with increased sleep problems and daytime sleepiness of children. *The Tohoku Journal of Experimental Medicine, 219*(2), 85–89.

Koranyi, N., Brückner, E., Jäckel, A., Grigutsch, L. A., & Rothermund, K. (2020). Dissociation between wanting and liking for coffee in heavy drinkers. *Journal of Psychopharmacology, 34*(12), 1350–1356.

Kraft, M. A., & Monti-Nussbaum, M. (2020). *The big problem with little interruptions to classroom learning* (EdWorkingPaper No. 20-227). Annenberg Institute at Brown University. https://edworkingpapers.com/sites/default/files/Interruptions%20-%20 FINAL.pdf

Kraft, M. A., & Rogers, T. (2015). The underutilized potential of teacher-to-parent communication: Evidence from a field experiment. *Economics of Education Review, 47*, 49–63.

Kraybill, J. H., Kim-Spoon, J., & Bell, M. A. (2019). Focus: Attention science: Infant attention and age 3 executive function. *The Yale Journal of Biology and Medicine, 92*(1), 3–11.

Kruger, J., & Dunning, D. (1999). Unskilled and unaware of it: How difficulties in recognizing one's own incompetence lead to inflated self-assessments. *Journal of Personality and Social Psychology, 77*(6), 1121–1134. https://doi.org/10.1037/0022-3514.77.6.1121

Kuczynski, L., & Kochanska, G. (1990). Development of children's noncompliance strategies from toddlerhood to age 5. *Developmental Psychology, 26*(3), 398–408. https://doi.org/10.1037/0012-1649.26.3.398

Kuhl, P. K., Conboy, B. T., Coffey-Corina, S., Padden, D., Rivera-Gaxiola, M., & Nelson, T. (2008). Phonetic learning as a pathway to language: New data and native language magnet theory expanded (NLM-e). *Philosophical Transactions of the Royal Society B: Biological Sciences, 363*(1493), 979–1000.

Kuhl, P. K., Stevens, E., Hayashi, A., Deguchi, T., Kiritani, S., & Iverson, P. (2006). Infants show a facilitation effect for native language phonetic perception between 6 and 12 months. *Developmental Science, 9*(2), F13–F21.

Kühn, S., Kugler, D. T., Schmalen, K., Weichenberger, M., Witt, C., & Gallinat, J. (2019). Does playing violent video games cause aggression? A longitudinal intervention study. *Molecular Psychiatry, 24*(8), 1220–1234.

Kurth, S., Dean III, D. C., Achermann, P., O'Muircheartaigh, J., Huber, R., Deoni, S. C., & LeBourgeois, M. K. (2016). Increased sleep depth in developing neural networks: New insights from sleep restriction in children. *Frontiers in Human Neuroscience,10*, 456.

Kurz, T. B., & Knight, S. L. (2004). An exploration of the relationship among teacher efficacy, collective teacher efficacy, and goal consensus. *Learning Environments Research, 7*(2), 111–128.

Kyriakides, L., Creemers, B. P. M., Papastylianou, D., & Papadatou-Pastou, M. (2014). Improving the school learning environment to reduce bullying: An experimental study. *Scandinavian Journal of Educational Research 58*(4), 453–478. https://doi.org/1 0.1080/00313831.2013.773556

Ladd, G. W. (1983). Social networks of popular, average, and rejected children in school settings. *Merrill-Palmer Quarterly, 29*(3), 283–307.

Laemmle, J. (2013). Barbara Martin: Children at play: Learning gender in the early years. *Journal of Youth and Adolescence, 42*(2), 305–307. http://dx.doi.org/10.1007/ s10964-012-9871-7

Laflamme, D., Pomerleau, A., & Malcuit, G. (2002). A comparison of fathers' and mothers' involvement in childcare and stimulation behaviors during free-play with their infants at 9 and 15 months. *Sex Roles, 47*(11), 507–518.

Lafuente, M. J., Grifol, R., Segarra, J., Soriano, J., Gorba, M. A., & Montesinos, A. (1997). Effects of the Firstart method of prenatal stimulation on psychomotor development: The first six months. *Journal of Prenatal & Perinatal Psychology & Health, 11*(3), 151–162.

Laghzaoui, M. (2007). Berber in the Netherlands: A minority language in a multilingual society. In *Proceedings of the conference: Multilingualism across Europe* (pp. 69–76). EURAC Research.

Laghzaoui, M., & Kurvers, J. (2006). De ontwikkeling van schooltaalvaardigheid in het Tarifit en het Nederlands. Een eerste beschrijving van codering in het Tarifit. In Koole, T. (Ed) *Artikelen van de Vijfde Sociolinguistische Conferentie* (pp. 330–341). Eburon.

Lamiell, J. T. (2003). *Beyond individual and group differences: Human individuality, scientific psychology, and William Stern's critical personalism*. Sage.

Lansu, T. A., & Cillessen, A. H. (2015). Associations of group level popularity with observed behavior and influence in a dyadic context. *Journal of Experimental Child Psychology, 140*, 92–104.

Larsen, N. E., Lee, K., & Ganea, P. A. (2018). Do storybooks with anthropomorphized animal characters promote prosocial behaviors in young children? *Developmental Science, 21*(3), e12590.

Larson, R. W. (2000). Toward a psychology of positive youth development. *American Psychologist, 55*(1), 170–183.

Lau, M., Markham, C., Lin, H., Flores, G., & Chacko, M. R. (2009). Dating and sexual attitudes in Asian-American adolescents. *Journal of Adolescent Research, 24*(1), 91–113.

Laursen, B., Altman, R. L., Bukowski, W. M., & Wei, L. (2020). Being fun: An overlooked indicator of childhood social status. *Journal of Personality, 88*(5), 993–1006.

Lave, J., & Wenger, E. (1991). Learning in doing: Social, cognitive, and computational perspectives. *Situated learning: Legitimate peripheral participation*. Cambridge University Press.

Lavecchia, A. M., Liu, H., & Oreopoulos, P. (2016). Behavioral economics of education: Progress and possibilities. In E. A. Hanushek, S.J. Machin, & L. Woessmann (Eds.), *Handbook of the economics of education* (Vol. 5, pp. 1–74). Elsevier.

Lazaratou, H., Kalogerakis, Z., Economou, M., & Xenitidis, K. (2017). Socioeconomic crisis and aggressive behaviour of Greek adolescents. *International Journal of Social Psychiatry, 63*(6), 488–491.

Leary, T. (1957). *Interpersonal diagnosis of personality: A functional theory and methodology for personality evaluation*. Ronald Press.

Lee, K., & Ashton, M. C. (2014). The dark triad, the big five, and the HEXACO model. *Personality and Individual Differences, 67*, 2–5.

Leen-Feldner, E. W., Reardon, L. E., Hayward, C., & Smith, R. C. (2008). The relation between puberty and adolescent anxiety: Theory and evidence. In M. J. Zvolensky & J. A. J. Smits (Eds.), *Anxiety in health behaviors and physical illness* (pp. 155–179). Springer Science + Business Media.

Legassie, J., Zibrowski, E. M., & Goldszmidt, M. A. (2008). Measuring resident well-being: Impostorism and burnout syndrome in residency. *Journal of General Internal Medicine, 23*(7), 1090–1094.

Legg, S., & Hutter, M. (2007). A collection of definitions of intelligence. *Frontiers in Artificial Intelligence and applications, 157*, 17–24.

Lehto, J. E., Juujärvi, P., Kooistra, L., & Pulkkinen, L. (2003). Dimensions of executive functioning: Evidence from children. *British Journal of Developmental Psychology, 21*(1), 59–80.

Lepp, A., Li, J., & Barkley, J. E. (2016). College students' cell phone use and attachment to parents and peers. *Computers in Human Behavior, 64*, 401–408.

Lester, S., & Russell, W. (2010). *Children's right to play: An examination of the importance of play in the lives of children worldwide.* Working Papers in Early Childhood Development, No. 57. Bernard van Leer Foundation.

Levine, S. C., Huttenlocher, J., Taylor, A., & Langrock, A. (1999). Early sex differences in spatial skill. *Developmental Psychology, 35*(4), 940–949. https://doi.org/10.1037/0012-1649.35.4.940

Lewin, K. (1951). *Field theory in social science: Selected theoretical papers.* D. Cartwright (Ed.). Harpers.

Lewis, C., Freeman, N. H., Kyriakidou, C., Maridaki-Kassotaki, K., & Berridge, D. M. (1996). Social influences on false belief access: Specific sibling influences or general apprenticeship? *Child Development, 67*(6), 2930–2947.

Lewkowicz, D. J. (2002). Heterogeneity and heterochrony in the development of intersensory perception. *Cognitive Brain Research, 14*(1), 41–63.

Lewkowicz, D., & Ghazanfar, A. (2012). The development of the uncanny valley in infants. *Developmental Psychobiology, 54*(2), 124–132. https://doi.org/10.1002/dev.20583

Liberman, Z. (2020). Keep the cat in the bag: Children understand that telling a friend's secret can harm the friendship. *Developmental Psychology, 56*(7), 1290–1304. https://doi.org/10.1037/dev0000960

Lick, D. J., Durso, L. E., & Johnson, K. L. (2013). Minority stress and physical health among sexual minorities. *Perspectives on Psychological Science, 8*(5), 521–548.

Light, P. (1983). Piaget and egocentrism: A perspective on recent developmental research. *Early Child Development and Care, 12*(1), 7–18.

Lilienfeld, S. O., Lynn, S. J., Ruscio, J., & Beyerstein, B. L. (2011). *50 great myths of popular psychology.* Wiley-Blackwell.

Lillard, A. S. (2015). The development of play. In Lerner, M. (Ed) *Handbook of child psychology and developmental science* (pp. 1–44). Wiley.

Linsey, E. W., & Colwell, M. J. (2003). Preschoolers' emotional competence: Links to pretend and physical play. *Child Study Journal, 33*(1), 39–53.

Lipsitt, L. P., & Rovee-Collier, C. (2012). The psychophysics of olfaction in the human new-born. In G. M. Zucco, R. S. Herz, & B. Schaal (Eds.), *Olfactory cognition: From perception and memory to environmental odours and neuroscience. Advances in consciousness research, 58* (pp. 221–235). John Benjamins.

Liszkowski, U., Carpenter, M., Striano, T., & Tomasello, M. (2006). 12- and 18-month-olds point to provide information for others. *Journal of Cognition and Development, 7*(2), 173–187. https://doi.org/10.1207/s15327647jcd0702_2

Liu, Y. H., Lee, C. S., Yu, C. H., & Chen, C. H. (2016). Effects of music listening on stress, anxiety, and sleep quality for sleep-disturbed pregnant women. *Women & Health, 56*(3), 296–311.

Livingstone, S., Blum-Ross, A., Pavlick, J., & Olafsson, K. (2018). *In the digital home, how do parents support their children and who supports them?* Parenting for a Digital Future (Survey Report 1). Department of Media and Communications, The London School of Economics and Political Science.

Livingstone, S., & Haddon, L. (2009). *EU kids online: Final report*. LSE, EU Kids Online.

Locke, J., & Nidditch, P. H. (1979). *The Clarendon edition of the works of John Locke: An essay concerning human understanding*. Clarendon Press.

Locke, J. Y., Kavanagh, D. J., & Campbell, M. A. (2016). Overparenting and homework: The student's task but everyone's responsibility. *Journal of Psychologists and Counsellors in Schools*, *26*(1), 1–15.

Loeber, R., Drinkwater, M., Yin, Y., Anderson, S. J., Schmidt, L. C., & Crawford, A. (2000). Stability of family interaction from ages 6 to 18. *Journal of Abnormal Child Psychology*, *28*(4), 353–369.

Logan, J. A., Justice, L. M., Yumus, M., & Chaparro-Moreno, L. J. (2019). When children are not read to at home: The million word gap. *Journal of Developmental & Behavioral Pediatrics*, *40*(5), 383–386.

Long, M., Wood, C., Littleton, K., Passenger, T., & Sheehy, K. (2010). *The psychology of education*. Routledge.

Lopes, D. R., Van Putten, K., & Moormann, P. P. (2015). The impact of parental styles on the development of psychological complaints. *Europe's Journal of Psychology*, *11*(1), 155–168.

Love, A., & Burns, M. S. (2006). 'It's a hurricane! it's a hurricane!': Can music facilitate social constructive and sociodramatic play in a preschool classroom? *The Journal of Genetic Psychology*, *167*(4), 383–391.

Luria, A. R. (1966). *Human brain and psychological processes*. Harper & Row.

Lynn, R., Harvey, J., & Nyborg, H. (2009). Average intelligence predicts atheism rates across 137 nations. *Intelligence*, *37*(1), 11–15.

Lynne, S. D., Graber, J. A., Nichols, T. R., Brooks-Gunn, J., & Botvin, G. J. (2007). Links between pubertal timing, peer influences, and externalizing behaviors among urban students followed through middle school. *Journal of Adolescent Health*, *40*(2), 181.e7–181.e13.

Lyons, J. (1981). *Language and linguistics*. Cambridge University Press.

Maccoby, E. E., & Martin, J. A. (1983). Socialization in the context of the family: Parent–child interaction. In P. H. Mussen (Ed.), *Handbook of child psychology: formerly Carmichael's manual of child psychology* (Vol. 4, pp. 1–101). Wiley.

Macnamara, B. N., Hambrick, D. Z., & Oswald, F. L. (2014). Deliberate practice and performance in music, games, sports, education, and professions: A meta-analysis. *Psychological Science*, *25*, 1608–1618. https://doi.org/10.1177/0956797614535810

MacWhinney, B. (1991). Connectionism as a framework for language acquisition theory. In J. Miller (Ed.), *Research on child language disorders: A decade of progress*. ProEd.

Main, M., & Solomon, J. (1990). Procedures for identifying infants as disorganized/disoriented during the Ainsworth Strange Situation. In M. T. Greenberg, D. Cicchetti, & E. M. Cummings (Eds.), *Attachment in the preschool years* (pp. 121–160). University of Chicago Press.

Mani, A., Mullainathan, S., Shafir, E., & Zhao, J. (2013). Poverty impedes cognitive function. *Science*, *341*(6149), 976–980.

Manning, W. D., Giordano, P. C., & Longmore, M. A. (2006). Hooking up: The relationship contexts of 'nonrelationship' sex. *Journal of Adolescent Research*, *21*(5), 459–483.

Mansfield, C. F., Beltman, S., Broadley, T., & Weatherby-Fell, N. (2016). Building resilience in teacher education: An evidenced informed framework. *Teaching and Teacher Education*, *54*, 77–87.

Maples, M. F. (1988). Group development: Extending Tuckman's theory. *Journal for Specialists in Group Work, 13*(1), 17–23.

Marchiori, D. R., Adriaanse, M. A., & De Ridder, D. T. (2017). Unresolved questions in nudging research: Putting the psychology back in nudging. *Social and Personality Psychology Compass, 11*(1), e12297.

Marcia, J. E. (1966). Development and validation of ego-identity status. *Journal of Personality and Social Psychology, 3*(5), 551–558.

Mares, S. H., Van der Vorst, H., Engels, R. C., & Lichtwarck-Aschoff, A. (2011). Parental alcohol use, alcohol-related problems, and alcohol-specific attitudes, alcohol-specific communication, and adolescent excessive alcohol use and alcohol-related problems: An indirect path model. *Addictive Behaviors, 36*(3), 209–216.

Marker, C., Gnambs, T., & Appel, M. (2018). Active on Facebook and failing at school? Meta-analytic findings on the relationship between online social networking activities and academic achievement. *Educational Psychology Review, 30*(3), 651–677.

Marlowe, F. (2000). Paternal investment and the human mating system. *Behavioural Processes, 51*(1–3), 45–61.

Marschik, P. B., Einspieler, C., Strohmeier, A., Plienegger, J., Garzarolli, B., & Prechtl, H. F. (2008). From the reaching behavior at 5 months of age to hand preference at preschool age. *Developmental Psychobiology: The Journal of the International Society for Developmental Psychobiology, 50*(5), 511–518.

Martin, C. L., & Ruble, D. (2004). Children's search for gender cues: Cognitive perspectives on gender development. *Current Directions in Psychological Science, 13*(2), 67–70.

Martin, C. L., Ruble, D. N., & Szkrybalo, J. (2002). Cognitive theories of early gender development. *Psychological Bulletin, 128*(6), 903–933.

Martínez-Loredo, V., Fernández-Artamendi, S., Weidberg, S., Pericot, I., López-Núñez, C., Fernández-Hermida, J. R., & Secades, R. (2016). Parenting styles and alcohol use among adolescents: A longitudinal study. *European Journal of Investigation in Health, Psychology and Education, 6*(1), 27–36.

Marx, R.W. (1983). Student perception in classrooms. *Educational Psychologist, 18*(3), 145–164. https://doi.org/10.1080/00461528309529271

Masataka, N. (2003). *The onset of language* (Vol. 9). Cambridge University Press.

Masuda, T., Ellsworth, P. C., Mesquita, B., Leu, J., Tanida, S., & Van de Veerdonk, E. (2008). Placing the face in context: Cultural differences in the perception of facial emotion. *Journal of Personality and Social Psychology, 94*(3), 365–381.

Matlin, M. W. (2003). From menarche to menopause: Misconceptions about women's reproductive lives. *Psychological Science, 45*, 106–122.

Matricciani, L. A., Olds, T. S., Blunden, S., Rigney, G., & Williams, M. T. (2012). Never enough sleep: A brief history of sleep recommendations for children. *Pediatrics, 129*(3), 548–556.

Maurer, D., & Barrera, M. (1981). Infants' perception of natural and distorted arrangements of a schematic face. *Child Development, 52*(1), 196–202.

Mayer, R. E. (2004). Should there be a three-strikes rule against pure discovery learning? *American Psychologist, 59*(1), 14–19.

Mazur, J. (2016). *Learning and behavior* (8th ed.). Routledge.

McAlister, A., & Peterson, C. C. (2006). Mental playmates: Siblings, executive functioning and theory of mind. *British Journal of Developmental Psychology, 24*(4), 733–751.

McCabe, M. P., & Ricciardelli, L. A. (2006). A prospective study of extreme weight change behaviors among adolescent boys and girls. *Journal of Youth and Adolescence, 35*(3), 425–434.

McClure, E., & Barr, R. (2017). Building family relationships from a distance: Supporting connections with babies and toddlers using video and video chat. In R. Barr & D. N. Linebarger (Eds.). *Media exposure during infancy and early childhood* (pp. 227–248). Cham.

McGinnis, E. (2012). *Skillstreaming in early childhood: A guide for teaching prosocial skills.* Research Press.

McGonigle-Chalmers, M., Slater, H., & Smith, A. (2014). Rethinking private speech in preschoolers: The effects of social presence. *Developmental Psychology, 50*(3), 829–836.

McGowan, A., Hanna, P., & Busch, J. (2017). Learning to program: Choose your lecture seat carefully! *Proceedings of the 2017 ACM Conference on Innovation and Technology in Computer Science Education.* ITiCSE '17, New York. https://doi.org/10.1145/3059009.3059020

McGue, M., & Lykken, D. T. (1992). Genetic influence on risk of divorce. *Psychological Science, 3*(6), 368–373.

McHale, S. M., Dariotis, J. K., & Kauh, T. J. (2003). Social development and social relationships in middle childhood. In R. M. Lerner, M. A. Easterbrooks, & J. Mistry (Eds.), *Handbook of psychology. Vol. 6: Developmental psychology* (pp. 241–265). Wiley.

McMillan, B. T., & Saffran, J. R. (2016). Learning in complex environments: The effects of background speech on early word learning. *Child Development, 87*(6), 1841–1855.

Mealey, L. (2000). *Sex differences: Developmental and evolutionary strategies.* Academic Press.

Mehta, C. M., & Strough, J. (2009). Sex segregation in friendships and normative contexts across the life span. *Developmental Review, 29*(3), 201–220.

Meins, E., Fernyhough, C., Arnott, B., Turner, M., & Leekam, S. R. (2011). Mother-versus infant-centered correlates of maternal mind-mindedness in the first year of life. *Infancy, 16*(2), 137–165.

Meins, E., Fernyhough, C., Wainwright, R., Clark-Carter, D., Das Gupta, M., Fradley, E., & Tuckey, M. (2003). Pathways to understanding mind: Construct validity and predictive validity of maternal mind-mindedness. *Child Development, 74*(4), 1194–1211.

Meisinger, E. B., Blake, J. J., Lease, A. M., Palardy, G. J., & Olejnik, S. F. (2007). Variant and invariant predictors of perceived popularity across majority-Black and majority-White classrooms. *Journal of School Psychology, 45*(1), 21–44.

Meltzoff, A. N. (2002). Elements of a developmental theory of imitation. In A. N. Meltzoff & W. Prinz (Eds.), *The imitative mind: Development, evolution, and brain bases* (pp. 19–41). Cambridge University Press.

Meltzoff, A. N., & Moore, M. K. (1977). Imitation of facial and manual gestures by human neonates. *Science, 198*(4312), 75–78.

Meltzoff, A. N., & Moore, M. K. (1983). New-born infants imitate adult facial gestures. *Child Development, 54*(3), 702–709.

Meltzoff, A. N., & Moore, M. K. (1994). Imitation, memory, and the representation of persons. *Infant Behavior and Development, 17*(1), 83–99.

Meltzoff, A. N., & Moore, M. K. (1999a). Persons and representation: Why infant imitation is important for theories of human development. In J. Nadel & G. Butterworth (Eds.), *Cambridge studies in cognitive perceptual development. Imitation in infancy* (pp. 9–35). Cambridge University Press.

Meltzoff, A. N., & Moore, M. K. (1999b). Resolving the debate about early imitation. In A. Slater & D. Muir (Eds.), *The Blackwell reader in development psychology* (pp. 151–155). Blackwell.

Meltzoff, A. N., Waismeyer, A., & Gopnik, A. (2012). Learning about causes from people: Observational causal learning in 24-month-old infants. *Developmental Psychology, 48*(5), 1215–1228. https://doi.org/10.1037/a0027440

Mendle, J., Turkheimer, E., & Emery, R. E. (2007). Detrimental psychological outcomes associated with early pubertal timing in adolescent girls. *Developmental Review, 27*(2), 151–171.

Mennella, J. A., Kennedy, J. M., & Beauchamp, G. K. (2006). Vegetable acceptance by infants: Effects of formula flavors. *Early Human Development, 82*(7), 463–468.

Merritt, A. C., Effron, D. A., & Monin, B. (2010). Moral self-licensing: When being good frees us to be bad. *Social and Personality Psychology Compass, 4*(5), 344–357.

Merton, R. K. (1948). The self-fulfilling prophecy. *The Antioch Review, 8*(2), 193–210.

Mervis, C. B., & Bertrand, J. (1994). Acquisition of the novel name–nameless category (N3C) principle. *Child Development, 65*(6), 1646–1662.

Michel, F. T., & Tyler, A. N. (2005). Critical period: A history of the transition from questions of when, to what, to how. *Developmental Psychobiology, 46*, 156–162.

Milgram, S. (1963). Behavioral study of obedience. *Journal of Abnormal and Social Psychology, 67*, 371–378.

Milgram, S. (1974). *Obedience to authority.* Harper & Row.

Miller, J. L., & Eimas, P. D. (1995). Speech perception: From signal to word. *Annual Review of Psychology, 46*, 467–492.

Miller, N., & Campbell, D. T. (1959). Recency and primacy in persuasion as a function of the timing of speeches and measurements. *The Journal of Abnormal and Social Psychology, 59*(1), 1–9. https://doi.org/10.1037/h0049330

Mills, C. (2013). Why nudges matter: A reply to Goodwin. *Politics, 33*(1), 28–36.

Minagawa-Kawai, Y., Van Der Lely, H., Ramus, F., Sato, Y., Mazuka, R., & Dupoux, E. (2011). Optical brain imaging reveals general auditory and language-specific processing in early infant development. *Cerebral Cortex, 21*(2), 254–261.

Mischel, W. (2014). *The marshmallow test: Understanding self-control and how to master it.* Random House.

Mischel, W., Shoda, Y., & Rodriguez, M. I. (1989). Delay of gratification in children. *Science, 244*(4907), 933–938. https://doi.org/10.1126/science.2658056

Mitchell, P. (2017). Acquiring a theory of mind. In A. Slater & J. G. Bremner (Eds.), *An introduction to developmental psychology.* Wiley.

Mizuno, K., & Ueda, A. (2004). Antenatal olfactory learning influences infant feeding. *Early Human Development, 76*(2), 83–90.

Moilanen, K. L., & Manuel, M. L. (2019). Helicopter parenting and adjustment outcomes in young adulthood: A consideration of the mediating roles of mastery and self-regulation. *Journal of Child and Family Studies, 28*(8), 2145–2158.

Montgomery, C., Fisk, J. E., Murphy, P. N., Ryland, I., & Hilton, J. (2012). The effects of heavy social drinking on executive function: A systematic review and meta-analytic study of existing literature and new empirical findings. *Human Psychopharmacology: Clinical and Experimental, 27*(2), 187–199.

Moon, C., Cooper, R. P., & Fifer, W. P. (1993). Two-day-olds prefer their native language. *Infant Behavior and Development, 16*(4), 495–500.

Morales, J., Calvo, A., & Bialystok, E. (2013). Working memory development in monolingual and bilingual children. *Journal of Experimental Child Psychology, 114*(2), 187–202.

Moreno-Delgado, D., Puigdellívol, M., Moreno, E., Rodríguez-Ruiz, M., Botta, J., Gasperini, P., ... & McCormick, P. J. (2020). Modulation of dopamine D1 receptors via histamine H3 receptors is a novel therapeutic target for Huntington's disease. *Elife, 9*, e51093.

Morris, D. H., Jones, M. E., Schoemaker, M. J., Ashworth, A., & Swerdlow, A. J. (2011). Secular trends in age at menarche in women in the UK born 1908–93: Results from the Breakthrough Generations Study. *Paediatric and Perinatal Epidemiology, 25*(4), 394–400.

Mõttus, R., Soto, C. J., & Slobodskaya, H. R. (2017). Are all kids alike? The magnitude of individual differences in personality characteristics tends to increase from early childhood to early adolescence. *European Journal of Personality, 31*(4), 313–328.

Mueller, E., & Brenner, J. (1977). The origins of social skills and interaction among playgroup toddlers. *Child Development, 48*(3), 854–861.

Mullainathan, S., & Shafir, E. (2013). *Scarcity: Why having too little means so much.* Macmillan.

Müller, U., Liebermann-Finestone, D. P., Carpendale, J. I., Hammond, S. I., & Bibok, M. B. (2012). Knowing minds, controlling actions: The developmental relations between theory of mind and executive function from 2 to 4 years of age. *Journal of Experimental Child Psychology, 111*(2), 331–348.

Mullinax, M., Mathur, S., & Santelli, J. (2017). Adolescent sexual health and sexuality education. In A. L. Cherry, V. Baltag, & M. E. Dillon (Eds.), *International handbook on adolescent health and development* (pp. 143–167). Cham.

Munzar, P., Cami, J., & Farré, M. (2003). Mechanisms of drug addiction. *New England Journal of Medicine, 349*, 2365–2365.

Murdock Jr, B. B. (1962). The serial position effect of free recall. *Journal of Experimental Psychology, 64*(5), 482–488. https://doi.org/10.1037/h0045106

Murdock, G. P. (1981). *Atlas of world cultures.* University of Pittsburgh Press.

Murray, A., & Egan, S. M. (2014). Does reading to infants benefit their cognitive development at 9-months-old? An investigation using a large birth cohort survey. *Child Language Teaching and Therapy, 30*(3), 303–315.

Nation, M., & Heflinger, C. A. (2006). Risk factors for serious alcohol and drug use: The role of psychosocial variables in predicting the frequency of substance use among adolescents. *The American Journal of Drug and Alcohol Abuse, 32*(3), 415–433.

National Center for School Crisis and Bereavement. (2018). *Talking to children about terrorist attacks and school and community shootings in the news.* www.school crisiscenter.org/wp-content/uploads/2020/08/guidelines-talkingto-Kids-About-Attacks-Two-Sided-Onesheet-Format.pdf

National Society for the Prevention of Cruelty to Children. (2017). *Supporting children worried about terrorism.* www.nspcc.org.uk/what-we-do/news-opinion/supporting-children-worried-about-terrorism/

Neal, J. W., Neal, Z. P., & Cappella, E. (2014). I know who my friends are but do you? Predictors of self-reported and peer-inferred relationships. *Child Development, 85*(4), 1366–1372.

Nederlandse Organisatie voor Wetenschappelijk Onderzoek. (2018, April 6). *Hoe goed kinderen lezen is in hoge mate erfelijk.* www.nwo.nl/cases/hoe-goed-kinderen-lezen-hoge-mate-erfelijk

Neisser, U., Boodoo, G., Bouchard Jr, T. J., Boykin, A. W., Brody, N., Ceci, S. J., ... & Urbina, S. (1996). Intelligence: Knowns and unknowns. *American Psychologist, 51*(2), 77–101.

Nelson, P. B., Adamson, L. B., & Bakeman, R. (2008). Toddlers' joint engagement experience facilitates preschoolers' acquisition of theory of mind. *Developmental Science, 11*(6), 847–852.

Newbury, D. F., Bishop, D. V., & Monaco, A. P. (2005). Genetic influences on language impairment and phonological short-term memory. *Trends in Cognitive Sciences, 9*(11), 528–534.

Newcomb, A. F., & Bagwell, C. L. (1996). The developmental significance of children's friendship relations. In W. W. Bukowski, A. F. Newcomb, & W. W. Hartup (Eds.), *The company they keep: Friendships in childhood and adolescence* (pp. 289–321). Cambridge University Press.

Newman, B. M., & Newman, P. R. (2020). Dynamic systems theory. In B. M. Newman & P. R. Newman (Eds.), *Theories of adolescent development* (pp. 77–112). Elsevier.

Newman, S. J., & Holupka, C. S. (2015). Housing affordability and child well-being. *Housing Policy Debate, 25*(1), 116–151.

Nicolai, S. (2001). Hechting en psychopathologie: Een literatuuroverzicht. *Tijdschrift voor psychiatrie, 43*(5), 333–342.

Nicolas, S., Andrieu, B., Croizet, J. C., Sanitioso, R. B., & Burman, J. T. (2013). Sick? Or slow? On the origins of intelligence as a psychological object. *Intelligence, 41*(5), 699–711.

Nihart, M. A. (1993). Growth and development of the brain. *Journal of Child and Adolescent Psychiatric and Mental Health Nursing, 6*(2), 39–40.

Ninio, A., Snow, C., & Gullickson, T. (1997). *Pragmatic development.* Westview.

Nisbett, R. E., Aronson, J., Blair, C., Dickens, W., Flynn, J., Halpern, D. F., & Turkheimer, E. (2012). Intelligence: New findings and theoretical developments. *American Psychologist, 67*(2), 130–159.

Noble, C., Sala, G., Peter, M., Lingwood, J., Rowland, C., Gobet, F., & Pine, J. (2019). The impact of shared book reading on children's language skills: A meta-analysis. *Educational Research Review, 28*, 100290.

Norman, D. A., & Shallice, T. (1986). Attention to action. In Davidson, R. J., Schwartz, G. E., & Shapiro, D. (Eds.). *Consciousness and self-regulation* (pp. 1–18). Springer.

NOS. (2015 February 27). *#TheDress: meerderheid ziet blauw-zwart.* https://nos.nl/op3/artikel/2021672-thedress-meerderheid-ziet-blauw-zwart.html

NOS. (2018 May 16). Dit zegt de wetenschap over dat gekke 'Laurel of Yanny'-fragmentje. https://nos.nl/op3/artikel/2232059-dit-zegt-de-wetenschap-over-dat-gekke-laurel-of-yanny-fragmentje.html

O'Boyle, E. J. (2009). The origins of homo economicus: A note. *Storia del Pensiero Economico, 6*(1), 195–204.

O'Connor, M. J., Kogan, N., & Findlay, R. (2002). Prenatal alcohol exposure and attachment behavior in children. *Alcoholism: Clinical and Experimental Research*, *26*(10), 1592–1602.

Odgers, C. L., & Jensen, M. R. (2020). Annual research review: Adolescent mental health in the digital age: facts, fears, and future directions. *Journal of Child Psychology and Psychiatry*, *61*(3), 336–348. https://doi.org/10.1111/jcpp.13190

Offer, D. (1969). *The psychological world of the teenager: A study of normal adolescent boys*. Basic Books.

Okbay, A., Beauchamp, J. P., Fontana, M. A., Lee, J. J., Pers, T. H., Rietveld, C. A., ... & Oskarsson, S. (2016). Genome-wide association study identifies 74 loci associated with educational attainment. *Nature*, *533*(7604), 539–542.

O'Keefe, P. A., Dweck, C. S., & Walton, G. M. (2018). Implicit theories of interest: Finding your passion or developing it? *Psychological Science*, *29*(10), 1653–1664.

Olivardia, R., & Pope, H. (2002). Body image disturbance in childhood and adolescence. In Castle, D., Phillips, K. A. (Eds.), *Disorders of body image*. Wrightson Biomedical, Hampshire, p. 1.

Open Science Collaboration. (2015). Estimating the reproducibility of psychological science. *Science*, *349*(6251), aac4716.

Ormrod, J. E. (2020). *Human learning* (8th ed.). Pearson.

Orben, A. (2020). Teenagers, screens and social media: A narrative review of reviews and key studies. *Social Psychiatry and Psychiatric Epidemiology*, *55*(4), 407–414.

O'Reilly, T., Wang, Z., & Sabatini, J. (2019). How much knowledge is too little? When a lack of knowledge becomes a barrier to comprehension. *Psychological Science*, *30*(9), 1344–1351.

Orth, U. (2018). The family environment in early childhood has a long-term effect on self-esteem: A longitudinal study from birth to age 27 years. *Journal of Personality and Social Psychology*, *114*(4), 637–655.

Ozawa, M., Kanda, K., Hirata, M., Kusakawa, I., & Suzuki, C. (2011). Influence of repeated painful procedures on prefrontal cortical pain responses in new-borns. *Acta Paediatrica*, *100*(2), 198–203.

Pace, A., Alper, R., Burchinal, M. R., Golinkoff, R. M., & Hirsh-Pasek, K. (2019). Measuring success: Within and cross-domain predictors of academic and social trajectories in elementary school. *Early Childhood Research Quarterly*, *46*, 112–125.

Palincsar, A. S. (1998). Social constructivist perspectives on teaching and learning. *Annual Review of Psychology*, *49*, 345–375. https://doi.org/10.1146/annurev.psych.49.1.345

Palmer, S. B., Fais, L., Golinkoff, R. M., & Werker, J. F. (2012). Perceptual narrowing of linguistic sign occurs in the 1st year of life. *Child Development*, *83*(2), 543–553.

Paludi, M. A. (2012). *The psychology of love* (Vols 1–4). Praeger/ABC-CLIO.

Papadimitriou, A. (2016). The evolution of the age at menarche from prehistorical to modern times. *Journal of Pediatric and Adolescent Gynecology*, *29*(6), 527–530.

Paquette, D., Carbonneau, R., Dubeau, D., Bigras, M., & Tremblay, R. E. (2003). Prevalence of father–child rough-and-tumble play and physical aggression in preschool children. *European Journal of Psychology of Education*, *18*(2), 171–189.

Park, K. A., Lay, K.-l., & Ramsay, L. (1993). Individual differences and developmental changes in preschoolers' friendships. *Developmental Psychology*, *29*(2), 264–270. https://doi.org/10.1037/0012-1649.29.2.264

Park, M., Brain, U., Grunau, R. E., Diamond, A., & Oberlander, T. F. (2018). Maternal depression trajectories from pregnancy to 3 years postpartum are associated with children's behavior and executive functions at 3 and 6 years. *Archives of Women's Mental Health, 21*(3), 353–363.

Parke, R. D. (2007). Fathers, families, and the future. In G. W. Ladd (Ed.), *Appraising the human developmental sciences: Essays in honor of Merrill-Palmer Quarterly.* Wayne State University Press.

Parker, P. D., Jerrim, J., & Anders, J. (2016). What effect did the global financial crisis have upon youth wellbeing? Evidence from four Australian cohorts. *Developmental Psychology, 52*(4), 640–651.

Parten, M. B. (1932). Social participation among pre-school children. *The Journal of Abnormal and Social Psychology, 27*(3), 243–269. https://doi.org/10.1037/h0074524

Paruthi, S., Brooks, L. J., D'Ambrosio, C., Hall, W. A., Kotagal, S., Lloyd, R. M., ... & Rosen, C. L. (2016). Recommended amount of sleep for pediatric populations: A consensus statement of the American Academy of Sleep Medicine. *Journal of Clinical Sleep Medicine, 12*(6), 785–786.

Pastoor, R. (2019). *GRIP: Het geheim van slim werken.* Uitgeverij NZ.

Paul, I. M., Savage, J. S., Anzman-Frasca, S., Marini, M. E., Mindell, J. A., & Birch, L. L. (2016). INSIGHT responsive parenting intervention and infant sleep. *Pediatrics, 138*(1), e20160762.

Pearl, J., & Mackenzie, D. (2018). *The book of why: The new science of cause and effect.* Basic Books.

Pedersen, S., Vitaro, F., Barker, E. D., & Borge, A. I. (2007). The timing of Middle-Childhood peer rejection and friendship: Linking early behavior to early-adolescent adjustment. *Child Development, 78*(4), 1037–1051.

Pellegrini, A. D., & Smith, P. K. (1998). Physical activity play: The nature and function of a neglected aspect of play. *Child Development, 69*(3), 577–598.

Peltz, J. S., Rogge, R. D., & Connolly, H. (2019). Parents still matter: The influence of parental enforcement of bedtime on adolescents' depressive symptoms. *Sleep, 43*(5), zsz287.

Perone, S., & Simmering, V. R. (2017). Applications of dynamic systems theory to cognition and development: New frontiers. *Advances in Child Development and Behavior, 52*, 43–80.

Persky, J. (1995). The ethology of homo economicus. *Journal of Economic Perspectives, 9*(2), 221–231.

Peterson, D. J., & Berryhill, M. E. (2013). The Gestalt principle of similarity benefits visual working memory. *Psychonomic Bulletin & Review, 20*(6), 1282–1289.

Petitpas, A. J., & Champagne, D. E. (2000). Sports and social competence. In S. Danish & T. P. Gullotta (Eds.), *Developing competent youth and strong communities through after-school programming* (pp. 92–108). Child Welfare League of America.

Phillips, T. (2015, October 29). China ends one-child policy after 35 years. *The Guardian.*

Piaget, J. (2013). *The moral judgment of the child.* Routledge. (Original work published 1932.)

Piaget, J., & Inhelder, B. (1967). *The child's conception of space.* Norton.

Pietschnig, J., & Gittler, G. (2015). A reversal of the Flynn effect for spatial perception in German-speaking countries: Evidence from a cross-temporal IRT-based meta-analysis (1977–2014). *Intelligence, 53*, 145–153.

Pietschnig, J., & Voracek, M. (2015). One century of global IQ gains: A formal meta-analysis of the Flynn effect (1909–2013). *Perspectives on Psychological Science, 10*(3), 282–306.

Pijnacker, J., Geurts, B., Van Lambalgen, M., Buitelaar, J., & Hagoort, P. (2010). Exceptions and anomalies: An ERP study on context sensitivity in autism. *Neuropsychologia, 48*(10), 2940–2951.

Pinker, S. (1994). *The language instinct.* Morrow.

Pinker, S. (2003). *The blank slate: The modern denial of human nature.* Penguin.

Pinquart, M. (2016). Associations of parenting styles and dimensions with academic achievement in children and adolescents: A meta-analysis. *Educational Psychology Review, 28*(3), 475–493.

Pinquart, M. (2017). Associations of parenting dimensions and styles with externalizing problems of children and adolescents: An updated meta-analysis. *Developmental Psychology, 53*(5), 873–932. https://doi.org/10.1037/dev0000295

Pintner, R., Forlano, G., & Freedman, H. (1937). Personality and attitudinal similarity among classroom friends. *Journal of Applied Psychology, 21*(1), 48–65. https://doi.org/10.1037/h0060037

Planinšec, J. (2001). A comparative analysis of the relations between the motor dimensions and cognitive ability of pre-school girls and boys. *Kinesiology, 33*(1), 56–68.

Plomin, R., Corley, R., DeFries, J. C., & Fulker, D. W. (1990). Individual differences in television viewing in early childhood: Nature as well as nurture. *Psychological Science, 1*(6), 371–377.

Plomin, R., & Deary, I. J. (2015). Genetics and intelligence differences: Five special findings. *Molecular Psychiatry, 20*(1), 98–108.

Plomin, R., DeFries, J. C., Knopik, V. S., & Neiderhiser, J. M. (2016). Top 10 replicated findings from behavioral genetics. *Perspectives on Psychological Science, 11*(1), 3–23.

Polletta, F., & Jasper, J. M. (2001). Collective identity and social movements. *Annual Review of Sociology, 27*, 283–305.

Ponton, L. E. (1999). Their dark romance with risk. *Newsweek, 133*(19), 55.

Porges, S. W., & Lipsitt, L. P. (1993). Neonatal responsivity to gustatory stimulation: The gustatory-vagal hypothesis. *Infant Behavior & Development, 16*(4), 487–494. https://doi.org/10.1016/0163-6383(93)80006-T

Posthuma, D., De Geus, E. J., Baaré, W. F., Pol, H. E. H., Kahn, R. S., & Boomsma, D. I. (2002). The association between brain volume and intelligence is of genetic origin. *Nature Neuroscience, 5*(2), 83–84.

Poulin-Dubois, D., Serbin, L. A., Eichstedt, J. A., Sen, M. G., & Beissel, C. F. (2002). Men don't put on make-up: Toddlers' knowledge of the gender stereotyping of household activities. *Social Development, 11*(2), 166–181.

Power, T. G. (2013). Parenting dimensions and styles: A brief history and recommendations for future research. *Childhood Obesity, 9*(s1), S-14–S-21.

Proulx, M. F., & Poulin, F. (2013). Stability and change in kindergartners' friendships: Examination of links with social functioning. *Social Development, 22*(1), 111–125.

Pugatch, T., & Wilson, N. (2018). Nudging study habits: A field experiment on peer tutoring in higher education. *Economics of Education Review, 62*, 151–161.

Quigley, A., Muijs, D., & Stringer, E. (2018). *Metacognition and self-regulated learning: Guidance report.* Education Endowment Foundation.

Quinn, P. C. (2008). In defense of core competencies, quantitative change, and continuity. *Child Development, 79*(6), 1633–1638.

Raag, T. (2003). Book review: Racism, gender identities and young children: Social relations in a multi-ethnic, inner-city primary school. *Archives of Sexual Behavior, 32*(4), 392–393.

Ramsey-Rennels, J. L., & Langlois, J. H. (2006). Infants' differential processing of female and male faces. *Current Directions in Psychological Science, 15*(2), 59–62.

Rancourt, D., Conway, C. C., Burk, W. J., & Prinstein, M. J. (2013). Gender composition of preadolescents' friendship groups moderates peer socialization of body change behaviors. *Health Psychology, 32*(3), 283–292. https://doi.org/10.1037/a0027980

Rasmussen, K. (2008). Halo effect. In N. J. Salkind & K. Rasmussen (Eds.), *Encyclopedia of educational psychology* (Vol. 1). Sage.

Ratcliffe, S. (2017). Oscar Wilde 1854–1900 Irish dramatist and poet. In Ratcliffe, S. (Ed) *Oxford essential quotations* (5th ed.). Oxford Reference. www.oxfordreference.com/view/10.1093/acref/9780191843730.001.0001/q-oro-ed5-00011525

Ray, E., & Heyes, C. (2011). Imitation in infancy: The wealth of the stimulus. *Developmental Science, 14*(1), 92–105.

Reddy, V., & Barrett, M. (1999). Prelinguistic communication. In Barret, M D. (Ed) *The development of language* (pp. 25–50). Psychology Press.

Reeve, J., & Jang, H. (2006). What teachers say and do to support students' autonomy during a learning activity. *Journal of Educational Psychology, 98*(1), 209–218. https://doi.org/10.1037/0022-0663.98.1.209

Rescorla, L., Alley, A., & Christine, J. B. (2001). Word frequencies in toddlers' lexicons. *Journal of Speech, Language, & Hearing Research, 44*, 598–609.

Resing, W., & Drenth, P. (2007). *Intelligentie.* Uitgeverij Nieuwezijds.

Rhodes, I., Long, M., Moore, D., Benham-Clarke, S., Kenchington, R., Boyle, C., ... & Rogers, M. (2019). *Improving behaviour in schools: Guidance report.* Education Endowment Foundation.

Ribner, A., Fitzpatrick, C., & Blair, C. (2017). Family socioeconomic status moderates associations between television viewing and school readiness skills. *Journal of Developmental & Behavioral Pediatrics, 38*(3), 233–239.

Rice, K. G., FitzGerald, D. P., Whaley, T. J., & Gibbs, C. L. (1995). Cross-sectional and longitudinal examination of attachment, separation-individuation, and college student adjustment. *Journal of Counseling & Development, 73*(4), 463–474.

Rice, M., & Dixon, W. (1998). There's a long, long way to go. *PsycCRITIQUES, 43*(4), 264–265.

Richards, M. H., Crowe, P. A., Larson, R., & Swarr, A. (1998). Developmental patterns and gender differences in the experience of peer companionship during adolescence. *Child Development, 69*(1), 154–163.

Rietveld, C. A., Medland, S. E., Derringer, J., Yang, J., Esko, T., Martin, N. W., ... & Albrecht, E. (2013). GWAS of 126,559 individuals identifies genetic variants associated with educational attainment. *Science, 340*(6139), 1467–1471.

Rinaldi, C. M. (2002). Social conflict abilities of children identified as sociable, aggressive, and isolated: Developmental implications for children at-risk for impaired peer relations. *Developmental Disabilities Bulletin, 30*(1), 77–94.

Ritchie, S. (2015). *Intelligence: All that matters.* John Murray.

Ritchie, S. J., & Tucker-Drob, E. M. (2018). How much does education improve intelligence? A meta-analysis. *Psychological Science, 29*(8), 1358–1369.

Rivera-Gaxiola, M., Silva-Pereyra, J., & Kuhl, P. K. (2005). Brain potentials to native and non-native speech contrasts in 7- and 11-month-old American infants. *Developmental Science, 8*(2), 162–172.

Robertson, K. F., Smeets, S., Lubinski, D., & Benbow, C. P. (2010). Beyond the threshold hypothesis: Even among the gifted and top math/science graduate students, cognitive abilities, vocational interests, and lifestyle preferences matter for career choice, performance, and persistence. *Current Directions in Psychological Science, 19*(6), 346–351.

Robinson, K. (2006) *Do schools kill creativity?* [Video]. Ted Conferences. www.ted.com/talks/sir_ken_robinson_do_schools_kill_creativity

Robinson, V., Hohepa, M., & Lloyd, C. (2009). *School leadership and student outcomes: Identifying what works and why.* Best evidence synthesis iteration [BES]. New Zealand Ministry of Education.

Rochat, P. (1989). Object manipulation and exploration in 2- to 5-month-old infants. *Developmental Psychology, 25*(6), 871–884. https://doi.org/10.1037/0012-1649.25.6.871

Rock, I., & Palmer, S. (1990). The legacy of Gestalt psychology. *Scientific American, 263*(6), 84–91.

Rodkey, E. N., & Riddell, R. P. (2013). The infancy of infant pain research: The experimental origins of infant pain denial. *The Journal of Pain, 14*(4), 338–350.

Roediger, H. (1985). Remembering Ebbinghaus. *PsycCRITIQUES, 30*(7), 519–523. https://doi.org/10.1037/023895

Roediger, H., & Pyc, M. (2012). Inexpensive techniques to improve education: Applying cognitive psychology to enhance educational practice. *Journal of Applied Research in Memory and Cognition, 1*(4), 242–248. https://doi.org/10.1016/j.jarmac.2012.09.002

Roeling, M. P., Willemsen, G., & Boomsma, D. I. (2017). Heritability of working in a creative profession. *Behavior Genetics, 47*(3), 298–304.

Rohrer, D. (2012). Interleaving helps students distinguish among similar concepts. *Educational Psychology Review, 24*, 355–367.

Ronen, T., Hamama, L., Rosenbaum, M., & Mishely-Yarlap, A. (2016). Subjective well-being in adolescence: The role of self-control, social support, age, gender, and familial crisis. *Journal of Happiness Studies, 17*(1), 81–104.

Rosa, E. M., & Tudge, J. (2013). Urie Bronfenbrenner's theory of human development: Its evolution from ecology to bioecology. *Journal of Family Theory & Review, 5*(4), 243–258.

Rose, A. J., & Asher, S. R. (1999). Children's goals and strategies in response to conflicts within a friendship. *Developmental Psychology, 35*(1), 69–79. https://doi.org/10.1037/0012-1649.35.1.69

Rosenstein, D., & Oster, H. (1988). Differential facial responses to four basic tastes in new-borns. *Child Development, 59*(6), 1555–1568.

Rosenthal, R., & Jacobson, L. (1968). Pygmalion in the classroom. *The Urban Review, 3*(1), 16–20.

Rothbart, M. K. (1989). Temperament and development. In G. A. Kohnstamm, J. E. Bates, & M. K. Rothbart (Eds.), *Temperament in childhood* (pp. 187–248). Wiley.

Rothbart, M. K., Ahadi, S. A., & Evans, D. E. (2000). Temperament and personality: Origins and outcomes. *Journal of Personality and Social Psychology, 78*(1), 122–135.

Rousseau, J. J. (2010). *Emile ou de l'éducation*. Flammarion.

Rubie-Davies, C., Hattie, J., & Hamilton, R. (2006). Expecting the best for students: Teacher expectations and academic outcomes. *British Journal of Educational Psychology, 76*(3), 429–444.

Rubie-Davies, C. M., Peterson, E. R., Sibley, C. G., & Rosenthal, R. (2015). A teacher expectation intervention: Modelling the practices of high expectation teachers. *Contemporary Educational Psychology, 40*, 72–85.

Ruda, M. A., Ling, Q. D., Hohmann, A. G., Peng, Y. B., & Tachibana, T. (2000). Altered nociceptive neuronal circuits after neonatal peripheral inflammation. *Science, 289*(5479), 628–630.

Rybanska, V., McKay, R., Jong, J., & Whitehouse, H. (2018). Rituals improve children's ability to delay gratification. *Child Development, 89*(2), 349–359.

Sackett, P. R., Schmitt, N., Ellingson, J. E., & Kabin, M. B. (2001). High-stakes testing in employment, credentialing, and higher education: Prospects in a post-affirmative-action world. *American Psychologist, 56*, 302–318.

Saiegh-Haddad, E. (2007). Epilinguistic and metalinguistic phonological awareness may be subject to different constraints: Evidence from Hebrew. *First Language, 27*(4), 385–405.

Sameroff, A. (1975). Transactional models in early social relations. *Human Development, 18*(1–2), 65–79.

Sameroff, A. (2009). *The transactional model*. American Psychological Association.

Sanchez-Garrido, M. A., & Tena-Sempere, M. (2013). Metabolic control of puberty: Roles of leptin and kisspeptins. *Hormones and Behavior, 64*(2), 187–194.

Saucier, G., & Srivastava, S. (2015). What makes a good structural model of personality? Evaluating the Big Five and alternatives. In M. Mikulincer & P. R. Shaver (Eds.), *APA handbook of personality and social psychology* (Vol. 4, pp. 283–305). American Psychological Association.

Savage-Rumbaugh, E. S., Murphy, J., Sevcik, R. A., Brakke, K. E., Williams, S. L., Rumbaugh, D. M., & Bates, E. (1993). Language comprehension in ape and child. *Monographs of the Society for Research in Child Development*, i–252.

Savin-Williams, R. C. (1998). *'--and then I became gay': Young men's stories*. Routledge.

Sawyer, R. K. (2011). *Explaining creativity: The science of human innovation*. Oxford University Press.

Schimanke, F., Mertens, R., & Vornberger, O. (2013, October). What to learn next? Content selection support in mobile game-based learning. In *E-Learn: World Conference on E-Learning in Corporate, Government, Healthcare, and Higher Education* (pp. 2503–2512). Association for the Advancement of Computing in Education (AACE).

Schlam, T. R., Wilson, N. L., Shoda, Y., Mischel, W., & Ayduk, O. (2013). Preschoolers' delay of gratification predicts their body mass 30 years later. *The Journal of Pediatrics, 162*(1), 90–93.

Schmader, T. (2012). *Stereotype threat: Theory, process, and application*. Oxford University Press.

Schmalz, D. L., & Kerstetter, D. L. (2006). Girlie girls and manly men: Children's stigma consciousness of gender in sports and physical activities. *Journal of Leisure Research, 38*(4), 536–557.

Schonert-Reichl, K. A., Smith, V., Zaidman-Zait, A., & Hertzman, C. (2012). Promoting children's prosocial behaviors in school: Impact of the 'Roots of Empathy' program on the social and emotional competence of school-aged children. *School Mental Health, 4*(1), 1–21.

Schreier, J. (2013). From Halo to hot sauce: What 25 years of violent video game research looks like. *Kotaku Longreads.* https://kotaku.com/from-halo-to-hot-sauce-what-25-years-of-violent-video-5976733

Schwarz, T. F., Huang, L. M., Medina, D. M. R., Valencia, A., Lin, T. Y., Behre, U., ... & Descamps, D. (2012). Four-year follow-up of the immunogenicity and safety of the HPV-16/18 AS04-adjuvanted vaccine when administered to adolescent girls aged 10–14 years. *Journal of Adolescent Health, 50*(2), 187–194.

Sedgh, G., Finer, L. B., Bankole, A., Eilers, M. A., & Singh, S. (2015). Adolescent pregnancy, birth, and abortion rates across countries: Levels and recent trends. *Journal of Adolescent Health, 56*(2), 223–230.

Sen, A. K. (1977). Rational fools: A critique of the behavioral foundations of economic theory. *Philosophy & Public Affairs, 6*(4), 317–344.

Serbin, L. A., Poulin-Dubois, D., Colburne, K. A., Sen, M. G., & Eichstedt, J. A. (2001). Gender stereotyping in infancy: Visual preferences for and knowledge of gender-stereotyped toys in the second year. *International Journal of Behavioral Development, 25*(1), 7–15.

Servin, A., Nordenström, A., Larsson, A., & Bohlin, G. (2003). Prenatal androgens and gender-typed behavior: A study of girls with mild and severe forms of congenital adrenal hyperplasia. *Developmental Psychology, 39*(3), 440–450. https://doi.org/10.1037/0012-1649.39.3.440

Settle, J. E., Dawes, C. T., & Fowler, J. H. (2009). The heritability of partisan attachment. *Political Research Quarterly, 62*(3), 601–613.

Shafto, C. L., Conway, C. M., Field, S. L., & Houston, D. M. (2012). Visual sequence learning in infancy: Domain-general and domain-specific associations with language. *Infancy, 17*(3), 247–271.

Shakeshaft, N. G., Trzaskowski, M., McMillan, A., Rimfeld, K., Krapohl, E., Haworth, C. M., ... & Plomin, R. (2013). Strong genetic influence on a UK nationwide test of educational achievement at the end of compulsory education at age 16. *PLOS One, 8*(12), e80341.

Shala, M., & Bahtiri, A. (2011). Differences in gross motor achievements among children of four to five years of age in private and public institutions in Prishtinë, Kosovo. *Early Child Development and Care, 181*(1), 55–61.

Shaver, P., & Hazan, C. (1987). Being lonely, falling in love. *Journal of Social Behavior and Personality, 2*(2), 105–124.

Shi, G., Xing, L., Wu, D., Bhattacharyya, B. J., Jones, C. R., McMahon, T., ... & Krystal, A. (2019). A rare mutation of β1-adrenergic receptor affects sleep/wake behaviors. *Neuron, 103*(6), 1044–1055.

Shi, L. (2003). Facilitating constructive parent–child play: Family therapy with young children. *Journal of Family Psychotherapy, 14*(3), 19–31.

Shin, H. B., & Bruno, R. (2003). *Language use and English-speaking ability: 2000.* Census 2000 Brief.

Shonkoff, J. P., Garner, A. S., Siegel, B. S., Dobbins, M. I., Earls, M. F., McGuinn, L., & Wood, D. L. (2012). The lifelong effects of early childhood adversity and toxic stress. *Pediatrics, 129*(1), e232–e246.

Shonkoff, J., Levitt, P., Bunge, S., Cameron, J., Duncan, G., Fisher, P., & Fox, N. (2015). *Supportive relationships and active skill-building strengthen the foundations of resilience*. Working Paper 13. National Scientific Council on the Developing Child, Harvard.

Siegler, R. (1996). *Children's thinking: Beyond the immaculate transition*. Oxford University Press.

Sierens, E., & Vansteenkiste, M. (2009). Wanneer 'meer minder betekent': Motivatieprofielen van leerlingen in kaart gebracht. *Begeleid zelfstandig leren, 24*, 17–35.

Simmons, J. P., Nelson, L. D., & Simonsohn, U. (2011). False-positive psychology: Undisclosed flexibility in data collection and analysis allows presenting anything as significant. *Psychological Science, 22*(11), 1359–1366.

Simon, E. B., Rossi, A., Harvey, A. G., & Walker, M. P. (2019). Overanxious and underslept. *Nature Human Behaviour, 4*(1), 100–110.

Simon, H. A. (1996). *Models of my life*. MIT Press.

Simons, D. J., & Chabris, C. F. (1999). Gorillas in our midst: Sustained inattentional blindness for dynamic events. *Perception, 28*(9), 1059–1074. https://doi.org/10.1068/p281059

Simons, P. R. J. (1999). Competentieontwikkeling: Van behaviorisme en cognitivisme naar sociaal-constructivisme. *Opleiding en Ontwikkeling, 12*, 41–46.

Simons, S. H., Van Dijk, M., Anand, K. S., Roofthooft, D., Van Lingen, R. A., & Tibboel, D. (2003). Do we still hurt new-born babies?: A prospective study of procedural pain and analgesia in neonates. *Archives of Pediatrics & Adolescent Medicine, 157*(11), 1058–1064.

Simpson, J. A., & Belsky, J. (2008). *Attachment theory within a modern evolutionary framework*. In J. Cassidy & P. R. Shaver (Eds.), *Handbook of attachment: Theory, research, and clinical applications* (pp. 131–157). Guilford Press.

Skinner, B. F. (1957). *Verbal behavior*. New York: Appleton-Century-Crofts.

Skinner, B. F. (1975). The steep and thorny way to a science of behavior. *American Psychologist, 30*(1), 42–49.

Skoe, E., Krizman, J., & Kraus, N. (2013). The impoverished brain: Disparities in maternal education affect the neural response to sound. *Journal of Neuroscience, 33*(44), 17221–17231.

Slater, A., & Bremner, J. G. (Eds.). (2017). *An introduction to developmental psychology*. Wiley.

Slater, A., & Kirby, R. (1998). Innate and learned perceptual abilities in the new-born infant. *Experimental Brain Research, 123*, 90–94. https://doi.org/10.1007/s002210050548

Slater, A., Von der Schulenburg, C., Brown, E., Badenoch, M., Butterworth, G., Parsons, S., & Samuels, C. (1998). New-born infants prefer attractive faces. *Infant Behavior and Development, 21*(2), 345–354.

Slaughter, V., Imuta, K., Peterson, C. C., & Henry, J. D. (2015). Meta-analysis of theory of mind and peer popularity in the preschool and early school years. *Child Development, 86*(4), 1159–1174.

Smidts, D. (2007). Executieve functies in ontwikkeling. *Het jonge kind, 44*(7), 22–25.

Smilansky, S. (1968). *The effects of sociodramatic play on disadvantaged preschool children*. Wiley.

Smith, L. B., & Thelen, E. (2003). Development as a dynamic system. *Trends in Cognitive Sciences, 7*(8), 343–348.

Smith, M., & Firth, J. (2018). *Psychology in the classroom: A teacher's guide to what works.* Routledge.

Smits, I., Soenens, B., Vansteenkiste, M., Luyckx, K., & Goossens, L. (2010). Why do adolescents gather information or stick to parental norms? Examining autonomous and controlled motives behind adolescents' identity style. *Journal of Youth and Adolescence, 39*(11), 1343–1356.

Snow, C. E., & Kang, J. Y. (2006). Becoming bilingual, biliterate, and bicultural. In Richard, M. L. (Ed), *Handbook of child psychology* (Vol. 4). Wiley.

Sokol, K. (2016, October 31). Directere aanmaningsbrief levert fiscus 18 miljoen euro op. *VRTNWS.* www.vrt.be/vrtnws/nl/2016/10/31/directere_aanmaningsbrieflevert fiscus18miljoeneuroop-1-2807919/

Solberg, O. K., Filkuková, P., Frich, J. C., & Feragen, K. J. B. (2018). Age at death and causes of death in patients with Huntington disease in Norway in 1986–2015. *Journal of Huntington's Disease, 7*(1), 77–86.

Sorkhabi, N., & Mandara, J. (2013). Are the effects of Baumrind's parenting styles culturally specific or culturally equivalent? In R. E. Larzelere, A. S. Morris, & A. W. Harrist (Eds.), *Authoritative parenting: Synthesizing nurturance and discipline for optimal child development* (pp. 113–135). American Psychological Association.

Sosnowska, J., Kuppens, P., De Fruyt, F., & Hofmans, J. (2020). New directions in the conceptualization and assessment of personality: A dynamic systems approach. *European Journal of Personality, 34*(6), 988–998. https://doi.org/10.1002/per.2233

Soto, C. J. (2016). The Little Six personality dimensions from early childhood to early adulthood: Mean-level age and gender differences in parents' reports. *Journal of Personality, 84*(4), 409–422.

Soto, C. J. (2019). How replicable are links between personality traits and consequential life outcomes? The life outcomes of Personality Replication Project. *Psychological Science, 30*(5), 711–727.

Souza, A. L., Byers-Heinlein, K., & Poulin-Dubois, D. (2013). Bilingual and monolingual children prefer native-accented speakers. *Frontiers in Psychology, 4*, 953.

Sperry, D. E., Sperry, L. L., & Miller, P. J. (2019). Reexamining the verbal environments of children from different socioeconomic backgrounds. *Child Development, 90*(4), 1303–1318.

Spessato, B. C., Gabbard, C., Valentini, N., & Rudisill, M. (2013). Gender differences in Brazilian children's fundamental movement skill performance. *Early Child Development and Care, 183*(7), 916–923.

Spielman, R. M., Dumper, K., Jenkins, W., Lacombe, A., Lovett, M., & Perlmutter, M. (2014). Gestalt principles of perception. In Spielman, R. M., Dumper, K., Jenkins, W., Lacombe, A., Lovett, M., & Perlmutter, M. (Eds.), *Psychology.* OpenStax CNX. http://cnx.org/contents/4abf04bf-93a0-45c3-9cbc-2cefd46e68cc@10.24

Sroufe, L. A. (1996). *Emotional development: The organization of emotional life in the early years.* Cambridge University Press.

Steinberg, L. (2008). A social neuroscience perspective on adolescent risk-taking. *Developmental Review, 28*(1), 78–106.

Steinberg, L. (2015). *Age of opportunity: Lessons from the new science of adolescence.* Houghton Mifflin Harcourt.

Steinberg, L., & Monahan, K. C. (2007). Age differences in resistance to peer influence. *Developmental Psychology, 43*(6), 1531–1543. https://doi. org/10.1037/0012-1649.43.6.1531

Steinberg, L., & Morris, A. S. (2001). Adolescent development. *Annual Review of Psychology, 52*, 83–110.

Steiner, D. D., & Rain, J. S. (1989). Immediate and delayed primacy and recency effects in performance evaluation. *Journal of Applied Psychology, 74*(1), 136–142. https://doi.org/10.1037/0021-9010.74.1.136

Steiner, J. E. (1979). Human facial expressions in response to taste and smell stimulation. *Advances in Child Development and Behavior, 13*, 257–295.

Sternberg, R. J. (2008). Increasing fluid intelligence is possible after all. *Proceedings of the National Academy of Sciences, 105*(19), 6791–6792.

Stevens, J., & Quittner, A. L. (1998). Factors influencing elementary school teachers' ratings of ADHD and ODD behaviors. *Journal of Clinical Child Psychology, 27*(4), 406–414.

Stewart, S. M., & Bond, M. H. (2002). A critical look at parenting research from the mainstream: Problems uncovered while adapting Western research to non-Western cultures. *British Journal of Developmental Psychology, 20*(3), 379–392.

Strack, F., Martin, L. L., & Stepper, S. (1988). Inhibiting and facilitating conditions of the human smile: A nonobtrusive test of the facial feedback hypothesis. *Journal of Personality and Social Psychology, 54*(5), 768–777.

Straughan, R. (1986). Why act on Kohlberg's moral judgments? (Or how to reach Stage 6 and remain a bastard). In Woodward, M., Mogdil, S., & Mogdil, C. (Eds.) *Lawrence Kohlberg* (pp. 157–165). Routledge.

Strice, E. (2003). Puberty and body image. In C. Hayward (Ed.), *Gender difference at puberty*. Cambridge University Press.

Sullivan, H. S. (Ed.). (1953). *The interpersonal theory of psychiatry*. W. W. Norton.

Sunstein, C. R. (2014). *Why nudge? The politics of libertarian paternalism*. Yale University Press.

Suor, J. H., Sturge-Apple, M. L., Davies, P. T., Cicchetti, D., & Manning, L. G. (2015). Tracing differential pathways of risk: Associations among family adversity, cortisol, and cognitive functioning in childhood. *Child Development, 86*(4), 1142–1158.

Swearer, S. M., & Espelage, D. L. (2004). Introduction: A social-ecological framework of bullying among youth. In Espelage, D. L., & Swearer, S. M. (Eds.). *Bullying in American schools* (pp. 23–34). Routledge.

Swearer, S. M., Espelage, D. L., Vaillancourt, T., & Hymel, S. (2010). What can be done about school bullying? Linking research to educational practice. *Educational Researcher, 39*(1), 38–47.

Sweller, J. (1988). Cognitive load during problem solving: Effects on learning. *Cognitive Science, 12*, 257–285.

Sweller, J. (2008). Instructional implications of David C. Geary's evolutionary educational psychology. *Educational Psychologist, 43*(4), 214–216. https://doi.org/10.1080/00461520802392208

Sweller, J., Van Merriënboer, J. J. G., & Paas, F. G. W. C. (1998). Cognitive architecture and instructional design. *Educational Psychology Review, 10*(3), 251–296. https://doi.org/10.1023/A:1022193728205

Sweller, J., Van Merriënboer, J. J. G., & Paas, F. (2019). Cognitive architecture and instructional design: 20 years later. *Educational Psychology Review, 31*, 261–292. https://doi.org/10.1007/s10648-019-09465-5

Swick, K. J., & Williams, R. D. (2006). An analysis of Bronfenbrenner's bio-ecological perspective for early childhood educators: Implications for working with families experiencing stress. *Early Childhood Education Journal*, *33*(5), 371–378.

Swingley, D. (2008). The roots of the early vocabulary in infants' learning from speech. *Current Directions in Psychological Science*, *17*(5), 308–312.

Taddio, A., Shah, V., Gilbert-MacLeod, C., & Katz, J. (2002). Conditioning and hyperalgesia in new-borns exposed to repeated heel lances. *JAMA*, *288*(7), 857–861.

Taga, K. A., Markey, C. N., & Friedman, H. S. (2006). A longitudinal investigation of associations between boys' pubertal timing and adult behavioral health and well-being. *Journal of Youth and Adolescence*, *35*(3), 380–390.

Talwar, V., Williams, S. M., Renaud, S. J., Arruda, C., & Saykaly, C. (2016). Children's evaluations of tattles, confessions, prosocial and antisocial lies. *International Review of Pragmatics*, *8*(2), 334–352.

Tan, L., & Ward, G. (2000). A recency-based account of the primacy effect in free recall. *Journal of Experimental Psychology: Learning, Memory, and Cognition*, *26*(6), 1589–1625. https://doi.org/10.1037/0278-7393.26.6.1589

Taylor, M., Cartwright, B. S., & Carlson, S. M. (1993). A developmental investigation of children's imaginary companions. *Developmental Psychology*, *29*(2), 276–285. https://doi.org/10.1037/0012-1649.29.2.276

Teasdale, T. W., & Owen, D. R. (2005). A long-term rise and recent decline in intelligence test performance: The Flynn Effect in reverse. *Personality and Individual Differences*, *39*(4), 837–843.

Thaler, R. H., & Sunstein, C. R. (2009). *Nudge: Improving decisions about health, wealth, and happiness*. Penguin.

The Learning Scientists (2020, March 4). *Six strategies for effective learning*. www.learningscientists.org/downloadable-materials

Thelen, E., & Smith, L. B. (1996). *A dynamic systems approach to the development of cognition and action*. MIT Press.

Thelen, E., & Smith, L. B. (2007). Dynamic systems theories. In Lerner, M. (Ed) *Handbook of child psychology* (Vol. 1). Wiley.

Thompson, R. A. (2013). Attachment theory and research: Précis and prospect. In Zelazo, P D. (Ed) *The Oxford handbook of developmental psychology* (Vol. 2, pp. 191–216). Oxford University Press.

Thorndike, E. L. (1920). A constant error in psychological ratings. *Journal of Applied Psychology*, *4*(1), 25–29.

Thorne, B. (1993). *Gender play: Girls and boys in school*. Rutgers University Press.

Tian, A. D., Schroeder, J., Häubl, G., Risen, J. L., Norton, M. I., & Gino, F. (2018). Enacting rituals to improve self-control. *Journal of Personality and Social Psychology*, *114*(6), 851–876.

Tincoff, R., & Jusczyk, P. W. (1999). Some beginnings of word comprehension in 6-month-olds. *Psychological Science*, *10*(2), 172–175.

Titova, O. E., Hogenkamp, P. S., Jacobsson, J. A., Feldman, I., Schiöth, H. B., & Benedict, C. (2015). Associations of self-reported sleep disturbance and duration with academic failure in community-dwelling Swedish adolescents: Sleep and academic performance at school. *Sleep Medicine*, *16*(1), 87–93.

Tomasello, M. (2006). Acquiring linguistic constructions. In R. Siegler & D. Kuhn (Eds.), *Handbook of child psychology* (pp. 255–298). Wiley.

Tomasello, M. (2009). *Why we cooperate*. MIT Press.

Tomasello, M., & Carpenter, M. (2007). Shared intentionality. *Developmental Science*, *10*(1), 121–125. https://doi.org/10.1111/j.1467-7687.2007.00573.x

Tortella, P., Haga, M., Ingebrigtsen, J. E., Fumagalli, G. F., & Sigmundsson, H. (2019). Comparing free play and partly structured play in 4-5-years-old children in an outdoor playground. *Frontiers in Public Health*, *7*, 197.

Toste, J. R., Didion, L., Peng, P., Filderman, M. J., & McClelland, A. M. (2020). A meta-analytic review of the relations between motivation and reading achievement for K–12 students. *Review of Educational Research*, *90*(3), 420–456.

Trahan, L. H., Stuebing, K. K., Fletcher, J. M., & Hiscock, M. (2014). The Flynn effect: A meta-analysis. *Psychological Bulletin*, *140*(5), 1332–1360.

Trainor, L. J., Austin, C. M., & Desjardins, R. N. (2000). Is infant-directed speech prosody a result of the vocal expression of emotion? *Psychological Science*, *11*(3), 188–195.

Trawick-Smith, J., & Dziurgot, T. (2011). 'Good-fit' teacher–child play interactions and the subsequent autonomous play of preschool children. *Early Childhood Research Quarterly*, *26*(1), 110–123.

Tricot, A., & Sweller, J. (2014). Domain-specific knowledge and why teaching generic skills does not work. *Educational Psychology Review*, *26*(2), 265–283. https://doi.org/10/gdj34w

Truelove, S., Vanderloo, L. M., & Tucker, P. (2017). Defining and measuring active play among young children: A systematic review. *Journal of Physical Activity and Health*, *14*(2), 155–166.

Tucker-Drob, E. M., Briley, D. A., & Harden, K. P. (2013). Genetic and environmental influences on cognition across development and context. *Current Directions in Psychological Science*, *22*(5), 349–355.

Tuckman, B. W., & Jensen, M. A. C. (1977). Stages of small-group development revisited. *Group & Organization Studies*, *2*(4), 419–427.

Turiel, E., & Rothman, G. (1972). The influence of reasoning on behavioral choices at different stages of moral development. *Child Development*, *43*(3), 741–756. doi:10.2307/1127628

Turkheimer, E. (2000). Three laws of behavior genetics and what they mean. *Current Directions in Psychological Science*, *9*(5), 160–164.

Turkheimer, E. (2018). The nature-nurture question. In Butler, A. (Ed.), *General Psychology (Fall 2018)*. Psychology Curricular Materials. 2.

Turner, H., Rubie-Davies, C. M., & Webber, M. (2015). Teacher expectations, ethnicity and the achievement gap. *New Zealand Journal of Educational Studies*, *50*(1), 55–69.

Tversky, A., & Kahneman, D. (1983). Extension- al versus intuitive reasoning: The conjunction fallacy in probability judgment. *Psychological review*, *90*(4), 293.

Tversky, A., & Kahneman, D. (1991). Loss aversion in riskless choice: A reference-dependent model. *The Quarterly Journal of Economics*, *106*(4), 1039–1061.

Twenge, J. M. (2017, September). Have smartphones destroyed a generation. *The Atlantic*. www.theatlantic.com/magazine/archive/2017/09/has-the-smartphone-destroyed-a-generation/534198/

Twenge, J. M., & Park, H. (2019). The decline in adult activities among US adolescents, 1976–2016. *Child Development*, *90*(2), 638–654.

Unsworth, N., Fukuda, K., Awh, E., & Vogel, E. K. (2014). Working memory and fluid intelligence: Capacity, attention control, and secondary memory retrieval. *Cognitive Psychology*, *71*, 1–26.

Urberg, K. A., Luo, Q., Pilgrim, C., & Degirmencioglu, S. M. (2003). A two-stage model of peer influence in adolescent substance use: Individual and relationship-specific differences in susceptibility to influence. *Addictive Behaviors*, *28*(7), 1243–1256.

Uylings, H. B. M. (2006). Development of the human cortex and the concept of 'critical' or 'sensitive' periods. *Language Learning*, *56*(s1), 59–90. https://doi.org/10.1111/j.1467-9922.2006.00355.x

Valenti, C. A. (2006). Infant vision guidance: Fundamental vision development in infancy. *Optometry & Vision Development*, *37*, 147–155.

Valkenburg, P. (2014). *Schermgaande jeugd: Over jeugd en media*. Prometheus.

Van Bergen, E., Snowling, M. J., de Zeeuw, E. L., van Beijsterveldt, C. E., Dolan, C. V., & Boomsma, D. I. (2018). Why do children read more? The influence of reading ability on voluntary reading practices. *Journal of Child Psychology and Psychiatry*, *59*(11), 1205–1214.

Van Cauwenberge, V., Wiersema, R., Hoppenbrouwers, K., Van Leeuwen, K., & Desoete, A. (2012). *Evolutie in temperament tijdens het eerste levensjaar en het verschil bij jongens en meisjes*. Steunpunt Welzijn, Volksgezondheid en Gezin. Rapport 33.

Vanden Abeele, M., Campbell, S. W., Eggermont, S., & Roe, K. (2014). Sexting, mobile porn use, and peer group dynamics: Boys' and girls' self-perceived popularity, need for popularity, and perceived peer pressure. *Media Psychology*, *17*(1), 6–33.

Van den Berg, Y. H., & Cillessen, A. H. (2015). Peer status and classroom seating arrangements: A social relations analysis. *Journal of Experimental Child Psychology*, *130*, 19–34.

Van den Bergh, B. R., Van den Heuvel, M. I., Lahti, M., Braeken, M., de Rooij, S. R., Entringer, S., ... & Schwab, M. (2017). Prenatal developmental origins of behavior and mental health: The influence of maternal stress in pregnancy. *Neuroscience & Biobehavioral Reviews*, *117*, 26–64.

Van den Bos, W., Van Dijk, E., Westenberg, M., Rombouts, S. A., & Crone, E. A. (2011). Changing brains, changing perspectives: The neurocognitive development of reciprocity. *Psychological Science*, *22*(1), 60–70.

Van der Horst, F., Lucassen, N., Kok, R., Sentse, M., Jooren, L., & Luijk, M. (2016). *Opgroeien in het hedendaagse gezin*. LannooCampus.

Van de Wiel, A., Poppelier, A., Van Dalen, W. E., & Van de Mheen, D. (2002). Hoeveel alcohol is te veel en waarom? Kanttekeningen bij sociaal geaccepteerd overmatig alcoholgebruik. *Nederlands Tijdschrift Voor Geneeskunde*, *146*(51), 2463–2465.

Van IJzendoorn, M. H., & Bakermans-Kranenburg, M. J. (1996). Attachment representations in mothers, fathers, adolescents, and clinical groups: A meta-analytic search for normative data. *Journal of Consulting and Clinical Psychology*, *64*(1), 8–21.

Van IJzendoorn, M. H., de Ruiter, C., & Kranenburg, M. J. (1991). *Intergenerationele overdracht van onverwerkte verlieservaringen*. In J. D. Boer (Ed.), *Infantpsychiatrie; De gezonde en verstoorde ontwikkeling van de vroege ouder-kindrelatie* (pp. 56–77). Van Gorcum.

Van Jaarsveld, C. H., Fidler, J. A., Simon, A. E., & Wardle, J. (2007). Persistent impact of pubertal timing on trends in smoking, food choice, activity, and stress in adolescence. *Psychosomatic Medicine*, *69*(8), 798–806.

Van Kesteren, M. T., Rijpkema, M., Ruiter, D. J., Morris, R. G., & Fernández, G. (2014). Building on prior knowledge: Schema-dependent encoding processes relate to academic performance. *Journal of Cognitive Neuroscience*, *26*(10), 2250–2261.

Van Merriënboer, J. J. G., & Kirschner, P. A. (2017). *Ten steps to complex learning: A systematic approach to four-component instructional design* (3rd ed.). Erlbaum.

Van Oosterdorp, M. (1999) *Klank en letter.* Universiteit Leiden.

Van Ouytsel, J., Walrave, M., Ponnet, K., Heirman, W., & d'Haenens, L. (2014). Prevalentie van sexting bij Vlaamse jongeren: een verkennende studie. *Tijdschrift voor orthopedagogiek, kinderpsychiatrie en klinische kinderpsychologie, 39*(4), 114–126.

Van Reekum, A. C., & Schmeets, M. G. J. (2008). De gen-omgevingsinteractie en de psychiatrie: Nieuwe visie op de invloed van de vroege omgeving. *Tijdschrift voor Psychiatrie, 50,* 12. 771–780.

Vansteenkiste, M., Sierens, E., Soenens, B., & Lens, W. (2007a). Willen, moeten en structuur in de klas: Over het stimuleren van een optimaal leerproces. *Begeleid zelfstandig leren, 16*(2), 37–58.

Vansteenkiste, M., Sierens, E., Soenens, B., & Lens, W. (2007b). Willen, moeten en structuur: Over het bevorderen van een optimaal leerproces, *Begeleid ZelfstandigLeren, 37,* 1–27.

Vansteenkiste, M., & Soenens, B. (2015). *Vitamines voor groei: Ontwikkeling voeden vanuit de Zelf-Determinatie Theorie.* Acco.

Vansteenkiste, M., Soenens, B., Sierens, E., & Lens, W. (2005). Hoe kunnen we leren en presteren bevorderen? Een autonomie-ondersteunend versus controlerend schoolklimaat. *Caleidoscoop, 17*(4), 18–25.

Vasiljevic, M., & Crisp, R. J. (2013). Tolerance by surprise: Evidence for a generalized reduction in prejudice and increased egalitarianism through novel category combination. *PLOS One, 8*(3), e57106.

Veitch, J., Timperio, A., Crawford, D., Abbott, G., Giles-Corti, B., & Salmon, J. (2011). Is the neighbourhood environment associated with sedentary behaviour outside of school hours among children? *Annals of Behavioral Medicine, 41*(3), 333–341.

Veldkamp, S. A., Boomsma, D. I., de Zeeuw, E. L., Van Beijsterveldt, C. E., Bartels, M., Dolan, C. V., & Van Bergen, E. (2019). Genetic and environmental influences on different forms of bullying perpetration, bullying victimization, and their co-occurrence. *Behavior Genetics, 49*(5), 432–443.

Veling, H., Van Koningsbruggen, G. M., Aarts, H., & Stroebe, W. (2014). Targeting impulsive processes of eating behavior via the internet. Effects on body weight. *Appetite, 78,* 102–109.

Vergauwe, J., Wille, B., Feys, M., De Fruyt, F., & Anseel, F. (2015). Fear of being exposed: The trait-relatedness of the impostor phenomenon and its relevance in the work context. *Journal of Business and Psychology, 30*(3), 565–581.

Visser, J. (2017, February 16). Waarom we de 'dromers, denkers En doeners' uit het onderwijs moeten verbannen. *De Correspondent.* https://decorrespondent. nl/6197/waarom-we-de-dromers-denkers-en-doeners-uit-het-onderwijs-moeten-verbannen/492370241-51cd584e

Vu, T., Magis-Weinberg, L., Jansen, B. R., Van Atteveldt, N., Janssen, T. W., Lee, N. C., ... & Meeter, M. (2021). Motivation-achievement cycles in learning: A literature review and research agenda. *Educational Psychology Review.* Advance online publication. https://doi.org/10.1007/s10648-021-09616-7

Vygotsky, L. (1978). Interaction between learning and development. *Readings on the Development of Children, 23*(3), 79–91.

Wade, N. (2001, October 4). Researchers say gene is linked to language. *New York Times.*

Wahi, G., Parkin, P. C., Beyene, J., Uleryk, E. M., & Birken, C. S. (2011). Effectiveness of interventions aimed at reducing screen time in children: A systematic review and meta-analysis of randomized controlled trials. *Archives of Pediatrics & Adolescent Medicine, 165*(11), 979–986.

Walden, T. A. (1991). Infant social referencing. In J. Garber & K. A. Dodge (Eds.), *The development of emotion regulation and dysregulation* (pp. 69–88). Cambridge University Press.

Walton, G. E., Bower, N. J. A., & Bower, T. G. R. (1992). Recognition of familiar faces by new-borns. *Infant Behavior and Development, 15*(2), 265–269.

Wang, M., & Lynn, R. (2018). Intelligence in the People's Republic of China. *Personality and Individual Differences, 134*, 275–277.

Warne, R. T., & Liu, J. K. (2017). Income differences among grade skippers and non-grade skippers across genders in the Terman sample, 1936–1976. *Learning and Instruction, 47*, 1–12.

Warnock, F., & Sandrin, D. (2004). Comprehensive description of new-born distress behavior in response to acute pain (new-born male circumcision). *Pain, 107*(3), 242–255.

Watson, J. S. (1972). Smiling, cooing, and 'the game'. *Merrill-Palmer Quarterly Of Behavior and Development, 18*(4), 323–339.

Wentzel, K. R. (2002). Are effective teachers like good parents? Teaching styles and student adjustment in early adolescence. *Child Development, 73*(1), 287–301.

Wentzel, K. R., & Asher, S. R. (1995). The academic lives of neglected, rejected, popular, and controversial children. *Child Development, 66*(3), 754–763.

Werner, L. A., & Marean, G. C. (1996). *Human auditory development*. Westview Press.

Whalley, B., & Hyland, M. E. (2013). Placebo by proxy: The effect of parents' beliefs on therapy for children's temper tantrums. *Journal of Behavioral Medicine, 36*(4), 341–346.

White, R. W. (1959). Motivation reconsidered: The concept of competence. *Psychological Review, 66*(5), 297–333. https://doi.org/10.1037/h0040934

Whitebread, D., Coltman, P., Jameson, H., & Lander, R. (2009). Play, cognition and self-regulation: What exactly are children learning when they learn through play? *Educational and Child Psychology, 26*(2), 40–52.

Whiting, B. B., Edwards, C. P., Edwards, C. P., & Ember, C. R. (1988). *Children of different worlds: The formation of social behavior*. Harvard University Press.

WHO Multicentre Growth Reference Study Group, & de Onis, M. (2006). WHO Motor Development Study: Windows of achievement for six gross motor development milestones. *Acta Paediatrica, 95*, 86–95.

Widding, G., & Berge, B. M. (2014). Teachers' and parents' experiences of using parents as resources in Swedish primary education. *Procedia-Social and Behavioral Sciences; 5th World Conference on Educational Sciences, 116*, 1587–1593.

Wigdor, A. K. (1982). Ability testing: Uses, consequences, and controversies. *Educational Measurement: Issues and Practice, 1*(3), 6–8.

Wilkosz, M. E., Chen, J. L., Kenndey, C., & Rankin, S. (2011). Body dissatisfaction in California adolescents. *Journal of the American Academy of Nurse Practitioners, 23*(2), 101–109.

Willingham, D. T. (2009). *Why don't students like school?: A cognitive scientist answers questions about how the mind works and what it means for the classroom.* Wiley.

Winner, E. (1990). Development in the visual arts. In W. Damon (Ed), *Child development today and tomorrow*. Jossey Bass.

Winsler, A., Feder, M., Way, E. L., & Manfra, L. (2006). Maternal beliefs concerning young children's private speech. *Infant and Child Development, 15*(4), 403–420.

Woelfle, J. F., Harz, K., & Roth, C. (2007). Modulation of circulating IGF-I and IGFBP-3 levels by hormonal regulators of energy homeostasis in obese children. *Experimental and Clinical Endocrinology & Diabetes, 115*(1), 17–23.

Wolfson, A. R. (1998). Working with parents on developing efficacious sleep/wake habits for infants and young children. In J. M. Briesmeister & C. E. Schaefer (Eds.), *Handbook of parent training: Parents as co-therapists for children's behavior problems* (p. 347–383). Wiley.

Wood, A. C., Saudino, K. J., Rogers, H., Asherson, P., & Kuntsi, J. (2007). Genetic influences on mechanically-assessed activity level in children. *Journal of Child Psychology and Psychiatry, 48*(7), 695–702.

Wood, F. B. (2008). Grief: Helping young children cope. *Young Children, 63*(5), 28–31.

Woodley, M. A., te Nijenhuis, J., Must, O., & Must, A. (2014). Controlling for increased guessing enhances the independence of the Flynn effect from g: The return of the Brand effect. *Intelligence, 43*, 27–34.

Woods, R. (2009). The use of aggression in primary school boys' decisions about inclusion in and exclusion from playground football games. *British Journal of Educational Psychology, 79*(2), 223–238.

Woodward, A. L. (1999). Infants' ability to distinguish between purposeful and non-purposeful behaviors. *Infant Behavior & Development, 22*(2), 145–160. https://doi-org.proxy.library.uu.nl/10.1016/S0163-6383(99)00007-7

Woodward, A. L. (2003). Infants' developing understanding of the link between looker and object. *Developmental Science, 6*(3), 297–311. https://doi.org/10.1016/S0163-6383(99)00007-7

Woumans, E., Surmont, J., Struys, E., & Duyck, W. (2016). The longitudinal effect of bilingual immersion schooling on cognitive control and intelligence. *Language Learning, 66*(S2), 76–91.

Wright, S. H. (2002). *Papert misses 'Big Ideas' from early days of artificial intelligence*. MIT News, Massachusetts Institute of Technology. https://news.mit.edu/2002/papert-misses-big-ideas-early-days-artificial-intelligence

Wrulich, M., Brunner, M., Stadler, G., Schalke, D., Keller, U., & Martin, R. (2014). Forty years on: Childhood intelligence predicts health in middle adulthood. *Health Psychology, 33*(3), 292–296.

Wynn, K. (2000). Findings of addition and subtraction in infants are robust and consistent: Reply to Wakeley, Rivera, and Langer. *Child Development, 71*(6), 1535–1536.

Xu, F., & Garcia, V. (2008). Intuitive statistics by 8-month-old infants. *Proceedings of the National Academy of Sciences of the United States of America, 105*, 5012–5015. https://doi.org/10.1073/pnas.0704450105

Yang, C. (2006). *The infinite gift: How children learn and unlearn the languages of the world*. Scribner.

Yee, M., & Brown, R. (1994). The development of gender differentiation in young children. *British Journal of Social Psychology, 33*(2), 183–196.

York, B. N., Loeb, S., & Doss, C. (2019). One step at a time: The effects of an early literacy text-messaging program for parents of preschoolers. *Journal of Human Resources, 54*(3), 537–566.

Young, S. E., Rhee, S. H., Stallings, M. C., Corley, R. P., & Hewitt, J. K. (2006). Genetic and environmental vulnerabilities underlying adolescent substance use and problem use: General or specific? *Behavior Genetics, 36*(4), 603–615.

Yuan, A. S. V. (2012). Perceived breast development and adolescent girls' psychological well-being. *Sex Roles, 66*(11), 790–806.

Zeegers, M. A., de Vente, W., Nikolić, M., Majdandžić, M., Bögels, S. M., & Colonnesi, C. (2018). Mothers' and fathers' mind-mindedness influences physiological emotion regulation of infants across the first year of life. *Developmental Science, 21*(6), e12689.

Zhu, L., & Gigerenzer, G. (2006). Children can solve Bayesian problems: The role of representation in mental computation. *Cognition, 98*(3), 287–308. https://doi.org/10.1016/j.cognition.2004.12.003

Zimmer-Gembeck, M. J., & Gallaty, K. J. (2006). Hanging out or hanging in? Young females' socioemotional functioning and the changing motives for dating and romance. *Advances in Psychology Research, 44*, 81–112.

Zohar, A. H., Zwir, I., Wang, J., Cloninger, C. R., & Anokhin, A. P. (2019). The development of temperament and character during adolescence: The processes and phases of change. *Development and Psychopathology, 31*(2), 601–617.

Zortea, T. C., Gray, C. M., & O'Connor, R. C. (2021). The relationship between adult attachment and suicidal thoughts and behaviors: A systematic review. *Archives of Suicide Research, 25*(1), 38–73.

INDEX

cognitive dissonance 264
cognitive flexibility 226–8
cognitive load 195–8, 202–3
cognitive psychology 12, 260
cognitive stage of acquiring
 expertise 204
cohort research 10
collective student efficacy 136
collective teacher
 efficacy 2,134–5
'coming out of the closet' 113
communication 90
community schools 2, 133–4
competence of pupils 236,
 246, 254–5
competence stage of acquiring
 expertise 205
computer games 124, 227, 229
concrete recommendations
 60–1 151
conditioning 190–3
 classic 190, 235
 operant 135, 190–1, 235,
 238, 243
confirmation bias 263–4
conscientiousness 33
conscious and unconscious
 systems 295–6
conservation 75
conservation bias 264
consistency in teachers'
 behaviour 152
construction of knowledge 196;
 see also co-creation of stories
context blindness 220
continuity
 feeling of 37
 law of 179
control groups 7
control of young people 149–52
controlling style of teaching 249–5
Convention on the Rights of
 the Child 121
conventions 53–4
conversations 225
Conway, John 79
cooking with children 226
coping mechanisms 232
copying 192
correlation 6– 9, 22
COVID-19 244, 268
crawling 101, 155
criminality 57
crisis situations 231
cross-sectional research 9–11
cultural dependence 33

cultural differences 174–5
Culture Fair Intelligence
 Test (CFIT) 69
curiosity 101, 235
'curling' parents 147
cyberbullying 117,
 133, 168

Damon, W. 157 159
dancing 228–9
daring to do things at
 school 157–8
Darwin, Charles 4–5
Darwin, William (Doddy) 4
dating 113
Dawson, P. 29
death, dealing with 49–50
De Bruyckere, S. 136
DeCasper, A.J. 177
'deceptive box' task 57
Deci, E.L. 236
'deep end' method of
 learning 203
de Groot, A.D. 202
Dehaene, Stanislas 11, 77
Del Giudice, Marco 98
delinquency 144
depression 49, 141, 159
design phase of child
 development 103
development of children xi, 24–5,
 50, 97–103, 155
 before birth 73
 helping them with 102
 influences on 127, 132–3
 at primary school stage 104–6
developmental psychology 2–4
de Wild, Arie 271
Diamond, Adele 219–20
diaries 229
didactic approaches 135
differences between
 individuals 103, 106
'difficult' pupils 39, 264
diffuse-avoidant approach 39
digital technology 118
dimensions as distinct from
 typologies 30
discipline 146, 255
discovery learning
 195–7, 203
discrimination 184
discussion in the classroom 61
disregarded/disoriented
 attachment 44
distractions 229

Printed in the USA
CPSIA information can be obtained
at www.ICGtesting.com
JSHW062352070824
67754JS00005B/11